Henry
VIII

Henry VIII

THE LIFE AND RULE OF ENGLAND'S NERO

JOHN MATUSIAK

'*Let us cease to sing the praises of the English Nero*'
Philipp Melanchthon, 1540

First published 2013
This paperback edition 2014

The History Press
The Mill, Brimscombe Port
Stroud, Gloucestershire, GL5 2QG
www.thehistorypress.co.uk

British Library Cataloguing in Publication Data.
A catalogue record for this book is available from the British Library.

ISBN 978 0 7509 6089 2

Typesetting and origination by The History Press
Printed in Great Britain

Contents

For my mother
Helen Matusiak
(9.7.1920–15.2.2013)

Author's Note

Though authors may well be forgiven for thinking otherwise, most books are ultimately committee products, and none more so than those whose subject is the past. The reign of Henry VIII has, of course, attracted more than its fair share of exceptional scholars and gifted popular biographers, and many have left their own particular imprint upon this altogether humbler endeavour. As a result of their dedication, there appear, for now, to be few new facts to glean and even fewer genuinely novel trails of research to blaze. But if the highways and byways of Henry's reign have been well trod, fresh perspectives and new syntheses are always available, especially where the man himself is concerned. In this, perhaps, lies the permanent allure of much historical writing. Certainly it lies at the heart of what follows.

Acknowledgements

I am as indebted as any author can be to a host of influences and legion of authorities, too numerous, sadly, even to be remembered let alone listed. The efforts of Lacey Baldwin Smith, Carolly Erickson, John Bowle, Neville Williams, Charles Ferguson and Marie Louise Bruce have both inspired and informed my work. And though the blame for any flaws is mine alone, I shall remain grateful both to them and countless others who have helped the book on its way. For, if ever a work arrived at its final destination by twists of chance and gusts of unexpected good fortune, it is this one. To Mark Beynon, who plucked it from its attic resting place, I owe a vote of special thanks. Likewise, a timely word of remembrance is surely due to the trio of eminent men who set the template for my education at the University of London precisely forty years ago. The late S.T. Bindoff, A.G. Dickens and Joel Hurstfield were all magisterial figures, and if the first, in particular, was so much more devoted to 'archival positivism' than I, it remains to his infinite credit. In the years that followed, some of my own students also played no small role in helping frame my ideas. Yet it is to Barbara and the rest of my family, as well as my small circle of special friends, that I am especially indebted. To those others who supported and encouraged, I offer my hand. They know who they are.

I

The Child Within the Man

'You have vanquished your enemies; you have gained many kingdoms; you have subdued many empires; you have acquired sovereignty of the entire east: but all the same you have neglected to control, or have been unable to govern, the small domain of your mind and body.'

Aristotle's words to Alexander the Great, quoted to the future
Henry VIII by his tutor John Skelton.

The birth of Henry VIII, unlike that of his elder brother, Arthur, was a distinctly muted episode. When Arthur, Prince of Wales, was born four weeks prematurely on 20 September 1486, he was hailed at once as the 'rosebush of England', the living embodiment of lasting union between the rival houses of York and Lancaster. Accordingly, the place of his birth was chosen in careful symmetry with his first name both to conjure a sense of long tradition and to affirm the mystique of his exalted station. Winchester was, after all, the ancient capital of the country's legendary past and in its cathedral hung the Round Table itself, freshly painted with Tudor emblems. As riders sped through the late summer countryside to herald the 'comfortable good tidings', bells pealed and joyous *Te Deums* resounded in chapels far and wide. In thronging streets huge bonfires blazed and roared to mark 'the rejoicing of every true Englishman', while at court, the Italian poets Pietro Carmeliano and Giovanni Gigli soared into raptures of exultant Latin verse in honour of the baby prince sent at last to heal a nation's wounds.

If, however, there was like rejoicing nearly five years later on 28 June 1491 when Henry VIII slipped into the world, no chronicler records it. His christening in the church of the Franciscan Observants, to which the silver

11

font from Canterbury Cathedral had been specially transported, was duly elaborate and, having been cleansed supposedly of the evil spirit, he was borne from the service in reverent style, preceded by the jubilant sound of trumpets and pipes and a splendid array of his godparents' gifts of gold and silver plate. Yet though the king and queen considered their second son an entirely welcome addition, they hailed him more as safeguard than saviour, a hopefully unredeemed insurance policy for his elder brother against the vagaries of Renaissance medical science. On this occasion, too, just as poets were wholly underwhelmed, so posterity was largely overlooked. Amid the yawning propaganda vacuum, Bernard André, the royal historian, devoted no more than fifty words to the new prince's birth in his *Vita Henrici VII*, including in the same inconsequential passage an incidental announcement of the birth of an elder sister, Margaret.

A similar vaguely half-hearted attitude seems to have influenced the choice of Henry's birthplace. Neither Winchester nor Westminster (where Margaret had been born) was this time selected for the purpose. Instead, the lusty infant heaved his first breath at the palace named Placentia, better known to us today as Greenwich, which was then esteemed less for its weighty historic significance than for its sweet air, agreeable river setting and reassuring distance from the plague-ridden capital. It was here that Prince Henry, anointed with oil, sprinkled with rosewater and swaddled in blue velvet and cloth-of-gold, was first laid in the great cradle of estate. Like all newborn babies he was, as yet, an innocent genetic mystery waiting to unravel with circumstance.

Some six years earlier, in September 1485, the infant's father had been greeted in London for the first time as Henry VII. Though received at Shoreditch amid magnificent display, he was still as yet a mysterious king from nowhere, whose legitimacy was derived from little more than England's desperation in that hour. While his great-grandfather had gained infamy as a fugitive Welsh brewer wanted for murder, his paternal grandfather had found fortune and influence only by seducing Henry V's French widow after some years as an official of her household. It was true that the new king's mother, Margaret Beaufort, was descended from John of Gaunt, but only from the wrong side of the blanket and although a parliament had made her legitimate along with her children, it had also expressly barred them from the throne. If, in any case, Henry VII's claim came through his mother, it was she and not her son who should have been crowned. But, in spite of this inauspicious pedigree, it was the improbable victor of Bosworth Field who had ultimately come to lay his battle banners at St Paul's, with trumpets sounding, and it was he who would demonstrate the strength to hold as well as the will to get in a land accustomed to turbulence.

'The French vice is lechery and the English vice treachery', ran the saying, and no impartial observer could have doubted at least the second half of this maxim when the first Tudor cautiously mounted his throne. Though for nine-tenths of the population the protracted and disjointed squabbles that today we call the Wars of the Roses were little more than 'kings' games', a contemporary parliamentary petition had still complained how 'in divers parts of this realm, great abominable murders, robberies, extortions, oppressions and other manifold maintenances, misgovernances, forcible entries, affrays and assaults be committed, and as yet remain unpunished'. Estate jumping, abduction of heiresses and casual brigandage had become, in effect, a modish pastime for the high-born Englishmen depicted to this day on their tombs and brasses in plate armour. Indeed, no less a figure than Sir Thomas Malory, who had apparently written *Morte D'Arthur* 'that we fall not through vice and sin, but exercise and follow virtue', found himself in prison in 1485 for sheep-stealing, sacrilege, extortion, rape and attempted murder.

Yet after little more than a decade of Henry VII's coldly efficient application of the royal will, chroniclers' laments and prayers for good rule would be out of fashion. The Venetian envoy Sanuto rightly recognised that the king was 'a man of great ability' and nowhere was this better exemplified than in his restoration of respect for due authority. True enough, he had limited objectives but, in the words of Francis Bacon, 'what he minded he compassed' and if his meticulous attention to detail and cagey awareness of human weakness were no doubt unpopular virtues at times, he knew how to behave regally, refusing to others 'any near or full approach, either to his power or secrets'. Likewise, he chose and managed his servants well, won the disaffected to his cause by securing their 'loving dread', and had ensured by the time of his death that the royal coffers, while not bulging, were at least no longer achingly empty. If, however, Henry VII's methodical realism might win a crown and tame a realm against all odds, the bridling of a troublous son would prove, in due course, an altogether different proposition. That this same son would lay waste so much of his father's work and flout so many of the principles that had guided his rule had, of course, an irony all of its own.

It was not the least of the first Tudor's merits that, in an age when the moral laxity of royal courts was all too common, he remained unswervingly faithful to his wife. No less than her husband, Elizabeth of York had been battered by past insecurities. Born the eldest daughter of Edward IV, she had been compelled at the age of 5, when Henry VI was restored briefly to the throne, to flee with her mother, Elizabeth Woodville, into sanctuary at Westminster. Six months later she had ridden out of the same Abbey gates in the embrace of her triumphant father, only to be forced back once more into the Church's protection at his sudden death when she was all but eighteen. Thereupon, she and her sisters and surviving brothers (Edward aged 12 and Richard aged 9) had been declared illegitimate, while their mother was accused of sorcery. Nor was this the end of Elizabeth's troubles, for later, after her uncle had been crowned Richard III, her brothers disappeared from view in the Tower amid rumours that they had been murdered.

The funeral effigy of Henry VIII's mother in Westminster Abbey bears witness today to her graceful features, and the likeness of her now hanging in the National Portrait Gallery also suggests a woman of some considerable beauty with a well-proportioned face, fair complexion, golden tresses and long, elegant hands. Neither image lays bare the inner woman, however. To all who knew her, in fact, her reputation for piety was outstanding and wholly consistent with her undivided loyalty and subservience to her husband. Having stood by his side throughout the times of danger after his first landing in England, she proceeded to decorate his court dutifully and would bear him seven children, only three of whom would reach adulthood. But while she was described by contemporaries as 'a very handsome woman and of great ability', 'very noble' and 'much beloved' and 'of the greatest charity and humanity', a less buoyant note was sounded in two dispatches from Spanish envoys. The first described her as 'kept in subjection by the mother of the king' and in need of 'a little love', while the other observed that the king was much influenced by his mother and suggested further that the queen 'as is generally the case, does not like it'.

True to her motto, 'Humble and Reverent', Elizabeth remained a kind and gracious presence, but little else besides, and her spouse, though loving, was often autocratic in his personal relations with her. In common, then, with other high-born women of her day, Elizabeth's role as wife was limited entirely to passive obedience just as her maternal role would be confined to begetting rather than rearing, for she would neither feed her second son nor even live near him. Indeed, it was by dying, above all, that she eventually left her deepest mark upon the future Henry VIII. Predictably, she would also endure the intrusions of her mother-in-law with characteristic resignation and soon surrendered the care of the new prince to her without demur. In fact, only a few weeks after his christening, the infant Henry left his mother's abode for Eltham Palace in Kent and here it was that he would be raised in severe seclusion under the doting but leaden devoutness of his grandmother, Lady Margaret Beaufort.

Not surprisingly, the earnest piety and precision of the 'Venerable Margaret' are unlikely to have left her second grandson with many cheerful memories. Intensely devout in her religious faith and devoutly intense in her political schemings, she was one of the most remarkable women of the century. After four marriages she had been widowed finally in 1504 and, at 61 years of age, immediately saw fit to take a solemn and public vow of chastity. She had also been instrumental in the plots that finally brought her son the crown and had lived through more reigns, with more opportunity to influence their outcome, than any other person at his court. To the Spanish ambassador in 1498 she was among the half-dozen people with the greatest influence in England and perhaps to compensate for her disappointment at not being allowed to interfere directly in government during his own reign, Henry VII allowed his mother to rule his domestic affairs. In consequence, her obsessions and ambitions were to leave an indelible imprint upon her second grandson.

The countess was, in effect, all prayer and learning, which made her, at one and the same time, both the best and worst of influences upon the highly impressionable boy in her charge. At her happiest when reading and translating pious works, such as *The Imitation of Christ,* she would begin her devotions at five every morning, one hour before the general time of rising and though she suffered grievously from rheumatism, this never deterred her from spending long periods on her knees in prayer. Next to her skin, for good measure, she wore a hair shirt 'for the health of her soul' and instead of regal fineries she dressed in modest robes, much like a nun's habit. Nor was this the sum of her austerities. Always a sparing eater, she observed fast days meticulously and during Lent would restrict herself to one fish meal a day. In the meantime, she maintained twelve paupers in her house in Woking, washing their feet, serving them with meals when they were ill and studying them as they approached death, so that she might thereby learn how to die well when her own eagerly awaited appointment with eternity arrived.

Although not permanently resident with her, Henry is therefore likely to have feared his grandmother as much as he loved her, for she represented an oppressive mix of sharp wits, high expectations and maudlin piety, leavened by a pinch of slowly gnawing anxiety. She never forgot, after all, how history had turned at Bosworth Field and how her cherished son might have ended the day in King Richard's place, a broken and dishonoured corpse. It was John Fisher, her confessor, who noted her knack for 'marvellous weeping' and it was he, too, who remarked upon her morbid pessimism. 'Either she was in sorrow by reason of present adversities', he observed, 'or else when she was in prosperity she was in dread of the adversity to come.' Haunted by fortune's wheel, the 'Venerable Margaret' in her turn came to haunt her grandson's childhood.

Apart from God the father and her own son, the third person of Margaret's blessed trinity seems, in fact, to have been none other than Prince Henry himself, and it is tempting to think that she may well have seen in him something of the tenacious vigour and cunning instinct for survival that had sustained her in earlier adversity. In any event, family ambition as well as religion certainly burned behind the deep-set eyes in her narrow face and henceforth those eyes would be firmly set upon her second grandson. The Beaufort family had, of course, stood tantalisingly close to the throne for all of three generations and now that it was theirs, she was adamant that it must be held at all costs. As well as protecting Prince Henry's person, therefore, she was equally intent upon nurturing his rank and by the time of his tenth birthday, she had singled the boy out as her heir, begging the king to arrange 'that none of my tenants be retained with no man, but that they be kept for your fair sweet son, for whom they be most meet'. Moreover, as events would demonstrate, she was no less set upon imbuing in him a keen sense of his wider birthright.

Though two generations, gender and temperament divided grandmother from grandson, she succeeded admirably and momentously in encouraging at least one common bond between them: a strong sense of grievance against the French, which the boy would carry with him throughout his life. It was widely known that the King of France still owed Lady Margaret a large sum of money that had been advanced by her mother to the Duke of Orléans in 1440 to pay the ransom fee after his capture at Agincourt.

But notwithstanding Margaret's continual petitions, the debt remained stubbornly unpaid and such was her crafty frustration that she eventually chose to gift the sum to her son in the hope that he might attempt to recover it by force. His letter in response, though gentle, still left her in no doubt that now was not the time to plan for war against such a formidable foe, and the rankling impact of this filial palm-off may well be imagined. Doubtless the grandmother's indignation about the unremitted debt will have raked her sorely and it is hard to imagine that her smouldering sense of grievance will not have communicated itself to Prince Henry, fuelling in its own way, perhaps, his later naive urges to repossess land lost to France in the Hundred Years War.

In the old lady's capacity as mistress of court ceremonial, it was she, too, who fashioned the bustling microcosm of the Tudor nursery, at the hub of which, especially in the early months, was Prince Henry's wet nurse, Anne Luke. Though largely unregarded in the records, we can be sure of much about this young woman, for both her physical and her mental qualities would have had to match precisely the exacting paediatric standards outlined for posterity in Sir Thomas Elyot's *The Boke Named the Governour*. A 'sanguine complexion', for instance, suggesting the predominance of blood among the four humours, was an absolute essential. This meant that Anne would have needed glowing cheeks, thick auburn hair, a buxom figure and a hearty, outgoing, amorous disposition, since this was the type considered most apt to produce milk that 'excelleth all other both in sweetness and substance'. She was required, too, to be 'of ripe or mature age, not under twenty years or above thirty' and 'of approved virtue, discretion, and gratuity', since 'the child sucketh the vice of his nurse with the milk of her pap'. Accordingly, she would be expected to abstain from sex and, if any ill were to befall the baby, the fault would be hers alone to bear, for the philosopher-physician, Avicenna, had left no doubt that 'the first thing in curing infants is to regulate the nurse'. She could expect at any time, therefore, to be phlebotomised, cupped, 'cured by vomiting' or made to suffer 'the turmoil of purgation', and should her supply of milk wane, she would find herself treated to a special diet of stewed udders, dried cow's tongue or powdered earthworm.

Perhaps it was only fitting, therefore, that after his accession Henry decided to award Anne Luke a yearly pension of £20 in recognition of her efforts on his behalf. But whether even so diligent and self-sacrificing a nurse could really have offered the infant prince the kind of unconditional love that his absent mother might have provided remains open to question. Nor could Anne Luke, or anyone else in the prince's household for that matter, relate to him with the kind of informality or spontaneity that might have made his later interaction with others more rounded. Literally from the instant of his birth until the age of 7, the vast majority of individuals who surrounded Henry in his insulated nursery world were impassive, one-dimensional figures, attending and providing rather than interacting and amending, and this is likely to have been especially true for the one who first supplied his most basic needs at closest quarters. If, then, the prince's early upbringing succeeded admirably in fitting him for his future role by ridding him of the humilities usually derived from more conventional dealings with adults, it also helped spawn a disregard for the inner workings of others that would increase exponentially during his adolescence and early manhood.

As might be expected, all Henry's needs were cosseted tirelessly and none more so than those pertaining to his health. His ailments were treated in accordance with the very best conventions of Tudor child care, which recommended, amongst other things, bitches' milk or chicken fat mixed with hares' brains as a trusted remedy for sore gums, and plasters of oil and wax, clapped 'hot on the belly', for wind. Rather less drastically, the baby prince's earache would have been soothed by drops derived from myrrh and pulverised acorns in honey and wine. Meanwhile, when he cried in the cradle, his four rockers, who had been specially chosen by his grandmother, would bend to their task. And when later he had learned to walk outside the pen, the prince would always be followed anxiously by hovering, fussing dames lest he should stumble, damage his spine and develop a humped back. His faltering steps were likely to have been aided, too, by a small brass jousting toy of the type that appears to have been popular throughout the royal nurseries of Europe at this time. Mounted on wheels and featuring an armoured knight poised for combat, this was a toy with more than one purpose since, in addition to supporting a tottering infant, it could be hurled and crashed in noisy combat.

Such items were designed, of course, to begin a prince's meticulous initiation into the military skills considered so indispensable that they could not be taught too early. Indeed, there was an unapologetically bloodthirsty emphasis upon slaughter in the upbringing of all royal children at this time, as we can see from a contemporary woodcut by Hans Burgkmair of Augsburg, which depicts the Holy Roman Emperor Maximilian I at play with his offspring. The cosy family gathering is depicted in the midst of a spree of casual carnage with a lethal miniature cannon duly primed to wreak havoc upon any passing wildlife. One child is gleefully despatching a songbird from a tree, while a baited trap is being laid for another. Elsewhere, a longbow lies temporarily discarded. We can be sure, of course, that Henry's toys would have followed a similar pattern. And though he had other playthings, such as spinning tops, bone skittles and an almost life-size hobby horse, his toy weaponry would have assumed a special significance, for as well as being a would-be warrior against the French, he was also the son of a king whose fear of treachery and sudden death would never fully leave him.

Throughout Prince Henry's early years, in fact, his father was far from secure upon his throne and it seems hard to believe that the pervasive insecurity of this time would not have had an insidious influence upon his future development. There were, in 1485, at least ten people with a better blood claim to the throne than Henry VII and, in due course, there would also emerge two pretenders: the 'feigned boy', Lambert Simnel, and his more dangerous and persistent counterpart, Perkin Warbeck, who between 1491 and 1497 flitted menacingly around Ireland, France and Scotland. In the Latin treatise *Speculum Principis*, written for him specially by his tutor John Skelton, young Henry was said to be surrounded by 'grievous wounds and deaths, days of suspicion and fear, incalculable secret hates, loyal words and deeds the opposite, the frightening curse of war, rare friendship, a thousand nuisances, a pretence at love and cowardly hearts'. Therefore, as the diminutive prince toddled after his brother and sister and played with his toy weapons in the care of his attendants, the moated palace of Eltham in its rolling parkland was nothing less than a haven of security in a sea of menace.

The year 1497 would prove of particular crisis as the Scots threatened the border, and Cornishmen led by the lawyer Thomas Flamank and a giant blacksmith called Michael Joseph marched in anger across the breadth of England to protest against the 'crafty means' by which the king had elicited his 'outrageous sums'. Today there is still a plaque by the lychgate at St Keverne, one of the early centres of the rising, recording how the rebels 'marched to London and suffered vengeance'. But it was not until they reached Blackheath that they were finally thwarted. And as the Cornishmen had advanced on the capital, armed with bills, staves, scythes and whatever other instruments of harm might be at hand, the

5-year-old prince was forced to seek shelter with his mother in the White Tower. On that same day, 15,000 men from the West Country, 'stout of stomach, mighty of body and limb', encamped at Farnham. Now, Henry would witness at first hand the Tower's armourers honing their weapons as London's citizens piled up great mounds of timber against the city's gates. And as mother and son, bound by their common danger, awaited the approaching rebel host, the boy could not have failed to notice his mother's fears, which were heightened by the defeat of her own father at an almost identical age.

Nor was the young prince likely to have been any less jarred by the rebellion's aftermath. Soon after dawn on 16 June he would have risen to general excitement in the Tower and the far-off thunder of cannon as royal forces attacked the mob of farmers, fishermen and miners who, according to the chronicler, had been 'in great agony and variance' as to whether or not to yield to the king's mercy. By two o'clock that afternoon, Henry VII was riding across London Bridge, the summer sun glinting on his armour, to be welcomed by the Mayor and his 'brethren in scarlet'. He was followed by prisoners tramping in chains, or flung like so much rubbish into carts, while, back at Blackheath, grave mounds were being filled that would remain visible for two centuries. Later the quarters of Flamank's body were set on the four gates of London as ghoulish reminders of the penalties of rebellion, and these poor relics Prince Henry cannot have failed to see – a sight much closer, and so more frightful, than the severed heads already dangling balefully above London Bridge.

To Thomas More, the uprising would seem a pitiful affair: 'that disastrous civil war which began with a revolution in the West Country and ended with a ghastly massacre of the rebels'. Yet young Henry learned, instead, to scorn pity. True, the boy's long vigil with his mother was at an end, but the fear of sudden, violent dispossession lived on. And this was not all, for he learned from his father to despise these 'base Cornishmen' who had threatened a return to the lawless commotion so dreaded by contemporaries. Indeed, by the time that Perkin Warbeck's further insurrection had passed in the same year, Henry's conviction that to be lenient is to be weak was set in stone. Nor would his hatred of the 'many headed monster' of rebellion ever recede, for his confidence in his rightful superiority was unshakable even now.

Henry had, after all, already been accorded the first trappings of rank and the splendour that it entailed. Before he was 12 months old he had been officially appointed Warden of the Cinque Ports, and other honours followed thick and fast. In October 1494, when still only three, the boy was brought to Westminster to be made a Knight of the Bath and Duke of York in a series of ceremonies over three days that would have exhausted any adult. Then, in December of the same year, the new duke was appointed Warden of the Scottish Marches before receiving the garter in the following May. As usual, however, there was sound policy behind the promotions rather than any hint that the prince was being groomed for the possibility of his eventual succession. With his second son rather than a competent adult installed in the offices concerned, it would be easier for the king to exert control through his appointed deputies and the fees provided would also make a handsome contribution to his son's household expenses. All in all, the prince's present, like his future, remained resplendent but limited.

This is not to say, however, that the future Henry VIII was not even now a significant personage in his own right. As 'my lord of York' he appeared more and more frequently in the rolls of the king's expenditures, receiving money to play at dice, to pay his servants, to reward his fool John Goose and to fund his minstrels, who were independent of those of his father and brother. In 1498, moreover, we hear of him being fêted by the Lord Mayor and aldermen of London. Having cleared the streets of beggars and ensured the cheering rabble that lined the road was free from infection, the City fathers duly presented Henry with a pair of gilt goblets, in return for which the prince delivered a well-turned speech of thanks, declaring that he hoped to be worthy of the citizens' 'great and kind remembrance' in future. But it was at Windsor in September 1496 that he may well have carried out his first independent public act when he witnessed the grant of a royal charter to the abbot and convent of Glastonbury to hold two public fairs. If this was indeed Henry's official debut, then its irony is manifest, for forty-three years later he would reduce the abbey to ruins and hang its last abbot for treason on nearby Tor Hill.

In the meantime, though, there seems little doubt that Prince Henry was smitten at once by his exposure to the limelight. Largesse on a grand scale was, after all, a key feature of Henry VII's attempts to affirm the status of the monarchy and to this end he succeeded literally magnificently. It was not uncommon, it seems, for 700 people to dine at his expense at Westminster and on red-letter days the menu could extend to sixty separate dishes. Similarly, the court entertainments that enlivened the long winter evenings were also glittering affairs and had their own particular place in government propaganda. On Twelfth Night 1494, for instance, the royal children were all present as the king and queen processed 'through both Halls' at Westminster between the end of divine service and the start of a great banquet. For good measure, the feast was followed by 'a play with a pageant of St George with a castle and twelve lords and twelve ladies disguised, which did dance'. All in all, it was a typical theme, slanted to enhance the Crown and its wearer and generate the kind of heady chauvinism that would eventually have such costly repercussions in the next reign.

Nor should it be forgotten that Henry VII was responsible for introducing the term 'majesty' into the English language or that, in doing so, he consciously developed the practices of pageantry and invested the notion of kingship with a mystique all of its own. Processions, the shouting of loyal salutations, the doffing of caps and reverent genuflexions in the royal presence all formed part of the underlying propaganda message that such spectacle was designed to drive home. Meanwhile, grooms, pages, servers and sundry menials were all attired in the Tudor livery of white and green embossed with the Tudor rose. Indeed, lest any should doubt or forget the might and splendour of England's new dynasty, there were roses, too, in the chains and necklaces worn by the king and queen, on the wooden ceilings and tiled floors of all royal dwellings and even on the gilded harnesses of royal horses. And all the while, the growing Prince Henry was encouraged to believe without reservation that Tudor children, as the offspring of a political miracle, had a unique relationship with God himself.

Nevertheless, the splendour of 'noble and triumphant company' served only to whet rather than satisfy the young Duke of York's hankering for recognition, and as he grew into boyhood, intermittent tastes of everyday life at court could in no way compensate adequately for the general absence of his father on weightier business. The official seat of government was still the palace of Westminster, a royal residence since the days of Edward the Confessor, and there the second son rarely ventured at this time. With the Thames, then much wider, running murkily beneath its windows, the old palace was damp and insanitary, prone to flood and often wrapped in fog. Though tapestry hangings kept out the draughts and wood fires and charcoal braziers lessened the cutting edge of the chill in the air, behind all the pomp and pageantry at Westminster there was acute discomfort. Here, in a warren of medieval buildings, government was executed and justice administered. Here, too, resided the king – a whole mental world away from his younger son who continued to grow in isolation among the oaks of Eltham.

It was probably in 1498, upon reaching the age of 7, that the future Henry VIII was finally forced to bid a fond farewell to those who had tended him since birth, for this was the age when contemporaries believed that a high-born boy should be taken 'from the company of all women'. Now Henry would be placed under the charge of a formidable array of tutors who subjected him to the full rigour of scholastic and Renaissance learning. One was Friar Bernard André of Toulouse, a blind historian and humanist who glorified King Arthur as the ancestor of the Tudor dynasty. Another, Giles du Guez, taught Henry 'to pronounce and speak French trewly' and, for pastime, dabbled in alchemy. There was also the bitter-tongued figure of John Skelton, East Anglian poet laureate to Henry VII, who would claim to have taught 'the honour of England' to spell and 'sit at meat seemly'. It was he, too, who advised his pupil 'to pick out a wife for himself and love her alone'.

Though such advice was clearly in vain, Skelton's overall influence upon the boy is likely to have been particularly significant. Born in 1460, he had risen to prominence through his outstanding poetical gifts and his mastery of the newly fashionable classical Latin before being 'crowned with laurel' by the universities of Oxford, Cambridge and Louvain. Thereafter, he was dubbed the 'incomparable light of British letters' by none other than the great Dutch scholar Erasmus, and was duly invited to court in 1496 by Lady Margaret Beaufort, for whom he had translated Guillaume de Deguileville's *Le Pèlerinage de la Vie Humaine*. In the same year he became Prince Henry's principal tutor and by 1498 he had also become a priest of the Abbey of St Grace. But while he had not yet begun to produce the ribald satires, scurrilous attacks on enemies and bawdy denunciations of drunken women, which would make him the most famous poet of his generation, his talents would soon enough extend far beyond the generally accepted parameters of courtly poetic convention. And though 'Merry Skelton', as he was known, could be delightfully accommodating to those who pleased him, he was mainly vain and querulous and easily sworn to enmity.

For all the high ideals he espoused and lofty talents he possessed, Skelton would therefore prove an unfortunate choice as tutor, since he is very likely to have taught his young charge far more than spelling and table manners. He was, without doubt, an incorrigible extrovert and Henry would have lived in the ambience of his intellectual brilliance and dark prejudice from the age of 7 to 11. The prince would, of course, have experienced some of his schooling in the company of his sisters, Margaret and Mary, as well as John St John, Lady Margaret's great-nephew, who came to live at Eltham. But although the king believed in educating his daughters well, there were many lessons their different ages would have made it impossible for them to share with their brother, and as John St John seems to have been considerably younger than Henry, it can be assumed that the latter spent much of the day alone with Skelton, exposed not only to the creeping influence of his character, but also to the steady stinging stream of his observations on men and life.

This is not to deny, of course, that Henry's tuition was entirely effective from the scholarly standpoint and there is little doubt that, as a result of its rigours, he developed wide-ranging abilities from an early age. As the prince grew, he became fluent in French and Latin and competent in Spanish. In fact, his Latin soon became so accomplished that by the age of 10 he was demanding a piece from the pen of Erasmus himself. Likewise, he was a keen mathematician and talented musician, playing the lute, organ and recorder and composing a number of masses, which are now lost. Architecture and the design of ships also fascinated him and somewhat oddly, perhaps, for a child he soon began to develop a lifelong interest in concocting medicines for his own use. He devised, for instance, a plaster 'designed to heal ulcers without pain' along with an unguent 'to take away the itch'. There seemed to be, then, 'no necessary kind of knowledge' of which he did not have an 'honest sight'. Indeed, it may well have been the excellence of Henry's education, coupled to his father's later disinterest in planning for his marriage, which prompted Lord Herbert of Cherbury to suggest in 1649 that he was destined to become Archbishop of Canterbury. However, the likelihood that a boy second in line to the throne might be committed to vows of celibacy is remote. Not surprisingly, therefore, the only other 'evidence' suggesting as much is limited to Dr William Parron's astrological prophecy in 1502 that Henry would become 'a good churchman' and the casual remark made by the Italian Servite, Paolo Sarpi, in 1619, that 'Henry was destined by his father to be archbishop and so made to attend his studies from boyhood'.

Throughout his childhood and adolescence, in fact, Henry's intellectual gifts were described in the most glowing terms, but the conventional plaudits accorded to him should not necessarily be taken at face value, and much of the lavishly heaped praise must be suspected of at least some generosity. The young prince was described reasonably enough by Erasmus in 1499 when he visited Eltham with Thomas More. 'In the midst' (of his attendants), wrote the Dutchman, 'stood Prince Henry, now 9 years old and having already something of royalty in his demeanour.' Before long, however, Erasmus would be referring to Henry as 'a universal genius', while later, in 1507, it would be the turn of the Spaniard de Puebla to overdo it. 'There is', he waxed, 'no finer youth in the world.' Overall, Henry was an apt and diligent child, but the claims of Erasmus and others that he was 'a prodigy of precocious learning' need to be viewed in the context of a time when attempts to win royal favour by out-gushing Cicero led all too often to rhetorical overkill of the most excruciating kind.

John Skelton, meanwhile, continued to flout the moral standards he urged upon his pupils. He was quick, for instance, to warn his young charges to 'shun gluttony', to 'listen to the other side', to 'be always gentle, kindly, calm and humble', to 'learn pity' and to 'maintain justice'. But in his day-to-day behaviour the poet consistently failed to set a good example. Engaging in a poetic duel with Sir Christopher Garnish, one of the many men who offended him, Skelton flung himself into a typically brutal surge of poetic invective, recommending that his adversary be racked at Tyburn. He also remained preoccupied by fornication and adultery. Even the prettiest of his lyrics, *My Darling Dear, My Daisy Flower*, which would have been sung at court before Henry, is a tale of betrayal by a girl with two lovers. More often than not, Skelton also delighted to show up apparently respectable women as whores and so vicious were his attacks that one 'honourable gentlewoman' was driven to send this enemy of her sex a dead man's head 'as a token' – an incident young Henry may well have heard about, since it was probably sent while the poet was still employed at Eltham Palace.

Later, as a lovelorn youth, the prince would read romantic literature full of gallant indulgence to erring damsels and this too would leave a lasting influence. But when his ardour cooled, it was Skelton's voice, perhaps more than any other's, that would echo in his thoughts. And as his father's policies grew more ruthless and more cynical in these years, their impact on his son was unlikely to have been moderated by the counsel of the boy's tutor. Indeed, when in November 1499 there occurred the political murder of the Earl of Warwick, who had committed no treason and was reputed to be too dim 'to tell a goose from a capon', it was Skelton's cynical observations that would serve to guide the prince in the royal ethics of the matter. Moreover, the fact that Henry would recall him to court in 1512, nine years after his retirement, in order to appoint him 'Orator Regius' is clear proof of the warm feelings he retained for his old tutor.

By 1501, though, John Skelton had been too tactless even for the generally tolerant Henry VII. So after five years of service he was duly dismissed from his post and given an extra 40 shillings in addition to his annual stipend and sent to Norfolk to become rector of Diss. However, even as he made way for William Hone as royal tutor, Skelton produced a most curious passing gift in the form of an intriguing short treatise in Latin on how a king should rule. While *Speculum Principis* was unexceptional in itself, it was extraordinary that Skelton presented it to Henry rather than Arthur, who was heir to the throne and about to marry Catherine of Aragon. At the time, even though the text addressed both princes, the gift seemed a rudely inappropriate gesture, for Henry could become king only through rebellion or by Arthur's death. Skelton's apparent belief that Henry would inherit the throne seems to have been wishful thinking born of nothing more substantial than an ambition to share vicariously in his pupil's glory. But his vision of his pupil's future greatness had a resonance that is unlikely to have been purely coincidental.

There is, in fact, no direct evidence of tension between the brothers, but this is largely because the records are simply silent on all counts. Though Arthur's personality was unprepossessing and he was cast in a smaller, narrower physical mould than his brother, his mother's pleasure in him was particularly obvious and there was also a special bond between him and his younger sister Margaret. It is true that in the spring of 1501, by which time Henry was old enough to be a companion for Arthur, the latter was sent off to hold court at Ludlow as Prince of Wales and that after this they saw one another only on ceremonial occasions or when the family gathered for Christmas. But it was precisely on such occasions that Henry's discomfiture would have been most heavily intensified, as a result of the rigid court protocols emphasising his brother's precedence. According to his grandmother's ordinances, on entering Arthur's presence chamber Henry would be obliged to remove his hat and remain bareheaded until Arthur graciously told him to 'be covered'. Then there were numerous other subtle, but no doubt galling, conventions for Henry to endure. When, for instance, he deputised for Arthur on State occasions, he would sit under a royal canopy of State, but to emphasise his inferior rank, the front and roof would be rolled back demeaningly, exposing him to full public gaze. And while Henry would have to address his brother as 'my lord prince', he himself would have to make do with the title 'my lord of York'.

If, indeed, any seeds of brotherly disharmony had already been sown, then Arthur's marriage to Catherine of Aragon in the autumn of 1501 would germinate them. At the time of its conception, this marriage appeared with justification to be a landmark in the Tudor dynasty's success. The betrothal of Prince Arthur to Catherine of Aragon had been brought about by the Treaty of Medina del Campo in 1489, when both were less than 3 years old. But it was not until September 1501, after years of haggling and two proxy marriages, that the 16-year-old Catherine finally embarked upon the month-long sea journey to England from the port of Laredo on the Basque coast. She would never return to her homeland. There had been further diplomatic delays and sundry postponements of her sailing due in turn to a revolt of the Moors, illness and a gale. Eventually, though, she bade farewell to her parents and was forced to endure a dire passage across the Bay of Biscay as violent squalls splintered masts and spars and her seasick retinue prayed for deliverance.

Landing finally in Plymouth on 2 October, she was overwhelmed by the spontaneous welcome accorded her by the people of the West Country and it would not be long before Prince Henry now began to make his mark, for the ensuing nuptials would allow him to court the publicity that he was already starting to crave. Not since Henry V conquered France and married the French king's daughter had there been an English marriage of such grandeur. It was exciting news for the whole court, but particularly so for the king's second son, since it had been decided that he should accompany the Spanish princess on her ceremonial entry into the heart of the kingdom, the walled city of London. For young Henry it was to be a triple milestone in his growing up. It would be the first time that he felt to the full the intoxicating adulation of the crowd and the first time that he drew close to the girl who was to play such a crucial part in his life. It was the first time, too, that he probably felt the full force of a pricking dart of envy at his brother's good fortune.

In the brief period that followed Catherine's arrival at the riverside town of Kingston on Thames in November 1501, Prince Henry performed his duties with aplomb. Two days after he had first escorted her through London 'amid greater rejoicings than if she had been the Saviour of the world', he led her in his suit of white velvet and gold along the nave of St Paul's to the scarlet-covered platform where Arthur awaited her. At five o'clock that same afternoon, the customary ceremonial bedding of the couple occurred. And after Catherine had been 'reverently laid and disposed' in the marriage bed, the younger brother would have been among the boisterous, laughing throng of courtiers who escorted Arthur in his nightgown into the bridal chamber to a merry tune of shawms, viols and tabors. There, said the Bishop of London, the din was so great that no one could hear a word. So it was, with the marriage bed having been duly blessed by the assembled bishops, that Arthur and Catherine were at last left alone to nature's devices. More than a quarter of a century later, the subsequent details of this public bedding were to be pored over equally publicly: this time by politicians and canon lawyers.

However, it was the celebrations thereafter that provided the younger brother with what may well have been the high point of his childhood. Two evenings after the wedding, the royal children were encouraged in turn to dance before the assembled courtiers and dignitaries and it was Henry who stole the show. After Arthur had trodden a sedate English measure before a respectful silence Henry's turn duly arrived. Accompanied by his sister Margaret, he gave, by contrast, such a lively performance of leaps and kicks that the onlookers demanded more. Amid smiles of approval and cries of delight, the prince and princess started again and now Henry delivered a theatrical flourish. 'Perceiving himself to be encumbered by his clothes', the chronicler tells us, he 'suddenly cast off his gown and danced in his jacket'. By the time, therefore, that he returned to the platform, where great cups of wine and plates of spiced cake were being passed, Henry had already set the first indelible mark of his own extraordinary exuberance upon England's history.

Yet the marriage only served in reality to underline the gulf between the two brothers in terms of their future prospects. Indeed, if and when Arthur eventually became king, Henry would at once exchange his present safe niche for an altogether more dangerous role. Then his love of publicity and restless energy would be sure to render him an object of distrust. His own great-uncle, the Duke of Clarence, an idol of the multitude and jealous of the Crown, had finally been drowned ingloriously as a traitor in a butt of Malmsey wine. Likewise, Richard, Duke of Gloucester, who had been loyal during Edward IV's lifetime only to seize the throne ultimately, had paid a heavy price on Bosworth Field. To be a king's brother, as Henry well knew, would also make him a future king's uncle, a relationship of the most hazardous kind that might be attended by dreadful choices of murder or extinction. Did not the fate of Thomas Woodstock, rudely done to death by order of King Richard II, prove as much?

There was also, it seems, the looming distrust of his father for Prince Henry to contend with. According to the Spanish ambassador, Miguel Pérez de Almazán, the king was 'beset by the fear' that his younger son 'might during his lifetime obtain too much power'. By July 1501, therefore, Henry VII had decided where his second son should reside when he was grown up and in framing his decision he had clearly in mind Arthur's long-term safety after he had become king. Being all too aware of the civil wars that had erupted in the past, figure-headed by an ambitious younger brother, the second son's main dwelling, his father decreed, was to be in Derbyshire, too far away for him to interfere in government. So, for the lavish sum of £1,000, the king bought him Codnor Castle, built by the lords Grey in the thirteenth and fourteenth centuries, surrounded by extensive estates and located 100 miles and more from London.

To set the seal upon his frustration, of all the royal children Henry alone appeared unlikely to occupy a throne. On 25 January 1502 in the queen's presence chamber in Richmond Palace, he witnessed the proxy 'marriage' of his elder sister Margaret to the King of Scots, James IV. She was twelve, while James was already in his mid-twenties and notorious for his many love affairs. But her younger brother knew full well that such considerations were insignificant when such a gain in status was involved. Even more vexingly, since at least 1499 his other sister, Mary, had been earmarked for the infant Charles of Ghent, heir to the vast Habsburg empire in Europe, as well as to the New World territories of Spain's Catholic Majesties. Although for three of his children, then, King Henry VII's dynastic ambition had soared high, there was no future match in sight for his second son. In fact, only one marriage of any kind had so far been considered, that to Charles's sister Eleanor, and the lack of further marriage plans for Henry again underlined his inferior status. Besides which, his father was in no hurry to make future trouble for Arthur by encouraging the creation of a rival branch of the royal family. As such, the junior prince had little to look forward to beyond an uninviting future that was at best arid and at worst perilous – or so, at least, it seemed.

2

A Prince Beyond Improvement

'It is not only from love that the king takes the prince with him. He wishes to improve him. Certainly there could be no better school in the world than the society of such a father as Henry VII. He is so wise and so attentive, nothing escapes his attention. If he lives ten years longer, he will leave the prince furnished with good habits, and with immense riches, and in as happy circumstances as a man can be.'

An observation made by the Spanish envoy, Hernán Duque,
six years before Henry VII's death.

In the small hours of 3 April 1502, an ageing Franciscan Observant friar was snatched from his meagre slumbers by a messenger of the Privy Council and told to attend his sovereign at the nearby palace of Greenwich without delay. The news that the old man was charged to convey 'in his best manner' was heavy indeed, even for one who had served for some years as the king's confessor. On the Welsh borders that spring the weather had been especially inclement and in the neighbourhood of Ludlow Castle the dreaded 'sweating sickness' had made an ominous appearance. A few recovered from its clutches but most died, 'some within three hours, some within two hours, some merry at dinner and dead at supper'. And among those now claimed by this remorseless universal leveller was the Prince of Wales himself, aged only 15½. Fate, in fact, could scarcely have played more cruelly with the House of Tudor. For not only had its best hope been taken, but the cause was that very disease first brought to these shores in 1485 by Henry VII's own Norman mercenaries. After a marriage of less than five months, then, the heir to the throne was dead, while his 'dearest spouse', at the age of 16 years and 3 months, also lay dangerously ill from the same contagion. King Henry and his queen 'took the painful sorrows together', we are told, and after the weary friar had left their presence, the royal couple comforted themselves with hopes of further offspring. 'God is where he was', the queen reflected bravely, 'and we are both young enough.'

So at that very point when Prince Henry's possibilities were evaporating beyond trace, fate had, it seemed, intervened decisively to rescue him from obscurity and deliver him from the political shadows. Yet although he was technically granted the office of Prince of Wales on 22 June 1502, it was not until 18 February 1504 that he was installed with full ceremony. Only then was he invested with the emblems of his new rank, the ring on the third finger of his left hand – a symbol, according to Margaret Beaufort's ordinance, that he was 'married to do justice and equity and to show right wisdom to all parties' – and the golden wand of office 'in token he shall have victory and deprive and put down his enemies and rebels'. Only at this time, too, so the parliament rolls of 1504 inform us, did he inherit the Prince of Wales' 'great and notable possessions'. Whether the reason for this postponement was simply a father's grief at the loss of his oldest son is unknown. What is certain, however, is that the lingering delay added considerably to the new heir's already mounting frustration. Moreover, while the prince bristled, a second family tragedy struck which would cut him still more deeply.

Though at the age of 36 the risks were considerable, Elizabeth of York was once more heavy with child within a year of Arthur's death. Redoubling her customary acts of piety in preparation for the impending ordeal, she arranged to wear for her delivery a special relic believed to be a girdle of the Virgin Mary. But divine protection, however ardently sought, was not forthcoming, for the birth was ten days premature. In consequence, the hapless queen was forced to her agonising task not at Richmond Palace as she had hoped, but within the dank, forbidding walls of the White Tower, no more than a stone's throw from the room in which her two brothers had previously been murdered. In this ominous setting, amid the stuffy, smelly fug considered so necessary for the health of newborn babies, Elizabeth of York gave birth on 2 February 1503 to a sickly daughter named Katherine. On her own birthday nine days later, wrapped in furs against the midwinter chill, the queen expired. The Princess Katherine meanwhile 'tarried but a small season after her mother', her only mark in history being the purchase of 4 yards of flannel at a shilling a yard to keep her from the perilous draughts.

If the loss of his new sister left Henry largely unmoved, his mother's demise was altogether another matter. Though their relationship had been lived mainly at a distance, this had, if anything, only served to enhance the prince's estimation of her qualities. This dutiful, but largely nondescript woman became, in effect, the perfect blank canvas upon which Henry would paint his ideal future partner. Indeed, he invested his mother with all the perfections that he later sought from his wives and in expecting heavenly bliss from union with them, he would more often encounter hellish disappointment. The death of 'my dearest mother', Henry wrote in a letter to Erasmus four years after the event, was 'hateful intelligence' and he seems to have construed the blow as yet one more of those sudden reversals of fortune so dreaded by his grandmother. Faced with the frustration of delayed recognition by his father, he now also came to harbour darker fears that would never recede: fears of death and mortal diseases that must be thwarted by continual vigilance. Disturbed by these worries and grieving sorely for his deceased mother, the second son now embarked uneasily upon his first lessons in kingship.

Since at least the middle of 1502, he had begun to eye his brother's exotic widow expectantly. Fate had whetted his ambition and, to all appearances, his star remained ascendant, since Princess Catherine's parents seemed eager to commit their daughter to a new circuit of the marital roundabout. Some two days before their letter of condolence to the English king had been composed, Ferdinand and Isabella of Spain despatched an envoy with instructions to propose a marriage between their daughter and 'the prince of Wales that now is'. If, however, young Henry's hopes were buoyed by the swiftness of this overture, they were soon immersed without trace in the unseemly mix of marriage broking and power politics into which his father now slithered with relish. In fact, there would be nothing gratifying or edifying about any aspect of the prince's first close brush with the practice of statecraft, as he rapidly discovered that both he and his hoped-for spouse were merely political counters to be lightly moved at will by their parents for any crumb of potential gain on offer.

The death of her husband had already left Catherine of Aragon in a particularly precarious position. The more strenuously Henry VII sought to acquire the unpaid second half of her dowry from King Ferdinand, the more resolutely the Spanish king resisted on the grounds that the widow's jointure due to his daughter should first be paid to him. Trapped thus between two feuding political giants, Catherine became more and more hopelessly squeezed. After her return from Ludlow Castle, she had been given initially the sum of £83 6s 8d a month by her father-in-law and although this matched the revenue of most contemporary noblemen of substance, it was still less than half the income she had renounced as Arthur's widow. Moreover, the amount was not nearly enough to maintain her household of fifty servants at Durham House, the mansion between the Strand and the Thames in which she had been installed by her father-in-law. Under the close supervision of William Holybrand, who had been appointed by the king to shackle her spending, she could neither pay her servants adequately nor even afford a wardrobe remotely compatible with her station. At the same time, her parents sent her nothing and when she asked in desperation to pawn a part of her plate to meet her growing arrears, they flatly refused.

Catherine was, of course, first and foremost a dutiful daughter who knew full well that the English alliance was essential to her parents' plans to oust the French from Italy and, as such, she was prepared to suffer almost any vagary that circumstance might contrive. Even so, the new matrimonial scheme now suggested by the King of England stretched political expediency too far even for Spanish taste. Henry VII was himself actively seeking a second wife at this time and the indecent keenness of his questing suggested interests and appetites that were neither wholly political in nature nor wholly appropriate to his age and dignity. 'If the king had been young', wrote Francis Bacon, 'a man would have judged him to be amorous.' So it was that England's monarch toyed distastefully with the notion of offering his own wrinkled hand to the Spanish princess, coolly disregarding a discrepancy of thirty years in their ages and the impediment in canon law entailed by their relationship. Unsurprisingly, the proposal left Catherine's parents aghast. 'Speak of it as a thing not to be endured', declared Ferdinand. Nor is it likely that such impropriety would have gone unnoticed by the new heir to England's crown, particularly when his own wishes were likely to be directly compromised.

Thus thwarted, King Henry settled instead for the original marriage option involving his second son and by the summer of 1503, with money wrangles and other details shelved somewhat untidily for the time being, the nuptial knot was duly tightened if not fully secured. On 24 June a treaty was signed with Spain at Richmond confirming that Prince Henry would marry Catherine on his fifteenth birthday and that, in the interim, the princess's parents should send to England a substantial marriage portion of 100,000 crowns' worth of plate and jewels. Two days later 'at the Bishop of Salisbury's place in Fleet Street', the boy found himself for the first time the focal point of a premier courtly ritual as Prince of Wales. After his father and the Spanish ambassador had solemnly consented to the betrothal, young Henry, only four days short of his twelfth birthday, took Catherine's right hand in his and spoke his carefully rehearsed lines. 'I am rejoiced', he declared, 'to contract matrimony with thee Catherine and take thee for my wife and spouse and all other for thee forsake during my and thine lives natural.'

Most curiously in the light of subsequent events, the considerable theological and legal complications posed by Henry's marriage to his brother's widow had been side-stepped with a lightness that bordered on abandon. An impediment clearly existed in canon law on the basis of the Book of Leviticus, which stipulated unequivocally that 'if a man shall take his brother's wife, it is an unclean thing' and went on to warn that any such marriage 'shall be childless'. But what was God's word when the affairs of kings were involved? Catherine was, in any case, adamant that her marriage to Arthur had never been consummated and her duenna, the ferocious Donna Elvira, confirmed that the sickly boy had been no true husband to her young charge. If the ladies were correct, then there was no significant barrier at all to future marriage with Prince Henry and the only legal oil needed to ease the match would be a so-called 'Dispensation from the Impediment of Public Honesty', entailing no direct intervention from the pope in person.

Momentously, however, both King Henry and his Spanish counterpart did indeed seek the Holy Father's personal involvement, in order, as they erroneously believed, to underpin the new marriage unshakably. Both, of course, wanted the marriage so badly by now and yet were so convinced of one another's incorrigible skulduggery that they were determined to leave no further room for further manoeuvre whatsoever. Ferdinand and Isabella were also anxious to press Catherine's dower rights, which could only be upheld if she had been Arthur's 'true' wife, however temporarily. So Catherine's assertion about the absence of sexual intercourse with her husband was conveniently ignored and it was assumed instead that Arthur had indeed been 'in Spain' on the night of his marriage, just as he had boasted next morning. After months of crude delay dressed up as weighty deliberation Pope Julius II therefore stated with characteristic pliancy that despite the affinity between them, Henry and Catherine might wed with Rome's blessing. And there, for the moment, the matter rested: like a heavy boulder finely perched upon a fragile mountain ledge.

For a short while, some of those loitering unthinkingly below were delighted by the happy prospects in store and none more so than the heir to the throne himself, who now plunged into a stylised adoration of his wife-to-be just as the courtly conventions of the day required. Henry had, after all, been thoroughly dowsed in the chivalric sentimentality of those new and old romances, which were now gushing forth in such profusion from the printing presses of Italy, France and Spain, as well as England. Anywhere and everywhere, it seemed, love's anthems resounded. At the elaborate 'disguisings' that so captivated the Tudor court young Henry saw laughing damsels 'in their hair' gaze down enticingly from mock castles as they awaited rescue by virile young knights on trusty steeds. And no tournament was complete unless embellished with a cooing throng of winsome maidens. Likewise, when the Children of the Chapel Royal raised their piping voices in the minstrels' gallery during dinner, it was usually on the theme of love's power, just like the songs sung by courtiers when the eating was done. The prince's mind was thus awash with words like 'truth and honour' and filled to overflowing with plaints of faithful swains scorned by heartless maidens. On those rare occasions, therefore, that he met his loved one in her once gorgeous but now fast-fading clothes, this would-be knightly paragon was stricken with noble pity and swollen by protective pride.

But as young Henry's heart fluttered, so his resentment towards his father was also taking wing. By 1504, he was already comfortably of an age when any self-respecting Prince of Wales could normally expect to be sent to live near his principality. Even the unfortunate little Edward V had taken up residence in Ludlow Castle earlier than this and for a boy of Henry's precocity and ambition the prospect of newfound freedom and status was irresistible. As winter had turned to spring and early summer, however, he continued to await the king's order with growing restlessness and when the command came finally, it was for Westminster rather than Ludlow that Henry was made to depart, since the king had decided that only there could the new heir to the throne be kept secure under his watchful eye. It was a judgement the boy would come to perceive, however erroneously, as near imprisonment, and his indignation is likely to have had far-reaching consequences. Firstly, it no doubt stoked his hatred of those treacherous rivals for the crown who had partly prompted his father's decision. Even more importantly, however, the command probably triggered the prince's reluctance to learn the art of kingship from his over-stringent father whose unrelenting efforts at his son's correction would create over time a damaging tension between the two: a tension which would serve only to compound rather than curb the heir to the throne's deficiencies.

For the short term, the consolations of young love might serve at least to dampen the prince's frustration, but fortune, as Catherine would discover soon enough, was as fickle as a dying mother's heartbeat. It was in November 1504, while Prince Henry was enjoying one of his 'wife's' rare, carefully chaperoned visits to the palace at Westminster that news arrived of her mother's death. With this single event the whole political nexus of which Catherine was the key link disintegrated and she went instantaneously from betrothed and beloved to bereft and benighted. Now that her father was no longer rightful king of Castile, Spain's future as a united entity was in grave doubt and her currency in the marriage market collapsed accordingly. Crucially, the dead queen's heir to the throne of Castile was not her husband but actually Catherine's unbalanced elder sister, Joanna, who was married to Philip the Handsome of Burgundy, son of the Holy Roman Emperor, Maximilian. No sooner had it become clear that Philip intended to rule Castile in his wife's name, it became equally clear to Henry VII that alliance with Philip was more valuable than alliance with Ferdinand. As such, the Spanish princess who resided at his palace was, in effect, largely extraneous to his political needs.

The heir to England's throne was already old enough to appreciate the changed political situation as well as the transformation in Catherine's political and personal status. Yet he was not so worn down by hard experience that he could perform the task now demanded of him by his father without the deepest misgivings. Though it was normal for betrothals such as his to be flippantly overturned, truth, honour and romantic love remained, ostensibly at least, unsullied ideals for Henry. It was no small matter, therefore, that on 27 June 1505, the day before his fourteenth birthday, he was made to renounce his previous promise of marriage to the Spanish princess upon whom he had lavished so much adolescent ardour. Moreover, he would have to do so secretly while she continued to consider herself bound to marry him. In this way, his father would have the option, if required, of engineering a more advantageous marriage with one of Philip's relatives as and when the opportunity arose.

Appropriately enough, the grubby deed was done and dusted not in the open daylight of the court but in a murky room beneath the kitchens of Richmond Palace's west wing. Here the prince presented himself before a black-gowned notary and a committee of privy councillors, huddled like conspirators. Presiding in a ceremonial chair and garbed in his formal robes of office was the aptly named Richard Fox, Bishop of Winchester, who had won royal favour long ago as a loyal servant to the Tudor cause during its supporters' dark days of exile in Brittany. Now, in these more comfortable times, he was used by Henry VII to smooth the moral creases in all the most subtle negotiations. Before this wily cleric, then (and the scribbling notary beside him), Prince Henry was made to declare gravely in the best manly tones he could muster that his marriage contract to Catherine was 'invalid, imperfect and of no effect or force' on the grounds of his minority at the time of the original contract. And as all good faith was duly shattered with this single hammer blow, so too was Henry's age of innocence.

If, as Fox insisted long afterwards, the king staged the protest only as a precaution, this is unlikely to have lessened its traumatic impact upon the boy significantly, for Henry was now being made to act in a manner wholly at odds with all the pretensions he had come to cherish. How, after all, could an aspiring hero of romance casually abandon his exiled princess, having hitherto rescued her single-handedly from a bitter fate? For his cold-blooded father there was no such dilemma involved in clinically selecting his priorities. Considerations of strategic advantage were of sole importance. But Prince Henry's finer instincts were as yet unsullied by reasons of State. Raised mildly amid lofty ideals of honour and courtly love, he could neither grasp his father's thinking nor readily accept his own complicity in what had passed. The only solution to this moral quandary was thus to lay the blame elsewhere, even perhaps upon the injured party herself. And so began the snake-like shedding of guilt that would become such a pernicious feature of Henry's behaviour from this time forth. Though what followed was approved by his father, it has nevertheless every appearance of being the future Henry VIII's first independent sally into the grimy world of policy.

In a letter to Pope Julius II, the heir to the throne was soon complaining that Catherine had threatened to make a religious vow dedicating herself to a life of rigorous contemplation and physical abstinence. Hearing, perhaps, of the prince's secret protest, she had indeed responded in the way suggested, and in doing so she not only threatened her physical health and child-bearing potential, but also challenged her 'husband's' authority over her. When, in October 1505, the pope responded by confirming that 'a wife does not have complete authority over her own body apart from her husband' and that 'the customary usages of her life can be revoked and undone' according to her husband's will, the results were of unimagined significance. Armed with what amounted to a papal imprimatur, Henry now had little difficulty in convincing himself that Catherine's intransigence provided further grounds for his recent denunciation of the marriage contract. By the summer of 1505, then, Prince Henry, budding humanist prince and would-be model of virtue and 'courtesy', had learned an invaluable political lesson for the future – how to sweeten misdemeanours by wrapping them in principles. Later on, by similar ingenious dance steps, he would extricate himself conscience-clear from other inconvenient relationships and come, more often than not, to perceive his victims as their own executioners.

Over the next three years the heir to the throne grew into an increasingly eye-catching figure, much more physically imposing than his father and all too conscious that a prince of State must also be a prince of fashion. Spangled and bejewelled, he sprinkled himself with musk, ambergris, lavender, rosewater and orangeflower, and bedecked himself in blue-and-red velvet and purple satin to emphasise the lustre of his skin. He began also to don the latest continental styles. His calves, which would become a particular source of pride for him, were enhanced by the latest knee-length bases from Italy and the sleeves of his doublets were puffed and slashed in the manner first favoured by Swiss and German mercenaries. Surcoats were cleverly topped to make his broadening shoulders appear even wider, while the loops of gold lace on his velvet cap served to emphasise the highlights in his hair. And naturally his locks were preened with the utmost care. Curled with tongs to meet the line of his chin, they also hung in bangs across his forehead 'like the priests in Venice'.

Yet while this dashing prince raced headlong towards magnificent manhood, his bride-to-be still struggled unavailingly to maintain regal appearances. Languishing in her cramped chambers on the edges of the sprawling palace of Westminster, where she had been made to reside since December 1505, she was, by her own admission, 'all but naked' for lack of funds. The fifteenth birthday of the Prince of Wales, which should have been her wedding day, came and passed, and piece by piece her jewels and plate were disappearing into Italian money-lenders' strong-boxes along Lombard Street. Every day her creditors came to insult her, the princess wrote. Already her cook had been sent back to Spain, captured en route and enslaved by the Moors of Barbary, and now she found herself attended only by Alonso de Esquivel, who served her as Master of the Hall, Juan de Cicero, her treasurer, a lone physician and her five remaining ladies, who were so wretched, Catherine claimed, that they were 'ready to ask alms'. Slowly but inexorably, then, she was sliding into shabby irrelevance and little by little her one and only hope was also perceiving her as a figure of no real significance beyond that laid down by his father.

If, however, the prince's relationship with his betrothed was at best one of magnanimous condescension, he had little reason to be satisfied with his own position in the broader scheme of things, for he continued to be held in numbing subordination by his father. The uneven nature of their bond is well illustrated by the events of the summer of 1508 when, at the age of 17 and within touching distance of the throne, Prince Henry was at last allowed to distinguish himself in his first competitive tournament. Fast approaching his final height of six foot three and clad in the finest Italian armour, astride his splendid horse caparisoned in rich cloth embroidered with ostrich feathers, he appeared to excel at every flamboyant feat in which he partook. Whether in running at the ring, or fighting on foot with sword and spear, or jousting in the tiltyard, he was eulogised by one and all. Yet little more than one month later on 24 July 1508 at Greenwich Palace, when Henry VII summoned Catherine to his privy chamber for a discussion lasting an hour and a half, the prince was still ordered from the room like a schoolboy.

There is a temptation, of course, to attribute the father's behaviour to simple resentment at the inevitable prospect of his own eventual eclipse by one more charismatic, dynamic and popular. But the king's misgivings about his son appear to have run much deeper, for by this time there was growing evidence that the new heir's lack of subtlety and self-restraint made him unsuited to the task of final consolidation that his father had earmarked for him. Chroniclers tell us how Henry VII would sometimes appear before ambassadors 'leaning against a tall gilt chair covered with cloth of gold, and a collar of many jewels' wearing 'a large diamond and beautiful pearl' on his cap. But money for such trappings was spent with a purely political end in mind: to convince men who equated rank with riches that he was truly king. In stark contrast to his son, he seems to have taken no intrinsic pleasure in clothes or trinkets and, if he countenanced a creeping hedonism among his younger courtiers, he did so dismissively. Nor is there any trace in the first Tudor of the braying self-advertisement so closely associated with the second. When Henry VII posed late in life for his portrait by Michael Sittow, he did so almost contemptuously, it seems, with scarcely tended hair and restless fingers suggesting a man eager to be done. This was clearly a man of business rather than pleasure who, even in the fullest flush of youth could never have flaunted himself at court revels dressed as a shepherd, Moor or Turk in the manner of his son. But times were changing and the future Henry VIII was already breathing deeply of the new spring air freshly stirring in the corridors and bays at court.

The conflicting priorities of father and son had much to do with the marked contrast in their upbringing. While Prince Henry, as the pampered son of a king, had known only security and privilege, his father had been schooled in struggle from his earliest days. And now the latter found himself in a predicament familiar to so many parents down the years. How could this father, whose duties had led him to overlook his son for so long, now establish a new, more personal relationship with him as the need arose? How, too, could this self-made ruler sympathise with the posturings of his indulged heir? How, for that matter, could he fully understand his son's elevated tastes and high learning, his novelties and flights of fancy, his love of ostentation? Alternatively, how could a headstrong youth comprehend the suspicions and sacrifices of a parent who had made his way against all odds? What began as mutual incomprehension hardened gradually into outright antipathy, as the prematurely ageing king applied an unyielding determination to keep his son in thrall for what he deemed to be not only the boy's own good but also that of the realm he would one day surely rule.

Until the very moment of his succession, in fact, England's heir was made to lead a stiflingly restricted life, which had the aggravating effect of fettering his egotism without suppressing it. According to the Spanish ambassador, Fuensalida, who came to England in 1508, the Prince of Wales was even at that late stage kept under such strict supervision that he might have been a young girl. Merely a year before his accession, Henry was often, it seems, 'as locked away as a woman' in a room leading off from the bedchamber of his ever-watchful father. He was apparently allowed to leave only through a private door and was surrounded at all times by attendants specially assigned by his father. No one, according to the ambassador, could approach or communicate with the young Henry and in public he scarcely opened his mouth. 'He is so subjugated', wrote Fuensalida, the Spanish ambassador, 'that he does not speak a word except in response to what the king asks him.'

None of this, however, should be taken to confirm the myth that the prince was confined to a single room throughout his time at Westminster. Contrary to what has been suggested by some of his biographers down the years, Henry undoubtedly retained some servants in his own right, including footmen, gentlemen ushers and chaplains, and also enjoyed his own minstrels and even a company of players. Indeed, a groom of Henry's privy chamber would later solemnly swear that the boy, just like his brother before him, had been accorded 'dignities proper to a king's son'. All this suggests, then, that the prince probably spent at least some of the time at the centre of his own miniature court, which though safely and conveniently hidden, was probably housed in comparative comfort. Within this microcosm, Henry could pose regally enough, eating his meals under his own canopy of State, while his servants looked on at a respectful distance lower down the room. And in the presence of his boon companions and tutors, not to mention his sister, Mary, who was five years his junior, he could even act out, however unconvincingly, the role of a budding Renaissance magnifico and make stirring promises of glorious martial deeds to come. But impressive as all this might appear to his tiny captive entourage, there was a growing realisation on the boy's part that the real world was largely eluding him and that his actual authority was desperately restricted.

Just as the heir to the throne rarely impinged upon the wider world outside, so the reverse was equally true. To visit the main thoroughfares of the palace Prince Henry needed the king's express permission and even upon entering the surrounding parkland for his afternoon recreation no one, except his specially designated companions, might speak to him 'for fear of his life'. At the same time, any visitor to the prince was first made to pass between the two yeomen of the guard who were always posted, with their gilded halberds, on each side of the door leading to the king's apartments. The very fact that Henry was mentioned so infrequently in ambassadors' dispatches during 1504 and 1505 gives the clearest possible indication of his anonymity. For if such insatiably gossip-hungry envoys could not engineer opportunities to meet him, then he must surely have been elusive indeed. Certainly, when he travelled with his retinue to Richmond, Windsor or any of the other royal houses he was every bit as closely kept as at the mighty palace of Westminster.

The heir to the throne was, however, most certainly encouraged to enjoy the exceptional company of at least one person – namely, William Blount, 4th Baron Mountjoy, an accomplished nobleman who was entrusted at the king's personal request to read history with him and improve his Latin composition. Appointed to his task as the prince's 'companion of studies' in 1499, only two years earlier Mountjoy had helped his sovereign crush the Cornish rebels. Like other members of the Blount family, then, this noble lord had firmly established his reputation for brave and loyal service to the Crown. But much more significant now was his glittering intellectual reputation. While still in his teens, he had become a valued member of the brilliant humanist circle that included Thomas Linacre, William Grocyn, John Colet and a young student of law at Lincoln's Inn, called Thomas More, who was already building a 'honey-tongued' reputation. Accompanied by his chaplain and Richard Whitford, a fellow of Queens' College, Mountjoy had been sent by his uncle to complete his formal studies in Paris, where Erasmus became one of his tutors. And after his recall to England to consummate his marriage to the young heiress, Elizabeth Saye, he invited the Dutchman to his house at Greenwich. Henceforth Mountjoy would be rewarded with the particular distinction of becoming the first English patron of Europe's foremost scholar. Indeed, it was as a result of his encouragement that Erasmus began work on the *Adagia*. All in all, therefore, the courtier seemed eminently suited to gild and burnish the Prince of Wales' intellect in the way that was now required.

Yet Mountjoy was intended to be much more than an occasional tutor to the Prince of Wales, for his chief function was to instruct the growing boy in the broader, even more rarefied skills of 'gentlemanly accomplishment'. Mountjoy's own exceptional grace and urbanity were renowned, and his involvement in so many of the welcoming committees arranged for important diplomatic occasions was no coincidence. In Castiglione's words, the consummate sign of nobility was 'to use in every thing a certain recklessness, to cover art withal, and [...] to do it without pain, and, as it were, not minding it'. All depended, therefore, upon the keenest self-knowledge as well as an intricate grasp of the inner workings of others. To this extent, true nobility was caught rather than taught and it was precisely here that Mountjoy laboured under insurmountable difficulties, since his pupil's acquaintances continued to behave not spontaneously and naturally, but like so many playthings and decorations. Indeed, such contrived deference was the only behaviour that Henry came to know and, with the passage of time, it became the only type of behaviour he would tolerate.

By observing his tutor in action, Henry would, therefore, only half-learn to play the game of courtship in both the wider and narrower senses. He would certainly discover how to adorn himself richly while feigning 'a gentle and familiar image' and how to gamble at tennis, bowls, shovelboard or dominoes with carefully contrived good fellowship. He would also see Mountjoy flirting effortlessly while playing card games like gleeke, ticktacke, cente or primero, and observe how courtiers delivered winning glances to their rapt admirers by candlelight. But as Henry watched woodenly on such occasions, he would be deceived into believing from sycophants of varied hues that the court was a clockwork toy merely created to dance to any tune of his devising. He would come to believe, too, that he alone was the vital spark that lit this court. If Mountjoy's task was, then, to initiate the prince into the finer points of right conduct, he succeeded, through no real fault of his own, in conveying only its showy periphery as opposed to its essence.

And while such a shining noble was, of course, perfectly suited to devise 'honest disports' for Henry's recreation, the prince's intimacy with him would also expose other facets of behaviour to be seized upon and readily misinterpreted. Mountjoy was certainly no wanton and it was from others that Henry would hear of the less seemly subterranean elements of court life. But though he was serious-minded, Mountjoy's predilection for women did lead him to marry four times. Moreover, he had married his first wife at nineteen and his peacock status at court along with that of others like him both reflected and reinforced the increasingly overt celebration of love in all its forms that was becoming widely accepted by younger courtiers as part of their culture. For the courtier at the start of the new century a love-struck look was as crucial a fashion accessory as the heavy gold chains on his breast and the exotic scent upon his body. Married or otherwise, whispers of a high-born paramour lent more glamour still to a man.

All this and more, the Prince of Wales will doubtless have learned at Mountjoy's side. And yet his own appearances at court were still confined almost exclusively to the more humdrum fringes of everyday activity. During these years, in fact, he was allowed no really significant role at all in front-rank functions and festivities. Shortly after his wife's death, for instance, Henry VII summoned the Earl of Kildare to England and for three months staged lavish entertainments in honour of his son Gerald, but Prince Henry did not feature. The same was true when sumptuous entertainments took place at Baynard's Castle and at Windsor to mark the visit of the Margrave of Brandenburg late in 1503. Even in February 1504, when a particularly lavish ceremony marked the investiture of the Prince of Wales, the prince himself remained largely anonymous. Two years later, when Philip the Handsome and his wife Joanna visited England, young Henry did spend a day and a night in their company under the careful supervision of Bishop Fox and was inducted ceremonially into the Burgundian Order of the Golden Fleece under the gilded ceiling of St George's Chapel. When, however, similar festivities occurred for the visit of Castiglione and other representatives of the Duke of Urbino, there was no contribution at all from the prince, and the same was true in 1508 when extravagant amusements took place at Richmond and Windsor to celebrate the detention of the Earl of Arran and his brother.

Meanwhile, if the boy's involvement in elite society was artificial and limited, his training in government up to the very time of his accession was virtually non-existent. He did, it is true, set his signature on a charter to the Earl of Ormond granting him the right to hold a weekly market and on a grant of certain revenues to the dean and canons of St Stephen's chapel in Westminster Palace. His name also appeared from time to time on commissions for the peace, as Arthur's had from infancy, and once on a commission of *oyer and terminer* at Westminster on 16 January 1503. But such acts were empty tokens and he was given no significant responsibility for State affairs whatsoever. Nor was he even encouraged to observe the operation of government at close hand. Only occasionally did he act as a witness to an official document and there is no record either of his ever having attended a council meeting. The plain truth was, then, that Henry VIII ascended the throne of England almost entirely untutored in the exacting art of kingship.

From some perspectives, of course, the stringent isolation imposed upon the prince was only to be expected. Great care had always been taken, for instance, to ensure that all talk in his presence was 'of virtue, honour, cunning, wisdom and deeds of worship, of nothing that shall move him to vice'. Likewise, the ever-present practical concerns about the threat from contagion will also have played some part in insulating him from unnecessary contact with the outside world. In 1508, after all, several servants in Prince

Henry's own household would contract a high fever before developing an infected rash and beginning to stink horribly in the final stages of what proved to be a fatal illness of unknown designation. Then again, there had already been some treasonous talk by the Lord Treasurer, Sir Hugh Conway, that, if the king died before his son reached majority, the latter might not have the support of influential figures at court. Nevertheless, when Henry VII habitually observed his son's scheduled exercise periods in the tiltyard from an upstairs window, his concerns were unlikely to have been stirred solely by issues of safety. The big question, perhaps, was not so much whether the son could be counted on to survive, but whether he could be relied upon to behave.

Since his initiation as Prince of Wales, Henry had taken his recreation in the company of other boys and youths known as 'henchmen'. Varying considerably in age and background, their number included Edward Neville, Henry Courtenay and Nicholas Carew, all of whom would be condemned to traitors' deaths in later life by the boy with whom they now revelled. Neville, who was a descendant of Warwick the Kingmaker, enjoyed the particular distinction of sharing Henry's colouring and husky physique to such an extent that he was even rumoured in some quarters to be the prince's bastard brother. Together the two teenaged boys would enjoy the same boisterous pastimes, competing in the lists and donning exotic costumes at splendid court functions, which invariably offered the chance to pose brashly before the fairest females on hand. But as well as servicing the prince's vanity by failing at every opportunity to excel him, Neville and his fellows also earned their keep as pages and were paraded as striking embellishments to great ceremonial spectacles. Sumptuously attired in black or blue velvet, as occasion demanded, and emblazoned with golden *fleurs-de-lys* and other majestic emblems, they acted as escorts and outriders, and in return for their efforts they were educated at royal expense in 'grammar, music and other cunning and exercises of humanity, according to their births and after their ages'.

Of all those who made up this thriving community of boisterous youngsters, one in particular, Charles Brandon, would have especial influence upon the prince. Seven years older than Henry, Brandon was in all respects the kind of dashing, reckless individual whom any hot-blooded boy with a showy streak would have been sure to follow. Though his blood pedigree was humble enough for Erasmus to refer to him later as a 'stable boy', in full adulthood he would come to be regarded as 'a second king […] one who does and undoes'. In fact, his father, William Brandon, was Henry VII's standard bearer at Bosworth Field and had been killed there, allegedly by Richard III himself. Thereafter, upon his mother's subsequent death in childbirth and the demise of his grandfather in 1491, the boy Charles became an orphan with no important title or great wealth. His luck was in, however, for, in recognition of his father's loyalty, he was now invited to court to become companion to Prince Arthur. Fate, moreover, would continue to smile upon him, since Brandon remained in London to be near the king's second son after Arthur's removal to Ludlow with Princess Catherine. Over the succeeding years, he became the closest thing to a best friend that Henry ever had, sitting as he did at the throbbing heart of a circle of 'boon companions' which would be crucial in shaping Henry's mental world as he grew to early manhood.

Already a young man in 1502, Brandon was impressively tall, broad-shouldered, black-haired, extrovert and glamorous. And though his gifts of mind were few, he more than made up for this by sharing to the full with his royal companion a marked physical exuberance and a headstrong delight in excelling at wrestling, hunting, tilting and jousting. He also exhibited a partiality for ladies, which was no doubt a particular source of adolescent admiration for Henry. By 1505, in fact, Brandon had already committed himself to marry Anne Brown, daughter of the Governor of Calais. And although no formal ceremony occurred at the time, the nuptial agreement had nevertheless been formally undertaken before Brandon's patron, the Earl of Essex. In effect, therefore, a binding contract had thus been established in canon law and Anne was soon pregnant.

But none of this would prevent Brandon from repudiating his betrothal after the subsequent birth of his daughter. Nor would it deter him from proceeding to marry Anne Brown's aunt, a very wealthy widow named Margaret Mortimer, as he demonstrated an asset-stripping opportunism that even contemporaries found somewhat distasteful. And even this was not the limit of Brandon's scandalous dealings, for the resulting marriage was swiftly dissolved when the outraged Brown family took their daughter's case to law – after which the double-dealing courtier eventually 're-married' her in a well-attended public ceremony which is likely to have occurred in 1508. Meanwhile, every juicy detail of the whole sordid business was no doubt imparted to the eager prince, who then went on, it seems, to draw his own merry conclusions about the proper place of marriage in the affairs of young men of vigour.

As companions, therefore, Brandon and his crew were certainly less than ideal. Yet they were also, as the king well knew, essential – not only for his son's happiness, but also to assist his education in military skill, which now began to take up many of the hours hitherto set aside for sport. War and mighty deeds became, in fact, a growing obsession for the young prince from this time forth. Though the chivalric tradition was already waning fast, it was far from dead in literature at least, and by the year of Henry's birth, more than a score of books extolling knightly virtues and heroic deeds had already left William Caxton's presses. It was Caxton who told his readers that 'it is most fair to men mortal to suffer labours and pain for glory and fame immortal' and this was a sentiment that would intoxicate the growing prince throughout his manhood and into gouty, bald-headed old age. He had been reared, after all, upon tales of Hector and Charlemagne. And stories of the Holy Grail and of Lancelot, Galahad, Tristram and Percival would remain a constant source of inspiration to him. He will have heard, too, of more recent exploits like those of the Chevalier Bayard, who, it was said, defended the bridge at Garigliano single-handedly against 200 Spanish soldiers. Until he had proved himself worthy of a similar reputation, Henry believed, he could never attain full stature as a monarch.

Above all things, he now longed to prove his worth against France, the traditional enemy of medieval English kings. Erasmus, who saw him a number of times during this period, later wrote to a friend that the prince's 'dream as a child had been the recovery of the French provinces'. The writings of Froissart, where all was talk of crushing victories on French soil, were duly devoured, and in the classroom the high points of English valour were further etched indelibly in his mind. He learned how the great triumph at Crécy had been followed by the capture of Thérouanne's sturdy fortress and came to know every detail of the Siege of Tournai, which Edward III had staged over many weeks. Above all, he dwelt upon the unparalleled exploits of Henry V, 'the flower and glory of all knighthood', who before the Battle of Agincourt had traversed his camp in driving rain, exhorting his dispirited army to rise up and seize victory against all odds. Henry was fixated, too, by the crusades at a time when it was still not finally appreciated that Christendom would never again raise its banners of war in the Holy Land. And as the prince's teenaged body steadily achieved heroic proportions, so his adolescent fantasies grew accordingly.

As a young man, then, Henry genuinely came to see himself as the perfect knight, and the gushing praise showered upon him only fuelled the unbridled romanticism that went hand-in-hand with his naive egotism. Having learned to fend off all-comers with sword, spear and poleaxe, he now learned to fight on horseback with Brandon and other henchmen in loud attendance. For the first time, too, he was fitted with dazzling plate armour fashioned in the smooth, rounded Italian style. Learning to mount and dismount without assistance, he was trained to move at speed under a weight of some 60 pounds, even in the scorching heat of summer, when the rays of the sun made the metal searingly hot. Furthermore, by the age of 16 he was said to be exercising every day in the lists and gaining his first serious instruction in the use of the lance. At every opportunity, he hacked, thrust and battered at man-sized quintains resembling scimitar-wielding Turks, and became familiar also with the use of guns and gunpowder and the wondrous destructive power of heavy artillery. There was not, it seemed, a single facet of the martial arts that was unknown to him. Nor is there likely to have been one in which he ever met a telling personal criticism or a serious challenge from his peers.

And as the prince's exploits continued to be vaunted so indiscriminately by one and all, so he began to exhibit a headstrong excitability that his father would find increasingly difficult to abide with the nagging advance of his own years. In 1504, when relations with Spain were at a peak, Hernán Duque had proclaimed that 'it is quite wonderful how much the king likes the Prince of Wales', but he added significantly that 'it is not only from love that the king takes the prince with him; he wishes to improve him'. According to Reginald Pole, a kinsman of the prince who was in a position to know, the king actually felt a deep aversion for his son, 'having no affection or fancy unto him'. Lord Montague, meanwhile, who was also ideally placed as an intimate of both the prince and the royal family as a whole, was another prepared to claim the same thing, only to find this used against him when charged with treason many years later. Certainly, the young Henry was capable by his defiance of driving his father into pathological rages, which left him in a trancelike state, 'his eyes closed, neither sleeping nor waking'. On one such occasion, according to Fuensalida, the king even fought so violently with his son 'as if to kill him' before shutting himself away for several hours to let his seizure pass.

As he approached manhood, the prince manifested a number of other disturbing traits, which his father could neither make good nor wholly contain. The observations of the Milanese ambassador may be particularly revealing in this regard. His comment, for instance, that Prince Henry was 'simple and candid by nature' has the appearance of a backhanded compliment highlighting the prince's regrettable tendency to overstep the mark on those rare occasions when he found himself able to play to the gallery. At sixteen, when a French courtier had complimented him on his archery, the prince responded naively and insultingly by pointing out that the courtier's own shot was 'good for a Frenchman'. Young Henry's vitality also fuelled a raging irritability and restlessness alongside his hearty bonhomie. The Milanese ambassador said of him that he 'wants to have his feet in a thousand shoes' and the same observer also implied that Henry displayed a particularly low boredom threshold, being 'never still or quiet'. Most worrying of all, perhaps, there was insecurity as well as pride. Erasmus noted that the prince 'could not abide to have any man stare him in the face when he talked to them'. And there was inordinate stubbornness, too. Thomas Wolsey would later say of Henry that once his mind was set, 'if an angel was to descend from Heaven, he would not be able to persuade him to the contrary'. 'Be well advised what ye put in his head', Wolsey warned, 'for ye shall never put it out again.'

The Prince of Wales' cloistered existence under the ever-watchful eye of his father had one further all-important ramification. Ironically, it was at the very time that the king was undergoing a marked physical and indeed moral decline that his heir became so firmly trapped beneath his smothering wing. Therefore, in these last claustrophobic years before his own assumption of power, the style of kingship that the son observed was that of an increasingly bad-tempered and obsessive father. And in this far from ideal setting, Prince Henry came to assume that an integral part of ruling involved the exercise of violent bad temper and the indulgence of personal whims. In spite of all his hard work and undoubted good intentions, therefore, Henry VII was unable to teach his son the cardinal principles of wise kingship: to discriminate between the use and abuse of power and to relegate personal concerns beneath the needs of one's subjects.

More and more in his declining years, the king resorted to the kind of bullying that later became the stock-in-trade of his heir. On one occasion the pompous and tactless Fuensalida so angered him that he refused 'to see or hear him' and gave orders that the Spaniard should not be allowed so much as to ride through the palace gates. When, nevertheless, Fuensalida arrived, the king had his servants seize the ambassador's horse by the bridle, in order to eject him by force. Another time, when the prince was fourteen, he was physically present as his father used a burst of unbridled wrath to solve a commercial dispute with Spain that had idled 800 English sailors. 'The words which came from his mouth were vipers', the Spanish ambassador complained, 'and he indulged in every kind of passion.' By the force of royal fury a crisis was for the moment averted, but the lesson, which was driven home to the onlooking prince, was that raging fury and a lascerating tongue were valid tools of everyday policy.

And as the king's fits of rage multiplied, so he also grew increasingly curmudgeonly and distrustful. The chief instruments of his oppression at this time were Sir Richard Empson, the base-born son of a Towcester sieve maker and his sidekick, Edmund Dudley, son of a gentleman of Atherington near Climping in Sussex. Both, in fact, were fundamentally loyal administrators. But both were also far too competent for everybody's good, including ultimately their own, when it came to their primary duty: the extortion of debts owed to the Crown. Possessing, it seems, 'a wonderful dexterity' in getting other people's money, they brazenly indicted a steady stream of great landowners for keeping retainers, failing to pay their feudal dues to the Crown, or occupying titles to which they had not been registered, until almost all of Henry's subjects who were worthy of notice found themselves entrapped in a webby system of bonds and financial guarantees of loyalty, from which there was no escape.

Nor, in these final years, was there the former lightness at court to compensate for the king's heavy rule and dark unpredictability. Indeed, as old age, infirmity and the loss of trusted advisers took their inevitable toll, the king encouraged little of the amusement that he had once enjoyed even in the simple slapstick of freaks and fools. 'For his pleasures', wrote Francis Bacon of Henry VII in old age, 'there is no news of them.' And after his queen's death especially, the court lost much of its former style and splendour. Older courtiers now harked back increasingly to the genial, open-handed Edward IV, who had made innovations at court 'after the manner of Burgundy', where successive dukes had set examples to all the courts of Europe in ceremonial and pageantry. But the king now wanted to pay only for as much splendour as was sufficient to impress observers, and the colourful festivities arranged in 1501 to mark the betrothal of Catherine of Aragon to his son, Arthur, were by this time little more than a dim and distant memory in the desert of comparative drabness that now prevailed.

So it was, with the approach of spring in his fifty-third year, that the wiry and chronically bronchitic king, whose teeth were by now 'few, poor and blackish', began his final creaking descent into a 'consuming sickness'.

And it was against this background of peace, quiet and aching dullness that Henry VIII was finally proclaimed king, just short of his eighteenth birthday and still technically a minor. Taking tranquillity for granted, there was little lasting grief among Englishmen when the time came. Indeed, the unleashing at long last of the new king's pent-up ego now resulted in an explosive euphoria that soon swept logic and all good sense before it. As the second Tudor burst upon his kingdom, therefore, his extravagance would merely be welcomed as liberality after the parsimonious days of his predecessor. Likewise, when Empson and Dudley were casually thrown to the wolves, the only cries to be heard were those of satisfaction that justice, long overdue, had at last been done. Nor were there protests when England's very own majestic troubadour made profligate war against the Scots and French, or plunged headlong into a legally suspect marriage with a Spanish princess, six years his senior, whom he had long neglected. Men yearn, it seems, for rest, only to become restless once it is finally theirs.

3

The Golden World of Coeur Loyall

'I am yours, Henry R., for ever.'

An inscription by Henry VIII in Elizabeth of York's missal, given as a gift to Catherine of Aragon.

As spring was quickening in April 1509, all England stirred mightily with hope, for the future was surely young and exciting. Henry VIII, freshly planted in his lush island realm, was set for romantic marriage and readying to lavish his inheritance on music, games and glory. Forceful of character, vital, hearty and ingratiating, this dashing prince was vaunted on all sides as a prodigy. The chronicler Edward Hall recorded that Henry was 'natural, young, lusty and courageous […] entering into the flower of pleasant youth', while Lord Mountjoy went much further, claiming that all England was now 'in ecstacies'. Thomas More even vied so gushingly with his praise that one French critic, Germanus Brixius, chided him for disloyalty to the deceased king. 'This day', More had written, 'is the end of our slavery, the fount of our liberty; the end of sadness, the beginning of joy.' The new monarch would be a ruler 'to cleanse every eye of tears and substitute praise for a long moaning'. Many foreigners, though, were no less fulsome. 'Love for the king', said one, 'is universal with all who see him, for his highness does not seem a person of this world, but one descended from heaven.' The plain fact was that in this new era 'called then the golden world', Henry VIII had a full hand of aces to play and ample scope to choose his game. Thanks to his father's statesmanship, he was the first English king in 100 years to succeed unopposed to a stable, peaceful and solvent realm. Furthermore, the second Henry Tudor, unlike the first, was of 'truly royal stock', embodying as he did the union of the red and white roses. Last, and by no means least, the new king literally looked the part.

Upon his accession in 1509 Henry VIII's eventual transition from semi-divine colossus to bloated tyrant in battered decline was an unimaginable prospect. Looks and stature were not everything in a king, of course. But to tower over all others helped considerably and a ruler who, according to one foreigner, was 'the handsomest potentate I have ever set eyes on' was in a most enviable position. Moreover, upon his succession the new King of England shone still more brilliantly by direct comparison to the paucity of competition on hand. He had, for example, every natural advantage over the Emperor Maximilian I with his snub nose and jutting jaw, not to mention the shifty-minded and shifty-looking Ferdinand of Aragon, who squinted in his left eye and lisped from the loss of a front tooth. Nor did that venerable debaucher, Louis XII of France, riddled with syphilis, cut any more dashing a figure. By contrast, Henry's auburn hair, 'combed short and straight in the French fashion', framed features so finely formed that they 'would become a pretty woman'. True, his neck was 'rather long and thick' and he had, too, a delicate, rather high voice, which he would retain throughout his life. When Henry was nearly fifty, an observer describing his daughter, the Lady Mary, reported that she had 'a voice more manlike for a woman than he for a man'. Even so, neck and vocal chords notwithstanding, Henry was, to all appearances, a physical paragon.

Ever restless, the new king danced, sang and jousted and seemed to care for nothing but spending his father's hoarded wealth. Yet the men who had been instrumental in amassing Henry VII's treasure were to be Henry VIII's first victims. Both the surgical skill with which the destruction of Sir Richard Empson and Edmund Dudley was legally sanctioned and the absence of qualm on the part of their sovereign were ominous signs of things to come. Very soon after his accession, in an effort to distance himself from his predecessor, Henry had pandered abjectly to public prejudice, by inviting all in the kingdom to lay charges of extortion against any of his late father's servants. Empson and Dudley were the king's obvious quarry, though in milking the realm during the previous reign they had been acting under royal instructions throughout and had no difficulty in proving this initially. Therefore, a totally fictitious charge of treason was subsequently concocted. Empson, it was alleged, seeing the old king on the verge of death, had 'resolved to seize the government for himself' in collaboration with Dudley, who was said to have 'summoned knights to repair to him with all their power'. Sensible precautions honestly conceived were thus neatly recast as conspiracy and in August both were executed while Henry and his courtiers were making merry at Windsor.

'Whoever yet saw any man condemned for justice?' complained Empson vainly and though the show trial and scapegoating of these newly rich dupes may not have been entirely of the king's own devising, it undoubtedly bore the stamp of many of his later injustices. Violent bolts from the blue and crude rationalisations of the indefensible would soon be familiar features of Henry's style of government and the tell-tale signs of future excess were already being recognised by those with eyes to see. Even when Thomas More was glorifying at full tilt at the time of the coronation, he acknowledged readily of his sovereign master that 'if my head could win him a castle in France [...] it should not fail to go'. Surely enough, in 1513, as a prelude to war in France, Henry would have his rival, Edmund Pole, summarily executed after seven years of helpless imprisonment in the Tower, so that men might learn the importance of loyalty during the king's absence abroad.

Nevertheless, for now at least, Mars was under wraps and all was love, headlong marriage and gay abandon. Within six weeks of his father's death the nuptial knot with Catherine of Aragon was impulsively tied in the chapel of the Franciscan Observants at Greenwich and there followed a riot of summer feasts, hunting, dancing and dressing up, which the death of Lady Margaret Beaufort a few days later did nothing to dampen. On the contrary, the demise of the king's grandmother in the abbot's house at Westminster on 29 June merely served to sever another link with a past that all around were busy forgetting. Though she was given a suitably grand funeral and buried, according to her wishes, beside her son and daughter-in-law in the Henry VII Chapel of Westminster Abbey, the new king would not allow her passing to curb his pleasures. Furthermore, the old lady's death would leave her grandson more at liberty than ever to plot his own unfettered course. By wilfully plighting his troth he had already directly flouted the advice of Warham, his Archbishop of Canterbury, who had raised once more the issue of Catherine's marriage to Arthur as a possible impediment. And now he was free to lavish his attentions upon his wife alone. Indeed, neither the queen's age, nor her previous marriage, nor the fact that at times she looked upon her new homeland as a freshly opened branch of her father's family business was enough to stay the king's ardour. Henry, it seemed, would have his wife quite literally at any cost, for from this point onwards he spared no expense in glorifying either his marriage or himself.

The gaudy centre of all the entertainments which now gripped the court was, of course, invariably the king. In a world where rank, appearance and conspicuous consumption were inseparable and princes vied for precedence, it was hardly surprising that the royal accounts were soon spattered with payments for precious items. We hear, for instance, of £335 despatched to a Parisian jeweller by the name of Jacques Marun and a further payment of £566 for assorted gems and a thousand pearls. 'His fingers were one mass of jewelled rings', wrote an Italian, 'and around his neck he wore a gold collar from which hung a diamond as big as a walnut.' Henry also sported, we are told, a pendant fashioned like a ship, its masts and decks outlined in diamonds. Predictably, the king's garments, fashioned from Venetian damask, sumptuous silks, sarcenets, satins and silver tissue, were no less magnificent. Doublets in cloth of gold costing the modern-day equivalent of more than £2,000 per yard and robes of shimmering bawdkin kept the Flemish tailor Stephen Jasper feverishly busy and earned Henry a reputation as 'the best dressed sovereign in the world'.

The new King of England gambled with gusto, too, though he did not always lose in good humour. Games of chance were popular at court, especially with the servants of royal ambassadors, and the Knight Marshal of the Household not only organised these competitions, but even acted as a bookmaker at tournaments. Banquets, in particular, rarely ended without the English game of mumchance, where the stakes were invariably high and in 1511, egged on by a group of Italian bankers, the king had a particularly heavy spell of wagering. Having lost a considerable amount of money, and feeling that he had been cheated by his Italian playmates, he proceeded to ban them from the palace.

In spite of appearances, however, the court was by no means entirely that of a dissolute, shallow pleasure-seeker. Even accounting for the sycophantic flannel heaped upon him, Henry's intellectual reputation was not without some substance. Eulogies about the king's accomplishments abound and one must assume that at least some of the hot air was generated by real fire. In this regard, it is significant, too, that a good deal of praise for Henry's gifts was often expressed in private letters. A rare man of principle like Philipp Melanchthon, for instance, called him 'most learned, especially in the study of the movement of the heavens'. But whether the king really did possess a 'lively mentality which reached for the stars' is, of course, another matter. In truth, Henry appears to have employed his gifts in a typically princely manner: enough to shine, but not enough to weigh him down.

Regrettably, Henry's love of God and learning did not entail a hatred of pride and bloodshed. Not content with pouring out his father's carefully garnered wealth at home, the new king was soon bent upon spending it even faster abroad by purchasing for himself what every young martial prince most desired, but Henry more so: the glories of war. It was only eighty years, after all, since an English king had been crowned in Paris itself and the new king lost no time in commissioning a translation of Titus Livius' life of that resounding legend Henry V, victor of Agincourt. Moreover, the bigoted whims of Henry's boisterous subjects suited his ends admirably. The hatred of the English, and especially Londoners, for their foreign brethren was well known throughout Europe and in the capital French, Venetian, Spanish and Burgundian merchants were ready targets for the rabble's barbs on the rare occasions they chose to roam abroad. Neither the mighty nor common folk had forgotten the bygone days of Edward III and Henry V, of which their grandfathers had told them, and it was still proudly boasted in those less thin-blooded days that every woman wore some jewel or trinket looted from France by her grandmother's husband or lover.

Even so, a war policy was not without its risks. South and east, over the water, lay the Great Powers – France, Spain and the Holy Roman Empire – and England, by comparison, was but a small and thinly populated island on the damp, misty fringe of civilised Europe. When Henry VIII was born, the King of England ruled less overseas territory than for 400 years. He held not one French province and Scotland was still a hostile independent realm. In Ireland, meanwhile, English control was confined to a thin strip of land around Dublin extending along the coast for about 30 miles and into the interior for less than twenty. Beyond this so-called Dublin Pale was the 'land of war' in which the only rulers, for Englishmen at least, were defiance and danger. Other than their boggy Irish foothold and the Channel Islands, the English kings ruled only Wales and, though they flattered themselves with spurious claims to the throne of France, the land they actually held there was confined to an area around Calais and the castle of Guisnes, about 8 miles in depth from the sea and stretching for about 20 miles along the coast. In fact, England's glory years had long since withered on the bough, and now the danger from abroad was real enough, for ships of the period had great difficulty sailing into the wind, and southern England was for most of the year a lee shore, easy to attack and difficult to defend.

In such circumstances, Henry VII had wisely followed caution's path and consequently by the start of the sixteenth century a Milanese envoy could write that he was 'perfectly secure against fortune'. It was England's good luck, in fact, that she had been blessed with a king prudent enough to seek safety in the diplomatic shade rather than risk the heat of conflict. 'His Majesty', said the Italian, 'can stand like one at the top of a tower looking on at what is passing in the plane' and the reason for this was the king's own sound judgement. Unlike his son, he had a keen awareness of his country's weaknesses and played to her strengths. He had a canny grasp, too, of his enemies' frailties and exploited them to the full. The Milanese ambassador, Soncino, noted in 1497 that Henry VII 'will always wish to have peace with France, though I think if he saw her up to the neck in water, he would put his foot on her head to drown her'. Eighteen months later he wrote to his master, Ludovico Sforza, that Henry 'seems to believe that even if the King of France became master of Italy, which he would not like, he would be so distracted in ruling it that no harm would ensue either to his Majesty or to his heirs'. What better for an English king, therefore, than to ride high by lying low?

But Henry VIII, by contrast, was now brashly set upon adventure. Indeed, one of his first declarations as king had already committed him to war against Louis XII, whose gout-ridden decrepitude seems to have rankled no less grievously than the youth and martial vigour of the next French king would do later. Nor could Henry curb his belligerent posturing. When, for instance, in September 1509 the Abbot of Fécamp came to congratulate him on his accession, he found himself gratuitously insulted for his trouble. Only the day after his arrival, at a mock battle he had been specifically invited to attend, the corpulent Frenchman found no place among the official spectators, making it plain, said the Venetian envoy, that Henry 'held the French king in little account'. Furthermore, the King of England was soon writing in secret to his father-in-law,

Ferdinand of Spain, to investigate the possibility of a two-pronged attack upon the common French foe.

In the event, it would be three long years and more before Henry's knights could trample the lilies of France for his greater glory, since he had inherited from his father those self-same councillors who had long governed England 'without sword and bloodshed' abroad. Though their motives varied, each member of the council's inner ring stood resolutely for the measured diplomacy of the previous reign. There was, for instance, Warham, chancellor as well as archbishop, who had married Henry to Catherine and crowned them both. Described by Erasmus as 'witty, energetic and laborious', he was a pliant, sceptical character who, it was said, 'only read' and would die with merely £30 in hand, 'enough for my funeral'. Frugal, then, and with no interest in sport, he seems to have seen war as little more than an expensive diversion from the ageing process. Similarly, Richard Fox, Bishop of Winchester, Lord Privy Seal and the man who had baptised Henry, also preferred peace, though more for business' than for goodness' sake, much like Thomas Ruthall, Bishop of Durham, whose narrow devotion to the everyday drudgery of accumulating vast lands made him the richest prelate in the realm. All feared lest, in the words of John Stow, 'such abundance of riches [...] the King was now possessed of should move his young years into a riotous forgetting of himself'. But though, as Stow added, they 'gate him to be present with them to acquaint him with the politique government of the realm, with which at first he could not endure to be much troubled', even the guile and gravity of such men could not indefinitely quell their master's growing war pangs.

For the time being, however, amid his frustrated anglings for conflict, there were other even more bitter surges of disappointment for Henry to endure. In November 1509, he had told King Ferdinand that 'Her Serene Highness, the Queen, our dearest consort, with the favour of heaven, has conceived [...] a living child and is right heavy therewith'. Accordingly, all the accoutrements of the birth chamber were made ready, including a 'groaning chair' upon which Catherine would perch throughout the delivery. Trimmed like a seat of honour in cloth-of-gold, it was suitably equipped with a gilded copper bowl to catch the royal gore. Nevertheless, such attention to detail proved unavailing, for in the last days of January 1510, after an agonising ordeal lasting a day and a night, the queen gave birth to a stillborn girl. The news was kept a closely guarded secret and, much to their fury, even Henry and his council were uninformed initially. It was not until May, in fact, that Catherine told her father, begging him pathetically 'not to be angry'.

Even as she wrote, though, the queen was already some two months pregnant once more and in the early hours of New Year's Day 1511 she was delivered of a son named Henry, leaving her husband beside himself with joy. He had cosseted Catherine in this pregnancy most cautiously and now that he was a father, it seemed truly as if providence had smiled upon him. Consequently, the celebrations may well have been the most lavish to date, for the banquets, costumes and pageant finery that accompanied the prince's birth were said to have cost Henry as much as sixteen ships of war. Nor could there be any doubt that the junketing at Richmond was as much a token of the king's devotion to his wife as a celebration of his fatherhood. At the high point of the festivities, he made his usual flamboyant appearance in the lists, this time as 'Coeur Loyall', flanked by five knight companions whose 'hose, caps and coats were full of posies' and bore the initials of the king and queen 'of fine gold in bullion'.

Yet only ten days later, England's hope was dead. The queen, it seems, was inconsolable at the news, while the father's response was oddly restrained. Though he gave his baby prince a most lavish funeral at Westminster Abbey, with 974 pounds of wax provided for candles on the hearse alone, he made no other outward sign of mourning. May Day was celebrated as usual with 'jousts against all comers' and no blame was laid at any stage. The midwife involved in the birth, Mistress Elizabeth Poyntz, was even rewarded for her efforts with an annuity of £20. Rather than pine or recriminate, Henry would busy himself almost at once with preparations for his first military expedition in assistance to his father-in-law. More and more, perhaps, the prospect of war now became a crutch as well as a glowing standard for this king of wounded pride.

Since the capture of Duke Ludovico Sforza nine years before, the French had intermittently controlled Milan and in May 1509, in alliance with Ferdinand, Maximilian and the pope, they had gone on to rout the Venetians at Agnadello and master northern Italy. 'In one day', wrote Machiavelli, 'the Venetians lost all they had acquired during eight hundred years of strenuous effort.' By the middle of 1511, however, both Ferdinand of Spain and Pope Julius II had become thoroughly disenchanted with the so-called League of Cambrai. Venice had submitted, but France had enjoyed both the pleasure and the profit as Ferdinand and the pope observed impotently from the sidelines. Therefore, Henry was now invited by Rome to join a Holy League that would set upon France and hopefully yield – in the name of God, truth and Christian piety – the most unholy profits for all the adventurers involved. As the diplomatic merry-go-round turned its giddy course, this time the Venetians were papal allies and, as such, they too fanned Henry's ambition to the full. The French king, they said, was 'elate and haughty' and 'wanted to be monarch of the whole world'. Behind the scenes, however, the pope still continued to eye Venice hungrily, while Spain, the League's third member, was concerned only with consolidating her control over Naples and annexing the kingdom of Navarre.

When John Stile, Henry's envoy in Spain, warned him that his father-in-law was only 'afeared for his realm of Naples' and cared not one jot for English interests, the observation fell on deaf ears. By now, indeed, Henry was already contracting with the gunmaker Hans Popenruyter of Malines for twenty-four 1,000-pound naval guns, known as serpentines, along with a further two dozen 'courtaulx', which, at over 7 feet in length, were equally substantial. He had even specified their names – Rose, Crown, York and Lancaster among others. 'Night and day and on all the festivals the cannon founders are at work', reported the Venetian ambassador. But while these preparations were unhappy news for Warham, Fox and Ruthall, they were much to the liking of a rising careerist called Thomas Wolsey, who was now to dominate the king's affairs increasingly. It was he, the king's almoner, who would order the thousands of handguns, the tons of saltpetre and gunpowder, the countless cartloads of victuals and every other conceivable provision for the coming business of war. And it was he, too, who would organise to the finest detail the transport of these items across the heaving Channel and beyond to the field of battle itself. Thus equipped, England's king was bent upon restoring some part of the empire which, until Joan of Arc's crusade, had stretched south of the Loire. All that was wanting was the necessary pretext and this was not long in coming.

Suddenly turned upon by his former allies, the French king did not smart for long without reacting. Having described his betrayal by the pope as 'a dagger plunged through the heart', he promptly besieged the papal forces at Bologna, while assembling at Pisa a schismatic Church council with a view to deposing the sharp-witted pontiff. In consequence, by November 1511, Pope Julius, 'this swarthy and pugnacious Genoese', had succeeded at last in enlisting English help 'to defend the unity of the Church'. Here, moreover, was a Vicar of Christ who once let it be known that he had pulled a galley oar in his youth, and had conducted his holy office ever since like a sailor on leave. Not long after the announcement of the new alliance, Erasmus caught sight of him in the midst of a procession at Bologna, a noisy spectacle of 'troops under arms, generals prancing and galloping, lovely boys, torches flaming, spoils, shouts that rent the heavens, trumpets blaring, canon thundering'. Over it all, above the general pandemonium, the pope was borne aloft in a gorgeous litter. 'I was dreaming of an age that was really golden', wrote the humanist, 'and isles that were really happy [...] when that Julian trumpet sounded all the world to arms.'

Already in the spring of 1510 the Holy Father had despatched to Henry a golden rose commemorating the Saviour's Passion and signalling the present need for war. But this was only the first of a series of blatant manoeuvres that had progressively inveigled the English king. When the French episcopacy had announced itself willing to recognise a rival, the pope responded by threatening to take back the title 'Most Christian King' from Louis and confer it instead upon Henry. And when subsequently the very throne of France itself was dangled before him, the snare was complete and the peace party on Henry's council undermined at a stroke. The bishops who had so far resisted the king's restless blustering could no longer constrain him, for his martial ambitions and dynastic fantasies were now unexpectedly sanctified. Bitterly denouncing the 'cruel, impious and unspeakable' French attempt to 'lacerate the seamless garment of Christ', Henry would now lead his nation straight into a Christian jihad which marked the revival of the Hundred Years War and the onset of a conflict that would dominate his reign and outlast his death. Ambition to cut a figure in Europe and a compulsion to break a lance for a righteous cause in France could not, after all, be suppressed forever. To play at soldiers at Greenwich was no substitute for leading a fully girded army into battle abroad.

While the Emperor Maximilian delayed in taking up arms against France, Henry determined to act with his father-in-law alone and, in June 1512, the Marquess of Dorset sailed out of Southampton Water bound for Gascony with 7,000 men. However, having reached the port of Fuenterrabia with the intention of attacking Bayonne, England's Spanish allies failed to materialise as arranged. In fact, while France was bracing itself for an English attack, Ferdinand, 'that ancient and politic prince', had sent his troops into Navarre, occupied it thoroughly and declared an abrupt end to the campaign. In the meantime, however, the English force, with negligible artillery and faced by novel continental formations of pikemen and arquebusiers, had sweltered through the summer looking hopelessly across the bay of St-Jean-de-Luz. 'Their victual was much part garlic', said one chronicler, 'and the Englishmen did eat of the garlic with all meats, and drank hot wines in the hot weather, and did eat all the hot fruits that they could get, which caused the blood so to boil in their bellies that there fell sick three thousand of the flux.' A bedraggled force of sullen and demoralised soldiers, 'glad that they had deported out of such a country', limped its way back to England.

Ferdinand's treachery was transparent. He had got what he wanted and, to forestall any protests, now bitterly criticised the English force, which had mutinied and sailed home without orders, bankrupt and diseased after four months of pointless waiting. In this humiliating manner Henry VIII's first foray into the perilous maze of European power politics ended. The expedition had wasted 200,000 ducats and the best part of 2,000 English lives, without striking a single worthwhile military blow. Moreover, Henry's response to this failure of Homeric proportions would set the tone for much of what was to come in later years. Having reacted at first to the news from Fuenterrabia by ordering that all the mutineers should be hanged, he opted finally for mercy at the specific request of the Spanish ambassador. However, after incurring his father-in-law's strictures without protest, Henry now summoned the captains of Dorset's army to the palace of Westminster, upbraided them in the presence of the Privy Council and Spanish ambassador, and ordered them to ask forgiveness of the Spaniard on their knees. By such means, Henry sustained his pride and maintained his conviction that all would be forgotten if only the next expedition against the French foe was greater still.

On 25 March 1513, while Henry still simmered, John Colet, Dean of St Paul's, preached the Good Friday sermon before his king at Greenwich and proceeded to condemn princes who were more eager to follow in the footsteps of Alexander the Great and Julius Caesar than those of their Saviour. Hearing that Colet was staying nearby at the house of the Franciscan Observants, the king went on foot to consult with him about his sermon. There, in the peaceful setting of the friary garden, he told Colet that he had come to ease his conscience, since he was disturbed by the dean's denunciations of war. Did he not, Henry asked, agree with Aquinas that some wars might be waged justly? Contrary to expectation, however, Colet remained resolute even after wine had been ordered. More unexpectedly still, perhaps, the king is said to have maintained a dignified composure throughout. Indeed, upon leaving his resolute interlocutor, Henry apparently assured him that he would continue to hold him in the highest regard. According to Erasmus, who probably heard of the incident from Colet himself, Henry told his courtiers that every king had his favourite doctor, but Colet was the doctor for him.

It was, then, a picture to stir the noblest sentiments: the gallant Christian prince, who would soon be twenty-two, preparing to lead his subjects in a just war for the defence of the Church and Holy Father, yet strong enough to countenance the sincere expression of pacifist sentiments. At the time, few noticed Henry's quiet orders for the dynastic murder of Edmund Pole and the transfer of his dukedom of Suffolk, with all its high connotations, to that upstart in the eyes of the old nobility, Charles Brandon. Moreover, by the hectic summer of the same year Catherine of Aragon would write to Wolsey that she and her ladies were 'horribly busy with making standards, banners and badges' for the imminent attack on France.

It was no surprise, therefore, that in Holy Week of 1513, around the very time that Henry was engaged in his earnest disquisition with Colet regarding the virtues of peace, the English fleet sailed down the Thames and out into the Channel under Sir Edward Howard, the 24-year-old son of the Earl of Surrey. Eighty ships in all ventured forth, including one boat named, with consummate irony, after Erasmus himself. In addition to a double complement of sailors, the fleet carried, according to one account, as many as 16,000 soldiers who would pour over onto the enemy's decks after his ships had been grappled. The objective was Brest and the force of Rhodes galleys, which, with their superior guns and lethal mounted crossbows, had been brought up by the French from patrolling the Barbary coast and harboured there under the command of Prégent de Bidoux. But Howard was soon writing of misfortunes and hindrances, and a crushing blow came when he personally led a force of light rowing craft to assault the galleys in their anchorage in the shallows of Blancs Sablons Bay, north of the Brest entrance which was inaccessible to the deeper English ships. From his own boat Howard was said to have boarded a galley, only to be forced overboard by morris-pikes and killed before his friends could follow.

Undeterred by his admiral's death, Henry made his final arrangements to cross to France. Indeed, the final formality in the preparation for a direct attack on France had already been sealed shortly before Howard met his watery end, for on 5 April 1513 the Emperor Maximilian had at last agreed to join the Holy League, leaving the way open for the prospect of a vast, four-pronged attack. Yet again, though, Ferdinand proved true to his character, if to nothing else. Betraying his allies to conclude a secret peace with Louis XII that left him in peaceful possession of Navarre, he coolly rebuked his son-in-law on whom the light was all too slowly dawning. Even so, the English campaign of operation, which involved a direct attack on northern France in the traditional fashion from England's bridgehead in Calais, could and would proceed without Ferdinand's cooperation. Though Spain's action brought an outbreak of hostility against its residents in London, the enthusiasm of Englishmen for war continued unchecked and the Venetian Pasqualigo still managed to declare to his brother, with no intentional irony, that there had been no king more noble or more valiant than Henry for a thousand years.

So at 4 p.m. on 30 June, on a fine midsummer afternoon, Henry parted from his queen at Dover in the midst of a fleet of 300 ships, the like of which, said one of his captains, Neptune never saw. Not one month earlier it was being rumoured that Catherine meant to cross with him despite the onset of her fourth pregnancy. Prudently, however, Henry had decided to leave his wife to rule as regent in his stead. Though it had caused the price of beef to triple, 25,000 oxen, 'the finest beasts from Lincolnshire and Holland', had been slaughtered and salted to feed his hungry troops, and 12,000 suits of armour had been ordered from drooling Flemish arms merchants. Nor had Henry skimped on himself. To enhance his personal magnificence he had ordered his goldsmiths to spend enough on the sumptuous adornments for his horse to buy twenty heavy brass field guns. His armour, too, was no less gorgeously appointed, since £1,000 had been lavished upon decorative chains and buttons alone. Over it all he would wear the simple tunic of a crusading knight.

Meanwhile, there had been both small sacrifices and large frustrations before the final day of departure. As the talk at court turned earnestly to saving money on clothes so that more might be spent on arms, Genoese and Tuscan cloth merchants felt the pinch. Special sumptuary laws had been issued forbidding all those below the rank of lord or knight to wear silk, and even the high nobility were expected to adopt a slightly less ostentatious mode of dress. Just as worryingly, a crisis developed over the soldiers' beer. Brew houses had been set up at Portsmouth to produce no less than 100 tons of it a day, but the soldiers complained that the country beer soured too quickly for their taste and could not rival that made in London with barley malt. When more was specially despatched from the capital, it was no better. 'Much of it is as small as penny ale', grumbled the admiral Thomas Howard, 'and as sour as a crab.'

Nevertheless, three hours after his departure from Dover, his ships brimming with men-at-arms, instruments of death and rancid beer, England's king approached Calais, where he was to be welcomed with great pomp on his first visit to the town. In making landfall to the west of the port, the English fleet had first succeeded in inadvertently terrifying the French garrison in Boulogne which had wrongly concluded that a direct assault was to be made on them. Indeed, it was only after an almighty crescendo of trumpet-blowing and cannon fire, probably intended as much to entertain the king as to fray the nerves of Frenchmen, that the ships finally turned eastwards. As Calais was finally sighted the salvoes from the fleet continued unabated and drew a joyous response from the mighty cannon set high on the town walls. So ferocious was the thunder of the guns by now that it could be plainly heard at Dover, more than 20 miles away, and Dr John Taylor, the king's chaplain, who was in the thick of things, duly launched into colourful, if inappropriate, comparisons with the Second Coming.

Upon his arrival the king was duly offered the keys to the town by its deputy, Sir Gilbert Talbot, while Charles Brandon, in his capacity as marshal of the army, and Thomas Wolsey, whose signature now adorned literally thousands of orders, receipts and authorisations, frantically supervised the unloading of the ships. In fact, Talbot had been teetering on collapse for some months past and only a few weeks earlier had been confined to bed for a fortnight. His own explanation of this indisposition was that in preparing so earnestly to receive the king's army he had forgotten to serve God and been duly punished. But perhaps the chief source of his troubles was better traced to the many wants of Wolsey, whose demanding presence was becoming increasingly apparent at all levels. Though Talbot had managed readily enough to lay in the tun of wine specified for the king's own use during his stay in Calais, the black 'gown cloth' which Wolsey insisted upon for himself had proven altogether another matter. Given, however, that the climbing cleric's every wish would have to be meticulously satisfied, messengers had been hurriedly despatched to St Omer and Bruges in search of the fabric. Only at the eleventh hour had the flagging deputy been able to report with palpable relief that the precious material had been duly acquired.

As Henry slept that night at the 'right goodly and sumptuous' Staple Inn, which was to be his headquarters at Calais, time was already of the essence, for even now it was nearly too late in the year to launch his invasion. If October should pass without a decisive outcome, mud would be as plentiful as shelter would be scarce and since it was much too expensive to pay the many mercenaries in the English force to remain inactive during winter, the whole army would have to be disbanded. However, since Henry's entire campaign in France was primarily a propaganda exercise, he felt no compunction in wasting all of three weeks upon banquets, tournaments and displays of archery, not to mention glittering daily processions to the church of St Mary's. In the meantime, when he was not knighting gentlemen he was pardoning petty criminals, though three 'Almayn' mercenaries, bearing their crusaders' banner in Tudor colours, were hanged early on for desecration of a church.

Ultimately, it was not until 21 July that Henry's force eventually left Calais and later that day the rain so typical of campaigns in Flanders and Picardy closed in. The king, however, travelled in all the style to which he was accustomed. Eleven tents made of cloth-of-gold and connected by covered galleries were his home en route and such was the attention to regal needs that the grandest of these pavilions boasted a huge gilded sideboard where wine was dispensed into golden cups. At his final destination, moreover, Henry would be sheltered within a specially prefabricated wooden house of six rooms boasting a special iron chimney. 'Therein', said a German visitor, 'stood the king's bed hung round with very precious cloth of gold, the gilt woodwork being carved and very well finished.' For good measure, his chamber attendants, which included the knights and squires of the king's body, gentlemen ushers, servers, grooms and pages, and a solitary lutanist, totalled 579, while his household, which comprised those responsible for the provision of his food and preparation of his meals, accounted for another 276 men.

For others there was neither pomp nor comfort. The invading force had mustered in fog and as the troops fell in, there was a cavalry stampede. In consequence, 'it was long ere ever the army might be set in order according to the bill devised by the council' and when darkness fell the entire contingent had covered no more than 3 miles before camping the first night in a driving gale at Coulogne. To compound matters, the tents of those fortunate enough to have them had already suffered in a storm of 4 July and were now further damaged. Perhaps this was the reason why the king himself did not sleep, but circulated in his saturated camp till the small hours encouraging his men with the thought that 'now we have suffered in the beginning, fortune promises us better things, God willing'. However, the common soldiers who were expected to improvise their own shelter under the stars 'as the men of other nations did', may well have been less than fully warmed by these words. Rumour had it already that the sweating sickness was at Brest, brought there by English sailors, and would surely spread to the army. Nor would it be long, in any case, before the moment of truth arrived, just before battle, when by long tradition yeomen soldiers would sink to their knees in prayer and take clods of earth into their mouths in token of the death and burial they faced imminently.

It was no coincidence that on 1 August 1513, Henry VIII arrived outside Thérouanne's sturdy walls, for this was the town captured by Edward III after Crécy. Here, Henry believed, he would begin to emulate his conquering forebears and seal his own glorious place in history. But as England's king prepared to act out his martial fantasies, Louis XII, that supposedly ferocious threat to all Christendom, had already sneaked timidly out of Paris in the opposite direction from his advancing foe. Ill, feeble and lacking heart, he took no part in any action to defend the fortress now sought so earnestly by Henry. And the hapless Frenchmen who found themselves stranded before the English host showed no more appetite for the fray. While they prepared for an onslaught that could have only one outcome, their king and fellow countrymen seemed but wistful spectators in a war that never quite came off.

Certainly, the chivalric posturing that drove Henry onwards bore little relation to the actual smashing of men's heads that now began in earnest at Thérouanne. Even in those far-off days war was becoming industrialised: the sport not only of kings, but of technicians and merchants, too. In the months before the English expedition crossed to France substantial purchases had been made of all types of mass-produced equipment. Thus John de Castro, a merchant of Spain, was commissioned to supply eighty handguns, each complete with its powder horn, for which he was paid 6 shillings per weapon, and there were innumerable similar transactions. De Castro's guns were relatively light and simple, but there were also 'harquebuses', more powerful weapons, which cost twice as much. There was the purchase, too, of thousands of 'complete harnesses': suits of 'almain rivets' for infantrymen, comprising breastplate and backplate, pairs of splints to protect the arms, gorgets for the neck and shoulder, and helmets, which cost around 16 shillings the set.

Then, of course, there were the great cannon: bombards, curtows, 'Nuremberg pieces', serpentines, falconets, multi-barrelled organs – all of which would belch and fume at one place and shatter men and property at a distance. These were the new fashion, and, at full fling, the batteries of these monsters now ranged outside Thérouanne's walls would require some 32 tons of gunpowder per day. Most famous of all were the dozen heavy guns provided by Wolsey and dubbed the 'Twelve Apostles'. These 'bumbardells', drawn by twenty-four Flanders mares, could fire a 260-pound shot five times a day. And while they were at their thunderous work, their smaller French cousins were busy, too. The hapless Gilbert Talbot, having followed from Calais, now lost a leg to enemy fire and Edward Carew, a Devonshire knight, was hit by a stray French bullet as he sat in Lord Herbert's pavilion, falling stone dead before the eyes of his dismayed audience. 'This is the chance of war', Herbert told those around about. 'If it had hit me you must have been content; a noble heart in war is never afeared of death.'

As for Henry himself, he was neatly insulated from such details. He would settle instead for all the glory of conflict without the gore, a circumstance that coloured his views of war throughout his life. He, of course, was the illustrious warrior-hero, the strong deliverer, escorted everywhere by fourteen young boys in golden coats, wearing scarlet mantles to keep them from the rain, their horses trapped in silver and adorned with silver bells that jingled gaily as they pranced. From Henry's own great bay stallion there hung 'little bells of gold marvellous costly and pleasant to behold' for which watching German soldiers scrambled in the mud after the beast had been made to rear before them for effect. In armour over cloth-of-gold, a shaggy, red-feather hat tilted above his jewelled cap, Henry, now bearded, towered over all and posed majestically. 'The King of England', wrote one German who seemed to like that sort of thing, 'is a very proper man.'

With the credulous Germans came Maximilian, their Austrian emperor, who was made of altogether shrewder stuff. His empire, which encompassed the Habsburg lands in Germany, as well as Switzerland, Burgundy and the Netherlands, was a sprawling, cumbersome entity, a patchwork garment of many seams, tacked together by countless conjugal threads. 'Let others wage war', ran the maxim, 'but thou, O happy Austria, marry; for those kingdoms which Mars gave to others, Venus gives to thee.' In fact, Maximilian was technically emperor in title only, since he had failed to reach Rome for his coronation, having been refused passage through the territories of Venice. Making an art of selling his allegiance to the highest bidder and a virtue of large-scale chicanery, he was known to contemporaries as 'the man of few pence'. And though he was full of imaginative schemes, they were never carried out, for he considered the task of implementing them beneath his dignity.

Affable, superficially charming and old enough to be Henry's grandfather, this new arrival at the English camp was, then, a tricky customer. But for all this, he was still Emperor of the Romans in line of succession to Charlemagne and, in spite of his cash balance at any one time, he was well connected. It was therefore taken by the young King of England as no small tribute when the great man joined his ranks, notwithstanding the awkward fact that the host he had brought with him was a far from potent force. Moreover, reading Henry like the open book he was, the canny emperor wasted no time in allaying English misgivings about his ragtag army by offering to fight not as Henry's ally but as a subordinate general under the banner of St George. For added effect, Maximilian even offered initially to fight for his noble ally as a simple pikeman. The imperial forces, too, would march under the English flag, he declared. The fact that Henry would have to pay them for their efforts did not diminish even slightly the artless pleasure he now derived from appearing to lord it over so august a lieutenant.

Not long after this most refined display of chivalric double-dealing, English forces did manage to win at least some small semblance of the glory that Henry VIII had invested so much of his father's money to acquire. On 16 August, a group of French cavalry, under strict orders not to fight, misjudged its position and, when confronted unexpectedly by the English, turned tail and fled. They left in their wake to be captured and ransomed an expensive and prestigious gaggle of noblemen that included the Dukes of Orléans and Longueville and that elderly military celebrity, the Chevalier Bayard himself. Over 100 other noble prisoners were captured and nine banners taken. Yet contemporary accounts greatly exaggerate the numbers involved in the encounter and the title given to this largely inconsequential skirmish, the 'Battle of the Spurs', precisely described the only sharp implements that the French actually brandished as they galloped pell-mell over the horizon in flight. For his part, the puffing King of England had, in any case, played only a supernumerary role in the engagement, though he had at least for a fleeting moment entered the immortal realm of chivalry – the realm of myth and fantasy.

In the meantime, while Henry was still savouring his victory, a far greater triumph in Scotland eclipsed every other event in France of that summer. For more than 300 years the Scots had been allies of the French against their common enemy, England. The international status of Scotland had risen sharply during the reign of James IV, who had set out to make his kingdom one of Christendom's leading nations. Well educated and a good Latin scholar, James could not only talk Gaelic with the Highlanders, as well as lowland Scots, but was also familiar with all the leading European languages. He built a navy, opened gunpowder factories in Fife, intervened in European politics and in 1503 married Henry VIII's elder sister, Margaret. His court was splendid and included, amongst other notables, the poets William Dunbar and David Lindsay, not to mention a bevy of beautiful ladies, several of whom he seduced. But though his realm boasted three universities as compared to England's two and its scholars taught in seats of learning throughout Europe, it remained for the people of other countries a mythical land inhabited by 'wild Scots' and bounded in the north by a great field of snow and ice.

The victory at Flodden on 9 September was a truly great one, if such a term can be aptly applied to bloody slaughter and the breaking of a proud nation. James IV had sold all his plate and 'eaten off pewter' to raise an army of 40,000 and pay for seven great guns, the so-called 'Seven Sisters', with which to gall the English foe. As the battle loomed, his nobles stood by him in the field in full strength, along with many churchmen too, who excused their collaboration in wholesale carnage by stressing that in setting off the guns that did the killing they were not killing with their own hands, which alone was sinful. At the same time, Thomas Howard, the indomitable Earl of Surrey, led an English force of 22,000. He had fought his first battle in the Wars of the Roses before the Scots king was born, and was as vigorous as ever at the age of 70. As he marched north, he took the great banner of St Cuthbert from Durham Cathedral and carried it at the head of his army, just as it had been carried to victory against the Scottish invaders in 1138 and 1346.

In spite of, perhaps because of, the fact that they had been deprived of beer for four days, the English fought with particular tenacity when battle was finally joined 'between 12 and 3 in the afternoon'. When James' great cannon opened fire with their 'filthey straw' from atop Branxton Hill, they were badly sighted and shot harmlessly over the heads of the enemy. The unarmoured Highlanders then took off their shoes and ran down the hill 'after the Almayn fashion' straight into English archers who for the last time in history played a decisive part in winning a battle. At the end, the Scots king, his bastard son and his quibbling clerics all lay broken on the field, waiting to be roughly plundered by dour Northumberland folk, who drove off Scottish horses in hundreds, and by armourers who swarmed over the butchered corpses for resale benefit. Thereafter, the surviving English soldiers slaked their four days' thirst with Scots ale. They would never have believed it to be so good, they said, 'had it not been tasted [...] by our folks'.

Queen Catherine, revelling in her new responsibilities as regent, had herself been moving north when the news of Flodden reached her. She had probably expected to lead her force into battle just as her mother had done three decades earlier and according to one account Catherine had already exhorted her captains 'in imitation of her mother Isabella', telling them 'that the lord smiled upon those who stood in defence of their own, and that they should remember that English courage excelled that of all other nations'. The news that she immediately despatched to Henry was therefore delivered as proudly as if the victory was entirely her own and may, for this reason, have been all the more double-edged for her husband. Though she was careful to attribute both this victory as well as the successes in France to her spouse's piety, she affirmed that, in defeating the braying Scottish foe, she had shown no less prowess than he. And though Henry had captured a duke, her men had killed a king. To prove it she sent her husband the plaid tunic of his fallen rival bearing the royal arms of Scotland and stained with his lifeblood. 'I think your Grace shall see how I can keep my promise', she wrote, 'sending you for your banners a King's coat. I thought to send himself unto you, but our Englishmen's hearts would not suffer it.'

In a vain effort not to be eclipsed by his wife after being so definitively outdone by her, Henry now set about the subjugation of the city of Tournai with especial fervour. 'We ordered our artillery', Henry boasted to the Duke of Milan, 'to be disposed for the assault. We greeted the inhabitants thereof with some shots, and conceded them, at their request, a two-day truce for the surrender.' It was true that the besieged considered themselves strong enough to resist the whole world, simply because of the great number of cannon in their possession; but as they had little gunpowder, they were hardly as strong as appearances might have suggested. One eyewitness, Brian Tuke, recorded, too, that there were no soldiers in Tournai, but only 'a great amount of peasantry and butchers with no commander-in-chief'. On 25 September, therefore, Henry and Maximilian entered their prize in a torchlight procession, with all bells ringing, to be presented with the keys and six barrels of burgundy. This impressive fortified citadel, known as the 'Unsullied Maiden', was, with its thick double walls, ninety-nine fine towers and resident bishop, an even richer prize than Thérouanne and Henry spared it in the vain hope that it might serve him as a prize to rival Calais in prestige.

That same autumn as the mist descended over Picardy and Flanders, the English trudged their way home through mysterious towns like Ypres and Dunkirk, which would become so much more familiar to their descendants. Among them was John Taylor, who had watched his countrymen arrive in summer from atop the walls of Calais, and Brian Tuke, who was eventually to become the first master of the royal posts. The former was mainly impressed by the emperor's deference to Henry during the campaign and by the great storms at night 'when the camp stood still'. Tuke, for his part, echoed Taylor's comments on the weather and added that, despite the various nationalities involved, the army was free of dissension – an outright inaccuracy, in fact, for fraught relations with the 'Almayns' and 'Burgundians' necessitated special orders from Henry's generals. Tuke also reflected gratefully that a force of such size was lucky to escape contagion, and noted that victuals were so plentiful that the men lived more cheaply at war abroad than they did in peace at home. They gained, he said, 'victories unparalleled, being always against many', which he took as clear proof of God's good offices.

In retrospect, though, the most that can be said about the campaign is that Henry achieved his personal objectives, however insubstantial. He had captured two important French towns, destroying one and claiming the other for his own. He had won the Battle of the Spurs and taken prisoner some of the leading noblemen and captains of France. Strictly speaking, however, he need not have gone to war at all, since the King of France had made peace with the new pontiff, Leo X, even before Henry's army had left Dover. And if Henry's knightly hankerings were temporarily satisfied, it was only at a truly staggering price. Antonio Bavarino reported to his

Venetian business colleagues that the king took with him fourteen wagons laden with gold and four with silver coin – 'facts which sound like tales of romance but are nevertheless true'. Meanwhile, another Italian, Lorenzo Pasqualigo, declared that the sums spent on artillery and camping gear alone could have filled a well of gold. Concluding his account of the first full-scale English invasion of France since the Hundred Years War, even Taylor rightly reflected that far too much English money, 'which greatly excels foreign coinage in value', had been expended. In the first three years of the reign, despite the extravagance of the court, annual expenditure had not exceeded £65,000. By 1512, however, it had climbed to £286,000 and stood by 1513 at nearly £700,000. Within another year, Henry and Wolsey had run through the limited capital in cash accumulated by Henry VII, and though by 1516 Wolsey had cut back war expenditure by almost 90 per cent, the reserves were all consumed.

Furthermore, the long-term consequences of the expedition were little short of disastrous. The main result was to burden England with a troublesome drain on scarce resources that would have been much better devoted to Calais. A strong Channel port had numerous advantages in commercial, political and military terms over the unhappy outpost of Tournai. And had England's five years of grinding effort there been turned instead to Calais, the precious harbour might not have been lost to the French by Queen Mary just over four decades later. In the event, England's position would also have been materially strengthened in the mortal struggle with Spain at the century's end. But the young king with money to burn, who was clay in the hands of older and wiser statesmen, could not wait to flesh his sword.

Meanwhile, the Holy Roman Emperor left tinsel and pipedreams to his ally and settled instead for the substance of genuine strategic gain. He had used the English army to keep France on the defensive for a whole campaigning season and to destroy Thérouanne while neutralising Tournai for more than five years. These were in themselves valuable services for which the emperor might have paid handsomely. But the full measure of Henry's naivety is revealed by the fact that it was he who treated Maximilian to the sum of £20,000 plus an additional living allowance of £20 a day. There is little wonder, then, that 'during this whole journey the emperor showed the greatest condescension, calling the king at one time his son, at another his king, and at another his brother'. Dr Taylor tells us also that at times of triumph Maximilian freely encouraged Henry to precede him, 'that he might not detract from the King of England's glory'. Sad to relate, the good doctor could not on these occasions have read the emperor's thoughts, which were surely awash with giggling contempt for the elated figure prancing before him. Was this not, after all, the puffed-up 'youngling' who was fighting his battles and paying him richly for the honour of doing so?

4

Brought Up Out of Nought

'It is a wonder to see the King how he is ordered these days, for the cardinal and the Duke of Suffolk, which the King hath brought up out of nought, do rule him in all things even as they list.'

Tavern gossip, reported by Thomas Wolsey's spies,
at Swineshead in Lincolnshire, 1517.

Like most other years in Tudor England, 1517 was a time of imbecile rumours among the poor and unemployed. In December, a certain Thomas Hykkes had claimed that 'Wolsey would put all beggars in a barn and burn them up'. But the king, said Hykkes, had refused consent without first consulting the Archbishop of Canterbury, who told him in no uncertain terms that such action could be condoned in Christ's name only if Wolsey himself 'was set in a pulpit and burnt with them'. Meanwhile, in the taverns of the capital, day by day, every unpopular act was laid to Wolsey's account and it was noised openly that he 'would destroy this realm'. Just as ominously, Charles Brandon's grandiose, pinnacled mansion in Southwark seemed to confirm widespread rumours that he, too, was a man of boundless ambition. And there was even darker talk of a king susceptible to sinister forces, ruled by others and seemingly unable to break the unwholesome bonds that held him. Together, it was said, Wolsey and Brandon 'meddled with the devil and by his puissance kept their master subject'. Nor was gossip of this kind confined to the tongues of yokels. At court, it was said that Brandon used magic to cause the leg of his rival William Compton to become diseased, and it was rumoured that Wolsey possessed a magic ring and had a familiar demon in his service. According to one creeping whisper, he had calculated the king's horoscope, then 'made by craft of necromancy graven imagery [...] wherewith he bewitched the king's mind and made the king to dote upon him more than ever he did on any lady or gentleman'. Even the hard-boiled Duke of Norfolk believed himself to be 'sore vexed with a spirit' sent to him by the cardinal.

So much, then, for any claim that the Renaissance somehow heralded an age of universal reason – though, in any case, the swiftness of Thomas Wolsey's rise would surely have stretched even the devil's ingenuity. Born some time between 1470 and 1473, this thrusting son of an Ipswich innkeeper and cattle-dealer had first risen to prominence by means of a powerful intellect that not even his bitterest enemies would deign to deny. For while John Skelton's references to Wolsey's 'greasy genealogy' were not entirely unfounded, the keenness of his mind had soon been confirmed by the fact that at only fifteen he took his degree at Magdalen College, Oxford. Even so, the academic life on offer could not hold him and after a short term as rector of Limington, where tradition has it he suffered the hospitality of the stocks for excessive gaiety at a fair, he began a fleet-footed ascent of the ladder of patronage. Emerging first as chaplain to Henry Deane, Archbishop of Canterbury, he then entered the service of Sir Richard Nanfan, deputy lieutenant of Calais, before becoming a royal chaplain to Henry VII. And such was his obvious impact that by November 1509 he had become both royal almoner and junior privy councillor. However, it was the backing and execution of Henry VIII's war policies that allowed him to quicken the pace of his promotion at a rate without precedent.

Wolsey was, said Polydore Vergil, 'to be taken by preferment as a fish by a worm' and though England had seen royal favourites before, never had there been one so ambitious or highly raised. Vain and greedy, as well as intensely loyal and hard-working, he had kept the English army fed, healthy and disciplined during the campaign of 1513, while winning his sovereign's affection with an earthy humour and worldliness that contrasted strangely with his religious calling and apparently insatiable appetite for minutely painstaking paperwork. Consequently, in 1514, after a mere five months as Bishop of Lincoln, the archbishopric of York fell into his grasp and only one month later he was granted the rich bishopric of Tournai as a personal spoil of war. Proving, moreover, that fortune tends to favour the already fortunate, Wolsey's accumulation of offices did not stop here. Not long afterwards, the pope was being urged to make him a cardinal, on the grounds that 'his merits are such that the king can do nothing of the least importance without him and esteems him among his dearest friends'. Accordingly, in November 1515 the red hat arrived in London 'with such triumph as though the greatest prince of Christendom had come into the realm'. As England's only cardinal, Wolsey now outshone even William Warham, Archbishop of Canterbury, and it was a natural step for him to succeed the primate as Lord Chancellor on Christmas Eve, 1515. Finally, in May 1518, reaching the peak of his giddy ascent, he was appointed papal legate. Thus far, no one man had ever amassed so many important offices in Church and State together. Nor, for that matter, would any ever again attract such hatred – though, as events would prove, the trappings of power were not the substance, since all now hung on the restless fancy of he whom the cardinal sought both to serve and harness.

At such a credulous time, there was more than enough similarity between Henry VIII and his minister to suggest to any superstitious dupe the existence of some sinister link between them. Both were rampant voluptuaries, extroverted, egotistical, ruthless and indifferent to the shame 'lesser' mortals might attach to certain base deeds. Both, too, were physically powerful men with apparently superhuman appetites. William Tyndale, a bitter critic, described Wolsey as 'a man of lust and courage and bodily strength to do and suffer great things'. Similarly, Wolsey was haughty and imperious, demanding the kind of deference usually reserved for royalty, and though, in general, he controlled his temper better than the king, this was not always so. On one occasion, it seems, he was not above striking the papal nuncio Chieregato, whom he then proceeded to bully in 'fierce and rude language'.

More than any other vice, however, Wolsey shared his master's irrepressible love of ostentation for ostentation's sake. No one who made their way at the Tudor court was unaware that 'outward esteem to a great man is as a skin to a fruit, which though a thin cover preserveth it'. As such, extravagant taste was no mere whim. In 1514, Andrea Badoer had been deeply impressed by the English nobles, who 'bore such massive gold chains that some might have served for fetters on a felon's ankles, and sufficed for his safe custody, so heavy were they, and of such immense value'. Yet the cardinal would outshine each and every one of his competitors in the brash art of opulent self-advertisement. Wolsey's 'upper vesture', wrote George Cavendish, his gentleman usher and biographer, 'was all of scarlet, or else of fine crimson taffeta, or crimson satin engrained'. Cavendish noted, too, how 'the broad seal of England' and his cardinal's hat were always borne before him. Indeed, his cardinal's hats appear to have become an outright obsession for him. Brought specially from France, they were dyed with a brilliant scarlet dye unobtainable in England. Gilt ones also adorned the bedsteads in his palaces, where nearly a thousand servants were entered on his household roll, all wearing his distinctive crimson velvet livery, emblazoned with the ubiquitous hat and the initials 'T.C.' for *Thomas Cardinalis*. And then, of course, there were those other beacons proclaiming Wolsey's status no less brazenly. Even the master cook of his privy kitchen, it was said, 'went daily in damask, satin or velvet with a chain of gold about his neck'.

Wolsey was, then, just as Cavendish described him, truly like a 'glorious peacock' and, as if to emphasise how far he had come, within five months of becoming Archbishop of York, he had acquired from the Knights Hospitallers a 99-year lease on the manor of Hampton Court. Here he established a household that would come to rival even the king's. Indeed, two Venetian ambassadors who visited him at the height of his pomp would both estimate the worth of his gold and silver plate to be £150,000 – and all this under the roof of a man whose father had earlier bought a house and some land in East Anglia for little more than £8. Outdoors meanwhile, Wolsey rode like Christ himself on a mule, though in this case the beast was bedecked 'in crimson velvet, with gold front-stalls, studs, buckles and stirrups'. Likewise, at banquets the cardinal was always served first, by virtue of his legatine status which made him the pope's direct representative in England, and whereas Henry was mainly accessible, Wolsey invariably remained remote. Not even a peer of the realm could obtain an appointment except through the cardinal's secretary and few were lucky enough to secure an audience before the fourth attempt.

All in all, then, it was hardly surprising that Thomas Wolsey should have his enemies, for few believed that his service to the king was anything other than self-interested. Cavendish observed that the cardinal's initial rise had sprung from the fact that 'he was most earnest and readiest of all the council to advance the King's pleasure and will, having no respect to the cause'. When the council had urged peace upon the belligerent king, Wolsey had, it seems, offered war, but would as readily have played the dove if the king's preferences had tended that way. By this means, it was said, Henry soon conceived 'a loving fantasy' for his almoner, who began before long to perform an unprecedented role, acting independently of the great officers of State as a confidential adviser to the Crown. This was, moreover, a function that he was ideally placed to exploit, since the magnates on the council, lay and ecclesiastical, were regularly distracted by their many other involvements. Unlike them, Wolsey was unencumbered during his early rise by the problems of estate management, building and the cares of diocesan duties. Instead, he could concentrate single-mindedly on the king's affairs and learn at leisure whichever tunes his sovereign cared for him to whistle.

All too often, it seemed, Wolsey was more inclined to give his sovereign what he wanted rather than that which might improve him. As those about him knew all too well, Henry was neither consistently nor exclusively focused on matters of State and he was determined from the outset to follow the practices in which he had been reared by having servitors fussing after him at every turn. Too often, he attended to State business only in fits and starts when the mood took him or the pursuit of pleasure allowed. He could, in fact, make slight illness a ready excuse for refusing to work for days on end and, by his own confession, he found the act of writing 'tedious and painful' – something which makes the copious letters that he later sent to Anne Boleyn all the more significant, perhaps. Government business might be shelved in favour of a special matins in honour of the Virgin or, more likely, in favour of his 'harts and hounds'. And, if he was tired after hunting, his ministers were wise not to bother him with official documents. Such was the king's inclination to dally that the Milanese ambassador recorded in 1513 how he 'put off our discussion to another time, as he was then in a hurry to go and dance and dine afterwards'. Therefore, accustomed as Wolsey was to gaining advancement through the simple and unfailing expedient of doing his masters' work for them, he made, from the young king's point of view, a perfect companion.

In fact, from the moment of his appointment as a privy councillor, Wolsey was prepared to transact his business without any recourse to the petty nonsense of protocol that might impinge on the king's sport. Though members of the council urged their sovereign to attend the meetings at which important decisions were being made, George Cavendish left no doubt that Henry 'loved nothing worse than to be constrained to do anything contrary to his royal will and pleasure'. This Wolsey grasped to the full, said Cavendish, 'and so fast as other councillors advised the king to leave his pleasure, and to attend to the affairs of his realm, so busily did the almoner persuade him to the contrary; which delighted him much, and caused him to have the greater affection to the almoner'. Even Henry's neglect of his wife was softened on occasion by the cardinal's personal intervention. It was he, for instance, who remembered on the 1513 campaign that Queen Catherine had entered the last months of her pregnancy and had begged for frequent letters, as she was without any other comfort in her husband's absence and was worried about his tendency to catch cold. When Henry was typically remiss, Wolsey duly filled the breach, assuring her that her loved one was being careful 'to avoid all manner of dangers'.

To his credit, Wolsey knew very well where his own gifts resided and how these could best be turned to the king's advantage. He was, without doubt, a marvellously gifted administrator – a one-man bureaucratic machine, with the stamina to work excessively long hours and a genius for recruiting talented staff, such as Richard Pace and Richard Whiting, Abbot of Glastonbury, to whom he could delegate routine matters. And though, of necessity, he neglected his archiepiscopal duties in the North, he never shunned even the most disagreeable tasks of secular affairs. He transacted unaided, we are told, the same amount of business as that which occupied 'all the magistracies and courts of Venice, both civil and criminal'. Cavendish described how, on a diplomatic mission in France, Wolsey rose at four in the morning and immediately sat down to write urgent letters to the king and others in England, stopping only to order his chaplain to prepare himself to say Mass. Twelve hours later he was still at his desk, 'all which season', Cavendish wrote, 'my lord never rose once to piss, nor yet to eat any meat but continually wrote his letters with his own hands, having all that time his night cap and keverchief on his head'. Finally, toward evening he despatched his correspondence, heard Mass and took a little walk, then went directly to bed after a light supper, ready to resume his labours the next day.

Even so, the general feeling among his enemies was that Wolsey had been propelled forward by a combination of elastic principles, supreme self-confidence and a knack for exploiting the young king's lightness. Henry's neglect of his regal duties had, it was generally thought, created an administrative vacuum at the centre of government which Wolsey freely exploited to his personal advantage. Equally, the anxious uncertainty underlying much of Henry's apparent self-confidence seemed to provide fertile ground in which Wolsey could plant his own policies. Certainly, the famous Holbein portrait of a strident Tudor giant bursting with majestic self-confidence and vitality was at odds with the living sovereign in many ways. In reality, the king's whole method of decision-making, when not explosively arbitrary, consisted of ponderous, mechanistic logic, which served as a convenient, if wholly inadequate, substitute for actual understanding and real responsibility. More often than not he preferred to postpone and, as it was reported in 1519, 'to sleep and dream upon the matter and give an answer in the morning'.

Not surprisingly, the cardinal's unbridled conceit reinforced the false but dangerous impression that he had taken over the reins of government from the king. The unparalleled splendour that accompanied his comings and goings, the increasingly dismissive self-confidence with which he seemed to merge his wishes with the royal interest, not to mention the near-regal fury of his displeasure all convinced foreign envoys that, in the words of Giustiniani, 'this cardinal is king'. Henry expressed himself only through Wolsey's mouth, it was said, and Richard Fox spoke for the whole council when he claimed that 'we have to deal with the cardinal, who is not cardinal, but king'. Indeed, by 1518, Wolsey was so thoroughly in command, or so Thomas More thought, that he appeared to be acting without the king's full knowledge, and the Venetians had begun to address all correspondence to the cardinal before Henry, 'lest he [Wolsey] should resent the precedence conceded to the king'. Meanwhile across the Channel, Francis I scoffed at the responsibilities the churchman had acquired, for it 'showed he held the honour of his king in small account'.

Nevertheless, those who came to confuse the servant with the master were largely deceived by appearances. In fact, the oft-quoted statement of Baltasar Tuerdus, envoy of Louis of Savoy, that Henry 'cared for nothing but girls and hunting', oversimplified a much more complex, multi-layered reality. Despite any evidence to the contrary, Henry still retained the keenest possible sense of his own sovereignty, which neither pastime nor good company would dull, and if he sometimes only played at the exacting task of kingship, he nonetheless played more than hard enough to confirm what Wolsey never doubted nor ever, for that matter, wished to doubt. Contrary to the common image, Henry did sometimes engulf himself in significant spurts of busy work – filing, annotating, quibbling over phrases in diplomatic correspondence and fussing over logistical questions where a clear-cut answer could be guaranteed ultimately. It was the king, for instance, not Wolsey, who went over the specifications for a new citadel at Tournai item by item, looking for ways to save money. It was Henry, too, who pored over the accounts of all his ships and the lists of their crews, and kept clearly in mind on a daily basis the locations and dispositions of his armies. On those occasions, therefore, when his mind was stretched but not overloaded either with anger or anxiety, the king performed his regal role convincingly enough.

Somewhat surprisingly, perhaps, the two men actually saw comparatively little of each other. Apart from important ceremonial occasions, such as the distribution of the Royal Maundy, king and cardinal were normally seen together in public much more rarely than might be expected, and it was the king's secretary who mainly acted as the intermediary between the two on a day-to-day basis. Each kept his own court and the two men tended to see more of each other at worship or around the banqueting table than in private discussions. Furthermore, the cardinal never accompanied the king on progress and his appearances at Greenwich and Richmond were relatively infrequent, which will almost certainly have suited the minister, since on those occasions when his master was inclined to intervene directly in plans, those plans would often be thrown into disarray.

But if the two men were often physically distant from each other, it was chiefly because of Wolsey's lurking assistance that Henry could project himself so authoritatively. Indeed, the king was kept so minutely informed that he could embarrass even ambassadors on occasion. When for instance, French envoys tried to boast to him that 10,000 Swiss mercenaries had been killed at the Battle of Marignano in 1515, Henry observed that the figure was remarkable, since there were at most 10,000 present. On the other hand, while the management of day-to-day affairs was left to the cardinal, the shadow of royal supervision remained all-embracing. Sometimes, usually after supper, Henry would keep his secretaries and his advisers busy for hours reading despatches to him and taking down his reactions, his plans and his directives to others. Richard Pace described, for instance, how Henry would read through letters three times, marking every passage he meant to answer, before dictating his replies, which were often accompanied by an instruction 'not further to meddle with the wording'. Furthermore, when an outbreak of plague necessitated the king's prolonged absence from court in 1518, he arranged for a special postal system to carry messages to and from Wolsey at seven-hour intervals.

The relationship between king and cardinal was, in fact, symbiotic. While the shark basked, his needs were tended continually, in return for which there was a constant harvest of rich pickings. Above all else, Wolsey's crucial task was to read the king's mind when he himself could not and for almost fifteen years, the cardinal performed this delicate task with consummate skill. Moreover, the foreigner who said that the king 'devotes himself to amusements and accomplishments day and night, and is intent on nothing else', was also quick to add that the Cardinal of York 'rules everything sagely and prudently'. But whether the dangerous art of deferential manipulation that Wolsey practised so deftly for so long could be conducted forever was altogether another matter.

Much would depend upon careful massaging of the king's ego and, in his heyday, Wolsey's attempts to drive home Henry's image as an archetypal Renaissance ruler succeeded admirably. Not only was the king presented alternately as warrior prince or Christian peacemaker, as occasion might demand, but he was also to be loved as 'Bluff King Hal'. Cavendish tells of an occasion when Henry suddenly appeared at one of Wolsey's lavish banquets in a mask, accompanied by sixteen others similarly disguised as shepherds, along with another sixteen bearing torches. Upon the aggressively incognito entry of the 'unexpected' guests Wolsey dutifully played the requisite game of startled incomprehension before Henry pulled off his mask and showed 'such a pleasant countenance and cheer' that all rejoiced. Taking the seat of honour that Wolsey had been occupying under the cloth of State, Henry then sat down amid general adulation to a new banquet comprising, so Cavendish informs us, fully 200 dishes. By such means, Wolsey succeeded in his ongoing task of helping to manufacture what amounted to a species of personality cult on his master's behalf.

Naturally enough, if the king's image were to be complete, it would need also to encompass both awe and mercy, and when in 1517, there were riots in London against merchants and craftsmen from Flanders, Florence, Genoa and the Baltic, Wolsey seized his opportunity with both hands. Incited by a preacher at Paul's Cross, and led by a disillusioned broker called John Lincoln, a mob of apprentices and assorted roughs used the May Day holiday to wreck and loot the foreign quarters and to overrun the city. Closing the city gates to prevent the king's soldiers from reinforcing the guard, the rioters temporarily took control, while Henry remained at Richmond confining himself to dire threats. Nevertheless, in a matter of hours royal forces under the Duke of Norfolk and his son the Earl of Surrey had made their way into the city to restore order. Remarkably, the damage was found to be light. 'This has been a great commotion', wrote one eyewitness, 'but the terror was greater than the harm done.'

Even so, Henry was now invited by Wolsey to come up to Westminster Hall from Richmond, in order to pass judgement in person on the hundreds of rioters who had been rounded up. Here, in full state, with Queen Catherine, his two sisters, his council, his nobles, and the Lord Mayor and Aldermen ranged about him, the king sat under his canopy of State. Then, down the long hall, came a miserable procession of 400 'poor younglings and old false knaves and a plain woman, in tattered shirts, halters about their necks, all along, one after the other'. Falling to the ground, they begged mercy, at which point Wolsey joined them on his knees, though the king remained adamant, even after his wife and sisters had added their supplications. Only when Wolsey, with tears gushing, pledged himself for the good behaviour of the prisoners, did the king relent, whereat all 'took the halters from their necks and danced and sang', making a great impression upon the spectators. 'It was', we are told, 'a very fine spectacle and well arranged.' Thus was the king's reputation for mercy sealed, though elsewhere in the capital the quartered bodies of forty others, denied pardon, made another sort of impression. 'At the city gates', wrote a visitor to London, 'one sees nothing but gibbets and the quarters of these scelerats, so that it is horrible to pass near them.'

Sadly, Wolsey's deference to the king was not matched by due respect for others, and both petitioners and courtiers alike declared that they would rather be ordered to Rome than approach the 'proudest prelate that ever breathed'. Such was Wolsey's reputation that even Lord Darcy, an ardent Catholic, eventually proposed a law that in future no papal legate should be allowed in the country. Not surprisingly, in his private moments, Wolsey must have felt the pressure weighing heavily upon him and, in 1517, Giustiniani caught a memorable glimpse of him deep in thought, his features troubled and his forehead furrowed in 'mental perturbation' as he gnawed distractedly at his cane. Above all, he was certainly acutely aware of the physical risks attending his rise and, therefore, when walking in the park 'would suffer no visitor to come near but commanded them as far off as a man could shoot with an arrow'.

Meanwhile, the king was doubtless purring inwardly at the readiness to hand of such a convenient and willing scapegoat, and when the time came, Henry's most loyal and tireless servant would be readily sacrificed at the drop of a cardinal's hat. Indeed, though he sat at the pinnacle for all of fifteen years, Wolsey was never more than a royal mood swing away from oblivion. But though the cardinal was undoubtedly a proud man with a crushing contempt for his inferiors, this was not the actual root of his jeopardy. The problem was, in fact, Henry's own vanity, which, unlike the cardinal's, fed off flattery and applause. Requiring worshippers, the king was always sensitive to public opinion and so it was that the worse deeds of 'Bluff King Hal' were always credited to his ministers. So it was, too, that these ministers were invariably sacrificed when they had done what was demanded of them.

Yet Wolsey was no mere selfless innocent. On the contrary, he was a political carnivore of the first order, whose addiction to status led him to glory in any opportunity to lord it over his betters. As early as 1511, while still officially only royal almoner, Wolsey was already circumventing the normal procedures of the king's officers and expressing himself too freely and cosily on affairs of the court. One of his earliest extant private letters was written on 30 September 1511 to tell Bishop Fox that Thomas Howard, Earl of Surrey, the chief noble around the king, had met with a cool reception at court and gone home the next day. Wolsey then proceeded to observe 'that with a little help he might be utterly excluded whereof in my poor judgement no little good should ensue'. This was, indeed, big talk from the son of an Ipswich commoner, whose native county had long stood cap in hand to the Howards of Norfolk.

There can be no doubt at all, then, that Wolsey sometimes exceeded his brief, just as there is no refuting that he was allowed to revel too glaringly in the reflected light of the king's power. And it was here, perhaps, that Henry's guile and culpability are both laid bare most fully. Not least of all, Wolsey's humble birth and utter dependence on the king plainly meant that Henry could unmake him at will. Yet Henry still quite consciously refused to rein the cardinal in, for only in the company of a base-born first minister could a ruler of his temperament feel entirely at ease. In such comfortable fellowship there was always service, never competition, only self-abasement rather than threat. Then again, Wolsey's apparent power and undoubted opulence suited Henry's needs nicely on two further counts. Firstly, they magnified and exposed the cardinal's function as a scapegoat. The more

Wolsey became the object of universal hatred, the less hatred there was to direct at Henry personally. Equally importantly, Henry construed Wolsey's magnificence as a means of magnifying his own. The logic here was as inexorable as it was crude. If Wolsey appeared so mighty, yet remained the king's chattel, how much mightier still must the king himself then be. Thus Henry could bide his time while Wolsey bore the burden of government conveniently until such time as the need arose to lop him.

In the meantime, opportunity had also arrived for one whose importance in Henry VIII's life and thinking has often been underestimated. According to the chronicler Edward Hall, there were, in fact, '*two* obstinate men who governed everything' at this time, for as well as Wolsey there was also Charles Brandon who appeared to be another 'scarcely inferior to the king himself'. The friendship between Henry and his hulking, spade-bearded shadow had, of course, been forged in childhood and it was this which gave their bond its enduring strength. It was Brandon who had led Henry into the tiltyard when he wearied of his tutors and sought blessed relief from the company of his father. It was Brandon, too, who had taught him the lore of the chase. Yet the real secret of this man's primacy in Henry's affections lay elsewhere and was captured much later, albeit unwittingly, by the Venetian ambassador who noted in 1531 that the king's best friend rarely dabbled in high politics, preferring to spend his time 'more pleasantly in other amusements'. More than any other figure at the Tudor court, Brandon was the nearest thing to a genuinely apolitical being, and it was precisely because he was guided by his glands rather than subtle stratagems that he became the king's *alter ego*. The things that mattered most to Henry – his wars, his women and his sport – were things he discussed more freely with Brandon than any other, and the fact that the mind of his childhood friend was an open book containing the simplest of plots made his company all the more conducive when the time for unburdening came. Higher even than Thomas More in the king's affection and more aware than Wolsey of his master's secret inklings, Brandon's careless indiscretions had so far bound him ever more closely to his sovereign, though soon even his charmed existence was to fall under a menacing shadow.

By 1512, Henry's boon companion had already whisked through two wives when he was given wardship of the heiress Elizabeth Grey, only child of the late John Grey, Viscount Lisle. And, true to form, he lost no time in laying claim to her title and fortune. Though she was only 8 years old at the time, a marriage contract was hastily drawn up which bound her to marry him when she came of age. One year later, letters patent had been duly issued granting Brandon the title of Viscount Lisle and referring to Elizabeth as his wife. Thereafter, the king's closest friend would show, just like Wolsey, that royal favour in time of war was a path that might lead to the very stars. As a direct result of his valour in the French campaign, where, as marshal of the army, he had been Henry's second-in-command and had taken possession of one of the gates of Tournai unaided, he became Duke of Suffolk: a promotion which outraged the Duke of Buckingham and led Polydore Vergil to remark that 'many considered it very surprising'. Moreover, as one of the two highest peers in the realm, he was now eligible to marry a high-born woman, irrespective of the fact that he was already on his third 'wife'. What the king had not counted on, however, was his own sister's infatuation with his boyhood friend, an infatuation which would, in due course, place the incorrigible duke 'in the greatest danger that ever man was in'.

For the time being, though, the King of England had returned from Tournai stuffed with delusions of might. And still craving a second, more ambitious campaign against France in 1514, he sought alliance with Ferdinand of Spain as well as the Emperor Maximilian. The ink had hardly dried on the Treaty of Lille, however, before those self-same old foxes had begun negotiating with the French, and in March 1514, John Stile was writing in bewilderment from Spain that 'all policy and craft be here used more for their own security [...] than for any natural love or kindness to their friends'. 'It passeth my poor understanding', Stile complained, 'and it please your Grace, wants others better learned than I am for to understand them.' So Henry was now left alone to launch the offensive against his French foe, from which his cheaters had nothing to lose and much, in the unlikely event that it should prove successful, to gain. Once more, Henry had planned for glory only to be treated to double-dealing contempt. Once more, too, the would-be arbiter of Europe had proven himself as blind to the realities of diplomacy as he was deaf to the small, still voice which should have counselled caution.

Yet neither of Henry's deceivers had counted on Thomas Wolsey's masterful counterstroke: a manoeuvre that beat Ferdinand and Maximilian at their own back-stabbing game and, in the process, sealed the wily cleric's rise. Wolsey had seen, as perhaps only he could, that Maximilian and Ferdinand had been too clever by half in their continual ruses, for in avoiding real confrontation with France for so long, they had lost their potency and Louis XII was no longer afraid of them. Instead, it was Henry, swollen with confidence and more pugnacious than ever, who was the real menace to French security and, in consequence, Wolsey was able to improvise a peace initiative with France of the most delectable kind. Though Louis was a gouty widower of fifty-two who gulped his spittle, he still hoped for a son and Wolsey had the perfect bride in mind. Naturally, in this subtle world of Renaissance diplomacy, where love in marriage was considered no more necessary than loyalty between allies, there was no difficulty in persuading Henry to offer the hand of his sister, the Lady Mary, who was seventeen and, so we are told, 'a nymph from heaven'. In return, then, for his sister's sacrifice on the altar of marital revulsion, Henry was to retain Tournai and receive from his slobbering former enemy a doubling of the 'pension' accorded by the French to his father under the Treaty of Étaples.

So Mary was duly packed off to France with a heavy heart and forty new gowns, awaiting she knew not what. Men had, it was said, never set eyes on 'a more beautiful creature, or one possessed of so much grace and sweetness'. The 'most attractive woman ever seen' was above average height, very fair and possessed of a wonderful complexion, which, according to the eagle-eyed humanist, Peter Martyr, was achieved 'without the aid of cosmetics'. But Mary was no less strong-willed than she was blithe, and when she agreed to accommodate her brother by making a marriage of State, it was only on condition that she could choose her next husband. Furthermore, there was no doubting that her next choice of husband would be Charles Brandon, with whom she had already fallen headlong in love.

In the main, Louis proved a generous husband to his new bride. But all did not run smoothly. Reports from across the Channel told how Louis 'loved to observe the good old French custom of dining at eight of the clock in the morning and going to bed at six in the evening; but now it suited his young queen that he should dine at noon, and not go to bed till midnight'. It was not long, too, before Louis dismissed Mary's English ladies, on the grounds that they came between husband and wife, and this widened the rift between the young queen and her dusty spouse. Yet Mary would not have to wait unduly for her new husband's demise. In November Peter Martyr wrote: 'If he lives to smell the flowers of spring you may promise yourself 500 autumns', and on New Year's Day he died. According to David Hume's later explanation, it seems that 'being of an amorous disposition, which his advanced age had not entirely cooled', the French king had been 'seduced into such a course of gaiety and pleasure, as proved very unsuitable to his declining state of health'. However, though she had been relieved of her aged romping burden, Mary's situation deteriorated in other respects, as did the prospects for continued peace between England and France.

The man now called to occupy the French throne was Francis, Duc d'Angoulême, who at twenty-two was greedy for fame, flesh and conquest. 'This great fellow will spoil everything', Louis XII had said of the man who now became Francis I, and events would bear him out, for the new king would help to keep Europe in turmoil for years to come. In marked contrast to his predecessor, Francis was strong, healthy and splendidly endowed for life in every way, it seemed. He talked boldly and continually, and seduced women every bit as energetically as he indulged in all other forms of violent exercise. He also patronised scholars, wrote verses of his own and built more grandly than any other monarch of his day, while in attire, deportment, dignity and easy grace, he was considered a paragon of fashion, nobility and good looks. Indeed, notwithstanding his tent pole legs and mighty shark's fin nose, he was, according to the unanimous view of contemporaries, 'as handsome a prince as the world has seen'. And though he had all the defects of a spoilt child, he fought so gallantly that Henry VIII was quick to identify him as an infuriatingly dangerous contender for the place he had earmarked as his own in the leadership of the new Europe. Most important of all, however, the new French king disposed of a power Henry's island kingdom could not hope to equal.

It was surely fate that Charles Brandon was already at the French court on a diplomatic mission when Louis gulped his last, although he had never, in fact, been far away. Even during the coronation festivities he had won great prestige at 'Barriers' when the French had set a colossal German to challenge him. For some time during the contest, odds were even, until at last Suffolk struck his foe with the butt end of his spear till he staggered, after which both men rested. Upon taking up the fight once more, it was said that 'the Duke so pommelled the German about the head' that blood spurted from his nose, 'which being done', the German was 'secretly conveyed away'. Though she had apparently been told by two English friars that she must stay away from the Duke of Suffolk, because of his traffickings with the devil, Mary now decided, in spite of all, to stake everything on Brandon's chivalry, affection and fear of a young girl's wrath.

Henry had sent Suffolk to France ostensibly to carry his condolences for the demise of Louis, but in reality to prevent the widowed Mary from being married off to the Duke of Savoy, another contender in the burgeoning bridal market which was growing up around her. And since the love affair between the king's sister and his best friend had long been known, an oath had been extracted from Brandon before he left England that he would not himself propose marriage. In February, however, with a remarkable economy of effort under the circumstances, Mary shamed him into making a runaway match and risking the full consequences. As she afterwards confessed to Henry, she had 'put my Lord Suffolk in choice whether he would accomplish marriage in four days, or else would never have enjoyed me'.

As the courts of both France and England buzzed, Suffolk wrote to Wolsey in a semi-literate patois that was all his own. 'I were like to be ondon', he struggled, 'if the matter should come to the knollag of the Kynge me master.' He would 'rather a died', he asserted, than that Henry should be 'miscontent'. 'Me known good lord', he begged simply, 'help!' Under growing stress, his writing became even more eccentric. 'Me lord', he wrote, 'Sche and I bouth rymittis this matter holle to your dyskrass: tresting ye in hall hast possebbyll wye schall her from you some good tydyngs.' ('My lord, she and I both remit this matter wholly to your discretion, trusting that in all possible haste, we shall have good tidings from you.') Both the contents of the letter and the language in which it was written speak volumes about the king's bosom companion. Invincible with sword or lance, expert on the pedigrees of hunting dogs, he could neither resist a testy woman's will nor form his words reliably on paper.

Of course, Henry took the news of the marriage 'grievously and displeasantly' and upon their return the couple were eventually forced to make over to him the whole of Mary's dowry from France and to pay a crippling fine of £24,000 in instalments. However, faced with a *fait accompli*, and well aware that it was his sister's impulsiveness that had overcome his friend's flaccid resistance, Henry made a rare decision to opt for moderation. Though the financial burden upon the couple was heavy, he gave them estates and lands enough in East Anglia to earn in rents what they owed him. Strangely, perhaps, he also indicated ultimately his full approval of the match by attending a second marriage ceremony for his sister and brother-in-law at Grey Friars church in Greenwich, and by accepting the compliment graciously when the couple named their first child after him. The friendship between Brandon and Henry was, after all, far too strong to be interrupted indefinitely and a crucial feature of that friendship on this occasion and others was that, just like Wolsey, the bumbling duke enhanced the king's celebrity without challenging or overshadowing him.

Sadly, however, Francis I was much less obliging, for in 1515 his armies had marched into Italy, sweeping all before them and, on 13 September, at Marignano, they convincingly overwhelmed the pro-imperial Swiss and Milanese in the so-called 'Battle of the Giants', which gave Francis control of all northern Italy. Even after the Venetian ambassador had told Henry that Francis had left Lyons and was on his way to Italy, Henry steadfastly refused to believe that Francis would dare to incur Tudor displeasure. 'The French king', he declared, 'will not go into Italy this year. I believe he is afraid of me, and that will prevent him from crossing the Alps.' 'If I choose', the boast continued, 'he will cross the Alps and if I choose he will not.' In an effort to make good this idle claim, Henry had even sent 100,000 gold crowns to Antwerp to pay the Swiss, but it was all to no avail. To rub salt into the English king's festering pride, Francis had also won great personal renown for his actions in the midst of the hand-to-hand fighting at Marignano. 'For two thousand years', the French king wrote to his mother, 'there has not been so grand or so hard a battle.'

Henry's response was simply to cast about for revenge by all means short of war and to throw good money after bad. Sir Richard Wingfield, the English ambassador, was duly instructed to suborn Emperor Maximilian into leading a force of 30,000 German and Swiss mercenaries against the French during the spring of 1516. When Francis had first crossed the Alps, Maximilian had done nothing, for he had been too busy paying his attentions to the Princess of Hungary, who was not yet in her teens. Now, however, at the sight of English gold, he became more warlike. Accordingly, in March 1516, the emperor came down over the Brenner pass and advanced menacingly on Milan before sundry bribes sent him marching boldly back to Innsbruck. After seven years of extravagant rule, Henry thus completed the bankruptcy of his father's treasury.

Meanwhile, in January 1516, Ferdinand of Spain, enthusiastically supporting the English king's plan for a pan-European alliance against

France, had dealt one last crooked hand by dying suddenly. Long ailing, he had expired, according to Peter Martyr, 'of hunting and matrimony, either of which are fatal to most men at the age of sixty-three'. His successor was Charles, grandson of both Maximilian and Ferdinand, and former fiancé of Mary Tudor. Solemn, spindle-legged and eighteen, the new King of Spain was already master of the Netherlands, but had never visited the realm that was now his. All in all, his personality was a mixture of grandeur and oddness, as complex as the patchwork Holy Roman Empire he would one day inherit. He excelled in no sport, was unpleasant in features and repellent in manner. No gleam of magnanimity or chivalry lightened his character, no deeds in war or statecraft declared his fame. Nevertheless, this unlikely ruler would, in the course of his life, become Europe's most powerful figure. For the time being, however, he was lisping, ineffectual and of worth only by descent. As such, he was more than delighted to conclude a treaty with his French counterpart at once.

Therefore, at Noyon in August, Spain professed every good will towards France, and the Emperor Maximilian was invited to join in the reconciliation – a possibility that sent shivers down the spines of both Wolsey and Henry. Charles had even undertaken to marry the infant daughter of the French king, an act which Henry declared scandalous, since the bridegroom was 17 and the princess not yet 1 year old. Predictably, however, more wagon trains of English money, amounting this time to 20,000 gold nobles, were despatched to keep the emperor on their side and, equally predictably, Maximilian received them as graciously as ever. 'My son', he is alleged to have chuckled to Charles, 'you are going to cheat the French, and I am going to cheat the English – or at least I shall do my best.' In the spring of 1517, therefore, he joined the signatories of Noyon, and England was, with scarcely concealed contempt, left to fend for herself in the diplomatic wilderness.

But luck, human treachery and Wolsey's consummate skill in exploiting both, would serve, yet again, to salvage at least glamour and the semblance of prestige for the King of England. Repeating the manoeuvre executed in 1514, Wolsey now made overtures to the French who were glad to dish their Spanish and imperial 'allies' before the same trick was played on them. To add to the delicious mix of circumstances, Maximilian was now poleaxed by an apoplectic stroke. His expected successor was his grandson, Charles, though the Holy Roman Empire's constitution meant that this could only be achieved by election: an election which Francis I could be guaranteed to contest. Therefore, both rulers suddenly became well disposed, for the time being at least, towards setting aside any talk of war, so that they could save their gold for the impending task of bribing the seven mighty electors who controlled the appointment of the new emperor.

The result of Thomas Wolsey's masterful exploitation of this extraordinary conjunction of events was the so-called 'Peace of London' or 'universal peace' between England, France, the Holy Roman Empire, Spain and the Papacy. The intention was a general settlement of the disputes between the states of Western Europe which would enable a united crusade to be undertaken against the Turks who were fast encroaching upon Central Europe and the Levant. At the high altar of St Paul's on Sunday 3 October, Wolsey celebrated sung Mass with a splendour that defied exaggeration. And though little comment was made about the meal provided by Henry in the Bishop of London's palace after the service, the State banquet Wolsey gave that night was said to have been more sumptuous than any feast 'given by Cleopatra or Caligula'. After dinner there was masqued dancing led by Henry and his sister, Mary, the Dowager Queen of France, and countless dishes of confections and other delicacies were served. Large bowls full of ducats were also brought in for those wanting to gamble at mumchance, even though, across the moonlit Channel swell, the tipstaff of Tournai's town watch was still waiting for the arrears on his salary of £4 a year to be made good.

Two days later, proxy marriage celebrations between the infant Princess Mary and the dauphin occurred at Greenwich and on the following day it was arranged by Wolsey that Henry and Francis should meet each other again near Calais at the place that would become known to posterity as the Field of Cloth of Gold. Fancying himself in a beard no doubt, Henry then swore as a token of goodwill not to shave until the two monarchs met once more. Not to be outdone, Francis also pledged to shun the razor. Alas, though, the tantalising prospect of the Kings of England and France greeting each other like desert island castaways was frustrated by Queen Catherine herself, who did not like her husband too hirsute. It was, perhaps, indicative of her tenacity or possibly a residue of some enduring affection on the king's part after ten years of childless marriage that she eventually prevailed. Daily, it seems, she 'made him great instance and desired him to put it off for her sake' until the razor was indeed finally brandished, leaving Henry to convince himself, as only he could, that the love between himself and his French brother lay 'not in the beards but in the hearts'.

5

Palace of Illusions

'Nor do I see any faith in the world save in me, and therefore God almighty who knows this, prospers my affairs.'

Henry VIII to the Venetian ambassador, Giustiniani, 1516.

On 19 January 1519, that gay old pauper the Emperor Maximilian died at Weltz, probably from laughter at those gullible enough to have been made fools by him down the years. In life, nothing had been too fantastic for his imagination, it seems, for though he lacked the might even to wrest a few towns from Venice, he had never ceased to delude himself with fond hopes of leading victorious hosts to the heart of the Turkish Empire or to the Holy City of Rome. In truth, he was only more inventive when it came to the fraudulent acquisition of money. 'The Emperor', Pope Julius II had once observed, 'is light and inconsistent, always begging for other men's money which he wastes on hunting the chamois.' But in the King of England Maximilian believed he had found an especially avid dupe. More than once he had offered Henry VIII his imperial crown and with each proposal the scheme involved grew wilder. The idea had first been mooted in 1513 and later Maximilian had talked of adopting Henry as his son. A further offer of the crown was made in 1516 when Maximilian suggested that the two brothers-in-arms should meet at Coire before crossing the Alps together in triumph. There the emperor proposed to invest the English king with the Duchy of Milan, after which he would take him on to Rome, resign the empire and have Henry crowned instead. For his part, Maximilian was to settle for being made pope. As an afterthought, the sovereign, whose main incentive in life was gold, also informed his daughter that he intended to be canonised so that when he died she would have to venerate him all the more diligently.

Until Maximilian finally shuffled off his earthly cares and made for an afterlife in which there would be better opportunity to pit his wits against beings of similar calibre, even Henry VIII had been able to resist these addled offers of the imperial crown. His advisers had told him of the folly of any potential quest and, for once, he had listened. 'The Crown of England', said Bishop Cuthbert Tunstall in a phrase that was to become famous later, 'is an empire of itself' and, as such, further dignities were incongruous and irrelevant. Besides which, the title of Holy Roman Emperor was mixed with little more than old lace and threadbare glories. Though by virtue of its earlier associations it carried with it, technically at least, a higher degree of rank and prestige than any other royal position in Europe, a long memory was needed to appreciate its worth. Indeed, the only immediate role performed by the emperor was to rule Germany and, amid the convulsions of the time, that alone should have persuaded any prospective contender to stand well clear.

When the latest contest began in earnest, moreover, it was, in any case, at best a two-horse race. Charles of Spain, as grandson of Maximilian, could lay claim to special preference on the grounds that he was heir to the Austrian House of Habsburg, which had for centuries worn the imperial crown. The King of France, on the other hand, being of much renown and superior in years of experience, was another possible ruler of the Germans. Certainly, his victory at Marignano and preparedness to pour 3 million crowns into the forthcoming election assisted his campaign considerably. By contrast, only once in the long history of the Holy Roman Empire had there been an English 'King of the Romans' with the appointment of Richard of Cornwall, brother of Henry III in 1257, and he had failed ultimately to be crowned as emperor. But none of this deterred Henry. In fact, the proposal became all the more romantic for the challenge involved. For him the Holy Roman Empire embodied the 'monarchy of Christendom', the highest honour to which any sovereign could aspire and by May 1519 his compulsive competitive streak had entirely overcome him.

Henry was driven, in fact, by a sour cocktail of vanity and jealousy, which seems to have been stirred above all else by insecurity involving the French king. From the first days of Francis' accession Henry had been embarrassingly envious of him. The Venetian Pasqualigo had, for instance, found himself fielding a whole series of questions about the French king when Henry intercepted him at breakfast in a bower at Greenwich in 1515. First, Pasqualigo was asked the following: 'The King of France, is he as tall as I?' to which the Venetian replied that there was only a little difference. 'Is he as stout?' was the next question and the answer was no. Finally, Henry turned to the all-important matter of the French king's legs, only to be told, much to his delight, that they were thin. At this, he was said to have opened the front of his doublet to display his leg, declaring, 'Look here; and I have also a good calf to my leg.'

In 1519, however, the King of England's looks would prove of little consequence, for even if he had indeed resembled an emperor, he had little else in practical terms to recommend his candidacy. Certainly, as Richard Pace hurriedly left England for Frankfurt on 17 May to push for Henry's election, he would have done well to offer up his prayers to St Jude, the patron saint of lost causes, for he had no real confidence in his prospects for success. His instructions from Wolsey, who lay sick with dysentery, were simply to gauge potential support and then to solicit the appropriate German banking houses for money to buy the necessary votes. In the meantime, Pace was to do nothing to help either Charles or Francis, but mislead both into believing that Henry was on their side.

The choice was to be made, as always, by the seven nominated electors, who would meet at Frankfurt to appoint the new emperor, though the successful candidate would be known as 'King of the Romans' until his coronation by the pope. Without exception, the electors were a sturdy, vigorous and utterly corruptible group of princes whose tattered morals closely matched the ragged muddle of lands that made up the empire itself. The Margrave of Brandenburg, for instance, who was known to the Austrians as 'the father of all greediness', was particularly influential because his brother, the Archbishop of Mainz, was also an elector. Therefore, he would need an especially exorbitant inducement to vote as required. Of the six remaining electors, two more were already in Charles's bag. The 12-year-old King Ladislaus of Bohemia and Hungary was engaged to marry Charles's sister, Mary, while Maximilian had already bought the votes of the Archbishop of Cologne. Three others – the Duke of Saxony, the Count Palatine of the Rhine and the Archbishop of Trier – were biding their time in considering the bribes on offer from Francis.

Not altogether surprisingly, the crushing impracticality of his sovereign's dreams became apparent to Pace soon after his arrival. When, for example, he asked the banker Hermann Rinck to make the necessary arrangements for bribing the electors, Rinck quickly learnt that they would insist on being paid in cash unless any bond was issued under the Great Seal of England. Pace was also told of the enormous sums that would be required, for in addition to the money already expended by Francis, Charles had made available another 1.5 million gold florins. To further complicate matters, the Archbishop of Mainz had demanded 52,000 florins for his vote before then increasing his price to 120,000. And while Rinck was of little use to Pace in mustering cash on this scale, Charles, by contrast, had the full elemental force of Fugger gold at his disposal. In the meantime, moreover, a very strong feeling had gathered ground in Germany that no foreigner should be made emperor, and armed bands were assembling to prevent any candidate except Charles from being chosen. Indeed, Pace felt his own life to be at risk.

It was not until the eleventh hour, however, that Henry finally abandoned the chase. As soon as Wolsey received Pace's dispatches, he became convinced that Henry should not pursue his candidacy and sent his chaplain, John Clerk, to Windsor to prevail upon the king to see sense. But during the long talk that Clerk conducted with his sovereign he found him difficult to persuade. Indeed, even after long and earnest entreaties, Henry refused to decide, telling Clerk merely to wait until morning. That same night at one o'clock, the troubled chaplain expressed his deep concerns to Wolsey: 'As touching his enterprise of the Empire, I have reasoned as deeply as my poor wit would serve me, not varying from your instructions; but His Grace, as methinketh, considereth no jeopardies.'

Nevertheless, as the new day dawned, the dead weight of the facts had even impressed themselves upon Henry. By this time, the electors were on the point of meeting at Frankfurt, and, as was customary, all foreign ambassadors were ordered to withdraw to Mainz until after the election. Orders were therefore swiftly despatched that no more money should be spent on the English king's candidature. Instead, Pace was to pay a series of small bribes to the electors on condition that they told Charles how they had been persuaded to support him only by virtue of Henry's efforts on his behalf. They were also to suppress the fact that Pace had made any suggestion that they might vote for Henry instead. For the time being, then, the King of England would have to content himself with playing the role of 'arbiter of Europe', which the cardinal had devised for him, without an imperial title to brandish. More ironically still, however, at the very moment when England's sovereign was convincing himself of his primacy among princes, Thomas Wolsey was attempting to purge his court of those very adolescent elements that he had so keenly fostered since the time of his accession.

From the earliest days of the reign, in fact, Henry had maintained at court a privileged circle of companions that included, among others, William Norris, his gentleman waiter, and also William Compton, chief gentleman of the bedchamber, who had been knighted for his service in the campaign of 1513 and was thought to have particular influence with the king. However, a small group of men of Henry's own age enjoyed a special status all of their own, for it was in their companionship that Henry sheltered from the cares of State. By virtue of the king's natural ebullience and gregarious nature these gentlemen of his privy chamber formed what amounted to an exclusive private club with their sovereign as president. It was they who jousted with him and let him win at tennis while taking his money at dice. They, too, formed the stage army for court masques, rode at his side on progress, shot with him at the butts, and caroused, carolled and cavorted with him into the small hours. By the spring of 1519, though, this high-spirited, laughing crew was becoming increasingly unwelcome to the council in general and to Thomas Wolsey in particular.

Of the six courtiers who were to be suddenly banished from court, John Peachy and Edward Poyntz appear only infrequently in the records. Henry Guildford, on the other hand, served as master of the revels and, in this capacity, was much sought out by both the king and the queen for the fairytale entertainments he designed and produced. Meanwhile, by virtue of his high Plantagenet blood, Edward Neville had been considered particularly suitable to occupy the prestigious office of 'sewer' (i.e. 'server') at the royal table. Nicholas Carew and Francis Bryan, in their turn, had come to prominence as young gentlemen whom Henry chose to 'set forth' and sponsor in feats of arms, even lending them horses and armour for this purpose in the spring of 1515. Bryan would become in due course an exceptional jouster, Carew an extraordinary one, and both men were to carve out glittering reputations in their master's service: the former as a soldier, sailor, cypherer, scholar and ambassador to France, the latter as a soldier and much-vaunted hero of countless tournaments. With a patch covering an eye he had lost in a tilting match, Bryan, more than any other of Henry's minions, had perfected the delicate art of retaining the king's favour, for he was as unscrupulous as he was dissolute. Nicknamed the 'Vicar of Hell', he owed his promotion, in part, to Anne Boleyn, but ditched her decisively upon foreseeing her fall. A poet, whose sonnets found their way into *Tottel's Miscellany*, and an ardent admirer of Erasmus, he was a gifted, charismatic and many-sided man. But in the spring of 1519 his star and those of all his dazzling company was in eclipse.

'Within the past few days', wrote the Venetian ambassador in May, 'King Henry has made a great change to his court', for he had dismissed some of those young companions 'who had enjoyed very great authority in the kingdom, and had been the very soul of the king'. Other officials had also been replaced by older, more experienced men. In itself, of course, this minor palace revolution was of only passing significance, but the exalted place that the fallen minions had held in Henry's affection and the suddenness of their fall from favour sheds much light upon the workings of his mind. From some perspectives, it was, indeed, more for dignity's sake than for high politics that the exhibitionist six were banished. According to Edward Hall, all were guilty of overexuberance and lack of due deference in the company of the king. 'Not regarding his estate or degree', said Hall, they were, too 'familiar and homely with him and played such touches with him that they forgot themselves'. But there was, from Henry's point of view, something much more disturbing and offensive about their behaviour.

By odd coincidence, some of these young bucks, including Neville and Bryan, had recently represented their sovereign at the French court, where they had made the unforgivable error of finding the even more roisterous and unbuttoned style of Francis I much to their taste. Each day they had accompanied him in disguise through the streets of Paris, 'throwing eggs, stones and other foolish trifles at the people'. More worryingly still, they learned during their stay to revel in 'French vices and brags' and upon their return, when reproving fingers were raised against them, these dedicated followers of Gallic fashion loudly decried the prim ways of Henry's court and English traditions. By now, in fact, 'they were all French' and found everything English, including their sovereign, ludicrously inadequate. It was this last feature of their behaviour, of course, which provided Wolsey and the council with precisely the opportunity they required to win the king's support. Suddenly, Henry's taste for his boon companions palled and he became ripe for action against the 'enormities and lightness' of his erstwhile soul-mates.

One day in May, therefore, the council, while meeting at Greenwich, called upon Henry to put a stop to the intolerable effrontery that was being given free licence within the confines of the court. The cardinal, Norfolk and Sir Thomas Boleyn were the most outspoken of the critics and, though the king was torn between love for what they did and anger at what they were doing, he agreed to punish his court's detractors by sending them away for a season. Accordingly, Carew was despatched to govern a fort in Calais, while Bryan, Neville, Peachy, Poyntz and Guildford were warned to tend their other offices more dutifully. But though their banishment 'grieved sore the hearts of these young men, which were called the king's minions', none, in fact, lost their standing with the king permanently. Indeed, within the year, they had resurfaced at Henry's side for what would be the most extravagant chivalric spectacle in which any of them, including Henry himself, had yet been involved.

The summit meeting between the Kings of England and France in June 1520 at what would become known as the Field of Cloth of Gold was loudly hailed on all sides as a watershed in Anglo-French relations, which was intended, in the words of Sir Richard Wingfield, to make 'such an impression of entire love between the two monarchs' that the resulting bond would 'never be dissolved'. The disappointment of the imperial election was, in fact, no more than a fast-fading interlude in Henry's plans and the cardinal now took up the threads for a meeting between the English and French kings on a scale more lavish than ever. Personal rivalry between the two monarchs had naturally enough bred mutual curiosity, too, and Wolsey firmly believed that relations between them could never be fully mended until both they and their courtiers had embraced and mingled cordially. To this end, the proposed meeting was intended to serve not merely as a political conference, but also as an unprecedented chivalric fantasia, which would banish long-standing distrust and weld old enemies in friendship. Now, instead of war, there was to be jousting, and in suspicion's place music, drama and feasting would hold sway.

In the real world, of course, ancient prejudice was deeply embedded at every level. The site chosen for the meeting lay between the English-held town of Guisnes and the French town of Ardres, and it was barely four years since English soldiers had sacked the latter and turned its dwellings to charcoal. French children, meanwhile, had long been reared on stories about the Hundred Years War when the English 'Goddams with tails' had pillaged and plundered their land. And many Englishmen, in their turn, were belchingly contemptuous of French peasants they believed so backward and exploited that they drank only water and tended their masters' fields unshod. In London, for instance, French merchants were cheated and intimidated and had even their most basic dignities flouted. Forbidden to attend English cloth fairs, they were stripped and searched at every opportunity and imprisoned as spies if found loose upon the streets at night without a candle. Furthermore, their English tormentors had long been arming themselves in readiness for the renewal of a conflict they now looked forward to with increasing relish. Indeed, since 1514, not only in a newly built armoury at Greenwich, but also in rented houses and cellars throughout the capital, German craftsmen had been fashioning weapons of all descriptions from the finest iron brought specially from Innsbruck.

The King of England, of course, bore his own intensely personal grudge against the French rival whom Wingfield described as 'young, mighty, insatiable'. Just like his English counterpart, Francis was flamboyant and ambitious, and his magnificence in dress and bearing was particularly galling for any would-be competitor. Adorned with a crown of uncut rubies and sapphires, and bearing a massive gold sceptre along with a royal staff of beaten gold, he was a sight to sicken Henry's soul. Nor was this the only cross for Henry to bear, since the women of the French court found their sovereign irresistible. Spurred on no doubt by the fact that his wife was the 'impotent, halt and naturally deformed' Queen Claude, Francis pursued beautiful women in droves and without compunction. In the words of one courtier he was 'of such slight morals that he slips readily into the gardens of others and drinks the waters of many fountains'. He was no less renowned either as a hunter of beasts. Upon the death of Hapequai, his favourite hound, Francis mourned for days before ordering that the dog be skinned, so that its hide could be made into gloves for sentiment's sake.

With so much pride involved, petty rivalries were inevitable in advance of the much heralded meeting between the two rulers. The English king retained, of course, his taste for bellicose bluster, telling all who would listen how it was Francis' fear of English arms that kept him cravenly hemmed within his own borders. The French king, claimed Henry, hated all Englishmen and especially their sovereign, but hid his malice under a false coating of warm words and sickly smiles. One day in the spring of 1518, while strolling arm-in-arm with the envoys, Giustiniani and Sagudino, Henry gave vent to his nagging insecurities with the kind of boastful threats that were his trademark. 'I know for certain that he wishes me worse than he does the devil himself,' Henry intoned, 'yet you see what kind of friendly language he employs towards me.' 'I prefer peace', he added, 'but I am so prepared, that should the King of France intend to attack me, he will find himself deceived. He will fall into his own pit.' It was amid such an atmosphere of simmering antagonism and covert treachery that a 'knot of perdurable amity' was now apparently to be tied.

However, if Henry bristled enviously at his French rival's accomplishments, Francis, too, was left mightily aggrieved when Charles V arrived at Dover from Spain on 26 May for discussions of his own with the King of England. Since the Treaty of London in 1518, of course, Henry's avowed objective had always been to mediate between France and the Holy Roman Empire, so that a crusade could be waged against the Turk. Therefore, from his point of view there was no inconsistency when imperial ships entered Dover to the salute of England's beflagged fleet, eagerly awaiting its own departure for Calais. Remarkably enough, even Henry's more humble subjects exhibited uncharacteristic forbearance in downplaying the emperor's lop-sided features and jumbled teeth, and taking delight in the 'benign manner of so high a prince'. The ruler who now rode over the downs to Canterbury in the midst of a splendid royal cavalcade had, after all, many other qualities to recommend him. Not only was he the natural and potent enemy of the French, but he was also master of the Low Countries and in particular Antwerp, which, as the chief entrepôt for English goods, was still central to the nation's wealth. No less significantly, he was the nephew of Queen Catherine, sweet and virtuous, beloved, it seemed, by each and all. Upon the emperor's arrival, wrote Thomas More, the felicity of all Englishmen was beyond description.

Though Charles had been King of Spain for four years, he was still but 20 years of age and had been elected emperor no more than twelve months earlier. Yet even in this state of comparatively raw inexperience he had the clearest understanding of the crucial task ahead. Throughout Henry's reign, England had been a stalwart ally of the Empire, but his recent dealings with France had created a pressing need for action on the emperor's part. Certainly, Charles's hand for the game ahead was not without its limitations. There was, for instance, no earthly possibility of forestalling the proposed meeting between the English and French kings at this late stage. Nevertheless, he could feed the worms of doubt in Francis' mind and at the same time ingratiate himself with his royal uncle. Most importantly, he could skilfully exploit the one ace at his disposal: the sacred bond of blood that he shared with the Queen of England. Next to his mother and his sisters, his aunt was his nearest living relative and she was as anxious as he to burn any incipient bridges between her husband's realm and France. Upon his arrival, therefore, Charles wasted no time in racing to meet her at Canterbury, and on the day after his arrival, in the midst of twenty-five of Catherine's most beautiful attendants and 'not without tears', they duly embraced at England's most hallowed place of pilgrimage.

In fact, it is not known precisely what took place on the political front in the remaining three days before the two rulers parted and the English royal party set sail for Calais. Not even Wolsey was privy to the confidential meetings between Henry and Charles, but it seems sure that the emperor's visit was a resounding triumph from his own perspective, for, strange as it may seem, his very vulnerability had proven his greatest strength throughout. As a shy and cringingly deferential youth, gangling hither and thither like a tasteless advertisement for the perils of inter-breeding, he had tickled the King of England's pride and caressed his vanity. Not only had the emperor listened attentively to every last drop of patronising nonsense that had cascaded from his host's lips, he had actively encouraged Henry to look upon him as a needy and defenceless son in desperate need of wise counsel. In due course, he would even complete the illusion of filial devotion by writing in gratitude for 'the advice you gave me like a good father when we were at Cantoberi'. Therefore, whatever else he did during his visit, the Holy Roman Emperor, consciously or otherwise, had won the King of England to his cause in the cheapest and most effective way possible: simply by making him feel big. Henry, meanwhile, bounced through the entire visit bulging with glandular vitality and goodwill, and emerged from proceedings utterly convinced that the fate of Christendom's nominal overlord was his alone to nurture, mould and protect.

How well Charles captured Henry's sympathies is clear from the fact that before both men left Canterbury in a torchlight procession, to make their farewells 5 miles outside the city, they had already arranged to meet again quietly at Gravelines, along the dune-fringed coast near Dunkirk, once the empty formalities of the Field of Cloth of Gold had been concluded. More importantly, they had tentatively agreed that Charles V might marry the Princess Mary, though she was still only seven and pledged at that time to the Dauphin of France. The imperial marriage, it was now thought, would be a more splendid prospect for England. Clearly, then, the pact of filial allegiance that Charles seemed to have established with Henry now turned the impending meeting between the Kings of England and France into a vacuous and costly farce. Nevertheless, it would, of course, have to be carried through at whatever cost. The eighth Henry's bushy beard had seen to that.

On 31 May 1520, Charles sailed from Sandwich for Flanders while Henry embarked at Dover for Calais. The King of England was accompanied by Wolsey, who was fortified for his sea crossing by the pension of 7,000 ducats that Charles had awarded him, and by the knowledge that the emperor had also promised his help when the next papal election occurred. One week later, in the awed presence of their followers and in the sight of thousands of the common people of France (who watched from the hills that created the valley known to Frenchmen as Val Dore), Henry VIII and Francis I would come face to face at last. They would meet as Wolsey had planned despite delays, difficulties and the inevitable subterranean double-dealing, and in the presence of the multitude they would proceed to bask in a chivalric spectacle that was blinding in both the literal and figurative senses. For not only was the luxury of the sixteen-day extravaganza utterly dazzling, it also concealed deep animosities and tensions that remained as real as ever.

It had been planned initially to lodge the English king and queen in Guisnes Castle, with Francis and his queen settled in the castle of Ardres across the valley. But the tumbledown edifice at Guisnes was found to have fallen into hopeless disrepair, its stagnant moat choked with weeds and its keep 'too ruinous to mend'. Therefore, making a virtue of necessity, English craftsmen raced madly against the calendar to complete in less than a month a fully fledged palace of brick and timber, precisely 328 feet square, on the castle green. It was a project that entailed truly awesome workmanship and the shipping of costly materials over considerable distances. Though the idea of a banqueting hall was abandoned ultimately in favour of a vast, highly ornate tent, the palace proper still included three chambers for the king on the first floor, the largest being more spacious than the White Hall at Westminster. The great hall in the palace was, according to the testimony of two astonished Italians, 'as lofty as that of the Pasaro palace at San Benetto, but longer, with a ceiling of green sarcenet and gold roses, decorated with hangings of silk and gold, woven with figures and horses represented to the life'. There was even a secret passage to take Henry to a privy lodging in Guisnes Castle, where he could take his ease. Meanwhile, outside his so-called 'palace of illusions', English ingenuity and foresight had conceived, as a definitive flourish, a gilt fountain of antique workmanship, with a statue of Bacchus 'birlying the wine'.

The magnificence of the occasion was also reflected in the garments on display. 'Never before was seen in England such excess of apparelment', said the flint-faced John Fisher. Everyone had been ordered to attend 'in their best manner, apparelled according to their estate and degrees', and Edward Hall considered it impossible to describe 'their rich attire, their sumptuous jewels, their diversities of beauties'. Henry, for his part, peacocked with a zest that surpassed even his usual extravagance, appearing each day in a series of increasingly spectacular costumes. For months in advance he had imported great quantities of rich fabrics, including 1,050 yards of velvet, and the bill for his jousting clothes alone topped £3,000.

Merely to provision the English host for the duration of the meeting meant that Wolsey had to plan every bit as meticulously as he had in the days of 1513. While some 400 French tents were pitched beside a small river at Ardres, Henry's retinue was accommodated in another 2,800 stretching away behind Guisnes. It was necessary to supply and transport to the spot 800 calves, 1,300 chickens, 9,000 plaice, 7,000 whiting, 19 bucks, as well as the numerous pots, pans and spits, which were supplied by London cooks at a cost of £337; 560 tuns of wine and beer, costing £7,409, and 4,000 pounds of wax for lighting were also provided. Whatever Wolsey's achievements as a diplomat, then, no one can ever deny him his place as the greatest stager of picnics in history. He attended to every detail from 700 conger eels to 26 dozen heron, 13 swans, and 4 bushels of mustard down to cream for the king's cakes costing £1 and tenpence. And always, beyond the 'great noise of artillery and music', the pounding of hooves, and the swelling cheers from the lists, could be heard the bleating of 2,200 sheep and the bawling of 340 beeves: sounds familiar enough to a man who had himself been reared within earshot of the market place at Ipswich.

It was late in the afternoon of Corpus Christi day that the monarchs themselves set out to meet each other for the first time. In the obsessive determination that neither king should gain precedence over the other, all proceedings were governed by a strict schedule, which ensured that each one did what the other did at precisely the same time. Accordingly, both men set out from their respective castles at the sound of carefully synchronised cannon fire. On the hills around about there had gathered a vast Brueghelesque swarm of witnesses – the unwashed and uninvited drawn from their squalid homes by curiosity and clinging tenaciously to their distant view, regardless of the dire threats scattered in their direction by the provost-marshal. Accounts suggest that no fewer than 10,000 had been made to turn back 'on pain of the halter'. But those who risked punishment were treated to a truly memorable scene.

When the climax arrived, Henry and his train approached the designated spot from one direction, Francis from the other, and when both parties reached artificial hillocks built up at opposite entrances to the valley there was said to be 'a breathless silence, followed by a slight stir on both sides'. Then, amid joyous cries from nobles, knights and beggars alike, 'two horsemen were seen to emerge' and, 'in the sight of both nations', they slowly descended into the valley from both sides. Approaching one another, 'they spurred their horses to a gallop' before reining them in and embracing in a lavish display of feigned affection, first on horseback and once more after dismounting. An Italian eyewitness swore that they threw their arms around each other more than twenty times before adjourning to a small pavilion in the company of Wolsey and the Admiral of France.

To be sure, it was a grand enough beginning and, in the three weeks of feasting and jousting that followed, Henry and Francis played at friendship with much bravado, if little real conviction. Neither king formally exchanged visits with his counterpart, though the King of England rode over to Ardres to call on the Queen of France, while Francis paid his respects to Queen Catherine. Even here, though, there was a tense undercurrent, since both men were effectively serving as hostages for each other before taking their leave upon the sound of more cannon fire synchronised to the nearest second. A rare act of spontaneity was provided when Francis, accompanied by only two gentlemen attendants and a page, rode straight to Guisnes, bypassing the guards to Henry's apartments, to tell him: 'I am your prisoner.' An exchange of gifts ensued, but even so, the French chronicler

Fleuranges recorded how Francis' advisers were horrified by the risk he had taken. It was duly noted also how the bracelet gifted by the French king was more than double the value of the collar of pearls bestowed by Henry in return.

However, amid the stifled snarls and petty sniping, there was one much more notable occasion when the taut rivalry between the monarchs would snap in a split second of near conflict. After defeating Francis at archery, Henry had, it seems, seized the long-legged Frenchman by the collar in the presence of both queens and given full vent to his overexcitement. 'Come', he shouted to Francis, 'you shall wrestle with me.' It was a gust of informality that ruffled the French king's better judgement and, in the unscheduled struggle that followed, the all too predictable happened. Released by surprise from his polite obligations as host, Francis threw Henry on his royal rump with a thud and, if the French king had been surprised by the challenge, the English one was dumbfounded by the outcome. No one since his father's day had ever laid a controlling hand upon him or thwarted a single one of his whims. It was said, therefore, that he rose to his feet smouldering, before squaring away with the single demand, 'Again!' In the end, only the gibbering intervention of attendants and the matronly appeals of the two queens rescued the combatants from the undignified spectacle of an all-out brawl. For as Catherine and Claude came forward promptly, a crowd of courtiers flocked round and smothered the flashpoint with a blanket of jolly palaver. But if they prevented the further round of grunt and groan demanded by Henry, they could never erase the significance of what had happened for posterity.

Even so, outward relations between the two sovereigns and their followers subsequently returned to their former stilted cordiality and were maintained until the end of the prescribed festivities. Guarded sociability had been ordered and was indeed delivered dutifully overall. There would be one more tricky moment of doubt among the heralds as to which monarch should first hang his shield on the so-called 'Tree of Honour' and in which position, but Henry settled the matter by causing Francis' arms to be placed on the right and his own on the left at the same height. Likewise, the drinking of English ladies at the jousts and in particular their habit of drinking from the same cup disconcerted French onlookers. Nevertheless, at a subsequent banquet, Francis surpassed himself with a display of gallantry by going round the hall, cap in hand, kissing all the English ladies in turn, 'save four or five that were old and not fair standing together'. And, to their credit, the two queens behaved themselves admirably throughout. At the parting benediction conducted by Wolsey there was a friendly dispute as to who should kiss the pax first, which they ended by kissing each other instead.

After three weeks of such self-conscious concord and forced back-slappery, it might be thought that the English and French had at least demonstrated a capacity to coexist with one another. At the elaborate concluding ceremonies, where Wolsey officiated at Mass, the two kings vowed, after all, to build a permanent church to 'Our Lady of Friendship' and to return to the Val Dore often. Effusive as always, Henry was also said to have looked 'as well pleased with this interview as if he had gained a great realm', and Francis seemed equally satisfied. But though the sovereigns parted with ham displays of sorrow, their followers retained the age-old hostility. 'If I had a drop of French blood in my body', Lord Leonard Grey grumbled audibly to a nearby companion, 'I would cut myself open to be rid of it.' 'And so would I,' came the equally loud reply. Though both men were arrested at Henry's order, the implication was clear enough. All the extravagance in the world – and most of it was there between Guisnes and Ardres in the summer of 1520 – could not conceal the apprehension and barely suppressed hostility of the governing classes of England and France.

Not only was Our Lady of Friendship never built, there was also no lasting political monument to emerge from the Field of Cloth of Gold. On the contrary, the meeting of the kings and the mingling of their most august subjects was merely a gross and costly formality. True, there was a strengthening of the French commitment to pay the arrears of the pension due under the treaty of 1475 and it was agreed, too, that the thorny matter of Anglo-French relations in Scotland should be discussed jointly at some later date by the Queen Mother of France and Wolsey. But beyond the hypocritical agreement to safeguard the betrothal of the Princess Mary to the dauphin, there was nothing of substance. Even before its occurrence, Erasmus had predicted that the meeting would be a waste of time and before the year was out Bishop John Fisher would preach a contentious sermon on the contrast between heavenly and earthly joys, in which he looked back with exasperation at the 'midsummer games' that had been played out between Guisnes and Ardres. Pouting yet again at the memory of the fine clothes on display, Fisher also recalled, with somewhat more satisfaction, the strong winds that had blown dust into the faces of the mighty and shaken the dwellings erected for their pleasure. But he could detect no benefit from all the high junketings. Moreover, the cost of it all had indeed brought monarchs and men nearer poverty. Henry alone spent an estimated total of £15,000, while it took the French ten years to pay for their share of the expense.

The meeting had come to pass ultimately, then, merely because the expense of Wolsey's preparations had made it impossible to draw back. In reality, the whole mealy-mouthed episode belonged to a set of bygone ideals, which the King of England professed to advocate, but flouted all the same, and as events would starkly demonstrate, any attempt at camaraderie was quite irrelevant to the problems of an increasingly nationalistic Europe. Paradoxically, the Field of Cloth of Gold sounded the death-knell of the age of chivalry and the end, too, of an era in which a churchman could cloak the intrigue of princes in the vestments of his office. It was swept into being on an irresistible flood tide of nobles, knights, gentlemen, calves, beeves, sheep, conger eels, canvas and candle wax mustered by the cardinal's indomitable will in response to his sovereign's weakness for an extravagant show at which he could be the star performer. Nothing, though, could alter what was plain for all to see: that the two protagonists remained implacable rivals and that the valiant victor of Marignano, who had already made the English king look foolish by his exploits, had no compelling need to make any sustained bid for friendship. In diplomatic terms, Francis would always regard Charles (with his encircling empire) as the figure of real significance. That Henry had met the emperor before leaving for Calais, and would now meet him as soon as his camp at Guisnes was dismantled, confirmed the crushing irrelevance of the spectacle in which he had just participated.

In early July, then, king and cardinal now hastened to consult with Charles at Gravelines, just as they had arranged earlier. Within a day of their initial rendezvous, Charles and Henry were making their way to Calais, where another, somewhat more modest, banqueting house had been erected 'upon the masts of a ship like a theatre'. And though when they arrived a mighty gale extinguished the torches and 'dashed' the rich chairs before blowing the entire structure to smithereens, the revelling was not abandoned. Undaunted by the elements and fortified by fine wines, the 'lusty maskers' danced on at the emperor's lodgings in their crimson cloaks and doublets of black velvet and cloth-of-gold. Wolsey, meanwhile, was confining himself to the business end of proceedings, reaffirming with imperial advisers the defensive alliance made tentatively at Canterbury and arranging to meet them the following year. Under cover of mediation, Wolsey thus devised a breathing space, during which Charles could once more go to settle a budding rebellion in Spain, while Henry looked after the Low Countries. As for the King of England himself, he was already conceiving 'a high and great enterprise' whereby English and imperial ships would jointly destroy the French fleet.

Naturally, the news of his enemies' meeting left Francis I deeply uneasy and he was further disconcerted to find that on 14 July, just before his return to England, Henry had signed a treaty with the emperor agreeing not to make any new alliance with France for the next two years. But even while his enemies' pavilion had been blowing down about their ears at Calais, Francis himself was planning for war in Navarre, next year: a war which, by 1522, Henry would have joined as Charles's ally. All too soon, in fact, the very timber used by the French for their pavilions at Ardres would be used for fortification against the English foe.

Flushed, then, with honour and delighted at his friendly dealings with the real enemy abroad, Henry now returned to England to pursue with equal zest his imagined enemies at home. When brewing war, he was, of course, always especially dangerous, as Edmund Pole had found to his cost before the 1513 expedition to France. But now, to boot, his prospects for an heir were less promising than ever and his malice and disquiet were magnified accordingly. Writing from Woodstock in July 1518, Richard Pace had informed Wolsey that 'the Queen did meet with his Grace at his chamber door, and showed unto him, for his welcome home, her belly something great, declaring openly that she was quick with child'. At the news, Henry had been beside himself, declaring that 'we should all be merry'. But Catherine soon miscarried once more, leaving Princess Mary still his only legitimate heir. If only, perhaps, to lessen the agony of his loss, it now became obvious to Henry that the main potential rival for his throne would have to suffer, too.

Born in 1478, Edward Stafford, Duke of Buckingham and High Constable of England, was a direct descendant of Edward III, and closely allied by ties of marriage to the cream of England's old nobility. Having been raised 'almost as a member of the royal family', he had therefore been a close companion of the king since childhood and was in the procession that set out to meet Catherine of Aragon upon her arrival in England, at which time he had been the only duke in the realm. As Lord High Steward, moreover, he had carried the crown at Henry's coronation and was prominent, too, at Henry's marriage. Nor would Queen Catherine ever forget her personal debt to him, for he had remained attentive to her needs throughout the darkest days after Arthur's death, sending her fruit and venison when her impoverished household was at its lowest ebb.

Yet Buckingham had far more than a queen's favour to bolster him. For though he was rattle-brained and imprudent, he also controlled what amounted to his own private fiefdom, extending over some dozen counties. With numerous liveried retainers at his call, he had entertained the king in great magnificence in August 1518 at his palatial Penshurst residence in Kent. And now he further flaunted his influence by regularly entertaining 130 local gentry to dinner in his newly built castle at Thornbury in Gloucestershire. In all respects, therefore, he stood out boldly as the lone survivor from a fast vanishing old-time feudalism. And in this capacity, he had steadily emerged as baiter-in-chief of the upstart Wolsey, upon whose shoes, it seems, he once deliberately spilt water while holding a basin for the king to wash his hands.

The claim, however, that the cardinal's lust for vengeance underlay the duke's eventual execution is far from accurate. Indeed, the 'fumes and displeasures' between the two rivals were greatly exaggerated in hindsight by those keen to ascribe a more sinister significance to comparatively innocent events. Though even Charles V would claim before long that 'a butcher's cur has killed the finest buck in England', it was mainly those with grudges, like John Skelton and Polydore Vergil, who probed most hungrily for their pound of Wolsey's flesh in this affair. Henry, after all, had ordered the cardinal in 1520 to 'make a good watch' on Buckingham, and it was he, too, who eagerly conferred behind closed doors with idle tale-tellers before summoning the duke to London to meet his fate. Nor was it Wolsey who benefited once the deed was done. On the contrary, it was the Dukes of Norfolk and Suffolk, his avowed enemies, who gathered up the richest spoils of the Stafford inheritance, while Wolsey, by contrast, was merely left to recommend that royal letters of condolence be sent to the victim's widow and sons.

Buckingham's jounal makes it quite clear, in fact, that he had no suspicion of his plight as he left for the capital in April 1521 to face what proved to be the testimony of discontented servants. Far from contriving the downfall of his sovereign he had, in fact, been mainly embroiled in purely domestic matters in recent months. The gardens of his beloved estates had, it seems, been of particularly pressing concern to him. Furthermore, from the detailed account that he kept of his expenditure along the way, there can be little doubt that he treated his journey like any other, until, that is, he reached Windsor. Here, however, he began to note that armed men were monitoring his movements and his anxiety mounted accordingly. Indeed, by the time he began the last stage of his trip by barge to Westminster, the duke was literally sick with fear. 'His meat would not down', we are told, because 'his spirit was so much troubled'.

Given his mortal danger, the duke had not spilled the contents of his stomach for nothing. Robert Gilbert, the duke's chancellor, and his chaplain, John Delacourt, had both turned informers, along with his former surveyor, Charles Knyvet, alleging that in 1511, the duke had 'imagined and compassed the death of the king'. Thereafter, according to the testimony of this motley Judas crew, Buckingham had planned to gather and arm fighting men, ostensibly to protect him while he toured his estates in Wales, but in reality to overthrow the king. He had also, it seems, consulted a treasonous Carthusian monk, Nicholas Hopkins, who 'pretended to have knowledge of future events'. In 1513, before the king's expedition to France, the monk was apparently asked how the war would turn out and whether James of Scotland would enter England, in response to which Hopkins had given out, amongst other things, that 'the king would have no male issue of his body'. Thereafter, in 1519, Buckingham had made another trip to the Hinton Charterhouse where the Carthusian lived, for the duke's accounts show 'to my ghostly father at Hinton, one hundred shillings'. Ultimately, so Knyvet testified, the duke planned to murder the king by coming into his presence, 'having upon him secretly a knife, so that when kneeling before the king he would have risen suddenly and stabbed him'.

Buckingham was tried in Westminster Hall, and the Duke of Norfolk, now seventy-eight and father-in-law to the accused man's son, conducted the case. He was supported by Suffolk, the Marquess of Dorset, seven earls and twelve barons, all of whom were terrified of the king and most of whom would benefit directly from Buckingham's death. The accused maintained throughout that the indictment against him was 'conspired and forged to bring me to my death' and, indeed, the outcome was never in doubt. At the end, after the axe of the Tower had been turned towards him to show the edge of death, it was said that if he would but seek royal mercy he might escape execution. However, Buckingham expressed no regret save for the manner in which he was to die, this being so far beneath the dignity of a duke that he marvelled at it. Four days after his condemnation, therefore, in response to the victim's final plea, the king relented and allowed his traitor to be decapitated without having his bowels burnt before his eyes.

As alarming as the charges against him undoubtedly were, public sentiment was, significantly, very much in the fallen duke's favour. And this was deeply unsettling to the king. That common folk should thus mourn such a manifest traitor shook him to the core, in fact. But Buckingham's trial had unearthed much besides that was equally perplexing. Rumbling discord had, in fact, been steadily eroding the affection that many Englishmen once undoubtedly held for their ruler. Now, though, more ominous murmurs abounded alongside further seething resentment of his upstart advisers. Indeed, such was the opposition to Buckingham's execution that both Charles V and Francis I came to convince themselves that an insurrection had broken out against Henry, and both competed to win his goodwill with offers of troops. Certainly, when the duke made his final grim journey, he was greeted not with the baying contempt usually reserved for traitors, but by anguished crowds who hovered respectfully to watch his final return to the Tower. His death, the Venetian ambassador wrote, was 'universally lamented by all London'. 'Our Italians', he added, 'had not the heart to see him die.'

Most worryingly of all, however, the growing hostility towards Henry's government had also infected broader sections of the English nobility who were already threatened by the shift in power that had been under way for more than a generation. The decline of their incomes from fixed rents at a time of rising costs fuelled their alienation just when their ancestral precedence in government was being disregarded and their customary prerogatives overlooked. Instead of ruling alongside the king, they were overruled by him, while men of lesser rank had been encouraged to crawl to eminence. Buckingham had allegedly hoped, therefore, that the nobles would 'break their minds' and reveal the extent of their displeasure, 'for few of them were contented, they were so unkindly handled'. As for himself, 'he would rather die than be ordered as he was'.

In the event, the kind of overt opposition that Buckingham desired was never an option when his peers were now more able and inclined to enforce their rank through fine garments and sumptuous entertainments than through civil warfare. Nevertheless, the nobility were deeply angered to see their places in power filled by mere rowdy 'boys' and social upstarts like Charles Brandon who, since his restoration to favour, had resumed his old role at the king's side, receiving foreign visitors to court and deliberating 'very earnestly' upon matters of State with ambassadors. Above all, though, the sullen fuming of England's elite continued to be directed at Wolsey who, according to John Skelton, considered them no more than 'pot shordes' and 'ribands not worth two plums'. Nor would it be long before men of the middling and common sorts were becoming more restive still.

6

Defender of the Faith

'Prithee, good Harry, let thee and I defend one another and leave the Faith alone to defend itself.'

A comment made by Patch, the king's fool, in February 1522.

As Henry VIII entered his thirtieth year of life, every outward sign proclaimed his heartfelt adherence to the old religion. In all the richly adorned tabernacles of his many royal chapels there lay the sacred Host, which, according to the Church's ancient teaching, was nothing less than the physical presence of Christ himself in the visible form of unleavened bread. Likewise, in strict accordance with Roman doctrine, there were for Henry a full seven sacraments and his year, too, was replete with saints' days. For him and his realm, the Latin Mass and Latin Vulgate Bible were still sacrosanct and just as his bishops solemnly wielded their gem-encrusted mitres, so the king himself clung to his holy relics, roods and rosary beads with no less reverence. Even while lying in his bed on the Vigil of All Hallows, Henry was comforted by the intermittent ringing of bells throughout the darkness of the night, secure in the prospect of priestly absolution and no less assured of the efficacy of right behaviour in bringing God's blessing. Immersing himself, therefore, in all manner of rituals, the king spent lavishly on tapers, smeared his forehead with ashes at the start of Lent and crept to the Cross on his knees uncomplainingly when Good Friday came. And as he fell headlong and willingly into that deep-seated psychological dependence with which Catholicism has always been associated, the same religion's potent mix of papally sanctioned certainties and darkest superstition both stoked and salved the fears which gnawed him.

Henry had, of course, been taught from earliest memory that passionate supplication in prayer, flattering promises of pilgrimage or crusade, sharp attention to ceremonial detail, and, above all, absolute obedience to God's laws as ordained by his Holy Church could bring contentment in this life and the certainty of paradise hereafter. But he had also been thoroughly dowsed by his grandmother and others in all the more compelling fixations of late medieval devotion. This, after all, was a religious tradition that did not give up its devotees easily: a tradition encapsulated most aptly in St Jerome's principle that 'in all my actions [...] my mind is on four things: first, that my days be short; second, death draweth near; third, mine end is dubitable and doubtful; and the fourth, my departing, painful, my reward, pain or joy'. Every family, not just Henry's, had buried newborn children. Every parish church had on its walls the sad, fading garlands that betokened the death of virgins. And at this time when funerals were among the most frequent of church services, hell itself was never more than a failed heartbeat or horse's stumble away. Moreover, the hell of this day was altogether less welcoming than the cosy oblivion now awaiting twenty-first century souls. There, soft resting places were transformed into beds of everlasting agony 'more grievous and hard than all the nails and pikes in the world'. There, too, the great retinues of kings and princes might readily be supplanted by legions of taunting demons.

Even the heralds of a newly dawning, supposedly more enlightened age had no doubts about the trials awaiting men after death. In his *Supplication of Souls*, Thomas More wrote of the dead enduring 'cruel, damned sprites, odious, envious and hateful, despiteous enemies and despiteful tormentors, and their company more horrible and grievous to us than is the pain itself [...] wherewith from top to toe they cease not continually to tear us'. And this, it should be emphasised, was not hell that More was describing, but merely purgatory, that long prison sentence assigned to even minor sinners. Men of all stations, then, continued to quake at images of eternal damnation and Henry VIII was no exception. On the contrary, his own egotism and the accompanying insecurity that it generated made him shrink all the more fearfully from death's approach and all the more inclined to seek the safe haven of Roman ritual. In Henry's own words, there was always much greater need 'to contemplate the severe and inflexible justice of God than the caprice of His mercy', and, in his case, such contemplation could always be conducted more comfortably under the umbrella of old habit.

Although his beliefs would evolve over time, for the moment, then, the very air that Henry breathed was heavy with Roman incense, and as was noted by the Venetian ambassador, he did not simply accept orthodox ways and ideas, but embraced them with a genuine passion. He was, we are told, 'very religious', hearing 'three masses daily when he hunted, and sometimes five on other days besides regularly attending vespers and compline'. He also, it seems, scrupulously received 'holy bread and holy water every Sunday' and daily used 'all other laudable ceremonies'. Even late in the reign, moreover, his reverence for the Mass was said to be 'always most profound'. When, for instance, it was suggested that, because of 'his weakness and infirmity', he did not have to 'adore the body of Our Saviour' on his knees but could 'make his communion sitting in a chair', he answered that 'if I lay not only flat on the ground, yea, and put myself under the ground, yet in so doing I should not think I have reverence sufficient unto His blessed sacrament'.

And though it is not, perhaps, so fashionable to admit it these days, the king was also firmly committed to a wide range of other practices associated with late medieval ways of devotion. Evidence can, of course, be mixed and matched to order, but Henry's 'Book of Payments' certainly records significant sums donated to shrines, for instance. Every year he sent 20 shillings to the shrine of St Thomas at Canterbury and always made appropriate donations on his visits to other places of pilgrimage. In September 1510, we find Henry making his first journey as king to the twelfth-century Augustinian priory at Southwick, where he gave amply to the shrine of Our Lady. Thereafter he also made numerous visits to other holy places, such as that of the miraculous black cross at Waltham Abbey, and those of St Edward the Confessor at Westminster Abbey and St Bridget of Syon, all of which were treated to his generosity. The tomb of the uncanonised Henry VI at Windsor, in its turn, was another site much hallowed by the king and when in 1512 a male child was born, alive but sickly, he sought to insure the infant's life by going on a secret and barefoot pilgrimage to the shrine of Our Lady at Walsingham, where he said his prayers, kissed the relic of the Virgin's milk and made offerings of £1 13s 4d. Significantly, the trip to the north Norfolk coast involved a round trip of some 200 miles and the outward journey alone took him ten days to make. On another occasion, in May 1521, Henry made plans for a pilgrimage in gratitude for his recovery from a serious fever.

Prayers for private resolutions were equally popular with the king, particularly when his own welfare or that of those close to him was involved. In January 1511, the gentlemen of the king's chamber were paid a handsome sum to pray for the queen's safe delivery of a child, and similar amounts were expended on other occasions. Henry also readily acknowledged the intervention of saints in earthly affairs. After the Battle of Flodden, for example, he was, in no doubt that victory had been gained under St Cuthbert's influence. So strong was this conviction, in fact, that his wife deemed it appropriate to tell him how the influence of God's own hand in the glorious events north of the border should not be forgotten. And when Henry went on to insist that the defeat of the Scots had resulted from the plundering of the saint's church by James IV, she felt obliged to remind him once more that 'this matter is so marvellous that it seems to be of God's doing alone'.

Nor was this the limit of Henry's dedication to the piety of his forefathers. The day before Good Friday he regularly took part in the Royal Maundy ceremony, which had its origins in the Middle Ages and is first known to have been performed in England by King John in 1210. In imitation of Jesus Christ at the Last Supper, wearing a voluminous white apron and armed with a towel, a basin and a nosegay to guard against infection, Henry would kneel to wash, sign with a cross and kiss the feet of a number of poor persons equal to the years of his age. Then, on Good Friday itself, he would bless 'cramp rings' made from the coins he had offered that day in the chapel, which were subsequently distributed to those suffering from a range of ailments, including rheumatism, epilepsy and palsy, in the belief that his blessing would effect a cure. And just like every other English monarch from the time of Edward II, Henry also 'touched' for the so-called 'King's Evil', a healing ritual believed to cure the skin disease scrofula.

More curiously still, the king also seems to have readily accepted the influence of other types of superhuman force in everyday life. Indeed, any attempt to interpret Henry VIII's religious beliefs without reference to the irrational elements which lapped against them at so many levels is to isolate his ideas from the whole context of the time in which they had developed. Not doubting in the slightest that the everyday operation of nature was loaded with occult meaning, the king crossed himself at the sound of thunder and interpreted any and all vagaries of climate as sure signs of God's judgement. Likewise, although it accounted for only part of his interest in the skies, astrology was not only a consuming fascination for Henry, but also a trusted guide to life. He looked upon comets, for instance, as divine portents and it was no coincidence that John Robyns, the Oxford astrologer and mathematician, became one of his most favoured chaplains. Moreover, as a firm believer in bad luck and omens, the king would prove unwilling throughout his reign to allow his bishops to denounce the existence of so-called 'dismal days' on which weddings, travel, blood-letting etc. were to be avoided. Nor for that matter would he submit later on to his own Archbishop of Canterbury's request that he assign both astrology and physiognomy to the list of 'unlawful and superstitious crafts'.

In other respects, too, Henry's mind was awash with concepts and assumptions linking him to an invisible realm that seemed as real in every detail as the material one over which he himself reigned. He did not doubt, for instance, that the celestial world was populated with highly corporeal and active agents in the form of cherubim and seraphim and other supernatural intelligences, including angels and archangels who, it was said, conducted divine services 'all the day long' and only took time off to listen to the appeals of men 'just before their matins and their evensong'. He had no doubt either that hailstones the size of eggs fell freely from the sky with the devil's face upon them, that rain turned readily to blood or that decapitated traitors chased about the country holding their heads in their arms. And when a high wind blew down St Alkmund's church steeple, the news that Satan's very own talons had left great scratches on the fourth bell would have come as no surprise to him. In times of crisis, after all, Henry would sometimes earnestly report that he had been visited at night by the legendary Herne the Hunter, and in due course he would be one of the first to claim a ghostly sighting of the deceased Anne Boleyn at Hampton Court. When, moreover, he complained shortly before Anne's disgrace that he now realised she owed her years of influence over him to witchcraft, the respect he paid to the occult gave his statement a particularly ominous weight.

Perhaps it was only to be expected, though, that the prevailing mind-set of the day should have left its mark upon the king so decidedly. Contemporary men and women, after all, routinely invoked supernatural assistance in their everyday affairs. There were charms to be spoken during childbirth and at the foaling of horses, while others helped ale to brew and milk to churn more quickly. In time of sickness, incantations were recited to staunch bleeding, and fevers and rheums were abated by a magical process known as 'casting of the heart'. Country folk, meanwhile, hung rue around their necks as an amulet against witchcraft, and put boughs of mountain ash and honeysuckle in their barns on the second day of May to turn aside spells cast on their cattle. Hot wax from a paschal candle dropped between the beasts' horns and ears gave additional protection, while burying an aborted calf in the roadway prevented cows from miscarrying. Equally, just as the future might be gauged from the chattering of birds, so lumps of coal could be relied upon to keep the evil one at bay.

Furthermore, this obsession with divination and wonder-working permeated all levels of society, including Henry's own court. Nobles had their horoscopes cast by court astrologers, while university doctors and students dabbled in necromancy and sought the philosopher's stone. Richard Jones of Oxford, for example, was a particularly notorious wizard of the day, who boasted a number of rich patrons attracted by the magical clutter of his dingy chamber – the stills, cauldrons, alembics and pestles, the carved sceptre used for conjuring 'the four kings', the box with a snake-skin inside and the shelves of magical and alchemical treatises. Even some of those intellectual luminaries who clustered around their king were, it seems, only partially immune to the prevailing superstitions of the day. No less a figure in the humanist firmament than John Colet, for example, was in regular correspondence with Agrippa von Nettesheim, whose practice as a physician subsidised his copious writings on magic as the surest path to knowledge of God. And the pope himself was careful to synchronise his religious services with the alignment of the stars.

The cult of saints, on the other hand, to which Henry subscribed so readily at this time, was merely the more respectable side of the same superstitious coin which had such wide currency amongst high and low alike. St Apollonia might be invoked for cure of toothache, while St Nicholas looked after pickpockets and St Osyth tended women who had lost their keys. The women at Arden, in their turn, made offerings to St Bridget for their sick cows and in St Paul's Cathedral stood the statue of St Wilgefortis, known appropriately as the Maid Uncumber, who was said to rid women of their husbands, if they offered her oats. There were, too, the immaculate deceptions involved in the Cult of Our Lady, which flourished at Walsingham, Ipswich, Worcester, Cardigan, Doncaster and a host of other resorts, and there were relics and wondrous images for the enlightened few to dismiss with equal gusto. Such was the celebrity attached to possession of holy objects, in fact, that one particular bishop of Lincoln was said to have bitten off and brought home part of Mary Magdalene's finger, which had been on display at Fécamp. Elsewhere, at Caversham, the head of the lance of Longinus, apparently delivered by an angel with a single wing, sat in a little chapel as fresh as the day it had pierced the Saviour's side. There, too, it seems, resided the 'holy halter' with which Judas had hung himself.

This is not to suggest, of course, that the king was a willing dupe to every old wives' tale and clerical confidence trick that came his way, or to deny, for that matter, that his religious outlook was also shaped by a considerable measure of hard learning. Indeed, the king was prepared to reinforce his religious beliefs with an omnivorous appetite for theological and other types of knowledge, which enabled him at times to wear down even the most learned of opponents. Certainly, he seems to have known the writings of the Church Fathers every bit as thoroughly as many of those distinguished ecclesiastics with whom he kept company and the contents of his libraries leave no doubt as to why. The one at Westminster, for instance, contained over a thousand volumes, many of which were imported from France and Italy, and other substantial collections of books also resided at Richmond, Greenwich and elsewhere. Alongside the inevitable manuals for hunting, hawking and chivalry, there also stood weighty scientific treatises and imposing classical works by Aristotle, Cicero and Thucydides, all of which testify to the king's intellectual aspirations. Nevertheless, a special place was always reserved for his closely annotated Bibles, his chronicles, his Church histories and, above all, for his much treasured collection of the writings of the great medieval schoolmen, which included texts by John of Salisbury, Abelard and Bonaventure, as well as his personal favourite, Thomas Aquinas, to whom he had been introduced by Wolsey.

Armed thus with an encyclopaedic knowledge derived from his own peculiar brand of rote-learning, Henry was able to hold forth unerringly in defence of his orthodox prejudices. And he would do so both orally and in print. From the 1520s onwards, in fact, he was to write extensively on a wide range of theological matters and became, in the process, an assiduous corrector of others' ideas. Predictably, too, he would display a typically naive willingness to rush in freely with his own sweeping ideas on subjects that professional theologians judiciously chose to avoid. The wording of the Lord's Prayer, and in particular the expression 'lead us not into temptation', would, for instance, come under Henry's critical scrutiny before long, and he was not above attempting to tone down the biblical condemnation of image-worship expressed in the Ten Commandments. Since the king was, in the words of one contemporary, 'a perfect philosopher', what, after all, could have been more natural and fitting for such a divinely inspired wit than to seek to improve upon God's own words?

Besides which, the truth was always, by Henry's own admission, 'so certain, so evident, so manifest, so open and approved' that it could be easily and definitively accessed by any intellect that was – just like his own – sufficiently adept and suitably well trained. At the same time, he was equally convinced that any truth so gained 'ought to be allowed and approved by all Christian men'. But what might have sounded like an appeal to reasoned unity in an enlightened Godly commonwealth amounted, in this instance, to nothing more than a licence for rigid intolerance. And it was precisely because of the king's surging self-confidence, too, that his faith appeared so empty in the eyes of many of the reformers he would later condemn. For Robert Barnes, Thomas Bilney and John Lambert, each of whom would die at Henry's hands, true religion could never be a matter of sterile rituals and mechanically applied canons. Nor could it be grounded on fear of damnation rather than the certainty of salvation. Yet for Henry, religion was, indeed, precisely a matter of strictly regulated deeds and clear-cut ceremonial guarantees against the eternal pit. 'My King does not care about religion', Robert Barnes would later declare and it is not difficult to see why, for from his point of view Henry had only a hollow faith, conceived mainly in the mind by a process of tank-like logic, and dead, for precisely that reason, to the heart.

Yet the threads that bound the king to the old religion in this way were as varied and subtle as they were resilient. He was, for instance, quite literally hemmed in on all sides by the Church's presence, and remained intimately linked to it through both the physical environment in which he moved and the rhythms of his everyday life. Near his palace at Richmond, to take but one example, there were the Carthusian monks of Sheen, and only a mile across the river from the palace itself stood the unique community of the Bridgettines at Syon Abbey, an aristocratic convent with wide influence among the elite of London and the English nobility generally. It was none other than the Protestant William Tyndale, in fact, who described, with undisguised hostility, the constant tolling of bells between Syon and Sheen in Richmond's royal enclave around the River Thames, which continually reminded the young king of Catholicism's all-encompassing influence. 'When', wrote Tyndale, 'the friars of Syon ring out, the nuns begin; and when the nuns ring out of service, the monks on the other side [at Sheen] begin; and when they ring out, the friars begin again, and vex themselves night and day, and take pains for God's sake.' So it was that Henry awoke each morning to Rome's calling, while the last sounds he heard at night were the Church's, too.

Within the palace itself, meanwhile, Henry found himself snugly cocooned from any violent theological undercurrents that may have been stirring in the world at large. The royal chapel, for instance, which was so much a part of the king's everyday life that he even discussed business in it in his own special pew during services, could well have served the pope himself. With its brilliant stained glass windows, wall paintings, splendid organ, designed by William Lewes, and statues of the Virgin and saints, it changed little throughout the course of the reign, just as its religious services would continue along essentially familiar lines. True, more emphasis was laid on preaching as the reign progressed, but in all other essentials, Henry's chapels continued to reflect the ease he experienced amid graven images. Likewise, in his private closet at Richmond, a team of twenty-six chaplains serviced Henry's religious needs during weekdays, once again in strict accordance with the ancient rites of Rome. And in the grounds outside the palace, just as at Greenwich, there stood a brand-new convent of the reformed order of Observant Friars, which further reflected and reinforced Catholicism's firm hold on the monarch. Though this building would eventually loom in Elizabeth's reign as a ruinous and baleful reminder of a bygone age, at this time it housed a thriving community that was one more affirmation of the triumph of tradition in the king's everyday world.

Nor would even the grossly sullied reputation of the papacy mar the king's allegiance to the faith he considered himself born to protect. Lewd tales heard outside the Flaminian Gate in Rome had certainly lost nothing in the telling by the time they reached English shores and stories that in Italy were regarded as merry yarns continued to excite grating indignation in London taverns and Cotswold cottages alike. Some popes, as the king well knew, had become far more renowned for their toxicological wizardry than for their pastoral gifts as 'Vicars of Christ', while others, such as Julius II, seemed to confirm the papacy's widespread reputation for greed and immorality. Not only did this particularly dazzling example of papal excess personally conduct an armed vendetta against his rivals in vice, the Borgias, but he did so in specially commissioned silver armour. Moreover, when not demolishing his enemies, he seemed to busy himself mainly with marvellously extravagant building projects, involving Raphael, Bramante and Michelangelo. It was he, for instance, who laid the foundation stone of the new Basilica of St Peter's and bequeathed to posterity the Sistine Chapel's painted ceiling. But he was also a builder and contractor in more than one sense, since he fashioned a family of at least three illegitimate daughters before finally falling prey to the scourge of syphilis in 1513. And his successor, Leo X, was, it seems, equally inclined to cherish visibility. The son of Lorenzo de Medici, he had been an abbot at the age of seven, a canon at eight and a cardinal at thirteen. Later, as pope, he would trade in more than 2,000 ecclesiastical appointments with a value of 3 million ducats and be accompanied on procession by Persian horses, a panther, two leopards and, for additional effect, his pet elephant, Hanno, whose portrait was painted by Raphael.

Yet still the King of England's single-minded devotion to his Holy Father remained untouched by such excess, not least because it conformed so neatly with his own ongoing perception of himself as a Christian warrior-prince. Piety was, after all, an integral part of the chivalric culture that Henry had absorbed from his Burgundian forebears, and his own knights of the Garter, too, were every bit as devoted to their faith as they were to deeds of heroism. Henry saw himself, therefore, quite literally in the mould of the Arthurian Sir Bedevere, and early in the reign when his blood was running especially freely, he had not hesitated to speak boldly of conquering Jerusalem with a mighty army of 25,000 men. Indeed, he had even seen fit to request four galleys from Venice to assist his proposed exploits. And although this particular rush of enthusiasm had soon abated, it was not long before he was stirred to even wilder flights of fancy. When, in 1516, Selim the Grim's Ottoman Turks subdued the Holy Land, Henry was soon aflame once more after Leo X's earnest appeal for aid from Christian knights. Similarly, when Cardinal Campeggio came to England in 1518 to preach a crusade, Henry had no hesitation in proclaiming that he would place everything in his possession at the pope's disposal. His personal wealth and treasure, his royal authority and even his kingdom itself, he declared, might all be gladly rendered up in the sacred cause of defending Christendom against the infidel.

Beneath such 'ardour of soul', of course, there were still undeniable tensions between the king's religious loyalties and his more selfish drives. This, it should be remembered, was the man who casually flattened the village church at Cuddington to build his fantasy palace at Nonsuch, and gladly redeployed the church windows of Rewley Abbey outside Oxford to light his bowling alley at Hampton Court. Besides which, Henry was a man of fashion in intellect as well as attire, and this was not without its side-effects. French diplomatists visiting Greenwich around this time amazed Francis I's court when they returned to Paris emphasising the important position Henry accorded to 'les savants' that he had gathered round him. Erasmus, in his turn, wrote that 'there are more men of learning in Henry's court than in any university'. These standard bearers of what has become known as humanism included Thomas Linacre, the king's physician, Thomas More, Master of the Court of Requests, John Colet, Dean of St Paul's, Lord Mountjoy, by now Lord Chamberlain, Richard Pace, the king's secretary, and others like Cuthbert Tunstall, Master of the Rolls, and John Stokesley, the king's confessor. All were front-rank scholars and all, significantly, were equally inclined to cock a snook at the more arcane and worldly features of contemporary Catholicism. In such modish company, therefore, Henry's very credibility depended heavily upon occasional outward shows of enlightened exasperation with certain features of the old religion. And, of course, he could never resist any opportunity to perform to order.

Upon hearing in 1521, for instance, that a society of 'Trojans' had been formed in Oxford to oppose the introduction of the study of Greek, the king wasted no time in posing as the righteous champion of true scholarship. His humanist heroes were, after all, continually emphasising the importance of 'rediscovering' the language and learning of the Ancient Greeks, so that the Church's teachings could be subjected to intensive investigation in the light of the original gospels. Therefore, Henry was quick to act when one of the university's preachers had fulminated against the evils of the 'New Learning' from the pulpit at Abingdon, where the royal party happened to be staying. In response, Henry appointed Thomas More to hold a solemn disputation with the man on the use of Greek, and it was not long after More had opened his case that the hapless don fell to his knees to beg the king's forgiveness, excusing himself by saying that his offensive claims had been prompted only by the Spirit. 'Not', Henry intoned gravely, 'the Spirit of Christ, but the Spirit of Folly.' And when the preacher subsequently admitted that he had never studied the works of Erasmus, he was roundly rebuked by his sovereign as 'a foolish fellow to censure what you never read'.

Henry had, moreover, already proven more than willing to assert his authority in the area of Church-State relations when, in 1514, the ecclesiastical hierarchy crudely bungled an attempt to assert its privileges. The macabre scandal involving a Whitechapel merchant by the name of Richard Hunne began innocently enough when Hunne's infant baby died at just a few weeks of age. However, the local parish priest then sparked an ugly chain reaction by refusing to bury the baby until Hunne gave him as payment the winding sheet in which the baby's corpse had been wrapped. Though the baby was eventually buried, this was not the end of the matter, for the priest concerned now prosecuted Hunne in the ecclesiastical courts for non-payment. The merchant's response was to escalate matters considerably by appealing to the king's council, alleging that by bringing his case before a Church court, his clerical adversary had exercised a power which was derived from a foreign prince – namely, the pope – and was therefore guilty of infringing the so-called Statute of Praemunire, which forbade the clergy to encroach on matters falling under the Crown's jurisdiction.

The strangest twist of all, however, followed after the Bishop of London's Chancellor, a certain Dr Horsey, accused Hunne of heresy and imprisoned him in the tower of St Paul's Cathedral. Two days later, Hunne was found hanged in his cell. But while his jailers claimed suicide, the subsequent inquest ordered by the London coroner suggested otherwise. The evidence proved conclusively, for instance, that Hunne had been found 'hanged with a fair countenance [...] without any staring, gaping or frowning. Also without any drivelling or splurging in any place in his body'. He had, moreover, bled as he died, although no drop of blood was found on his clothing. Similarly, the noose around his neck was both loose and made of silk, suggesting that it could not have been the cause of his broken neck. And though his hands were not tied when his body was found, there were marks on his wrists that suggested they had been tied beforehand. On this and other compelling evidence, the coroner's jury returned a verdict that Hunne had been murdered by his captors, on the orders of the bishop's chancellor.

The resulting shockwaves might still have been contained, had it not been for a further gross miscalculation on the part of the ecclesiastical authorities. For when Dr Horsey and the jailers were duly indicted in the Court of King's Bench, Bishop Fitzjames of London remained determined that the matter should not be allowed to rest. He could not, he told Wolsey, expect justice for his chancellor from any London jury, 'so set were they on heretical depravity', and it was now that he hit upon a swift and drastic expedient that would eventually unleash a tidal wave of resentment against his fellow clergy. Pressing ahead with heresy proceedings, Fitzjames recklessly secured Hunne's posthumous conviction and proceeded to exhume his corpse and burn it before outraged Londoners at Smithfield.

Amid seething controversy, two bills were subsequently brought before Parliament to vindicate Hunne and in spring the prosecution of Dr Horsey in a secular court was raised in the Convocation of Canterbury by the Abbot of Winchcombe, who claimed that the traditional privileges of the clergy had been infringed. Ultimately, however, the case would be argued before the king himself at Blackfriars. And when Archbishop Warham suggested that the dispute might be referred to the papal court in Rome, Henry could not have made his own position more apparent. 'We are', he declared, 'by the sufferance of God, King of England, and Kings of England in times past had never any superior but God. Know therefore that we will maintain the rights of the crown in this matter like our progenitors.' Only after Wolsey had made a partial admission before king, council and both Houses of Parliament did Henry allow the affair to lapse.

The king had therefore made it emphatically clear that he was more than willing to defend his prerogative against even the pope himself, if necessary. Yet the significance of this or any other early flicker of independence on Henry's part should not be misconstrued, for the Hunne case was neither an early glimpse of any irreconcilable rift, nor omen of things inevitably to come. Indeed, even when, much later, Henry consciously attempted to shift ground in keeping with political needs and intellectual fashion, the umbilical cord binding him to his Mother Church remained very much intact. Pre-Reformation Catholicism was, after all, a clockwork religion of bargains and contracts, which synchronised perfectly with his own cast-iron calculations of right and wrong. For the common man, meanwhile, the Church of Rome offered New Testament consolation, but still hid Old Testament punishment like a robber's cudgel within its seamless cloak, and this, too, suited the king's purposes, since men afraid of God were more apt to remain in awe of their ruler. Equally conveniently, this religion of salvation by taboo was also a religion of blind-eyed pragmatism, which was always prepared to accommodate the many moral shortcomings of its more important members. In sum, then, the Church of Rome was a massive, rambling mansion, owned by a temporarily absentee God and run by men who frequently rented rooms to the devil and his parties. As such, it remained the ideal dwelling for just such a man as Henry, King of England.

Ultimately, it would require a brilliantly neurotic Augustinian friar, an obscure Professor of Divinity in his mid-thirties at the University of Wittenberg, to light the touch paper for the Europe-wide religious explosion that rocked Henry VIII's natural spiritual home to its foundations. Obsessed with his sinfulness, Martin Luther had long been burdened by his inability to live up to the requirements for salvation imposed upon him by the Church's so-called 'doctrine of works', which taught that the fate of the soul was dependent upon an individual's behaviour whilst living. On this basis, Luther was, he believed, consigned to hell by his own humanity, which seemed shot through with sinful drives that he was incapable of taming. Just as the Church recommended, he sought in vain to ease his soul with 'human remedies, the traditions of men'. Confession of his sins, however, provided only momentary relief before the recurrence of overpowering temptation. In consequence, his conscience nagged him constantly by telling him: 'You fell short there [...] You were not sorry [...] You left that sin off your list.'

And there was the question, too, of whether the Church's claims to hold the keys to salvation could, in any case, be defended. How, after all, could men of any kind, even pontiffs, encompass God's intentions, let alone tether his judgements and mercy to petty rituals of their devising? For Luther, the ways of God were utterly awesome, wholly ungraspable and entirely beyond influence by mankind. God's 'omnipotence, combined with his eternal foreknowledge, absolutely and inevitably dispose of the idea of reason acting freely within us', Luther had concluded. Indeed, reason was, as he quaintly put it, no more than a 'harlot eaten up with the itch'. Therefore, just as man was inevitably sinful, so the Church's mechanical efforts for his salvation were completely vain. These convictions, which were coloured all too vividly with nightmare visions of demons and hell fire, pointed incontrovertibly, it seemed, to a constant war between flesh and spirit in which there could be only one victor and one possible outcome too ghastly to imagine.

1 The family of Henry VII at prayer, beneath an image of the Virgin Mary's parents embracing at the Golden Gate of Jerusalem. To the left kneels the king with Prince Arthur, Prince Henry (the future Henry VIII) and Prince Edmund who lived for only fifteen months. To the right is Elizabeth of York with Princess Margaret, Princess Elizabeth who died at the age of 3, Princess Mary, and Princess Katherine who died with her mother shortly after birth.

2 Sketched by an unknown artist, this is reputed to be the earliest ever image of the future Henry VIII. The drawing is inscribed '*le Roy henry d'angleterre*'.

3 Henry VIII's mother, Elizabeth of York, was the eldest child of Edward IV. She holds the white rose of her father.

4 This stained glass image of Prince Arthur is to be found in the 'Magnificat' window of Great Malvern Priory's north transept. It is thought to date from between 1499 and 1502.

5 Princess Mary Tudor and Charles Brandon, Duke of Suffolk, wed secretly in 1515, a mere six weeks after the death of Mary's first husband, Louis XII of France. Their granddaughter was the unfortunate 'Nine Days Queen', Lady Jane Grey. Brandon is wearing the collar of the Order of the Garter.

6 Sampson Strong's portrait depicts Thomas Wolsey at Christ Church, Oxford, in 1526. Though the 'proud prelate' had founded Christ Church as Cardinal's College two years earlier, it would become Henry VIII's property after his fall in 1529, and was subsequently re-established with its present name in 1546.

7 On 31 May 1520, Henry VIII set sail with over 6,000 members of his court to meet the King of France at the Field of Cloth of Gold. More than two decades after the event, he was still celebrating this vain chivalric spectacle as one of his crowning triumphs, and in around 1545 commissioned the above painting of his embarkation at Dover. The king himself can be seen beneath the golden sails of the *Great Harry*, his largest ship.

8 Bernhard Strigel painted this portrait of Emperor Maximilian I with his son Philip the Fair, his wife Mary of Burgundy, his grandsons Ferdinand I and Charles V, and Louis II of Hungary whom the emperor adopted after his father's death in 1516. Louis would die in battle against the Turks at Mohács ten years later.

9 In this painting of the Field of Cloth of Gold, dating from around 1545, Thomas Grey, Marquess of Dorset, carries the Sword of State, while Cardinal Wolsey rides alongside the king. The right-hand foreground is dominated by the splendid prefabricated palace specially erected for the occasion, behind which is Henry VIII's golden dining tent. The tournament field and Guisnes Castle are also depicted.

10 Born in 1478, Edward Stafford, Duke of Buckingham, was a direct descendant of Edward III, and closely linked by ties of marriage to the cream of England's old nobility. In 1521 he was accused of intending to kill the king and executed on the evidence of discontented servants.

11 This wool, silk, silver and gold tapestry, manufactured in Brussels, depicts the Battle of Pavia. One of the decisive confrontations of the entire Habsburg–Valois conflict, the battle was commemorated here by Bernard van Orley some three years or so after its occurrence in 1525.

12 In this copy of an original portrait by Holbein, Thomas Cromwell is dressed soberly in black and portrayed in a relatively simple setting. However, the wooden panelling, damask wall covering and Turkish carpet suggest an interest in fine things. On the table before him is a book – probably devotional – a quill, scissors to trim it, and a soft leather bag for his seal.

13 This woodcut illustration from John Foxe's *Book of Martyrs* (1570) depicts Henry VIII upon his throne, with Thomas Cranmer to his left, presenting him with a Bible, while Pope Clement VII is prostrated at the king's feet. Standing behind Cranmer is Thomas Cromwell. John Fisher supports the pope's head, Cardinal Pole the pope's back. Looking on in dismay is a group of monks.

14 Title page of a 'Great Bible', printed in 1539, which was probably Henry VIII's personal copy. It depicts the enthroned king receiving the Word of God and bestowing it upon his bishops and archbishops, who in turn deliver it to the rest of the clergy. Finally, the Word is transmitted to the laity who respond with loyal declarations of 'Vivat Rex' and 'God save the kynge'.

15 On the left of this portrait of Sir Thomas More and his family, from an original by Hans Holbein, is More's second daughter, Elizabeth Dauncy. Beside her is his adopted daughter Margaret Giggs, explaining a point to More's father, John More. Sir Thomas himself sits in the centre, with the engaged couple Anne Cresacre and his only son, John More, on either side of him. Beside John More is the household fool, Henry Patenson. On the right of the picture are More's youngest daughter Cecily Heron, and his eldest daughter Margaret Roper. More's second wife, Alice, is kneeling on the extreme right.

16 In April 1534, Bishop John Fisher was confined in the Tower of London for refusing to swear the oath attached to the Act of Succession. The following year he was beheaded, not long after the pope had made him a cardinal. Emaciated by years of fasting and the rigours of his final stay in the Tower of London, he was described at his execution as 'a very image of death and (as one might say) Death in a man's shape and using a man's voice'.

17 Portrait of a Carthusian monk by Petrus Christus. In May 1535, Humphrey Middlemore, William Exmew and Sebastian Newdigate from the London Charterhouse were confined to a stinking dungeon for refusing to swear the oath of succession. There they were left for seventeen days, loaded with lead, unable to sit and 'never loosed for any natural necessity' before being hung, drawn and quartered at Tyburn. Their prior, John Houghton, had suffered a similar execution earlier in the month.

18 Illuminated title page of *Valor Ecclesiasticus*, the survey of the lands and wealth of England's monasteries prepared for Henry VIII by Thomas Cromwell in 1535.

Luther's liberation from the false pretensions of the Church and the leaden weight of what might be termed 'guilt from nature' was afforded, however, by his reading of St Paul. There, at last, he found the doctrine that man could only be saved by God's mercy rather than by means of anything he could *do*. The sinner must, therefore, reject human intermediaries of any kind, for neither priests nor popes could help him. And he must avoid their vain remedies. God was vast and ineffable, while Rome had rendered the deity petty and bureaucratic, little more than a celestial accountant who totted up sins studiously and arranged generous rebates for sharp operators who exploited the rules skilfully. In reality, the only recourse for any man was to fling himself in abject humility and contrition at the feet of his sustaining Saviour. Only thus could his eternal soul be saved from the fiery pit.

Upon this revelation, it seems, Luther had felt at once as though he 'had been reborn altogether and had entered Paradise'. This doctrine of 'justification by faith alone', a notion already conceived by St Augustine, rendered futile in one sweep the religious hierarchies, 'loose blabber' and superstitious practices that were so central to Henry VIII's Catholicism. The whole Roman caboodle, including priests, pilgrimages and purgatory therefore appeared redundant and, if purgatory was a myth, then papal indulgences, which remitted the stay of dead souls there, were a cynical confidence trick. The logic was remorseless and so, too, was Luther. The final straw came, of course, when, in 1517, a papal indulgence seller called Tetzel arrived in Wittenberg offering salvation in return for contributions to the building of St Peter's Basilica. In a state of terminal frustration, Martin Luther nailed the '95 Theses' to the door of the local cathedral and raised his whirlwind.

Not surprisingly, then, the King of England observed the beginnings of disorder in Germany with disgust and horror. On 29 January, Bishop Cuthbert Tunstall had written to Wolscy, mainly in cypher, to give the facts as he saw them. 'The people of Almayn', he said, 'be so minded to Luther, whose opinions be condemned by the pope, that, rather than he should be by the pope's authority oppressed [...] [they] would spend a hundred thousand of their lives.' Luther's books, he continued, were in the hands of every man that could read and available even in the Hungarian tongue. 'The beginning of this', in Tunstall's opinion, had been 'the great sum of money that yearly goeth to Rome for annates, which the country would be rid of, and the benefices be given by the pope to such persons as do serve at Rome, unlearned as cooks and grooms, and not to the virtuous and learned men of the country as they say'. The pope, he declared, must act at once or 'lose the total obeisance of Almayn'. As for Luther's latest work, the so-called *Babylonish Captivity*, Tunstall prayed God to 'keep that book out of England'.

But the bishop's prayers went unanswered, for early in 1521 copies had reached his homeland and, by April, Henry was himself reading the book and 'dispraising' it. 'At mine arrival to the King this morning', wrote Richard Pace, 'I found the King looking upon a book of Luther's.' Nor was it long before Henry was indulging his appetite for new projects – an appetite that would ensure, incidentally, that he spent much of his life eating his own words. Since in his view it had always been his proper business both to champion Rome and to earn the praise of the learned, the time was now ripe, he reasoned, to take up writing, so that 'all might see how he was ready to defend the Church, not only with his armies but with the resources of his mind'. 'By one man's disobedience', Henry claimed, 'many were made sinners.' So naturally, therefore, it would take another more learned and more steadfast man to effect a famous rescue bid. Heresy was at large, defiling Christ's true message, degrading the Virgin Mary and saints, and endangering, too, God's hierarchy on earth, since this looming contagion 'robbed princes and prelates of all power and authority'. The danger, then, was manifest and dire, and in sensing this, Henry also sensed his chance to reassert that loyalty to the pope that had already brought him a golden rose from Julius II and might now win him a title he had long coveted. If the monarchs of Spain were 'Most Catholic' and those of France 'Most Christian', might not the Kings of England receive some such title themselves, confirming their status in the hierarchy of Christendom?

In the task before him, the king, who had already been generously lavished with a reputation as a 'sharp wit', mobilised the usual apparatus of scholastic argument and Latin cliché to assert the orthodox position. Luther, of course, would allege that the resulting book was never Henry's own and had been produced instead by Dr Edward Lee, who had, indeed, played some part in the editing. 'I expect', wrote Luther, that 'the King gave one or two ells of homespun to that good for nothing, who cut himself out a cape and then trimmed it with lining.' Certainly, the book was revised by a committee of professionals, which included John Fisher and, in particular, Sir Thomas More, who would soon be attacking 'lowsy

Luther' in his own right. But there is, in fact, no reason to question Henry's authorship of the so-called *Assertio Septem Sacramentorum adversus Martinum Lutherum*, which is known more commonly today as his *Defence of the Seven Sacraments*. Mountjoy, for instance, assured Erasmus that Henry was the actual writer and the content is, on the whole, sufficiently laboured to corroborate this view.

In truth, the king's *chef d'oeuvre* would prove a mightily clumsy anvil on which to beat out even a remotely convincing defence of his Mother Church and Holy Father. Consisting of 100 references from thirty books of the Bible and seventy questions from St Augustine and other patristic authors, the *Defence* largely missed the point of Luther's arguments, which denounced the sacraments of the Catholic Church as 'the devices of a human institution to hold its members'. Equally predictably, the king's fighting blood and wish 'to defend my Mother, the Spouse of Christ' seem to have got the better of any dialectical talent he may actually have possessed. Throughout, Luther was denounced in well-worn Latin phrases which look no less threadbare in translation – 'he belches out of the filthy mouth of the hellish wolf whose foul inveighings ...' and the like. And, of course, some of the book's more purple passages would continue to clang indecorously down the centuries. There was, for instance, the notorious reference to the sanctity of marriage: 'The insipid water of concupiscence is turned by the hidden grace of God into wine of the finest flavour. Whom God has joined together, let no man put asunder.' Elsewhere, in earnestly vindicating Rome's authority against Thomas More's somewhat surprising advice to the contrary, Henry also produced the following tirade: 'What serpent so venomously crept in as he who calls the Most Holy See of Rome "Babylon", and the Pope's authority "Tyranny" and turns the name of the Most Holy Bishop of Rome into that of "Anti-Christ"?'

The fact that Henry would eventually saddle More with responsibility for some of these more embarrassing claims concerning the papal supremacy was, of course, particularly reprehensible. But, in the short term at least, the king's purposes were served conveniently enough and finally, on 25 August, the book was ready, whereupon Wolsey wrote to John Clerk, the English ambassador in Rome, giving detailed instructions on how the text was to be presented to His Holiness. In all, twenty-eight copies were to be despatched, but Clerk was to present privately to the pope a single copy covered with cloth-of-gold and containing two verses in the king's own hand. The ambassador was also to deliver a heavy-handed hint to the effect that his sovereign master had already styled himself 'the very defender of the Catholic Faith of Christ's Church which (title) he had truly deserved of the Holy See'.

When the time came, the ailing connoisseur pope is said to have taken the book in his hands and admired the binding and 'the trim decking'. Then, upon opening it, he apparently read five leaves of the introduction without interruption. 'At such places as he liked', Clerk wrote, 'and that seemed to be at every second line, he made ever some demonstration.' Moments later, His Holiness declared to the Englishman that 'he would not have thought that such a book should have come from the King's grace, who hath been occupied necessarily in other feats, seeing that other men which hath occupied themselves in study all their lives cannot bring forth the like'. Declaring that Henry had displayed eloquence and wisdom in confuting 'this terrible monster', Pope Leo then thanked God for raising up such a prince to defend his Holy Church.

Clerk's next move, just as instructed, was to request that a public consistory of cardinals should be called to provide a formal reception of the king's book. This, however, Leo flatly refused, albeit much to the Englishman's surprise and frustration. There was, after all, nothing remarkable about the work save that it was written by a monarch and if the pope did owe Henry some token of gratitude for the sentiments on offer, he had no wish to overdo the special recognition being sought. As an alternative, therefore, the pope asked Clerk to meet him at the place where consistories were generally held, before merely calling into the chamber such prelates as were loitering about the halls, 'to the number of twenty'. All in all, it was much less of an occasion than Henry would have wished for or Wolsey might have planned. Nevertheless, it proved sufficient to the task, for next day the pope issued a bull rewarding Henry for his sturdy tilt at the devil with the title of 'Defender of the Faith'.

Ultimately the bull bearing the title was received in England with great ceremony. In February 1522, there arrived at Greenwich a magnificent legation, headed by Wolsey and the papal ambassador, and such was the importance of the occasion that Henry, we are told, came in person to meet them at his chamber door, 'as though they had both come from Rome'. Then, after fulsome compliments to the king, 'so formed and figured in shape and stature […] which signified the pleasure of our Lord God', the cardinal presented the papal bull declaring his new title. But although a fitting crowd had to be rustled up for the purpose, there was, in fairness, nothing half-hearted about Leo's prose, which rolled on and on in waves of sumptuous excess. Nor was there anything casual about his naming Henry as his friend and brother in the Lord's work, after which the whole glittering entourage of courtiers and clerics proceeded to high Mass, while trumpets blared and 'shalmes and saggebuttes' played in honour of the king's new title. In fact, the only frivolous note amid the high solemnity was heard from Patch, Henry's fool. Seeing his master jocund, Patch asked him the reason. When the king replied that it was because of his new title, the fool is said to have replied archly: 'Prithee, good Harry, let thee and I defend one another and leave the Faith alone to defend itself.'

And whether, of course, the mighty Church of Rome did, indeed, require such mighty defenders from the clamorous minority pitched against it, remains as doubtful as ever. True, there was more than superstition and the corruption of the papacy for Rome's detractors to seize upon. The supposedly heavy financial burdens imposed in the form of tithes, mortuary and probate fees, Peter's Pence, annates, indulgences, dispensations etc. were, for instance, a regular source of complaint for those with axes to grind. 'Is it not unreasonable', asked Thomas Starkey, 'the first fruits to run to Rome, to maintain the pomp and pride of the Pope, yea, and war also, and discord among Christian princes as we have seen by long experience?' Similarly, the materialism and worldliness of cardinals and bishops, which contrasted so blatantly with the ideals of apostolic poverty and Christian humility that they claimed to espouse, was also being loudly condemned in some quarters. It was John Colet, for instance, who first coined the phrase 'wolves in sheep's clothing' in connection with the English episcopacy, and nepotism, simony, pluralism and absenteeism had all become favourite targets of anticlerical bile. Furthermore, the leading clergyman in England, Thomas Wolsey, seemed to epitomise all that was wrong with the institution whose power he wielded so domineeringly. 'One cross', said Polydore Vergil, 'is insufficient to atone for his sins'.

Monks and the lower clergy, too, attracted more than their fair share of criticism. Tales of decadent 'abbey lubbers' abounded and it was said that if the Abbott of Glastonbury bedded the Abbess of Shaftesbury their bastard would surely become the richest landowner in England. Christopher St German, meanwhile, pointed to priests who played 'at Tables' and other illicit games, while Thomas More said of the parish clergy that 'many were lewd and naught'. And before the 1520s were out, Simon Fish, a barrister of Gray's Inn, would publish his famous *Supplication for the Beggars*, which reflected the full venom of the new challenge to the Church. In it, amongst other things, he denounced the pope as a 'cruel and devilish bloodsupper drunken in the blood of saints and martyrs of Christ'. The clergy, too, were depicted as immoral perverters of God's word, and Fish beseeched his sovereign accordingly 'to tie these holy idle thieves to the carts to be whipped naked about every market town'.

Nevertheless, a prudent judge reads the work of a political agitator like Fish with due caution and, in spite of his passionate rantings, the old religion, though embattled, was far from crisis. In fact, complaints about corrupt or decadent clergy were neither new, as any student of Langland and Chaucer can attest, nor especially widespread. By no means all members of the episcopacy were as corrupt as Wolsey and the much maligned parish clergy were, in the main, a willing enough bunch, in spite of all the anticlerical vitriol that the likes of Simon Fish might pour upon them. Nor were the judicial and financial burdens imposed upon Henry VIII's subjects as intolerable as high-profile scandals and lurid tales of the day might suggest. Moreover, the Church had the unyielding support of the political establishment in its favour and, far from undermining it, humanist learning was mainly serving to initiate the crucial long-term process of purging Catholicism of its defects. On the other hand, those self-same superstitious features, which so aggrieved a minority of middle class intellectuals, gave the old religion an unswaying hold over many more who were snugly cosseted by the familiar mummeries and mystifications of everyday worship.

If, then, the Church of Rome was no virgin incarnate, neither was she altogether diabolically mired. And while there is no denying that Roman Catholicism was confronted by a broad array of challenges, the old view that it was a moribund and decadent anachronism, confronted in the early years of the sixteenth century by an irretrievable crisis of credibility, holds little water. Equally unconvincing is any claim that Henry VIII eventually performed a necessary task in kicking down the decayed structure of an organisation that stood condemned in all senses of the term. These days, therefore, King Henry, the builder and creator, looks much more like King Henry the appetent bull in a china shop.

7

Puissance and Penury

'Ay, sir, have ye been with Master Henry King? A noble act ye did there!
Ye spent away my money and other men's, like a sort of vagabonds and
knaves!'

> John Brody of Shaftesbury in Dorset to John Williams,
> soldier of King Henry, 1524.

On the evening of 14 August 1521, England's cardinal arrived at last upon
his resplendent mule outside the gates of Bruges to lay his master's plans
for war and conquest. With the late summer foliage overhanging its canals
deferentially, the city was packed to capacity and primed for festival in
honour of this most high guest. Indeed, so exalted now was Wolsey's rank
and so pressing the imperial need for English assistance against French
aggression in Navarre that Charles V had waited a full half hour for him
in the company of his entire court. Accordingly, as the cardinal made his
eventual appearance along with 1,050 satin-clad horsemen, bells pealed, the
banners of the guilds were unfurled and Flemish hospitality was stretched
to its lavish best. Every lodging, we are told, was furnished with 'fuel,
bread, beer, wine, beeves, muttons, veals, lambs, venison and all manner of
dainty viands as well in fishes as in flesh'. Nor, upon his eventual meeting
with the emperor, did Wolsey dismount. Merely raising his precious hat,
he embraced his host from saddle to saddle as an equal, and in the journey
to his lodgings which followed, his only concession to royalty was to give
the emperor the place of honour on the right as they rode side-by-side. To
be escorted thus, 'familiarly', by the Holy Roman Emperor was an entirely
unprecedented honour for any subject of a foreign ruler and next day, to
confirm the cardinal's glowing status, Charles and he heard Mass together

in the city's cathedral, where they shared the same kneeling-desk under a single canopy of State.

Now, at last, the hypocritical posturings begun at the Field of Cloth of Gold were finally abandoned, and the altogether more meaningful negotiations for conflict could begin. Throughout the late summer and autumn of 1521, in fact, Wolsey would barter doggedly with the emperor 'sometimes with sharp winds, sometimes in pleasant manner', as he told Henry. And such was the gravity of the conference that for three days negotiations were suspended while Wolsey lay panic-stricken in bed, suspecting that he had been poisoned by the emperor's cook. Charles himself had also feared for his life when a small bladder filled with hair and foul-smelling powders was discovered in a platter of meat, though the mixture was later found to be nothing more dangerous than a stray love potion. Nevertheless, by November the cardinal had devised a treaty that paved the way for a joint invasion of France in 1523 and secured the proposed marriage contract between his master's daughter Mary and the emperor, which had first been proposed in 1520. He had done so, moreover, on what seemed the best possible terms, for Charles had not only settled ultimately on a modest dowry of £80,000, but had even agreed to pay Henry what he would lose in pensions by a breach with France. Not surprisingly, therefore, the English king was more than satisfied with his cardinal's diplomacy, telling Richard Pace in no uncertain terms how his affairs could not have been better handled. The king's 'contentment with all your acts', Pace told Wolsey, 'cannot be so well painted with a pen as it is imprinted in my heart'. Furthermore, Wolsey had also received into the bargain another clear guarantee of Charles V's support when the papacy itself next became vacant.

Nor was the wait for Pope Leo X to make way a long one and when he died in December 1521, Wolsey was at once widely mooted as successor. Here, it might be thought, was the realisation of a fitting ambition for a man approaching fifty who had reached his pinnacle as a commoner. But appearances were utterly deceptive, since this, at least, was one promotion that the so-called 'proud prelate' never seriously sought. For a cardinal supposedly aspiring to become pope, Wolsey had, in fact, always remained strangely ignorant of personalities and procedures in Rome. Not only did he remain consistently indifferent to the power struggles within the Roman curia, for example, but he had never even visited the Holy City and had scant patience with those who thought he should. Equally surprisingly, he made no attempt to build up a personal following by securing the election of his supporters to the cardinalate. Indeed, the only cardinal with whom he was personally acquainted was Lorenzo Campeggio, whom he had roundly slighted in 1518. Leo X, meanwhile, had frequently expressed his indignation that Wolsey should write to him so infrequently when he had so much to report. For once, then, Wolsey was being wholly frank in claiming, as he did later, that he entered the election only out of duty to his sovereign and master.

There is no doubting, in fact, that it was Henry himself who insisted so strenuously upon Wolsey's election, irrespective of the cardinal's own wishes or the practicalities involved. It was the king, of course, who was so intensely conscious that there had been no English-born pope since Nicholas Breakspear became Adrian IV in the twelfth century and it was Henry, too, who immediately despatched Pace to Rome upon Leo's death 'as if he had sent his very heart'. To secure Wolsey's election would, Henry believed, greatly redound to his own personal credit and help to secure obvious political advantages in his dealings with France. As always, then, the more unlikely the cause, the more ready the English king was to support it, so long as there was some hint of personal glory to be had for him. And as usual he was prepared to throw money in pursuit of his pipedreams. The election, he swore, 'should not be lost for the want of 100,000 ducats'.

The supreme irony, however, was that Henry was encouraging Wolsey to pursue a prize that was every bit as unwinnable as it was undesirable, for as the eventual deliberations ground out their weary course over fourteen days it was quite clear that the English candidate had no chance and that the emperor had never meant him to. Certainly, no one present seems to have considered the 'cardinal of York' a viable contender and he achieved in all only seven votes in the fifth and twelfth scrutinies. According to his would-be friend Cardinal Campeggio, it was Wolsey's relative youth that had ultimately disqualified him, and even though Campeggio claimed that on his own 'personal impression' Wolsey was nearer sixty than fifty, he was clearly unable to prove his hunch to the satisfaction of the conclave. Cardinal Petrucci, on the other hand, explained Wolsey's failure to Pace on the rather more convincing grounds that 'he would never come to Rome'. The deciding factor, however, was simply Charles V's decision not to deliver on the assurances he had given. Instead, it would be his former tutor, the aged, care-worn and ineffectual Adrian of Utrecht, who 'triumphed' under the emperor's patronage to become Adrian VI. Only eighteen months later, death would relieve him of his burden. 'Here lies Adrian VI', his epitaph declared, 'whose greatest misfortune was that he became Pope.'

Nevertheless, while Wolsey was enough of a realist to be more relieved than disillusioned by the outcome of his bid, there were still more than enough cares to occupy him nearer home. Events in Scotland, for example, were once again shaping menacingly, since that 'marvellous wilful man' the Duke of Albany, who in 1515 had virtually kidnapped the infant James V and ousted his mother, Margaret Tudor, was once more about to be unleashed by his French paymasters. The duke was French both by upbringing and in his sentiments, and, as such, keen to bedevil the English at any opportunity. Moreover, he was volatile in the extreme. 'So passionate' was he, according to the Earl of Surrey, 'that he be apart among his familiars'. If, said Surrey, the duke 'doth hear anything contrarious to his mind and pleasure, his accustomed manner is to take his bonnet suddenly off his head, and to throw it on the fire', so that 'no man dare take it out, but let it be burnt'. 'My Lord Dacre', Surrey added, 'doth affirm that at his last being in Scotland he did burn a dozen bonnets after that manner.' It was not altogether surprising, therefore, that this ranting duke had been quick to exploit the earlier indiscretion of Henry's sister Margaret when, after the death of her husband James IV at Flodden, she had swiftly married the unpopular Archibald Douglas, Earl of Angus. Indeed, it had been this reckless action which had led to her ejection from Scotland and separation from her son. Sadly for her brother, however, this would be neither her final foolhardy act nor the last time that she spoiled his policies.

By 1521, in fact, Margaret's temperament was once more conjuring storm clouds, as she tired of her second husband, and with tension mounting on all sides, Albany duly seized his opportunity. Returning to Scotland in December after lying low 'like a fox in a hole', he now once more removed the young king, this time from Stirling Castle to the 'windy and unpleasant castle and rock of Edinburgh'. And as a further defiant flourish, the passionate Gallic Scot had even, it seems, bent Margaret herself to his will by means of 'fair words'. Warned against scandal and urged to remember 'whereof she was come and of what House', she had nevertheless remained 'much inclined to the pleasure of the said Duke', and it was no secret that there was 'marvellous great intelligence' between the two, which went on 'all the day as much of the night'. Henry, in the meantime, fumed over the 'dishonourable and damnable abusing of our sister', but was already so irretrievably committed to war against France that he would have to live for the time being with the increasingly likely prospect of the traditional stab in the back through Scotland.

Ireland, too, would have to wait while Henry's one-track mind was turned to glory across the Channel. In the so-called *Remembrance* of 1519, which Wolsey had drawn up to encourage the king to take a more active role in government, it had been carefully considered 'how the lands of Ireland could be brought into order and obedience'. But the aim was more easily stated than achieved, for at the time that Henry VIII ascended the throne, the wastes of Connemara and the solitudes of Northern Ulster remained stubbornly unexplored. Nor were there were any safe estimates of the size of Ireland's population, let alone its distribution and composition. In an early sixteenth-century account the land was said to be divided into more than sixty counties or regions 'inhabited with the king's Irish enemies' and governed by over sixty chieftains 'that liveth only by the sword and obeyeth to no other temporal power, but only to himself that is strong'. And the clans and septs who lived 'west of the Barrow and west of the law' were indeed a pugnacious bunch, who further confirmed the dominant stereotypes associated with 'wild Irishry' by sporting mantles of Bronze Age cut and bearing names that made one Englishman complain they belonged rather to 'devouring giants' than to 'Christian subjects'. Even the Irish Church had remained untouched by humanist influences and, naturally enough, from the moment that the disdainfully uncomprehending English had arrived with their centralised government and all the exploitation it entailed, there had been and would continue to be an almighty clash of alien cultures and incompatible worlds. For the Gaelic chroniclers, Henry VIII was still, after all, 'King of the Saxons', and as such, their sworn and eternal enemy.

With his second French war now pressing in upon his thoughts, Henry would therefore have to reckon with this uneasy background in Ireland. He had declared early in his reign that 'none of his progenitors were so resolved to reduce that disordered land to good government as he was', but he did little to deliver on his promise, and though he did not make his usual mistake of overestimating his military options, he now harboured fond illusions about the possible success of political approaches:

> We and our Council [he informed the Earl of Surrey in 1520], think and
> verily believe that in case circumspect and politic ways be used, ye shall
> […] bring them to obedience […] Which thing must as yet be practised in
> sober ways, politic drafts and amiable persuasions, founded in law and reason
> than by rigorous dealing, comminations or other enforcement by strength
> or violence.

In reality, though, this uncharacteristically moderate approach, brought
on, no doubt, by one of the fleeting self-satisfied bouts of reason and light
to which Henry was occasionally prone, was wholly deluded. Surrey,
who already knew Ireland well, made a truer and, for that matter, more
truthful judgement. 'After my poor opinion', he wrote, 'this land shall
never be brought to good order and due subjection but only by conquest.'
However, when, in 1521, Surrey went on to claim that, with enough
men, he could subdue Ireland, he would not be spared the necessary funds.
More than that, he was soon writing that he and his soldiers 'have not
among us £20 in money'. Ireland, then, would remain another problem
shelved as every available penny in the coming months was anxiously
earmarked for France.

It was wholly apt, of course, that a war as archaic in intent as the one
now to be waged against the French should have been launched with all
the old devices of heraldry. The ceremonial flinging of insults and defiance
by means of heralds was, after all, a time-honoured feature of the dusty
furniture of feudalism, and however tawdry their backstage dealings,
Henry and Charles were determined to maintain their chivalric charade
to the bitter end. So it was that the noble task of tweaking the King of
France's honour fell, somewhat ironically perhaps, upon a herald whose
official name was Clarenceux. While Henry and Charles were worshipping
side-by-side at Canterbury, therefore, Clarenceux appeared before Francis
at Lyons, brandishing his weighty credentials, and was greeted with
due ceremony. Then in a stylised oration that was as pompous as it was
provocative, he set forth the charges Henry now laid against his former
brother and ally. Responding with the gracious but slowly simmering self-
control required by the occasion, Francis duly parried his detractor's claims
'with the proud assurance that if any man said the French king had failed
to keep his word, he would give his maligner the lie'. 'And', he added
manfully, 'if Henry took the field, he was ready to meet him.' But for all
the virile posturing involved, the challenge issued to Francis would, in any

case, prove premature, since Henry himself was far from ready for combat. It was, after all, one thing to declare a war, quite another to finance one. Before it could be fought, the whole nation would have to be squeezed to its limits and beyond for funds.

Though the art of destruction was increasing in sophistication all the while and its costs climbing accordingly, early efforts to finance the impending war would rely entirely on old expedients long grown rusty and deficient. At a time when almost £50,000 had already been earmarked to deal with the danger from Scotland, estimates of the cost for the proposed campaign in Flanders were deeply unsettling. The land army involved was expected to number 26,000 English and 8,000 'Almain' infantrymen, along with 8,000 cavalry, and with its consumption of beer alone calculated to run at some 882,000 gallons for every month of campaigning, it was hardly surprising that the overall cost of provisions had been calculated at close to £300,000. Meanwhile the 'sea army' of some 3,000 men was expected to consume at least 187 tons of grain, 600 oxen and 18,000 barrels of salt fish, not to mention a further 17,640 gallons of ale. In all, then, the cost of supplying the navy was estimated at £28,000, and when the additional cost of 'conduct money' to get the army to the waiting ships is added to the tally, the likely grand total for the war stood at a potentially crippling £372,404. Of necessity, such expenses would entail increased taxation, which would be bound to make Henry's government intensely unpopular.

In March 1522, therefore, two months before Henry's herald brashly bearded the French king, a demand for £20,000 had been inflicted upon the capital's merchants, while royal agents were loosed throughout the shires of England to ascertain the value of lands and all other items of fixed and movable property. At the same time, the wine casks and storage barrels of all Londoners, including foreign residents, were laid out, by royal order, throughout the narrow streets and alleys of the capital for the king's purveyors to purchase at cheap rates of their own choosing. Any item, however precious or humble, that might be deemed of use to the army was subject to such patriotic confiscation. And the inconvenience caused by Henry's grandiose schemes did not end here, for, later in the year, a property tax was imposed under the name of a loan, although the promise of repayment, which accompanied it, fooled no one. Greeted with grumbling dissatisfaction by all classes, there was not surprisingly especial resentment from the London merchants, who reminded the cardinal how it had been scarcely two months since the king had already demanded his payment of £20,000, 'whereby the city is bare of money'. But any sums procured by such means would not, in any case, remotely suffice to finance the military plans now in hand. By the early part of 1523, therefore, Henry saw that he would have to summon Parliament: a decision that amounted to his most eloquent admission of desperation to date, since MPs had not been called to Westminster in the previous eight years.

When Parliament subsequently convened on 15 April at the great hall of the Blackfriars in London, the king himself attended, flanked by his cardinal and council. But even this imposing gathering failed to flush the requisite funds at the first asking. Two weeks later, therefore, as Parliament continued to bristle in sullen indignation, the cardinal was forced to come once more before the House of Commons to specify what was expected of its members. Emphasising the king's moral obligation to chastise France, Wolsey explained the reasons and detailed the likely costs. 'The French King', he contended, 'had broken his promises made to England, by making war with the emperor; notwithstanding the meeting of the two princes at Guisnes, where the French King had solemnly swore to keep all the articles contained in the league.' He had also, it seems, 'withholden the payment of money agreed on as to the delivering up of Tournay' and 'refused to pay the French Queen's dowry'. 'Wherefore', Wolsey hoped, 'the Commons would cheerfully assist the king in vindicating his Honours by granting the supplies necessary on this urgent occasion.' The sum involved, Wolsey concluded, 'could not be less than £800,000'.

To the sound of not a few gasps, the cardinal then made his solemn departure, leaving the Commons, or so he hoped, to stand and deliver. It remained for the Speaker of the House, Sir Thomas More, to plead the government's case the following day, but on this occasion his half-hearted arguments fell on stone-deaf ears. Indeed, far from complying, the Commons now sought to drown Wolsey's demands in a bottomless trough of endless talk. Should the sum be paid, said one member, loyal subjects would be left 'to barter clothes for victuals and bread and cheese'. 'The realm itself', complained another, 'for want of money would grow in a sort barbarous and ignoble.' There was a call, too, for the formation of a committee to wait upon the cardinal in the hope that he might persuade the king 'to be content with a more easier sum' than the monstrous levy of 4 shillings in the pound entailed by the current proposal. When, however, the requested meeting took place, Wolsey, says Edward Hall, 'currishly answered' that he would rather have his tongue plucked out of his head with a pair of pincers than to move the king to take less. Somewhat insensitively, he cited, too, the growing costs that his master was already incurring, as a result of the sumptuous buildings, rich apparel and 'fat feasts' now fashionable. Annoyed by the babble 'blown abroad in every alehouse' and by the Commons' request that the king accept a reduced levy, Wolsey now demanded the right to return to Parliament to press the king's case, but this time with his full entourage in tow. Where reason had failed, it seems, theatre must surely prevail.

When, however, the time came for the cardinal to make his second appearance 'with all his pomp, with his maces, his pillars, his poleaxes, his crosses, his hat, and the great seal too', he was met not with the awed deference and compliance he had anticipated, but with what he himself termed 'a marvellous obstinate silence'. The man who had not hesitated in the past to thump papal nuncios or arrest vexatious ambassadors had run into a situation he could not comprehend and an atmosphere unreceptive to his tricks. Far from subsidising the king's grandiose plans, the Commons now expressed their concerns about the costs and risks of invading France more and more stridently, and after sixteen days of 'long persuading and privy labouring of friends', MPs remained adamant that they would concede no more than half the sum required of them. Therefore, in an almighty about-turn, both king and cardinal now had no choice but to profess themselves to be pleased with the offer, although even this proved of little real consolation to the country at large. On the contrary, there remained seething discontent, which was fanned further by general ignorance of the levy's proposed details. Especially resented in the country's outlying regions, this tax would be interpreted as nothing less than the preliminary onslaught in a calculated plan, hatched in London, to confiscate all and any property. And as reports now filtered into the capital of budding insurrection in East Anglia, there was news, too, from the middle shires of a plot to 'seize and rob the collectors of the subsidy, and then to hold Kenilworth against the king'. Though the rumours were idle, they matched the private wrath of common folk.

As was widely suspected, the grand strategy which the tax financed would prove hopelessly misconceived. True, the Holy Roman Emperor, the pope, Spain, Venice, Florence, Genoa and even the disaffected Duke of

Bourbon were all now arrayed against the French king, but hard experience should have taught Henry that such alliances were every bit as fragile as the military strategies that went with them. Moreover, what Henry had signally failed to grasp in his dizzy schemings was that, even in the highly unlikely event of any decisive victory over France, his country could only suffer in the long term from the resulting destruction of the balance of power in Europe. Prudence counselled that England should make herself strong, develop her resources and hold her strength in reserve, while her two rivals weakened each other steadily. This had been the policy that had stood Henry VII in such good stead. Yet Henry's desire to gain 'free entry into the bowels of France' propelled him onwards, in spite of the fact that when war finally came it failed to capture the interest of any of those who played their dreary parts in it. While French peasants and cattle were aimlessly slaughtered, and a few adventurers enriched, the war's engagements had no discernible effect upon the map. Nor was its dismal course redeemed by any hint of either bravery or strategy, which might have lent some colour or meaning to the bloodshed.

The business of wanton slaughter would begin ultimately with a preliminary sortie into France led by the Earl of Surrey, son of the glorious victor of Flodden. During July of 1522 he captured and burnt Morlaix in the Cherbourg peninsula, though with what aim in mind was far from clear, and the following month he duly ravaged Artois and the country around Boulogne. By this time, however, his main concern was already not so much laurel wreaths as the great scarcity of basic amenities for his men. Writing bitterly, at one point, that he had only enough beer for twelve days, he also bemoaned the great shortage of wood for the bakehouses. Besides which, the ships at sea were no better off, for Fitzwilliam's vessels, Surrey complained, were without either fish or flesh. It seemed, then, that the war was proving a failure even in the one area where Wolsey had earlier showed his most commanding talent: the provision of beer and victuals.

From all perspectives, in fact, it was a wretchedly conceived expedition in which only the destruction proceeded unerringly. While Henry himself was hawking in Essex and Hertfordshire, Surrey informed the cardinal that:

> all the country we have passed through has been burnt; and all the strong places, whether castles or fortified churches have been thrown down [...] When we have burnt Dorlance, Corby, Ancre, Bray and the neighbouring

country, which I think will be in about three weeks, I cannot see that we can do much more.

Closing his letter with the observation that 'there is universal poverty here, and great fear of this army', he added his hope that 'the King's grace and you will be content with our services'. That the king's grace would indeed be well satisfied with such a carefree record of premeditated and pointless savagery says much about the harsh realities of the chivalric ideal he claimed so vehemently to espouse. That such devastation should be inflicted, moreover, upon an area of France already stricken by drought, pestilence and poverty says even more.

And here, of course, was another noble exploit for the son of the victor of Flodden to boast of. Having himself played a gallant part in the defeat of a formidable Scottish army, the Earl of Surrey was now left to settle for the humdrum butchery of innocent French peasants, sparing neither their houses, nor even their places of worship. At Lottinghen, near Desvres, Surrey's forces incinerated everything they could find over an area of 40 square miles, and after one especially successful raid we hear of a single scorched church left standing, looking 'more like a house of war than the house of God'. But quite apart from its outrightly shameful features, the whole enterprise, which the Duke of Vendôme described as a 'very foul war', had soon assumed an almost embarrassing aspect as marauding English troops struggled vainly to find any broader purpose for their mission. Thus, having failed to take the town of Hesdin, the English were eventually prevailed upon by imperial generals to cease their play, and by 16 October 1522, Surrey was safely returned to Calais, left to reflect upon his deadly handiwork with whatever pride he could muster.

The whole worthless escapade had also sucked dry those few reserves of money raised so far for the war. Equally significantly, it had rendered the north of England virtually defenceless against the Scots, for while Surrey was eagerly swatting scattered French hamlets, the Duke of Albany had brought from France a force of 5,000 men and was marching purposefully towards a defenceless Carlisle. Though the Earl of Shrewsbury had been sent to improvise what resistance he could, scarce supplies delayed him at York, and, in consequence, the way to England now lay wide open for the invaders. This, it seemed, was Scotland's long-awaited moment of destiny, but as the window of opportunity opened wide before him, even Albany could not weld the Scottish lords into concerted action, for feeble as it was, the English party north of the border was just sufficient to divide the duke's supporters. And when Huntly, Argyle and Arran, the leading Scottish earls, proved unwilling to risk another Flodden, and the Gordons refused outright to cross the Tweed, Albany's plans were finally undone.

So it was that the potential Scottish juggernaut faltered. But the crisis, it should be emphasised, was not averted through any foresight or skill on the King of England's part. Sorely lacking the means to repel the impending invasion, the commander of England's northern forces, Lord Dacre, resorted ultimately to the diplomacy of desperation by offering a wholly unauthorised truce to the Scots at the very moment when they could have laid waste all before them. No doubt as a result of divisions among his followers and the unwillingness of Francis I to lend anything more than moral support, Albany duly accepted a cessation of hostilities, while Henry, of course, affected disappointment at the loss of an opportunity for a resounding victory over the Scots. Even the King of England, however, had gumption enough to know his luck on this occasion. Tear his hair as he might in feigned frustration, he had only been saved by Dacre's improvised strategy and Scottish rankling.

Nevertheless, in spite of countless ill omens, setbacks and close scrapes, the main assault on France now lumbered into motion in the late summer of 1523. Ultimately, against all odds, the Duke of Suffolk would lead his troops to within 40 miles of Paris itself and, from his camp in Compiègne, he sent word to Henry that there was 'good likelihood of the attaining of his ancient right and title to the crown of France to his singular comfort and eternal honour'. By then, though, it was November and winter had set in with a vengeance. And as the frost hardened, so the imperial soldiers in Suffolk's army began to melt away, leaving him no choice but to send an emissary to the king explaining the necessity of retreat. In his defence he cited the severe frosts that had killed 100 of his men in two days, the wet weather, the impassable roads, the short days and long nights, as well as 'great journeys and little victuals which cause the soldiers to die daily'. Even the 'profit of the spoil', which had at first been 'great encouraging to them', now held less and less attraction for the English troops. But Henry had already despatched a force of 6,000 men under Lord Moulsey to relieve Suffolk and was obdurate that the war should be waged to the bitter end. 'We wish', the king declared, 'that in no wise the army should break up.' Just as with Dorset's ill-fated expedition of 1512, however, the army now developed a will of its own and, in spite of the king's indignation, Suffolk acceded to the wishes of his men and broke camp. Though Henry's response was this time sullen and petulant rather than violent, he nevertheless made clear his disappointment by banning Suffolk and his captains from court. They 'came not to the King's presence a long season', it was said, 'to their great heaviness and displeasure'.

Meanwhile, as Suffolk's soldiers straggled back to their homes, spreading their frustration throughout the English countryside, the futility and cost of the imperial alliance was more apparent than ever. Bourbon had proven utterly ineffectual and Charles had contented himself with the conquest of Fuenterrabia, making no move toward the prearranged goal of Guienne and remaining impervious to the reproaches of his ally. Yet the long-term repercussions of Henry's folly were much greater still, for by yielding to the blandishments of the emperor, he had thus helped to plunge Europe into a major war at the very time when Christendom was threatened from within by Lutheran heresy and from without by the Turk; a war, moreover, which would rage, with only brief intervals of peace, for the next forty years and bring great sadness and disorder to his realm. The blunder had been Henry's, but the blame would fall to Wolsey. And this was not the sum of the cardinal's troubles in 1523, for now, at his sovereign's whim, he was made to take up the burden of a further challenge for the papacy.

With summer's last ripening, Adrian VI had been stricken by what would quickly prove to be a fatal renal disease. Six days before the end came, faltering in his speech 'like a man fatigated', the pope had informed his cardinals that he expected soon to depart to the mercy of God, and when news of his unlamented death arrived in England on 30 September, the mirage of a papacy under English control once again reared tantalisingly before Henry's eyes. Therefore, in spite of Wolsey's private protest to Pace that he would much rather end his days in the king's service, remaining in England, instead of 'mine old days approaching, to enter into new things', the die was cast. If the decision were his to make, Wolsey declared, he would rather remain the king's minister than be 'ten popes'. Even so, he was resigned to his fate. 'The mind and entire wish of His Highness, above all earthly things, is that I shall attain to the said dignity,' he wrote.

Once again, Charles would toy with Henry, even telling his ambassador to inform his gullible 'uncle' that he had despatched a special courier to Rome, and presenting him with copies of the letters of recommendation that he had written on Wolsey's behalf. What he did not say, however, was that he had deliberately delayed the courier. Not surprisingly, when the inevitable news of his non-election finally reached him, Wolsey's relief seems to have been palpable. In a letter to the new pope, Clement VII, which was by no means entirely the shallow exercise in flattery it may at first seem, he greeted him as 'his singular and especial lover and friend' and told him how he had deserved his election 'above all spiritual persons living'. 'Being far more joyful thereof than if it happened upon my own person', Wolsey went on to declare that his pen could not adequately express his great joy at Clement's appointment to the supreme governance of Christ's own Church. It seems certain, then, that any disappointment that Wolsey expressed elsewhere was merely a dutiful response to the undoubted frustration felt by his master, for if the heavy papal tiara had indeed become his, he would have found himself banished to a resentful community torn by feuding churchmen, many of whom were every bit as adept as he in the subtle art of self-aggrandisement. Furthermore, if by some miracle Henry's wish had been fulfilled, it is by no means certain that five years later the pope of his choice would have granted him the divorce he craved.

For the time being, at least, the alliance between the King of England and the emperor trundled on, while Henry remained as committed as ever to his French project. During 1524 he even sent 100,000 crowns to subsidise an offensive by Bourbon in Provence and pledged himself to invade France in person, should the duke prove successful. However, in spite of the usual surfeit of mighty talk on her sovereign's part, England took no further military action in the immediate aftermath of Suffolk's fruitless foray into France. The irony was, of course, that Henry's decision to opt out of the fighting at this point proved far more costly than the earlier move to enter it, for although the emperor's progress was by no means steady or straightforward, he now managed ultimately to do everything and more that Henry's forces had failed so abjectly to achieve in the previous year. Yet again, it seemed, the turns of the wheel of fortune had stopped at a point which favoured Charles and mocked the King of England, for in the middle of the night on 23 February 1525, the French finally received the most crushing of defeats with no English army on hand to share the fruits of victory.

The French fought fiercely and well at the Battle of Pavia, but to no avail. With Francis at their head, wearing a splendid silver surcoat with long plumes that swept down over his shoulders, they had charged a force of Spanish arquebusiers and pikemen, but as the attack continued from the imperial forces, the garrison of the besieged town sallied out and attacked the French in the rear. As a result, the confined space in which Francis' army had been caged up to that point now became, in effect, a meat grinder. Swinging a great gold-hilted sword, Francis himself fought valiantly, bringing down with his own hand several Spanish officers and an imperial standard bearer, but most of his army had already deserted him by the time he made his way toward a bridge that might have taken him to safety. It was a straggling musketeer who shot the king's horse from under him, and as he fell an imperial man-at-arms is said to have approached and bade him yield. 'Give me my life, for I am the King', said Francis, 'I yield myself up to the Emperor.' At which point, we are told, one soldier took off Francis' helmet, another removed the feathers from his crest and the remaining bystanders cut off pieces of his coat to carry with them as a memorial of their part in the overthrow of so renowned a prince.

Receiving the news from Pavia with his usual gravity, Charles V prohibited all celebrations at his court, choosing instead to express sympathy with Francis' misfortune. Henry by contrast was ecstatic at the news of the French defeat and was bent at once on gloating and gain. When the news reached him he was in bed, but no dream in his head could have matched the one that now became a reality for him. 'You are', he told the bearer of the glad tidings, 'as welcome as was the angel Gabriel to the Virgin Mary.' Upon hearing of the death of his English rival Richard Pole in the fighting, he then ordered more wine for the messenger and having sprung up to tell Queen Catherine the joyous news, he was soon regaling all and sundry with his lofty plans for a final reckoning with the French. 'Now is the time', he told an embassy from the Netherlands, 'for the Emperor and myself to devise full satisfaction from France. Not an hour is to be lost.' The ancient enemy of the realm of England had suddenly, it seemed, been consigned to oblivion. In less than two hours at Pavia 8,000 Frenchmen and mercenaries had fallen, and the pick of France's elite, including Fleuranges, Galiot, Montmorency and Henri d'Albret were captured. But these, of course, were the lucky ones, for many more were even now rudely stacked in the biggest funeral mounds to be dug for French nobles since Agincourt. Kingless, defenceless and newly impoverished, their country was, it seemed, helplessly stranded at a crossroads offering no sign of safety or hope.

Irresistibly, then, Henry was beckoned by his fantasy of recovering his 'true inheritance' and 'just title'. 'So long', he now wrote to Sir Robert Wingfield, his permanent ambassador to the emperor, 'as the realm of France […] situate in the heart and midst of all Christendom, shall remain in the hands of those who cannot, nor never will, cease to apply their wits, powers, thoughts and studies, to ampliate and extend their limits and dominions, never satiate nor contented with enough, there can never be rest, quiet and tranquillity in Christendom.' For Henry, it was 'notorious and manifest' that the French crown should be his, or at the very least, the right by line of succession to Picardy, Normandy and Brittany. And since these territories could only be won by 'violence and puissance' rather than by consent, Henry instructed Wingfield to propose to Charles V an immediate and utterly impractical joint invasion of France. It was 'for his high orgule, pride and insatiable ambition', Henry told Charles, that the King of France had been dealt divine retribution and unless king and emperor seized this heaven-sent opportunity to crush their enemy once and for all, it was to be feared 'that God should take high indignation against them, executing his terrible sword of correction and dreadful punishment upon them for the same'. Together, it was suggested, they could enter Paris whereupon Henry would snap up the French crown, leaving Provence, Languedoc and Burgundy for his ally. Thereafter, the new King of France would proceed with Charles to Rome 'to see the Crown imperial set upon his head', while the Princess Mary would be 'transported' to Paris to wed the emperor who would eventually stand to inherit England and Ireland as well as a title to Scotland, thereby becoming ultimately the 'Peacable Lord and Owner of all Christendom'.

Such a delirious enterprise could never, of course, even remotely appeal to the stolid, calculating mind of Charles V, who had no intention whatsoever of making his English counterpart King of France. Nor had he any interest, for that matter, in conquering France himself or any need of England in mastering the remainder of Italy. It was well known, in any case, that Charles's mighty empire was propped up on empty treasure chests. Even the pay of his household servants was said to be in arrears, 'some for twenty years, some for twelve months, and the least for nine'. As such, any troops that he could afford for campaigning were much better sent to the deeply troubled German states, where furious peasants, inflamed by apocalyptic preachings, were massing to dish out God's wrath to their masters. Therefore, in spite of the fact that the Princess Mary answered

Charles's commissioners in such fluent Latin that they thought her twelve rather than nine, and although she sent him an emerald ring, which he put on his little finger, Charles would not be swayed into assistance.

This much was made transparently clear by Dr Richard Sampson, the regular English ambassador at Madrid, who had already given the King of England to understand that the emperor would provide no help. 'They think here', he wrote, 'that the king should make the rest of any conquest at his own charge.' Having met with Charles, Henry's other envoys, who had been specially despatched to fire the emperor's interest, also 'thought it needless to blow any longer at a dead coal'. In consequence, it remained only for Charles to spurn his English bride as soon as a more attractive candidate was available, and such a female was not long in appearing. Whereas Mary Tudor was still a tender child, Isabella of Portugal was a perfectly marriageable 19 years of age, bearing a dowry of no less than a million crowns to further sweeten her appeal. The betrothal to Mary was therefore duly dissolved, and Charles, in a letter extolling the 'almost indissoluble tie' between himself and Henry, now severed that tie with a casual stroke of his pen.

But whatever the emperor might decide, Henry for his part remained resolved upon the invasion, even if such a venture would require huge amounts of money he did not have. The task of raising the necessary sums could, after all, be left to the care of his cardinal, and so it was that the dwindling energies of Thomas Wolsey, who had been increasingly exhausted by the bombast of his master and the double-dealings of an emperor nearly thirty years his junior, now had to be turned to the frightful task of raising funds for yet another invasion of France.

In fact, the method devised for lightening Englishmen's pockets was not of the cardinal's confecting, though to his misfortune the details of the plan's execution devolved upon him and he became inextricably identified with it. He had already been branded as the minister who had forced through Parliament the grant of 1523 and, as Henry well knew, he would now bear the full brunt of a much fiercer reaction still. The levy, which was to be known with ringing irony as the Amicable Grant, involved a demand of a sixth from lay property and a fourth from clerical property. Commissioners to collect it were appointed for the various shires, and to lend momentum to the whole proposal the highest nobles were assigned to enforce the king's demand. Wolsey, meanwhile, receiving as usual the short straw, was to be made Henry's commissioner for London, and his initial presentation to the city corporation and leading merchants showed clearly the kind of psychology and appeal upon which his sovereign would come to rely more and more often. When one of his audience weakly ventured to suggest that business had decayed and that times were hard, Wolsey cut him short with the uninspired riposte that 'it were better that a few should suffer indigence than that the king should at this time lack', adding in his best baritone, no doubt: 'Beware, therefore, and resist not, nor ruffle not in this case; otherwise it may fortune to cost some their heads.'

In the event, the Amicable Grant very nearly cost the cardinal his own head, for anger at Wolsey's part in its genesis was soon reaching fever pitch. Archbishop Warham, now a septuagenarian and retired from court, reported from Kent to say that the people spoke cursedly, declaring that they 'should never rest from such payments as long as *some one* was living'. The dukes of Suffolk and Norfolk, in their turn, made it clear that they feared general rebellion and informed the cardinal, with a warm tingle of satisfaction, that 'if any insurrection follow, the blame shall be only against you'. And even if London's merchants accepted the cardinal's high-handed treatment for the time being, rich and poor alike at once saw through any thin disguise of amicability. Edward Hall noted how 'the poor cursed, the rich repugned, the light wits railed; but in conclusion all people cursed the cardinal and his co-adherents, as subvertors of the law and liberty of England'.

The south-east proved the most dangerous flashpoint, as in sermons and taprooms alike the loan was roundly denounced. At Cambridge both town and university rose as one in opposition, and a mob of 20,000 milled menacingly when the commissioners sought to make their levies. In other parts of East Anglia, Lavenham, Sudbury and Hadleigh were especially affected by the disorders and there were similar rumblings in Huntingdonshire. Elsewhere, Sir Thomas Boleyn was roughly handled at Maidstone, while in Suffolk 4,000 spinners and weavers 'rose in a body, rang the alarm bell, and menaced the commissioners with death'. At Chelmsford and Stansted, on the other hand, there was outright refusal to pay and at other places in Essex the people refused to meet with the commissioners 'except in the open air'. There were reports, too, that 'some fear to be hewn in pieces' by their neighbours 'if they make any grant'. In fact, news of the resistance would ultimately spread as far as Lincolnshire and touch off faggots of rebellion in every town and village. The fear amongst Kentishmen, meanwhile, was that if the king were indeed to conquer France, which they did not believe was likely, he would spend all his time and all their money there. Such was the scale of general disaffection that both the Dukes of Suffolk and Norfolk reported every day from their respective bases at Eye and Norwich on the glowering dissatisfaction of the common people. In a letter written on 12 May they expressed the opinion that 'they never saw the time so needful for the king to call his council to determine what should be done', adding the highly significant request to Wolsey that he should not send for one of them without sending for the other. Clearly, this was no time for a tax collector to find himself alone.

Most ominously of all, the nightmare vision of a rampant peasantry unleashed at last to avenge generations of exploitation was now no longer a dreadful fantasy, since at that very time Charles V was facing just such a scenario in his own territories. The so-called Peasants' War had begun in the Black Forest area of Germany before spreading throughout Thuringia, and before long, a tidal swell of insurrection had swept all before it in Swabia, Franconia, Alsace and even the Swiss territories of Salzburg and the Tyrol. Led by Thomas Münzer, who believed that the living God was 'sharpening his scythe in me', there were by April 1525 in excess of 100,000 heavily armed and mightily angry peasants demanding the restoration of their ancient manorial rights and citing Luther's doctrines of Christian freedom as justification for their excesses. There had, of course, been rural insurrections before, but nothing on this scale, as peasants, drunk on plundered wine and violence, killed bailiffs, raped nuns and looted property at will; seventy monasteries were destroyed in Thuringia and another fifty-two in Franconia, while in Frankfurt alone more than thirty fortresses had been destroyed. And as events gathered momentum, Münzer and his lieutenants began to dream of an apocalyptic transformation of the whole of Europe into an egalitarian paradise purged of the ungodly rich.

Certainly, the potential parallels with events in Germany were plain to see. A Swiss cleric who had seen the rebels at close range wrote to the imperial ambassador in Venice likening the rioting in England to the German rebellion. He had letters from English friends, he said, telling him that King Henry's subjects were everywhere turning against him and that no one could say where the unrest might end. The dangerous similarity between events in England and Germany was all the more marked, of course, since the resistance to the Amicable Grant was encouraged and promoted by the clergy and the religious orders. Amid the general clamour, priests coupled their shrill vocal opposition with an equally robust refusal to pay any grant demanded of them unless it was approved by their bishops. In the diocese of Salisbury, for instance, not one priest chose to submit, while in Bedfordshire and Buckinghamshire, Huntingdonshire and Kent most of the heads of the religious houses declared that they simply had not the means to deliver the full amount.

Nevertheless, when the time came for the government to concede defeat, it was harsh reality rather than any dictates of conscience that encouraged a change of policy on the king's part. Early in May 1525 it became clear that Henry had no choice but to settle for a much moderated demand and in doing so he seized the opportunity to pose as the rescuer of his oppressed people from the ill-counsel which, he claimed, had been foisted upon him. It was against his honour, he now discovered, that the council should attempt so doubtful a matter in his name. Indeed, he had been misled, or so he suggested. 'Well', he complained, 'some have informed me that my realm was never so rich and that men would pay at the first request, but now I find all the contrary.' Then, with a familiar ham display of royal anger, he declared: 'I will no more of this trouble. Let letters be sent to all shires that the matter be no more spoken of. I will pardon all ...' And on this imperious note, he capitulated entirely, withdrawing the Amicable Grant and insisting that from the first he had known nothing about it. In place of the heavy burden of one-sixth of all their goods, he now asked only 'such as his loving subjects would grant him of their good minds', and did not punish those who had risen against the tax.

The failure was total and resounding and to compound the king's frustration he was now faced with the abandonment of his most precious desire. France was to Henry what Milan was to Francis. It was the keystone of his ego and now was the critical moment when the French crown was waiting to be plucked decisively from its fallen owner. Henry had, in desperation, even told his agent John Clerk to make representations to the pope in Rome, thinking that His Holiness might be willing to contribute to his invasion. But the pope had declined with the truly delicious excuse that 'it was his duty to be a common father of Christian princes, and not to enter any league to the offence of any other'. Left with no other option, Henry therefore accepted Wolsey's Treaty of the More, which was signed at the cardinal's Hertfordshire manor house in August 1525 to end hostilities with France.

The ensuing autumn and winter months would be a time of subdued reflection and comparative isolation for the king. Once his hopes for the conquest of France had collapsed amid the alarming advance of popular rebellion, Henry's horizons narrowed considerably and in the light of the mind-boggling extravagance of his previous plans and involvements, there is a striking mundanity and pettiness about what now preoccupied him. In fact, as his foreign ambitions hibernated during the so-called 'still Christmas' that he spent at Eltham, Henry now settled for pinching pennies nearer home by overhauling the functioning of his household. As a result, he produced in January 1526, with Wolsey's assistance, the Ordinances of Eltham, which not only reflect the government's financial straits, but also provide an intriguing insight into the everyday world of England's sovereign up to this time.

From the outset of his reign, the king's extravagance had encouraged his court to develop into a huge, chaotic establishment. Henry had been particularly lavish, for instance, in his appointments to his privy chamber, with the result that there were far too many carvers, cup bearers, ushers and servers in attendance, all of whom brought their own servants to court, to be housed and fed at the king's expense. Others with official duties to perform had their functions undertaken too often by deputies, and the ranks of these hangers-on were often further swollen by servants of servants of royal servants. Not altogether surprisingly, brawling and general indiscipline were commonplace among this parasitic horde and even the King's Guard was in no better state. Now, however, at the start of 1526, stringent economies were enacted and a range of abuses addressed. Henceforth, every morning by nine o'clock the remains of all candles were to be collected for reuse and scullions who had hitherto worked either naked or in garments of 'vileness' were to be properly clothed. At the same time, no serjeant of arms, herald, messenger, minstrel, falconer, huntsman or footman was to bring to court 'any boys or rascals'. Much more significantly, there were also wholesale dismissals, so that the gentlemen of the privy chamber were roughly halved in number, while the servers were reduced from forty-five to six and the grooms of the chamber cut from sixty-nine to fifteen. 'Alas', said Hall, 'what sorrow and what lamentation was made when all these persons should depart the court.'

Of course, even in the fine detail of the Eltham Ordinances, Thomas Wolsey's influence can be plainly discerned. Curiously enough, a cardinal when lodged at court was to be allowed stabling for twenty-four horses, while a duke would now have to make do with provision for six less. But much more significantly, Wolsey had also taken this opportunity to rid himself of the presence of some of his most threatening foes. The Groom of the Stool, Sir William Compton, was, for example, neatly excised from court, along with Sir Francis Bryan, Sir Nicholas Carew and George Boleyn. Yet the removal of these individuals marked only a temporary clearing of the decks for the cardinal-legate prior to the onset of his most critical challenge to date, since the disposition of any king who wished to grow fat on success would not be long satisfied with the petty detail of household reform. And surely enough, Henry's eyes had already begun to glaze with thoughts other than those of conquest and the tedious business of government. Moreover, just as the king's recent ambitions had taxed Wolsey to the limit, so his new stirrings would break the mighty cardinal once and for all.

8

Impulse Born of Passion

'When this King decides on anything, he goes the whole length.'

Eustace Chapuys, Imperial ambassador to the
court of Henry VIII.

Just as Henry VIII had been at first a loyal son of the pope, so he was also for many years a diligent spouse to Catherine of Aragon. Soon after her marriage Queen Catherine was described as being in 'the greatest gaiety and contentment that ever there was' and for almost a decade she and Henry were to live in harmony as, at the very least, close and devoted friends. They were, for instance, happy partners at revels, dances and a host of other entertainments, and both rode together in the hunt. The queen played her coyly simpering part, too, as the king jousted tirelessly in her honour, wearing her symbol, the pomegranate, on the trappings of his horse. Henry, in his turn, spent most afternoons in his wife's apartments 'taking his pleasure as usual with the Queen', discussing theology, reading books or receiving visitors. Likewise, when evening came, it was his habit to take supper in Catherine's company, after which he invariably joined her for Vespers. Such, indeed, was his ardour that in 1513, shortly after she had sent him the blood-soaked garments of the fallen King of Scotland as a sign of victory and token of her love, Henry had declared to her father: 'If I were still free, I would choose her for wife above all others.' Catherine was, then, manifestly a kindly, gracious, loving and humble wife, who had learned well the virtues of patience and discretion after the death of her first husband. Yet, sad to say, none of these qualities would now serve to spare her from rejection at the hands of the very man around whom she had so gladly rebuilt her life.

There was, of course, still much outward affection and warmth in evidence when, on 18 February 1516 at Greenwich Palace, the royal couple's procreative exertions had borne their first lasting fruit, for at last the king's manly honour and his nation's future seemed less doubtful. So vital had the delivery of a healthy child been this time that, as the queen endured a difficult labour, clutching the girdle of her patron saint and namesake, the news of her father's demise had been kept from her, lest grief affect the final passage of her pregnancy. And in view of her harrowing catalogue of previous failures, such grave precautions seemed most apt. A stillborn daughter had already fallen from Catherine's womb in 1510 and at the end of November 1514 she had also given birth to a premature child, 'a prince who lived not long after'. Indeed, before the Princess Mary's birth the queen had brought forth four sons in all, none of whom survived longer than a few weeks. But now, aided by her physician Dr Vittoria and providence too, no doubt, she delivered a new babe who was described by her glowing father as 'a right lusty princess'.

Nevertheless, only a year or so after his daughter's birth, Henry's infidelities began to make their mark. There had been earlier rumours of dalliance, but these seem to have been consistent by and large with the rather cloying and impotently flirtatious gallantries typical of the time. The king had, for instance, apparently shown an interest in one of Queen Catherine's ladies-in-waiting, Lady Anne Hastings, as early as 1510, though after a whiff of scandal it came to nothing. Then in Flanders, in 1513, it was noticed how gaily the 22-year-old king had danced with Margaret of Savoy. A year later, a young lady from Margaret's court called Etienette La Baume, whom Henry had met on campaign, wrote and reminded him of their encounter at Lille, where the king had spoken *'beaucoup de belles choses'*. All this denoted little of significance, however, and for almost the entire first decade of his marriage Henry appears to have been unique among his princely counterparts in terms of faithfulness to his spouse. In comparison to Henry's nil score up to 1519, the Emperor Maximilian, for instance, had sired eleven bastards.

Some time before this, though, *'coeur loyall'* had already begun a tip-toeing but inexorable descent into husbandly contempt, and at the sumptuous fêting of the French ambassadors during Michaelmas 1518, Elizabeth Blount, a lady-in-waiting to Queen Catherine, had caught his eye. Moreover, when on 18 November the queen gave birth to a dead princess, she did so in the cruel knowledge that Mistress Blount had just become pregnant by Henry. To add salt to the wound, the latter's healthy son was born in June 1519 and as the years unfolded he would be officially acknowledged and treated to a spate of high honours. While Henry's legitimate daughter, Mary, was eventually packed off to the Marches as Princess of Wales, his bastard son would be made Earl of Nottingham, Warden of the Cinque Ports, Warden of the Scottish Marches, Lord High Admiral and Lord Lieutenant of Ireland. Most significantly of all, he was created Duke of Richmond and Somerset – two combined titles that were of old and significant association among the Tudors. At the same time he was also given his own household, which at a cost of £4,000 per year, was significantly more substantial than that of his half-sister. And when the queen protested, Henry took no more notice than to dismiss three of her Spanish ladies as a lesson in wifely obedience. Worse still, he soon began to discuss with the council an altogether more startling project – that of entailing the crown upon his bastard son.

By the shaky sexual standards of the age, of course, the king might still be reckoned comparatively abstemious even after this first lapse, for he appears to have confined his adulterous exploits to the times when Catherine was either pregnant or recovering from childbirth. Nevertheless, the first bite of the extra-marital apple is almost invariably an hors-d'oeuvre and after Mistress Blount came Mary Boleyn, wife of William Carey since 1521 and sister of Anne. There was, too, a special piquancy about this particular liaison, for if Henry had already nibbled at temptation, then Mary herself had surely gorged and laid bare the orchard. Having been loosed at a susceptible age in the French court, she had succumbed too avidly to the *gallant* atmosphere pertaining there and had emerged 'as a very great wanton with a most infamous reputation'. Francis I himself was among her lovers and described this 'English mare' with typical sensitivity as 'a great whore, the most infamous of all'.

But then, after earlier dips, came Henry's fateful plunge. Some time during 1525 or 1526 what had begun as a light flirtation with a raven-haired woman in her mid-twenties grew into something much more momentous. The offspring of a clan of avaricious social climbers, Anne Boleyn had joined her sister at the French court in August 1513 to learn the subtleties of deportment, dancing, polite conversation, high fashion and etiquette. But the ladies awaiting her there sought new freedoms and displayed new audacities and though she would become, in due course, a committed advocate of the new religious thinking, she would also learn to shun austerity. Indeed, while Anne Boleyn and her French counterparts were attending to their prayer books, they were no less keen to apply their thoughts to the altogether less edifying pages of Marguerite of Navarre's *Heptameron*. And having fully gauged the ways of the world, they could titillate and captivate accordingly. So when eventually, in the early weeks of 1527, Mistress Boleyn was neatly installed in Queen Catherine's household, she was more than fully equipped to laugh and dance her way into England's history. And before the May blossom had fallen, she had become a lady in waiting in an altogether more significant sense.

If truth be told, the underlying reasons for Henry's decision to put paid to his marriage are much more murky than is sometimes recognised and all too often the fears of dynastic insecurity that appear to have haunted him have also deceived historians. There is no doubt, of course, that there was a serious political dimension to the king's perplexity concerning the succession issue. Compared to France, where there were prolific lines of princes and princesses of the royal blood, the families of both Henry VII and Henry VIII were indeed tiny. In England, however, the problem of rival claimants to the throne had been greatly eased by the early deaths or infertility of those descended from the Yorkist line. Apart from Henry VIII's own mother, who had been bound to the Tudor cause by marriage, only one of Edward IV's six other daughters produced a son, the future Marquess of Exeter. Nor were the two sons of Edward IV's hapless brother, the Duke of Clarence, ever serious contenders for the throne. Edmund Pole was, after all, already captive at the time of Henry's accession, only to be quietly executed in 1513. And although his exiled brother Richard had grandiosely styled himself the 'White Rose' and been proclaimed King of England by Louis XII of France in 1512, support for his claim was abruptly withdrawn only two years later when the French booted him unceremoniously from their country after peace had been made with Henry. Ultimately, he would end his exile only by being killed at the side of Francis I at the Battle of Pavia in 1525, an event that caused Henry to declare confidently at the time that 'all the enemies of England are gone'. Certainly, Richard Pole's sons, Lord Henry Montague, Reginald Pole and Sir Geoffrey Pole, were always irritants rather than genuine threats.

This, then, was in reality a comparatively flaccid brood to inconvenience the Tudor dynasty. The remaining Poles, meanwhile, confined themselves to armchair plotting and pungent comments, and by the late 1530s their sole threat seemed to progress along the lines that Henry 'will one day die suddenly; his leg will kill him and then we shall have jolly stirring'. Such was the measure of their subtle strategy. There was also, of course, the Stafford line, which had produced the most substantial potential rival to Henry VIII in the form of Edward Stafford, Duke of Buckingham, but as we have seen, he had been trapped neatly by his own indiscreet murmurings in 1521. And beyond Buckingham, there were what can at very best be termed fringe claimants, such as Thomas Howard, Duke of Norfolk, who could trace his descent from Edward I, and Henry Brandon, the young Earl of Lincoln. But the consistent submissiveness of characters like Norfolk, not to mention the desultory nature of the so-called 'Exeter Conspiracy' of 1538, serves as further ample proof, if any were needed, of the essential security of Henry VIII's position.

Indeed, having long ago realised that their best interests lay in cooperation rather than conflict, the dynastic 'enemies' of the Tudors were, in the main, actually offering loyal service and support to Henry *before* his decision to divorce Catherine and break with Rome. The 'White Rose' nobility, for instance, had emerged as notable favourites of the Crown in the early years of the reign. The Marchioness of Exeter had been Catherine of Aragon's special friend, while Lady Margaret Pole, who was made Countess of Salisbury, had been godmother to the Princess Mary. Reginald Pole was another to whom disloyalty did not come easily. Though Henry would later want him 'trussed up and delivered to Calais' for his outspoken opposition, the king himself had previously appointed him to a prebend in Salisbury in 1517 and shortly afterwards to the deaneries of Wimborne and Exeter. Pole also seems initially to have supported Henry's case for divorce. On the other hand, the earls of Rutland (who were descended from Edward IV's sister, Anne) and the earls of Bath, who traced their princely connection to Thomas Woodstock, offered loyal service throughout the reign and were fully honoured for their devotion to the Tudor cause. In fact, any threat from rival dynastic contenders was largely imaginary and, as and when any stirrings became perceptible, they were principally a result of Henry's own provocative miscalculations.

So at that very point when the king was, in all likelihood, beginning to ponder the annulment of his marriage to Catherine of Aragon, the threat of rival dynastic contenders was diminishing almost beyond trace. And if, in considering the succession issue, Henry overestimated his problems, he also underestimated his daughter's potential success as prospective heir to the throne. For, as the events of the second half of the century would ultimately prove, the need for a specifically male successor was never as imperative as either scholars or schoolboys have tended to assume.

It is true, of course, that in a society that considered women naturally inferior to men and subject to them by divine law, Henry had every right to be concerned about the prospect of a female successor. The moral inferiority of women was, after all, a commonplace of theology, and the patristic authorities of the Middle Ages had rehearsed countless vindications of this claim. Predictably enough, the customary starting point was the biblical account of creation, in which Adam was made directly from God, but Eve was made only indirectly, by means of her husband's rib. It was Eve, too, who was saddled with Adam's temptation and as such responsible for mankind's Fall. Were not queens, the argument ran, therefore liable to the same punishment as the rest of Eve's daughters: perpetual subjection to their husbands? Several New Testament passages also implied that men were to serve as mediators between their wives and Christ, just as Christ had served as mediator between man and God. St Paul had written, for instance, that 'the husband is the head of the wife, even as Christ is the head of the church'. In their turn, scholastic theologians had gone further still by assimilating the Aristotelian teaching that all female creatures were 'misbegotten males', or, in other words, mere biological accidents. On this basis, men were viewed as the perfect archetype of humankind, made in God's own image, while women were perceived as imperfect departures from the original divine model. Some authorities had even been ready to speculate that at the last judgement, women would necessarily rise from the dead not in their imperfect female form but as men.

Added to all this, female rule entailed significant practical and legal problems of which Henry would have been all too acutely aware, and there was also the further issue of historical precedent to consider. How, it was commonly asked, could a woman command her generals in time of war, govern Parliament, or negotiate on equal terms with foreign princes and their ambassadors? And if women must not speak in church, as Paul had instructed the Corinthians, how was a queen to direct her clergy? Most pressingly of all, perhaps, there were issues relating to marriage and inheritance. If a queen remained unwed, she could not produce legitimate heirs. On the other hand, if she married, her dependence upon her husband might undermine her magisterial powers as head of State. Likewise, if the queen's consort was of royal status, would not her political authority revert to him, just as a wife's property did? And of course the civil wars of the previous century had grown particularly large in Tudor mythology and propaganda. Nor was there any doubting that England's sole prior experience of a queen regnant had been far from auspicious. The Empress Maud's torrid fling at the political helm back in the twelfth century had been accompanied by usurpation and turmoil, and the vain attempts of Henry VI's wife, Margaret of Anjou, to wield power inspired no more confidence.

Yet surprisingly none of this served to justify an absolute prohibition of female rule under any and every circumstance, and this, too, the king fully understood. Apart from medieval sources produced by the likes of John of Salisbury, the first significant Tudor writings on the issue belong not to Henry VIII's reign, but to the mid-century and must, in consequence, be carefully contextualised. Moreover, the blatantly polemical writings of John Knox, Christopher Goodman, Thomas Becon and John Ponet are much better viewed as attacks on the iniquity of female *Catholic* rulers than as attacks upon the principle of female rule *per se*, and it is no coincidence that the few virulent reformist writings against female rulers in the reign of Mary contrasted strikingly with the almost unanimous reformist welcome for a queen at the time of Elizabeth I's accession.

Indeed, the last decade of Henry's reign would actually witness a range of literature expressing sentiments very different to some of the more extreme views presented thereafter. Although Sir Thomas Elyot, for example, fully acknowledged the more limited capacities of the female, his *The Defence of Good Women* (1540) regretted the outpourings of 'many men, which do set theyr delyte in rebukynge of women, althoughe they never received displeasure, but often tymes benefit by them'. There also followed a spate of works supporting the same much more moderate line. Sir Robert Vaughan's *A Dyalogue Defensyve for Women agaynst Malycyous Detractoures* and Edward Gosynhill's *The Prayse of All Women* were both published in 1542, as was a new translation of Agrippa's *De Nobilitate*, subtitled in this case, *The Excellencie of Women*. And if such texts were hardly designed to advance a comprehensive case for the virtues of rule by women, they serve, perhaps, to hint at the very least that the prospect of female rule might not have been as intolerable as is often assumed, particularly in the absence of viable alternatives.

The legal and constitutional situation was also much more ambiguous than might be imagined and allowed Henry considerable scope for creative interpretation in support of his daughter's succession. One of the greatest of Tudor tenets was, after all, the doctrine of obedience to God's providence by which all men were bound to submit to the mysterious will of their Creator. From this perspective, in fact, the acceptance of Princess Mary as rightful heir amounted to nothing less than a conscientious Christian duty on behalf of all loyal subjects. At the same time, the possibility of female rule was also securely underpinned by the principle of rightful inheritance, which was, arguably, the lynchpin of all contemporary social and political thought, for even though the Tudor dynasty had itself been established by force in 1485, all Tudor monarchs relied on the argument of legitimate inheritance as the foundation of their authority. And this was no less true, indeed, of the ruling elite in general.

More strikingly still, Henry would himself eventually accept the principle of female rule in both the third succession statute of his reign and his own will. Each document specified that any male heir was to be given precedence, but each also accepted quite categorically that, if none existed, first Mary and then her sister Elizabeth would succeed to the throne. Equally significantly, when Henry's son Edward eventually died the only constitutional uncertainty lay not in whether a female monarch might rule, but over which particular female ruler it should be. The statute of 1554 confirming Mary's succession to the throne would meet little significant resistance in declaring her the undoubted 'heir and inheretrix' to the crown and stipulating that the queen exercised royal authority in 'as full, large and ample manner' as any of her male predecessors. Nor did the Act suggest that any legitimate doubts had actually been raised about Mary's succession on the grounds of her gender, only that 'malicious and ignorant persons' might be persuaded into this 'error and folly' in the future.

But most importantly of all, what is so often overlooked is that Henry VIII was to place England in every bit as much danger by repudiating his marriage to Catherine of Aragon as he would have done by settling for a mature heiress in the person of his daughter. In effect, the King of England recklessly exchanged the measured risk attached to legitimate female rule for the gaping unknowns of a wild search for a male heir. If he had died during the ten-year period between 1527 and 1537, that is, between the time when the divorce became public and the birth of Edward, this would have left a menacing succession crisis, with Princess Mary, his bastard son (the Duke of Richmond) and (after 1533) Princess Elizabeth all being touted as potential successors. Even more ironically, in the seventeen months between the death of Anne Boleyn and Edward's birth, there were actually no legitimate heirs at all and the situation would have been even more perilous. For ten years, therefore, the succession was desperately insecure, precisely because of the king's divorce and even when a male heir did arrive, he was born too late. By the time that Prince Edward made his appearance, Henry would be 46 years old and an eventual minority government, with all its menacing concomitants, was a near certainty. Furthermore, if the precedents for female rule were not auspicious, it was also a fact that the glittering achievements of Henry V's reign had dissolved rapidly and irrevocably when he died leaving a 9-month-old child as his successor. Other cases, like that of Henry III's minority, provided no further grounds for optimism.

By contrast, there were sound marital possibilities for Mary and it was a testament to Henry's lack of political imagination that these alternatives went largely unexplored. Particularly if Mary had been married young, she might well have borne a son who would grow to manhood in his grandfather's lifetime, thus removing any potential awkwardness posed by a female ruler and offering a good chance of an heir who would be acceptably English by upbringing even if fathered by a foreigner. The minimum canonical age for cohabitation was, in fact, twelve and as Mary was already nine in 1525 when Henry's marital anxieties were ripening, a search for a suitable marriage contract could have begun at once. Another option, meanwhile, was far from straightforward and would have required substantial skill and imagination in execution, but the benefits accruing could have assumed historic proportions. The Princess Mary, might, in this case, have been married on favourable terms to her first cousin, James V of Scotland, thereby achieving at a stroke what was once claimed to have been a primary objective of Henry's foreign policy: the union of England with Scotland. Mary might also, for that matter, have been betrothed to Reginald Pole, the grandson of the Yorkist Duke of Clarence, dealing at a stroke with the supposed problem posed by the White Rose.

Alternatively, the King of England could even have explored a variety of more lurid options that many a contemporary pope might well have had the barefaced cheek to countenance. The pontiff had, of course, already sanctioned incest as an option in the case of Henry's own marriage and he was now equally prepared to tip the wink at old-fashioned adultery, which would have done the political, if not the moral, trick perfectly well. Sexual licence and Catholicism, after all, slept well enough together as a number of 'Holy Fathers' could attest from personal experience. Besides which, morality was never any kind of absolute imperative for Henry when his own interests were at issue. The Church might, then, have agreed to legitimise any extra-marital offspring issuing from the king's relationship with Anne Boleyn, or for that matter, it could also have blessed the so-called 'pharaonic option', entailing a marriage between the bastard Duke of Richmond and the Princess Mary. Even this last most drastic of all solutions might well have been acceptable to a papacy desperate to maintain England's allegiance by any and all means.

Ultimately, of course, both the grim upsets of his son's reign and the evident success of his youngest daughter in the second half of the century would make a mockery of Henry's matrimonial convulsions. And it remains as hard as ever to see how any monarch could be so possessed of folly as to plunge his nation into potential chaos merely to unload a homely if unattractive wife. Yet this appears to be precisely what Henry VIII did. Certainly, when Henry's interest in Anne Boleyn first emerged, the lustre of Catherine of Aragon's attraction had already faded. The six-year age difference between him and his wife seemed greater and though the queen was forty-three when Cardinal Campeggio visited England in 1528, he described her as 'nearly fifty' in appearance. According to a contemporary ambassador, meanwhile, Catherine was 'of low stature, rather stout, very good and very religious'. In other words, she was dumpy and pious: a stodgy enough confection to quell the ardour of many a man. She was also menopausal. In 1531, indeed, Henry was to claim that Catherine's menstruation had finally ceased some six years earlier, and that as a result of a gynaecological condition that repelled him, he had thenceforth ceased to have sexual relations with her.

To compound matters, following Mary's birth in 1516, the routine of abortive pregnancy had resumed, albeit briefly, when the queen miscarried once more in the autumn of 1517 and again in November 1518. Even in an age when perhaps half of all infants died within their first year, Catherine's chequered history of stillbirths, miscarriages, menstrual irregularities, swellings and deflatings placed her abject record well outside the norm. Plainly, her English physicians offered no solution and this was hardly surprising at a time when common remedies for infertility included drinking the urine of pregnant sheep or treating the cervix with steam funnelled into the vagina by means of a pessary. Moreover, when the importation of Spanish doctors, such as Dr de Vittoria proved equally unavailing, it is not hard to imagine the impact on the king's morale. Though Catherine endured all amenably, it seems that the gynaecological battering to which she had been subjected over the years had finally taken its toll, not only on her spent body, but also on her husband's affections. Yet, even now, the only sensible course was for the queen to be unfussily bypassed rather than outrightly rejected. Both common sense and worldly wisdom dictated as much. Faced, however, with a wife who could neither conceive nor allure and a seductive would-be mistress who was refusing to submit without the ultimate guarantee of marriage, Henry duly crumbled.

If it is true that Anne Boleyn's denial of her sexual favours to the king may have encouraged him finally to unravel the conjugal knot that bound him, then he appears to have been as weak as he was foolish, for she had but one ace to play and the king should have trumped it decisively. In brief, Henry should either have had her and left her or simply left her and had done. Certainly, it seems hard to believe seriously that the former was not an option, given the indirect pressure that could so surely have been applied on Anne by means of her father, Thomas Boleyn, and her uncle, the Duke of Norfolk. Nevertheless, in August 1527, Mendoza, the imperial ambassador, wrote from London to Charles V: 'In truth the King is so swayed by his passions [...] It is generally believed that if he can obtain a divorce he will end by marrying a daughter of Master Boleyn.' Notwithstanding any token resistance, Henry was, of course, entirely at liberty to enjoy Anne as courtesan without the encumbrance either of matrimony or political upheaval. That he should seek adultery was regrettable, but that he did not demand it would prove, in political terms, far more sinful still.

It is a mistake, therefore, to perceive political necessity as the spur to Henry VIII's actions, for the Henrician Reformation was not so much an 'act of state' as an 'act of emotional impulse'. True, his fears concerning female rule were reinforced by a lumbering popular prejudice, but even this was by no means utterly insurmountable. To put it another way, the king's 'insoluble' problem was neither dynastic nor religious in origin, but psychological. In essence, Henry VIII was the victim of what amounted to little more than an intense infatuation, fuelled by frustrated fatherhood and a curious flood tide of superstition masquerading as conscience.

Time and again, as events unfolded, Henry made frequent references to 'the tranquillity of consciences and the health of his soul'. In 1529, he would write to Charles V, explaining that he could not 'quiet or appease his conscience remaining longer with the queen, whom, for her nobleness of blood and other virtues, he had loved entirely as his wife, until he saw in Scripture that God had forbidden their union'. The source of the doubts to which Henry referred was the famous reference cited in the Book of Leviticus (xx 21): 'And if a man shall take his brother's wife it is an unclean thing: he hath uncovered his brother's nakedness; they shall be childless.' Henry's marriage to Catherine had, of course, initially necessitated a papal dispensation in 1503 from Pope Julius II, and since at least 1522 the possibility that he was a victim of God's punishment as a result of his breach of biblical law had been exercising his mind. In the event, a combination of ponderous logic, obstinacy and deeply ingrained superstition sparked by the black-and-white revelation of God's own word in the king's head could lead in one direction only.

Yet the Levitical seed, which supposedly tormented him, was, in reality, more pip than acorn. John Fisher, Bishop of Rochester, whom Henry had once described as the most learned theologian he had ever known, demonstrated that there were ready antidotes to Henry's scriptural headache. The Book of Deuteronomy (xxv 5), for instance, actually contained a direct invocation for a man to marry his deceased brother's wife when that brother had died without children. There was also the small matter that Henry was not actually childless. The birth of Princess Mary surely stood large in the midst of this theological minefield. However, the king's conscience was more often than not merely the lubricant that allowed him to force square pegs into round holes and his response was simply to appoint another scholar to give him the answers he wanted. Robert Wakefield, a gifted young scholar of Hebrew with no eye for either professional or any other kind of martyrdom, duly obliged his king by contending that the 'childless' reference in Leviticus referred exclusively to male offspring and that Deuteronomy was using the word 'brother' in the wider sense of male relatives in general.

Having been readily convinced, Henry was now rocked on every side by portents of God's displeasure, which multiplied as they reverberated. In July 1525 the worst plague in a decade seemed to descend straight from heaven to chastise the kingdom. Fifty people a day died in London and, as Henry well knew, not even royal blood was a guarantee of safety. Then, in

January 1526, two gentlemen of his household died, and for the next two years the terrible disease was endemic. Moreover, these fears will have been compounded by the king's own close scrapes with death. In March 1524, for instance, he entered the lists with the visor of his helmet open while jousting with the Duke of Suffolk. Though, according to *Hall's Chronicle*, the horrified spectators shouted to the duke to hold, he could neither hear nor see, and Suffolk's lance struck and shattered against the king's helmet less than an inch from his exposed face. A year later, whilst hawking, he vaulted a ditch, but broke his jumping-pole and fell head-first into the water, his face stuck firmly in the mud. On this occasion, only the timely arrival of panting attendants saved their master from the kind of earthy earthly exit that would have led to merry banqueting barbs throughout the courts of Europe.

But it was during the 1528 epidemic of the 'sweating sickness' that Henry's fears reached truly exceptional heights. The mere name of 'the sweat', Bishop Gardiner wrote, 'is so terrible to his highness' ears that he dare in no wise approach where it is noised to have been'. Immured in Wolsey's residence at Tittenhanger, it now became his practice to shut himself away for long periods – sometimes in a high tower where he often took his supper alone or consulted with his physician Dr Chambers. At times like these he feared to sleep alone and ordered Sir Francis Bryan to attend him in his privy chamber throughout the night.

No doubt, too, the creeping onset of age and infirmity will also have played its part in fuelling Henry's preoccupation with Leviticus. His tomb, a towering marble structure, had been commissioned in 1519. And did its image now rear before him from time to time in his quieter moments? Henry was, after all, thirty-five in 1526, in a century where a man's forties offered old age and his fifties held out only the release of the grave. In 1521 he had been struck down by fever and complained of sinus trouble. Then, in 1528 his chronic headaches were recorded for the first time and four years later the gout would come calling. If pain was God's megaphone, then Henry, it seems, was receiving the divine message loud and clear.

As it transpired, Henry's strategy for unpicking the complex legal knots that attached him to Catherine was the equivalent of brain surgery by bulldozer, for by 1527 he had committed himself to a series of unnecessary frontal assaults on both papal authority and his wife's word. With utter insensitivity to Catherine's vehement denials and against Wolsey's express advice, Henry duly protested that his wife's marriage to Arthur had been consummated and was, as such, contrary to God's law. Therefore, having been adulterously bypassed, Catherine would now also, it seemed, have no choice but to lose her honour in favour of a woman of no substance or reputation. Naturally enough, for a Trastmara princess such as she, this was utterly intolerable and in response to her husband's secrecy, contempt and bullying, Catherine would ultimately throw away for good the keys to her cooperation. Equally damagingly, the king's chosen course also ignited the whole issue of papal authority by implying that no pope had the capability to dispense with God's law as laid down in the Bible. In short, Henry was determined to challenge his wife's honesty, to lecture the doctors of the Church on divinity and biblical exegesis, and to tell the pope his job. Meanwhile, as the king flailed with knuckledusters, Wolsey suggested a neat and comparatively painless excision based on canonical technicalities, which had an altogether better chance of success were it not for his master's insistence upon ignoring it.

The ever astute cardinal favoured the position that Pope Julius II's marital dispensation had, in fact, nullified a non-existent 'affinity', since Catherine's marriage to Arthur had never, it seems, been consummated. In doing so, Wolsey noted, the dispensation had not dealt with the remaining bar to the marriage resulting from the issue of 'public honesty', i.e. that Henry and Catherine were technically 'in-laws' and as such forbidden to marry by canon law. If all this was the case, the marriage had remained illegal, in spite of the dispensation. Moreover, the clinical beauty of this approach was that neither the pope's authority nor the queen's honesty would thereby be impugned. Catherine's claim that she had been a virgin upon her marriage to Henry would not be at issue and the pope's predecessor would merely have been deemed responsible for a straightforward technical oversight. For good measure, Wolsey also contended quite rightly that there could be a further neat, effective and non-confrontational challenge to the assumptions under which the bull of dispensation was issued in the first place. If, as was claimed in the bull's contents, it was granted primarily for the political purpose of maintaining peace between England and Spain, then this premise was also flawed, since England and Spain were already in a state of long-standing peace at the time.

However, Wolsey's fond hopes that he could confine legal proceedings to a secret legatine court at which he would preside, thus ensuring an expeditious and neatly sanitised resolution of the whole problem, were soon dashed. As soon as proceedings began, the imperial ambassador,

Mendoza, informed Charles V and sent a secret message to Catherine, informing her that a hearing was to be convened. This single note shattered the queen's peace of mind and initiated her gradual descent from fear and insecurity into the dogged, desperate resistance that would ultimately force Henry into the breach with Rome he wished so much to avoid. Now she would insist upon appealing to the pope and enlist her nephew, the Holy Roman Emperor, to support her case – a move that at once transformed Henry's domestic dispute into a thorny issue of international diplomacy. And as the case escalated, so Henry's hopes of success were dealt a grievous blow when, on 6 May 1527, Spanish and German troops sacked Rome, killing up to a quarter of the Holy City's population in the process, and leaving the pope, in effect, a captive of Charles V. Henceforward, it would be impossible for the pontiff to make even the slightest move without the emperor's permission.

Only Wolsey now proferred any hope of salvation for Henry. He was, after all, a past master at snatching victory from the jaws of defeat and with great dexterity he duly plotted a masterstroke, designed to mend Henry's fortunes in one fell swoop. The very captivity of the pope could, he reasoned, actually be turned to advantage, since it created a vacuum in the leadership of the Church, which he could fill both *de jure* and *de facto*. The cardinal's initial plan, then, was to convoke a meeting of free cardinals under his chairmanship at Avignon. As the leading ecclesiastic of the west not under imperial sway, he would induce the current pope, Clement VII, to assign him full authority to act on his behalf during his captivity. The gathered assembly would therefore settle the annulment of Henry's marriage at a stroke and lay plans for a general council to deal with heresy. This concordat, as well as liberating the Holy See and bringing peace to Europe, would make Henry VIII the most respected ruler in Europe – all of which was delightfully Wolseyan in its grandiose conception. But given the cardinal's international status and the condition that there were no seismic shifts in the diplomatic status quo, it was, perhaps, worth the try.

In the event, the proposed Avignon summit was eventually stymied both by the pope, who forbade his cardinals to attend, and, much more frustratingly still, by the King of England himself. A month before Wolsey sailed for Calais on 22 June, Henry had blabbed to Catherine his grievous doubts concerning their marriage, which was a blunder of truly disastrous proportions, since, at this stage, the queen is unlikely to have had any idea of the full danger posed to her interests by Anne Boleyn. In fact, a delicate and respectful discussion of the succession problem and a humble entreaty for her dutiful self-abnegation might well have elicited a positive response from Catherine. However, her husband's shocking revelation had been delivered with such cold force that she wept long and piteously and was too distraught to reply. More importantly, the king's behaviour also encouraged Catherine to despatch Felipez, her trusted servant, to convey the news to Charles V, cutting the ground from under Wolsey's feet at a stroke. The emperor appears to have been genuinely shocked and immediately pledged full support to Catherine. He also wrote to the pope insisting that he prohibit Wolsey from hearing the case.

But even though the Dukes of Norfolk and Suffolk and Anne Boleyn herself were busily spinning their webs against him in his absence, the cardinal's hand was still not quite played out. Pope Clement VII was, after all, a muddle-headed procrastinator who had once been described as 'the most secretive man in the world' and Wolsey realised astutely that it was not only Charles V who could apply persuasive threats against the Holy Father. In January 1528, therefore, England joined the League of Cognac with France, making a formal declaration of war against the emperor on 28 January, though no hostilities followed, for Wolsey's plan was merely to bluff Clement into concessions. Stephen Gardiner and Edward Fox were then duly despatched to Rome to apply pressure and upon their arrival on 20 March they found Clement bearded and benighted. The pope, it seems, wept and waved his arms like one distracted as he paced his bedchamber. He talked of the danger he would be in should he offend Charles, in response to which the envoys threatened him with the loss he would sustain if England and even perhaps France chose to sever their links with the Holy See. It was impressed upon Clement, too, that at this very moment French forces under Lautrec were marching triumphantly through Italy to besiege Naples. By 8 April, therefore, faced with unremitting intimidation, Clement had finally capitulated and granted a commission for Wolsey and Cardinal Campeggio to hear the case in England.

So it was that Cardinal Lorenzo Campeggio, absentee Bishop of Salisbury and a seasoned practitioner in the weasel ways of contemporary diplomacy, said goodbye on 25 June to his two children, neither of whom, surprisingly enough, were bastards, for they had been born before the death of his wife, after which he had taken holy orders. Racked by gout, Campeggio could travel from Corneto only at snail's pace and when, finally, he entered London on 28 October, he was booed by the crowd, for the divorce was already unpopular. Furthermore, upon meeting Henry he found him furiously impatient and utterly convinced of his cause. The king was, it seems, stuck to Leviticus like a bull to the ring in his snout. However, in spite of all Henry's high expectations, neither Cardinal Campeggio nor Wolsey was permitted to employ the decretal papers they held with them and without which the marriage could not be dissolved. Furthermore, even before Campeggio's arrival in London the international situation had shifted fatefully. While Lautrec had been killed and the emperor's cause in Italy bolstered by Andrea Doria's galleys, there had also been a regrouping of the Italian states, and Florence had once more declared itself a republic. Only by coming to terms with the emperor, therefore, could the Medici pope now save his own family. Accordingly, in December he would write to Campeggio ordering him to burn the decretal commission and consign Henry's hopes and Wolsey's fortunes to ashes.

In consequence, there was now only one hope as far as Campeggio was concerned – the good offices of the queen herself. If she could be persuaded to enter a nunnery, there would be an adequate canonical case to allow her husband to remarry on the grounds that entry into a convent entailed a form of physical death for the person involved. This idea, which had been formulated first by St Bonaventure, had much to recommend it. Such an arrangement had already occurred when Jeanne de Valois, sometime wife of Louis XII, had humbly retreated to a nunnery at her husband's wish. Furthermore, the queen's staunchest supporter, Bishop John Fisher, was said by Campeggio to have warmed to the proposal when it was put to him. Catherine's religiosity was, after all, known to be intense and she would still have enjoyed all the comforts and privileges of her royal station, for Henry, who was enthused by this ingenious solution, even hastened to asssure Campeggio that Catherine would lose only 'the use of his person'. Grievous though this loss would doubtless be, in all other respects she would be accorded due honour and privilege. Most important of all from the queen's point of view, her beloved daughter's legitimacy and birthright would remain intact.

Unfortunately, however, shortly after Catherine had declined Campeggio's initial proposal on 26 October, another intemperate outburst by her husband put paid once and for all to any hope of breakthrough. In a fit of rage, the king had, it seems, insisted that the queen should accept Campeggio's proposal without delay. In October, too, Henry complained to the Privy Council about her behaviour. She was, he grumbled, too lighthearted and dressed too richly. She should be prayerful for justice rather than presenting herself in public. He even implied, at one point, that she was involved in a mysterious plot to kill him. All this prompted a letter from the Privy Council in which Catherine was told with cudgel bluntness that she was 'a fool to resist the King's will'. Henceforth, the main barrier to divorce was no longer international power politics, but simply a slighted woman's pride in the face of a torrid husband's mistreatment and bluster. Now Catherine would remain an immovable object to the bitter end, which she demonstrated to perfection at the legatine hearing convened on 18 June 1529 at Blackfriars to weigh her marriage.

The gap in time between Henry's tirade and Catherine's summons to court was a particularly long one of more than half a year, because, in desperation, Campeggio had chosen to take whatever shelter he could find in an impenetrable thicket of delay. When, however, the legatine court finally creaked into action like an arthritic sloth, it was the queen's turn to be obstructive. First she protested against the court's legitimacy and formally appealed her case to Rome. Then she protested against Wolsey's appointment as judge and withdrew regally, declaring 'I be no Englishwoman but a Spaniard born!' However, the plump figure, dressed in a gown of crimson velvet edged with sable, saved what was indubitably her greatest performance of all for her last appearance in the court. Ignoring official procedure, she weaved her way with high drama through crowded benches and tables to fall on her knees before the king, pleading to him not to dishonour her or disown their daughter. Henry sat all the while staring past his wife, making no comment when she had finished. After this Catherine participated no further. There was no need. John Fisher, Bishop of Rochester, made a great speech in her absence in favour of the marriage, but the undoubted eloquence of his words could by no means match the power of what had been the queen's defiant parting gesture.

By 27 July the case had become bogged down in technicalities, but events in London were now, in any case, already irrelevant. In June, imperial forces had crushed the French at Landriano and on 13 July the pope agreed to the Treaty of Barcelona, which pledged him to support Charles. Unbeknown to the participants at Blackfriars, the pope had also yielded to the emperor's pressure, annulled the legatine commission and summoned Henry to appear before the Rota in Rome. In fact, this news did not reach England for some time, but the situation was dire enough even without such a thunderbolt, for on 31 July, only ten days before the final decision that Henry expected, Campeggio declared that the court would follow the Roman calendar and adjourn for the vacation. This meant that there would be no further proceedings until October.

With this announcement there was, not surprisingly, outrage and tumult in the court. 'By the mass', thundered the beetle-browed Duke of Suffolk, 'it was never merry in England whilst we had cardinals amongst us', whereupon Wolsey smartly reminded the fuming peer of the help that he had been given at the time of his marriage to the king's sister. 'If I, a simple cardinal, had not been', retorted Wolsey loudly, 'you should have had at this present time no head upon your shoulders wherein you should have had a tongue to make any such report in despite of us!' However, the power of the cardinal's language was not matched by the strength of his position, for the king had suffered a shattering blow and now retired to Waltham Abbey to nurse his wrath and ponder all the hard things that Anne Boleyn and her grasping tribe of relatives would now be sure to say about his minister.

Although Henry's personal interventions had continually undermined the efforts of Wolsey, it was, of course, the latter who would always carry the blame. By the time that the Franco-Imperial Peace of Cambrai was signed on 3 August, Henry's patience was at an end and so, in effect, was the cardinal's primacy. Within a month this great potentate of Church and State, the great panjandrum whom Cavendish would call 'the haughtiest man alive', was teetering on the brink and Anne Boleyn and the faction around her were exercising all their influence to lever him over the edge.

Surely enough, on 9 October 1529, therefore, Wolsey was finally charged under the Statute of Praemunire of 1393 on the grounds that he had used his ecclesiastical authority to impinge upon the legal jurisdiction of the Crown. The charge was, of course, purely a pretext and a smokescreen, for Wolsey's only real offence was failure to satisfy the caprice of his master, but one week later he was stripped all the same of his Lord Chancellor's office and made to deliver up the Great Seal. Then, in a desperate attempt to placate the king, the stricken cardinal surrendered York Place and indeed most of his other property. Nevertheless, a bill of attainder was brought against him on 3 November. The king, who had relied so heavily on Wolsey's resourcefulness, had personally scuppered his chief minister's stratagems and then proceeded to spurn him for failure.

Thereafter, with one of those rich ironies that are so common in history, York Place was renamed Whitehall and an elated Henry duly handed it over to Anne Boleyn for use as her personal residence. Soon after the cardinal had made his exit, moreover, Anne was brought in secret to view the fine tapestries and plate of her new dwelling. Thrilled by the splendour of it all, now she would have her own court and truly be queen in all but name. Accordingly, great changes were put in hand to enlarge the palace and satisfy her fastidious requirements. Neighbouring houses were compulsorily acquired to extend the site and make room for gardens. 'All this has been done', reported the imperial ambassador, 'to please the lady, who likes better that the king should stay in Whitehall than anywhere else, as there is no lodging in it for the Queen.' By contrast, the queen herself had been cast once and for all into political and marital limbo.

9

The Infinite Clamour of Deadlock

'In substance, he plainly confesses that he finds himself in such perplexity that he can no longer live in it.'

Jean du Bellay, French ambassador, describing
Henry VIII in January 1530.

As winter's grip steadily tightened in 1529, Anne Boleyn's grasp on the man of her ambition seemed increasingly secure. Now installed in her own apartments at Greenwich, she 'kept an estate more like a Queen than a simple maid', while elsewhere in the same palace, Catherine of Aragon continued to mend her husband's shirts, regally contemptuous of her upstart rival and stoically resigned to her chosen path of fruitless resistance. In the cold world around her, there was nothing, it seemed, to insulate her from further mistreatment. On 8 December, Anne's father, Thomas, was created Earl of Wiltshire and a grand celebration followed at Whitehall, over which Anne herself presided at Henry's side. Courted and attended like a queen and sitting on the queen's throne, 'the King's wench' could not have seemed more snugly placed amid the seasonal blazes and hangings. To all appearances, the festivities seemed to betoken triumph, rejoicing and imminent conjugal bliss. Wolsey had been vanquished, Catherine's stubborn resistance was being circumvented and Henry's heart and conscience were, for the moment, light of their burdens.

For around a year and a half relations between the king and his wife would be maintained for formal occasions and they continued to visit one another 'every few days' for appearances' sake. However, in the summer of 1531 the council ordered Catherine to vacate her apartments and move to Wolsey's former house at the More. Thereafter began a long, dreary and humiliating exodus, encompassing a series of distant royal manors at Ampthill, Buckden and finally Kimbolton. She was forbidden either to write to the king or see her daughter, and her household would now be progressively whittled away until it became a paltry embarrassment to all concerned. Before long it consisted of little more than a confessor, a physician, an apothecary, and three women, including the ever loyal Lady Willoughby: a retinue even more inadequate than in Catherine's days of hardship at Durham House twenty-five years earlier. Now, as her little court became a home for lost causes, she would be 'scantily visited by courtiers'.

That the king's Gordian knot was all but cut even before the end of 1529 seemed manifestly clear to most outside observers and especially Eustace Chapuys, the 40-year-old imperial ambassador, who was in that year newly arrived at the English court. This doctor of canon law and former ecclesiastical judge was to serve in England for the next sixteen years and though a consistently passionate ally of Catherine, he left detailed records of his activities and opinions, which, if not always entirely objective, were invariably perceptive. As a scientist of the wagging tongue and miner of the secret heart, he left no court luminary unsounded, no merchant or maidservant untapped. His staff from Flanders and Burgundy were all hand-picked for their fluency in English and their familiarity with English ways, and Montoya, his principal secretary, knew every nook and cranny of court life, having served for some twenty years in England as Catherine's gentleman usher. Even the imperial ambassador's martyrdom to gout was turned to good advantage as he painfully circulated the court, leaning upon Fleming, his English valet, in order to gain the use of yet another pair of keenly pricked ears. 'It seemed', said Chapuys, 'as if nothing were wanting but the priest to give away the nuptial ring and pronounce the blessing.'

In private, however, the king's dealings with the new woman in his life were anything but tranquil, for like so many silverback males of his kind, he was frequently barracked and buffeted in private by the tongue of the woman whom he claimed publicly to dominate. Now in her late twenties, Anne was increasingly impatient. 'Did I not tell you', she railed in early November 1529, 'that when you disputed with the queen she was sure to have the upper hand [...] I have been waiting long and might in the meantime have contracted some advantageous marriage [...] But alas! Farewell to my time and youth spent to no purpose at all!' Later, in January 1531, she would threaten to leave Henry, reducing him to abject pleas before the Duke of Norfolk and her father that they might intercede on his behalf. Such, indeed, was Henry's fawning deference to his mistress that he attracted a good deal of outright disdain. He 'showed himself so forgetful of what is right and of his dignity and authority', wrote one visitor from the Holy Roman Empire, 'that everybody thinks little of him, as of a man who is acting against the truth and honour of his conscience'. To display such weak-kneed solicitude for a wife would have been foolish enough, but to be distraught on account of a mistress was, it seemed, nothing short of absurd.

Though after their spats, as Chapuys observed, their love was invariably 'greater than before', the frying pan of Henry's previous marriage had begun to look no less forbidding than the fiery rows by which he was more and more frequently singed. Now, ironically, instead of forcing favours from the pope, the king was forced increasingly to court Anne's compliance. Peace offerings proliferated in the form of ornate French saddles and harnesses, fine linen for night clothes, as well as gold embellishment for Anne's desk. There were purses of coins for playing and spending money and large sums of £100 or more as New Year's gifts. There were also expensive furs and diamonds and pearls in abundance, while, in December 1529, £180 was spent on purple velvet for Anne's gowns.

No one, even at court, pretended to like the turn that events were taking. The Duchess of Norfolk, at Anne's request, had to be packed off home 'because she spoke too freely and declared herself more than was liked for the Queen'. Even her husband who as Anne's uncle probably knew too much already of his niece's shrewish temper to be glad of her advancement, said that 'it was the devil and nobody else who was the inventor of this accursed dispute'. In Parliament the Speaker had to rebuke those who suggested that 'the King pursued this divorce out of love for some lady and not out of any scruple of conscience'. And while country folk cheered the queen and the princess, the women of Oxford would soon be hurling stones at the Vice-Chancellor when he sought to set the seal of the university upon the document declaring the king's first marriage incestuous.

Anne's prominence had much broader ramifications, too. In September 1532, Henry disconcerted his courtiers by creating a place for her among the nobility, in spite of the fact that the Boleyn ancestry was far from inherently distinguished. Her great-grandfather Geoffrey Boleyn had risen from obscure rural origins to enjoy a prosperous career as a silk and wool mercer before becoming Lord Mayor of London in 1479. Subsequently, her grandfather Sir William Boleyn had also shown a keen eye for opportunity by marrying the daughter of the Earl of Ormond at a time when her family found itself languishing under a cloud. Having thus gained access to elite society through the back door, it was left to Anne's father, Sir Thomas, to complete the final leg of the long haul to advancement by linking himself through marriage to a daughter of the future Duke of Norfolk, who was soon to become one of the most powerful men in England.

But though Sir Thomas would be made an ambassador to the court of Francis I and by 1530 had become Earl of Wiltshire and Lord Privy Seal, the Boleyns were stuck fast to their inauspicious bloodline and neither lofty rank, nor a considerable estate at Hever in Kent, nor, for that matter, profitable timber mills at Rochford in Essex could fully make good this sore deficiency. Therefore, in order to cover up the somewhat ill-shod footprints of his mistress's forebears, Henry was left with no choice but to conjure up two more notable ancestors for her – one a twelfth-century Norman lord, the other a fourteenth-century Picard. These, it was hoped, might lend a sheen of sorts to the somewhat dowdy heraldic shield of the Boleyn family, and with her aristocratic credentials duly manufactured, Anne was created Marquess of Pembroke on 1 September 1532 at a ceremony held at St George's Chapel in Windsor. Wearing her hair long so that Henry could more easily slip a coronet over her head, she was deemed to hold her new title in her own right and duly granted lands worth more than £1,000 a year in Hertfordshire, Somerset and Essex.

Among many courtiers Anne's newfound nobility would have been a source of wry amusement, but among the common people it stirred a much more violent reaction, which would nearly result in her violent death. Anne had, it seems, been subject to much 'hooting and hissing' from the very time that her affair with the king had become public, but what followed now was of an altogether different magnitude. According to a report reaching Venice from France, a furious mob of from 7,000 to 8,000 women gathered in London on the night of 24 November 1531 and marched to the riverside house where she was dining in the company of only her host and a few attendants. The crowd, which was said to have included a number of men dressed as women, was apparently set upon lynching the king's mistress, and might well have succeeded had word not reached her of their approach. Making her way to safety across the river, Anne escaped, it seems, in the very nick of time. Somewhat surprisingly, though, the incident evoked little official response, on the grounds that it had been, according to the French report, 'a thing done by women'. Nevertheless, it reflected a growing groundswell of opposition to the king's dealings, which could not be lightly dismissed in the long term.

Moreover, if Henry's new relationship was proving an increasing liability at all levels, the inadequacy of the advisers who had supplanted Wolsey was equally glaring. By the end of 1529 a new regime had been created, with the Duke of Norfolk, as president of the council, heading a triumvirate completed by the Duke of Suffolk and the Earl of Wiltshire. However, any semblance of a 'new order' was an unconvincing fiction, and fresh approaches, let alone novel solutions, to the central issues of Henry's marital dilemma were not to be had. Nor was this surprising, for the three stalwarts of the English nobility, who now served as the king's chief acolytes, were wholly unequal to the task confronting them. The Duke of Norfolk, for instance, though an able enough soldier and administrator, was an inherently conservative and unoriginal thinker. More than that, he was a self-avowed philistine who had once boasted how 'he had never read the scriptures nor ever would', and declared for good measure that 'it was merry in England before this New Learning came up'. A servile creature whose ambition outstripped his ability, he may well have been a fitting enough servant for an absolute monarch, but he lacked entirely the imagination to make a monarch absolute. The Duke of Suffolk, in his turn, was an admirable sportsman, a competent soldier and little else besides. If Henry were seeking to breed the finest hounds in England, then he would have good counsel from this man. Canon law, international diplomacy and political legerdemain were, however, wholly beyond him. In the Earl of Wiltshire, meanwhile, Henry had the father of Anne Boleyn and, in terms of strategic acumen, naught else. Besides which, this was a man who, according to the Bishop of Tarbes, 'would sooner act from self-interest than any other motive'. To accord any of these men even stopgap status is, then, to grant them a substance they do not deserve. In effect, they were merely washed into government like so much detritus on a tide of misplaced ambition.

There was, however, the new Lord Chancellor, Sir Thomas More, who was anything but second-rate. Born in 1477, More was the most outstanding English humanist scholar of his age, a skilful diplomat, an accomplished courtier and a trenchant – sometimes rabid – controversialist. Although attracted in early manhood to a life of contemplation and isolation with the Carthusian monks, he had opted ultimately for the call of the flesh rather than the summons of the cloister and took to marriage. In the words of Erasmus, 'he resolved to be a chaste husband for fear that he might become a lascivious priest' and after his first wife, Jane Colt, died, he chose to wed Alice Middleton, a well-to-do widow who was some seven years older than himself. She was, said More, 'neither a pearl nor a girl' and Erasmus would describe her nose as 'the hooked beak of a harpy'. In fact, More's keen asceticism seems to have been driven, at least in part, by a strong sensual streak that he sought to overpower by means of a hair shirt and, perhaps too, by his marriage to the matronly Alice. With intentional irony, he dubbed her his 'shrewd wife' and appears to have loved her in the way that some men love their favourite armchair. Nevertheless the family tie featured strongly in More's priorities and his household at Chelsea, according to Erasmus, 'breathed happiness'. In a broader context, Richard Pace called More 'a laughing philosopher', while Erasmus told Ulrich von Hutten that 'he seems to be made for friendship'.

Of course, there was a man beneath the piety and bonhomie, and these days the spiteful as well as the ambitious aspects of More's character are often stressed at the expense of his saintliness. Certainly, the first biography of More produced by his son-in-law, William Roper, underplays or overlooks a number of inconvenient but salient facts about the saint's personality. More's contemporary Edward Hall noted his great wit, but added that 'it was mingled with taunting and mocking', probably of the kind that many gifted people exhibit in their dealings with those whom they perceive, perhaps unconsciously, to be lesser mortals. Much more disconcertingly, the future saint was prepared, if we believe his detractors, to persecute heretics ruthlessly. Indeed, he would be demonised by both John Foxe and William Tyndale for his anti-heretical excesses and a good deal of the mud thrown at the time has now re-adhered as a result of the writings of the current generation of historians. According to the martyrologist Foxe, there was an accusation that a heretic called Tewkesbury was apparently held 'hand, foot, and head in the stocks, six days without release' in the porter's lodge of More's house after which he was whipped and tortured with ropes applied to his head 'so that the blood started out of his eyes'. In fairness, More always denied these charges and claimed that he had only ever twice sanctioned the flogging of heretics. In the first instance, when one of his servants was profane about the Blessed Sacrament, he had, on his own admission, felt no compunction in having him 'striped like a child'. Similar treatment was also meted out to a heretic who had made an unseemly habit of lifting up women's skirts in church.

But whatever More's many virtues or shortcomings, the crucial consideration for now was that he would be of no use at all in helping Henry progress along his chosen path regarding Rome. The new Lord Chancellor had taken office only on condition that he should not be involved in the divorce and with all the unconscious irony of a man who has no idea whatsoever of his own inner drives, Henry had firmly promised him that 'he would never put any man in ruffle or trouble of his conscience'. Since these years were dominated by issues relating to the king's marital status, it was inevitable, therefore, that More's active role in government would be marginal as he confined his activities by and large to the Court of Chancery which he set out to acclimatise to the common law.

None of Henry's current advisers were, then, the men to succeed where Wolsey had failed. Norfolk, Suffolk and Wiltshire were incapable by nature, whereas More was incapable by inclination, and so for the next two years the king was thrown back wholly upon his own inadequate resources. Never remotely grasping that it is as much the task of a leader to contain and wait upon events as it is to push them, he now plunged impetuously into a political and religious whirlpool which would result ultimately in discord, foreign war and national insolvency, the full and heavy consequences of which his son and eldest daughter would have to contend with. Nor was this by any means the limit of Henry's deficiencies. Continually absorbed in the short-term priorities of the present and lacking, too, the skill of adaptation to evolving circumstances, he was a slave to his reflexes. So when Luther declared that 'Junker Heintz will be God and does whatever he lusts', he could not have hit the nail more squarely on the head. More than ever now, whim was Henry's compass and ego his rudder. And with the passage of the years, he would become even more of a careless, random spark igniting a series of fuses leading he knew not where.

It was small wonder, of course, that the king would soon be informing the clique surrounding him that 'Wolsey was a better man than any of you'. Even at the time of the cardinal's fall in 1529, Henry had demonstrated some residue of feeling for him. He had, for instance, allowed his former servant to retain not only his archbishopric, but also a pension of £3,000, as well as plate worth more than £1,750, eighty horses with their apparel worth £150, tapestries and beds worth £800, fifty-two oxen worth £80 and clothing to the tune of £300. But if such provision was enough for Wolsey to maintain at least some semblance of rank, it was, nevertheless, wholly inadequate to his inflated needs, and the portion of the pension that the king had advanced to him was swiftly spent. Initially, he lacked even the money needed to repair the decayed episcopal residence at York to which he had eventually retreated in the spring of 1530. For months, therefore, he was forced to endure the leaking roof of his shabby dwelling, 'wrapped in misery and need on every side, not knowing where to be succoured or relieved'. To compound his despondency, he found himself subjected to 'very hungry' leeches, as well as 'vomitive electuary', after his health had given way. He had never in his life been so wretched, he confessed, and in a letter to Stephen Gardiner he signed himself 'Thomas the miserable, Cardinal of York'.

But even now, Wolsey's enemies feared his glorious resurrection. Ominously, when the cardinal fell ill just after Christmas in 1529, the king declared that he 'would not lose him for £20,000' and sent his personal physician Dr Butts to him with instructions to accept no fee. At the same time, Anne herself was bidden to 'send the Cardinal a token with comfortable words' and though it must have mortified her to do so, even she knew that there were times when Henry was indeed he who must be obeyed. As a result, she duly despatched a gold tablet from her girdle to the hated eminence. More provocatively still, Wolsey was formally pardoned on 12 February 1530 and confirmed in his see of York. In fact, his apparent rehabilitation was striking enough for Chapuys to be convinced that 'to reinstate him in the king's favour would not be difficult, were it not for the Lady'.

As it transpired, Anne's hostility towards Wolsey remained unabating and George Cavendish, the cardinal's gentleman usher, noted how she never slept 'but studied and continually imagined his destruction'. Oddly enough, the cardinal himself had long believed 'that a woman should be his confusion', but ultimately it was Henry's fickleness and Wolsey's own carelessness that provided Anne Boleyn and her party with the tools they required. Though the cardinal was well aware of Anne's 'serpentine' intent, he reacted to the threat with a naivety that was most untypical. During the summer of 1530, he would fall into regular contact with

Chapuys and in July supported Charles V's call for Pope Clement to order Henry's separation from Anne. Moreover, in August, he wrote to the Holy Father asking why Queen Catherine's cause was not more energetically pursued. These were reckless miscalculations for which he would pay dearly.

Seizing his opportunity, the Duke of Norfolk now bribed Wolsey's physician, Dr Agostini, into falsely accusing the cardinal of urging the pope to excommunicate the king and place England under a papal interdict, which might provoke an uprising on Catherine of Aragon's behalf. And for once Henry acted decisively, although in a way that he would ultimately come to regret. On 1 November a warrant was drawn up for Wolsey's arrest, and though the fallen minister attempted over a period of days to starve himself, 'hoping rather to finish his life in this way than in a more shameful one', he was forced, nevertheless, to start the journey south. As a final degradation, the king had given him the humiliating task before his departure of writing out in his own hand an immensely long list of all that he possessed, under strict instructions that nothing be left out. At the same time, watches were set at the port cities to make certain that he did not try to smuggle any of his treasures abroad.

In London a traitor's death certainly awaited Wolsey, as did the opprobrium of high and low alike. Courtiers abused by him for so many years now gloated eagerly over his fate. For them he had been 'double both of speech and meaning', 'vicious of his body', 'a stinking mass of iniquity and corruption', 'a crafty scabby wether'. Common people, too, cursed his memory. Thomas Cromwell, the cardinal's former servant, heard one particular rustic lout declare that Wolsey 'was not worthy to wipe his horse's feet'. Mercifully, however, the broken minister was at least to be spared the baying indignities of the gallows, for he died at Leicester Abbey, stricken by a terrible dysentery on the way back to face his fate at the Tower. That night, the pious canons of Norwich recorded how a great storm swept over England such as occurred only when the Prince of Darkness himself came in person to carry off one of his own. Harried to the end by demands from the king that he reveal the whereabouts of £1,500, which he had allegedly stowed away, the fallen minister was finally entombed by torchlight at the abbey, next, we are told, to none other than Richard III in what Chapuys wryly designated 'the tyrants' sepulchre'. 'Oh, the slippery turns of the world!' exclaimed Erasmus when he had heard of Wolsey's fall. Anne, meanwhile, staged a jubilant masque at court entitled 'The going to hell of Cardinal Wolsey'.

Ironically, in the months since Wolsey's disgrace, the government of England had proven not so much lame as outrightly paraplegic. Quite apart from the incompetence of his replacements, the cardinal's fall had merely produced a reconfiguration rather than a solution of Henry's problems, since Catherine of Aragon was still intransigent and the international situation remained wholly inimical to the king's cause. So it was at this critical juncture that Henry found himself seized by abject indecision born of deep insecurity and, as so often, he recoiled from finishing what he he had started. In direct contrast to the steely ruler of legend, Henry's mind now became lumbered and cluttered with contradictory impulses, which disabled him. Indeed, of all Henry's many deficiencies, the most serious may well have been his inability to perceive, acknowledge and follow the logical courses dictated by events. Having come thus far, circumstances now surely demanded that he proceed to cut his links with Rome, but his inherent conservatism and fears and intuitions prevented him from doing so. Ravelled and snared in a predicament wholly of his own making, he writhed, wriggled, whined, wheedled, blustered and teetered unavailingly.

And as the walls closed in upon Henry, so increasingly the despot emerged. His sole strategy now was to exert hostile pressure on the Church in an effort to force it to bend to his demands, though the pope would always be more frightened by the cold reality of the emperor's threat than by any coercion that Henry could ever hope to apply through blasts of hot air. For two years after Wolsey's fall, then, the King of England was reduced to the role of the fairytale wolf, huffing and puffing at the pope's door in blatant disregard of the fact that this door was bound to remain firmly bolted shut. Imperial invasion of the papal domain was, it should not be forgotten, always an imminent possibility and there was also, for that matter, no cast-iron guarantee that Charles would not alter the stand that he had taken against Luther in 1521. This would, after all, have gained him a good deal of popularity amongst some of his subjects, not to mention a good deal of ecclesiastical booty into the bargain.

Charles V was, therefore, the figure who was always bound to loom largest in Pope Clement's thinking and he was unbendingly committed to family pride and justice for his aunt. Indeed, he now urged Clement as forcefully as he could to remain steadfast against Henry and his mistress, for it was, he said, 'a strange and abominable proceeding that to suit the lust of two fools a law suit should be held up'. And yet the more circumstances conspired against his wishes, the more determined Henry became to have his own way, even if it meant ultimately that he would need to alter the process of law to achieve his ends. The main lever that would be used for this purpose was the so-called 'Long Parliament of the Reformation' or 'Reformation Parliament', first summoned in November 1529, which would remain in existence over seven separate sessions until April 1536.

It is often assumed that Henry VIII called the Reformation Parliament with the intention of marshalling and exploiting the kind of anticlerical sentiments that MPs had vented back in 1515 after a coroner's jury had accused the Bishop of London's chancellor and two of his servants of murdering the merchant tailor Richard Hunne. In this way, we are told, Henry was intending to force from the papacy an abject cry of submission. But even if this interpretation wholly conforms with Henry's general ignorance of the art of negotiation, it is actually unsatisfactory on a number of counts and not least of all because it accords him some credit for strategic thinking, which is belied by actual events. The fact is that nobody at the time and probably least of all the king himself had a wholly clear idea of precisely what the new parliament was intended to achieve. When, for example, the Lord Chancellor, Sir Thomas More, spoke at the opening ceremony, he made a broad reference to the need for new laws to remedy 'divers new enormities', but was unspecific. According to Chapuys, on the other hand, Catherine was certain that Parliament would be used against her. However, if this was so, then it must be admitted that Parliament remained remarkably inactive for more than two years. In fact, it was not until its third session that it went on to pass the crucial legislation of the 1530s which would finally seal the breach with Rome. By that time Thomas Cromwell would be the conductor calling its tune.

To all intents and purposes, therefore, Henry seems to have been concerned initially with nothing more than the appearance of action. He could not, in his view, be seen to be idle, so Parliament must be called. But if the king was wishing to unleash a slavering parliamentary hound in pursuit of the Bishop of Rome, then what he had to hand, at this stage at least, was a largely toothless puppy, for the much-vaunted raging anticlericalism of MPs was by no means self-evident. The main contemporary commentator to suggest that Parliament was indeed raring for action against Rome was, after all, the London lawyer Edward Hall, who was himself an overtly anticlerical Member of Parliament. In his account of the proceedings of the Commons, Hall laid great emphasis on the 'griefs wherewith the spirituality had before time grievously oppressed them' and the determination of MPs to have these dealt with. Yet this determination bore fruit in only three of the twenty-six acts passed in the first session of the Reformation Parliament. Two dealt with mortuary and probate fees and the other attempted to curb the problem of clerical non-residence and pluralism. Furthermore, the Mercers' Company of London rather than the government was behind the action on probate and mortuary fees, and even then only as the fifth of a five point programme otherwise concerned with trade. For some members, too, the target of the legislation is likely to have been not so much the clergy in general as the fresh, bitter memory of one particular cleric, Thomas Wolsey. After six weeks, when Parliament was prorogued owing to plague, precious little of any substance had actually been achieved.

Overt support for the Church during the first session of the Reformation Parliament was limited, admittedly, to the lone voice of John Fisher, Bishop of Rochester. 'Now', said Fisher, 'with the Commons there is nothing but Down with the Church; and all this meseemeth is for lack of faith only.' Consequently, he urged the Lords in response to 'resist manfully [...] this heap of mischief'. And in spite of the bravery of such words Fisher's resistance in the House of Lords is almost always remembered as an articulate, stinging, brave and essentially Canute-like stand against the overwhelming thrust of anticlerical feeling issuing from the Commons. Nevertheless, some of Fisher's rhetorical questions are illuminating and suggest neither a Church on its knees nor one that was under new and imminent threat: 'Or is there any of these abuses that the clergy seek not to extirp and destroy?' he asked. 'Be there not laws already provided against such and many more disorders?' In other words, any anticlerical sentiments being expressed by the Commons were, by implication, of the usual tired variety, which focused on problems already being addressed.

Ironically, it may even have been the forcefulness of Fisher's defence that actually served to inflame matters. As his Jesuit biographer Francis van Ortroy later made clear, Fisher was an identikit saint: a hair-shirted, hard-praying, uncompromising flagellant. But if he was a scholar and ascetic worthy of beatification, he also exhibited a pugnacious ego fit to match the undoubted grandeur of his principles. And though Fisher was a genuinely blessed man, he had now, not altogether necessarily, magnified the issue dangerously. The truth was that the bishop displayed as much indiscretion as heroism by his show of what many considered to be ecclesiastical arrogance. The parallel he drew with the earlier heretical calamity involving Jan Hus in Bohemia was, for instance, especially provocative: 'For God's sake, see what a realm the Kingdom of Bohemia was, and when the Church went down then fell the glory of the Kingdom.' The Commons certainly 'took the matter grievously' and sent a deputation of thirty members led by their 'wise and discreet Speaker', Thomas Audley, to complain to the king that they 'which were elected for the wisest of all the shires, cities and boroughs within the realm of England, should be declared to lack faith, which was equivalent to say that they were as ill as Turks or Saracens'. Perhaps, then, it was in the light of his overreaction that Fisher's fellow bishops declined to follow his lead – not out of cowardice in the face of a coming tidal wave that might sweep them away, but rather from a desire to ride out what they saw more as a troublesome squall than a typhoon.

Even so, Fisher's stand had clearly made him enemies who would stop at nothing to be rid of him. On 20 February 1531 his cook, a man named Rouse, who was said by some to have been acting on the instructions of either Thomas or Anne Boleyn, poisoned a cauldron of broth with a mysterious white powder, which was served to the bishop and his household. Two men died at table and seventeen others, including some beggars who were unlucky enough to be treated to the leftovers, fell seriously ill. Fisher, however, ate sparingly, as was his wont, and survived, albeit only after excruciating abdominal pains. Such was the publicity of the case that in its aftermath Henry VIII went in person to the House of Lords and in a speech lasting one and a half hours declaimed upon the barbarity of poisoning. In truth the fuss raised by the king had much less to do with Fisher's plight or justice *per se* than with his own morbid terror of poison, which is well documented. But a law was nevertheless enacted making murder by poison high treason and punishable by boiling in oil. And so it was that the bishop's hapless cook was duly braised at Smithfield before the usual crowing rabble.

Some time before Rouse was cruelly immersed, however, the wheel of fortune had turned much more happily for a comparatively obscure Cambridge divine. As Stephen Gardiner, former secretary to the king and newly appointed Bishop of Winchester, was returning from Rome in September 1528 in the company of the king's almoner, Edward Fox, the pair had happened to lodge in a house belonging to Waltham Abbey in Essex. There they came upon 40-year-old Thomas Cranmer, who had been formerly a student with them at Cambridge. Cranmer's academic career had been cut short initially by his marriage to, of all people, a barmaid called Black Joan. When, however, she died in childbirth, Cranmer was readmitted to the university and took holy orders, and by the time of his meeting with Gardiner and Fox, he had become a little known Fellow of Jesus College, Cambridge, of broadly evangelical outlook.

Except on horseback, where he is said to have ridden with breakneck abandon, Cranmer was by nature timid, confessing once that all 'audacity' had been whipped out of him by a 'mervelous severe and cruell scholemaster'. Not altogether surprisingly, therefore, he disliked pomp and shrank from publicity. Nor did he seek to enrich himself. Indeed, in years to come he would readily allow the king and Cromwell to rob him of some of his finest manors. All in all, he was a shy, unworldly and diffident man with a scholarly rather than a sharply political turn of mind, who had, it seemed, long ago settled for the comfort of the shadows. And it was precisely this that now endeared him to the king and would lead Cromwell to remark: 'You were born in a happy hour; for, do and say what you will, the king will always take it well at your hand.'

Nevertheless, there was another side to Cranmer, which is often overlooked these days. Though gentle and devout and with no craving for power, he was not without the vanity of a scholar. In fact, having no sympathy with the prejudices and superstitions of the unlettered multitude, he regarded with impatient contempt all opposition from those who were unacquainted with the 'results' of German scholarship. This side of him would become best known later to his prebendaries and the county justices of Kent. And when the time came, he would also prove jealous in maintaining the authority of his office. Ultimately, as Archbishop of Canterbury, he continued to issue dispensations which had previously been reserved for the pope and on one occasion he would even have the impertinence to send a pallium to Bishop Holgate, who succeeded Lee as Archbishop of York. Nor would he conceal his appreciation of honours and titles, which he took to confirm the authority of his ideas and served to protect him from the need for tireless debates with inferiors.

At Waltham, then, Cranmer made a strong impression with Gardiner and Fox by proposing that the whole question of the validity of Pope Julius II's dispensation be submitted to the universities of Europe, where it might be settled in the most rational, impartial manner. When it was eventually brought to his attention, this idea immediately captivated

Henry, who was often prone to such eureka moments. 'Marry!' he is said to have exclaimed, 'This man hath the sow by the right ear!' Accordingly, Cranmer now benefited from the full gust of Henry's enthusiasm, for his rise from this point onwards was rapid. Attached initially to the Boleyn household, in 1530 he was sent on a diplomatic expedition to Charles V at Bologna, along with Thomas Boleyn, after which he went to Rome and, ironically, pleased the pope sufficiently to be appointed Penitentiarius of England. Next, in 1531, he was despatched to Charles V at Vienna and both the emperor and his worldly-wise minister Granvelle also took to him, although both seem to have assumed quite wrongly that he sympathised with their viewpoint. Finally, he travelled through Germany meeting Lutheran divines like Osiander whose niece, Margaret, he married in defiance of canon law.

In spite of the recognition it brought him, though, Cranmer's proposal for an appeal to the universities was never the Archimedean lever he had hoped for. Indeed, in many respects the plan perfectly demonstrated both the strengths and the weaknesses of his mind. To Cranmer's credit, he was consistently an advocate of gradualism and persuasion in a thrusting and intolerant age. But he was also more often than not unable to appreciate or control the strong pressures that mould political decisions and in spite of Henry's initial enthusiasm for it, his plan was clearly flawed, since the 'intellectual' inclinations of the leading universities of Europe bore, not surprisingly, a striking resemblance to their political loyalties. In England, France and northern Italy, where anti-Habsburg feeling was strong, the universities therefore found in favour of Henry. After Poitiers had supported Catherine, for instance, Francis intervened on behalf of his ally and Paris was bullied into compliance. Orléans, Bourges and Toulouse followed suit. On the other hand, Alcalá and Salamanca did as they were bid by Charles and found in favour of the pope, as did those German universities under the emperor's thumb. In Italy, not surprisingly, only Ferrara, Padua and Bologna were for the divorce, although Vicenza would also have supported Henry, had their bishop not arrived, with a beefy gang of minders in attendance, to tear up the theses which nine learned doctors were ready to maintain. Most of the decisions were, in fact, paid for.

And as Henry scraped every available scholarly barrel for support that was to prove academic in all senses of the term, other learned individuals were also treated to the material benefits of partisan scholarship. Most notably, Richard Croke, the great Greek scholar, boasted that he had secured 110 adherents to Henry's cause, not to mention numerous needy Jewish rabbis, fished out of their ghettos to support Henry's interpretation of Deuteronomy at twenty-four crowns apiece. Predictably, Croke was always petitioning for more money on his travels, though he maintained, with stirring sincerity, that he did not bribe, but only paid men for the trouble they took in mastering the case.

Curiously enough, Protestant theologians were largely unconvinced by the English king's case for divorce and they would remain so even throughout the mid-1530s when the break with Rome was being confirmed. When, in 1531, Grynaeus was employed to canvass Protestant scholars, he obtained favourable answers only from Oecolampadius and Phrygian. Zwingli, however, was dubious about the king's position and Bucer outrightly negative. Likewise, although Melanchthon hedged his bets somewhat by suggesting that Henry could take another wife in the manner of the patriarchs, he concluded, all the same, that the marriage was legal, while Luther, for his part, was unequivocally in favour of Catherine and prayed 'that she might bear this great evil as her cross, but never approve or consent to it'. Furthermore, Protestant disavowal of Henry's case would actually increase over the next few years. In 1534, Robert Barnes failed to convince Alpinus in Hamburg and in 1536 Lutheran theologians would unanimously decide against Henry, though for reasons that varied.

In the meantime, whenever Henry attempted independent diplomatic initiatives, they backfired. His decision in 1530 to send Anne Boleyn's father to the pope while the latter was meeting Charles at Bologna merely afforded the Holy Father a splendid opportunity for gleeful disrespect. Seizing his opportunity with both hands, Clement did not hesitate to serve the Earl of Wiltshire with a writ citing his master to appear before him at Rome. Then, as if to scotch rumours that he was privately expressing a wish for the king to marry Anne and thereby settle the matter once and for all without involving the Holy See, he issued a series of bulls threatening excommunication if Henry should do any such thing. For good measure, he prohibited anyone from speaking or writing against the validity of Catherine's marriage, and any court or other body from attempting to pass judgement on it.

At home, meanwhile, Henry continued to remain hesitant during 1530, albeit more and more aggressively so. His first response to the news of his possible excommunication was to remind the papal nuncio of the law of *praemunire*, which declared that those who brought or received papal bulls into England relating to 'our Lord the King, against him, his crown, and royalty of his realm' should be 'put out of the King's protection, and their lands, tenements, goods and chattels forfeited' to the Crown. Moreover, in the summer of 1530, writs of *praemunire facias* were actually issued against fifteen clergy, which included all of Catherine's supporters with the exception of Cuthbert Tunstall. The specific charge was that they had aided Wolsey in his offences by handing over part of their income to him.

Before a decision had been reached in this case, however, the charge was extended in December to the whole English clergy. 'No one', Chapuys said of the Statute of Praemunire, 'can fathom the mysteries of this law. Its interpretation depends wholly on the King, who limits or amplifies it according to his will, and applies it to anyone he pleases.' Nor were the penalties any less arbitrary, for in surrendering, the provinces of Canterbury and York paid fines of £100,000 and £18,840 respectively in return for a royal pardon. And in addition to their financial submission, the clergy were also forced, most significantly, to recognise Henry as their 'singular protector, only and supreme lord [...] even Supreme Head' – an acknowledgement that clearly set a potentially handy precedent for the Crown if it should choose at some time in the future to press its control of ecclesiastical affairs.

Yet, in spite of appearances, the clergy's acceptance of a royal pardon on these terms was by no means a clear sign that Henry was already intent upon a breach with Rome's authority, for in recognising the king as Supreme Head of the Church, the clergy were carefully permitted to append the key phrase 'as far as the law of Christ allows'. In reality, then, Henry's defiant posturing, spiteful threats and token gestures of confidence were more indicative of growing frustration and impasse, since his attempts at irresistible force were, in effect, foundering on the immovable position of a pope, hemmed in on all sides by circumstances beyond his control. Indeed, in the twelve months following the ending of the legatine court at Blackfriars, the king's policy was remarkable only in terms of its confusion. In June 1530, for instance, when his case was finally revoked by the pope to Rome, Henry summoned his leading subjects to court to give speedy judgement on his behalf, since, or so he claimed, informed opinion in

England and Europe as a whole was in no doubt of the rectitude of his case. At this very time, however, he was also urging his representative in Rome, William Bennet, to procrastinate at all costs.

Of course, there may have been at least a little more to Henry's antics in this period than mere foot-stamping frustration and bullying. It is possible, for example, that the king was well aware the pope would not be made to bend by intimidation, and that the real purpose of the continual threats and bluster was simply to dissuade Clement from dismissing the divorce case. Hence, on this model, Henry was primarily concerned with achieving delay, or, in other words, preventing the papal administration from finding against him, until some variable in the situation altered, allowing further progress. Clement VII might die, for instance, or perhaps some unforeseen development in international affairs would loosen the emperor's control of the situation. Such a gloss on events would certainly seem to reflect slightly more favourably upon Henry, although still not well, for we are left, nonetheless, with a leader waiting on events, unable to complete the process he has initiated.

Yet, for all this, like a sleepwalker in a maze, Henry did indeed appear during this time to stumble on at least the right direction, if not a precise route, to his desired ends. Though a severance with the underlying doctrinal principles of Roman Catholicism remained unthinkable for the defender of the faith, a juridical breach had its attractions both for his ego and ultimately, of course, his purse. And throughout 1530 this realisation appeared to grow upon him. On Christmas Eve 1529, for instance, Henry had given notice to Catherine of Aragon that 'he prized and valued the Church of Canterbury as much as the people across the sea did the Roman' and in April 1530 he told the French ambassador that he intended to settle the matter of his divorce within his own kingdom and without recourse to the pope, 'whom he regards as ignorant and no good father'. Then, in September 1530, he declared stridently that he had 'a pinnacle of dignity' and 'no superior on earth' and it was proclaimed also in this month that the King of England 'was absolute both as Emperor and Pope in his own Kingdom'. Henry's references to himself as Supreme Head of the Church in his letters to Bishop Tunstall further suggested a growing preparedness to contemplate the ultimate step, as, indeed, did the recorded remarks that the king made intermittently to the papal nuncio. All of this might, of course, be interpreted as little more than yet another fit of bellicose foot stamping to intimidate the pope. Very significantly, however, the first drafts of the treason laws, which were later used to crush opposition to the royal supremacy, are known to have been drawn up without advertisement as early as 1530.

Thus, as Henry's frustration grew, there does appear to have been a nascent reorientation of his thinking, which was produced, in part, by his introduction to ideas that now neatly served his interests. It seems, for instance, that he had by this stage – most probably under Anne's influence – read William Tyndale's *The Obedience of a Christian Man*, notwithstanding the fact that around six years earlier, he had hounded the author out of the country in fear of his very life. 'This book', Henry now declared solemnly, 'is for me and all kings to read.' Although the evidence of the king's written words is somewhat contradictory, he was also maintaining more and more frequently at this time that he had no case to answer before the pope, because he was not subject to papal authority and the jurisdiction of the papal courts. The 'Levitical curse' was, it seems, receding in importance and being replaced by the new notion of *privilegium Angliae*. Therefore, gropingly and falteringly, Henry was transferring his emphasis from the shifting sands of scripture, the mire of canon law and the tangled grey beards of the scholars of Europe to what he considered to be the bedrock of political theory and hard historical fact.

Moreover, the researches of Edward Fox, Thomas Cranmer and John Stokesley were playing a major role in feeding Henry a diet of evidence that would help him fuel the rationalisations and self-justifications that he was always inclined to embrace so ardently. Working together, the three divines had compiled for Henry's benefit by September 1530 a massive collection of legal and historical evidence, entitled *Collectanea satis copiosa*, supporting the judicial independence of the Crown from Rome. The pre-eminence of the king was confirmed from Old Testament examples connected with Solomon and David, and on the basis of medieval Catholic authorities, such as Ivo of Chartres. The Council of Nicaea of 325 and subsequent councils had, it was argued, affirmed the principle that no legal case should be taken outside the ecclesiastical province of its origin. Furthermore, the *Collectanea* included a letter, written supposedly by Pope Eleutherius around AD 187, in which he addressed the mythical King Lucius I of Britain as 'vicar of God'. At the same time, William Bennet and Sir Edward Carne were now given the impossible task in Rome of reading all the Vatican Registers to abstract entries that would support Henry's claim to 'authority imperial'.

Henry turned, too, to British sources. The Constitutions of Clarendon of Henry II's reign, for instance, had enshrined England's jurisdictional privileges. Another favourite source for Henry's legal burrowers was the largely mythical chronicle of Geoffrey of Monmouth, which favoured a version of English history based on the claim that Christianity had been brought here in biblical times by Joseph of Arimathea independently of the Roman Church. Henry's archivists also tried to trace the descent of the kings of England back to the Roman Emperor Constantine via King Arthur. The fact that such myths had already been exposed by Polydore Vergil did not dissuade Henry's seekers. Given, they argued, that it was the so-called Donation of Constantine which had first granted papal authority, and that this document had, in any case, been proven to be a forgery, it followed that England's rulers had always been independent of the papacy. By twisted logic and dubious scholarship of various kinds, Henry thus sought to press home his case that the Christian world had started as, and still should be, a federation of autonomous, local churches, each ruled over by a prince appointed by God and rejecting the fraudulent universal authority of the Bishop of Rome.

If, however, Henry was contemplating a new strategy, his tactics for achieving it remained hopelessly inadequate. And the attempt to smother the pope with a welter of archival evidence remained, like Cranmer's appeal to the universities before it, a powder puff effort. Like it or not, the pope remained diplomatically manacled and neither words nor sticks nor stones could force him to comply. So while Henry was slowly beginning to identify the correct objective, he remained hopelessly unable, nevertheless, to strike upon the appropriate method for achieving it. By the end of 1530, in fact, both Henry's ministers and his strategies were proving nakedly unproductive. Chapuys, for his part, noted that 'Parliament is prorogued from time to time as though they do not know their own minds about the measures proposed therein'. And there was no denying either that if Henry had, indeed, hit upon the notion of a national church under his direct control, it would require somebody else to furnish the means for its achievement and the intellectual case upon which it might be founded. Someone was required, too, to drive the sluggish Reformation Parliament towards a more 'constructive' goal.

10

Plenary, Whole and Entire Power

'Let the King, with the consent of Parliament, declare himself Head of the Church of England, and all his difficulties would vanish. England at present is a monster with two heads. If the King should take to himself the supreme power, religious as well as secular, every incongruity would cease; the clergy would immediately realise they were responsible to the King and not to the Pope, and forthwith become subservient to the royal will.'

Words ascribed to Thomas Cromwell in Reginald Pole,
Apologia ad Carolum Quintum.

Thomas Cromwell, whose origins may well have been rather more modest and unhappy than is generally recognised these days, was born in the small village of Putney, which then lay some 4 miles from the capital. Though not, therefore, quite a Londoner, it is certain, nevertheless, that he will soon have felt the irresistible pull of the many-spired and malodorous city in which his years of power were to be passed. Appropriately enough, the time of his birth is thought by some to have coincided with the Battle of Bosworth and the triumph of the Tudor dynasty with whose fortunes he would be so closely linked. And if Cromwell's arrival did indeed occur in 1485 or thereabouts, he is likely to have shared his birth year with any number of famous figures: Zwingli, the Swiss reformer, Cortés, the conqueror of Mexico, and Arthur, Prince of Wales, whose early death was destined to have such an influence on Cromwell's own rise to eminence, all ventured forth around this date. Yet the chronological link between the boy from Putney and these individuals would have surely seemed the probable limit of any connection, for when he entered the world wrapped in anonymity and burdened with the dead weight of humble parentage, none could have predicted so prominent a place in history for him. If, as some have suggested, he was descended from the rich Nottinghamshire magnate Ralph Lord Cromwell, there was little evidence of it in his upbringing. Bereft of rank, connection or fortune, even the prospect of formal schooling was to be denied him. Indeed, his will of 1529 made more than one reference to 'poor kinsfolk' still living and in later life he is known to have shaken the hand of an old bell-ringer at Syon House before a crowd of courtiers, confessing, according to one source, that during his childhood 'this man's father had given him many dinners in his necessities'.

Cromwell's own father, meanwhile, had been a man of many parts with few of them particularly worthy. Though often described as a brewer, Walter Cromwell, was primarily a blacksmith and fuller, who, as a sideline, apparently brewed bad beer, for he was more than once condemned at the assize of ale. Moreover, as well as being prone to dishonesty and occasional bouts of drunkenness, he was also quarrelsome and known to the local magistracy for assault and overgrazing the common. But in spite of the fact that he led a life of more than typical commotion, the elder Cromwell was not without his fair share of native wit and it is highly probable that the influence of such an artful, devil-may-care fellow upon his son was considerable. Certainly, the younger Cromwell appears to have acquired a patina of tough unconventionality, which he carried into adulthood, even proudly. Never one to hide behind airs and affectation, he later confessed to the ever-earnest Cranmer, doubtless with some glee, that 'he had been a ruffian in his youth' and Chapuys would confirm that 'for some offence he was thrown into prison and obliged afterwards to leave the country'. Yet if this may sound an unpropitious start, it was not without benefit, too, for it set him upon a European odyssey lasting a decade, which would equip him most fittingly for the tasks ahead.

Although we cannot be sure if Chapuys was correct about the reasons for Cromwell's departure from England, we do know that in December 1503, at the age of 18, he was with the French army in Italy as either a soldier or page. We know, too, that after his military adventures ceased, he remained in Italy in the service of the Florentine banking family of Frescobaldi and travelled widely there, operating mainly in Florence, but also in Pisa and Venice. Significantly, it was during his Italian sojourn that he came into contact with a range of new ideas and approaches, and readily absorbed the emerging rationalistic ethos of the day, which would prove so important in equipping him for his later role. Not least of all, he was introduced to Marsiglio of Padua's seminal work *Defensor Pacis*, which emphasised the primacy of the secular ruler in ecclesiastical affairs. But more importantly his considerable commercial experience reinforced his natural tendency to think in terms of efficiency and outcomes rather than hidebound traditions. On his travels, too, he encountered and was genuinely influenced by the writings of religious reformers, although contrary to what is still a widely held misapprehension, the impact of reforming ideas upon him at this stage may not necessarily have been quite as substantial as is often assumed. Curiously, the inventory of his London home for the year 1527 mentions numerous pious objects which were wholly in keeping with the devotion of the old religion, including two images in gilt leather of Our Lady and St Christopher, as well as a golden leather image of St Anthony tucked away under the stairs. Furthermore, the centrepiece of Cromwell's 'new chamber' appears to have been an ornate gilded altar of Our Lord's Nativity. Even his jewels, for that matter, included a golden *Agnus Dei* with an engraving of Our Lady and St George.

In truth, almost all aspects of Cromwell's early years are obscure, but what can be said with certainty is that upon his return to England he was a highly marketable commodity in his own right. This, after all, was the age when a quick-witted pachyderm with a practical knowledge of men and affairs and an eye for the main chance could vie with lords and dukes, provided that he doffed his cap with all due humility to those who held the keys to advancement. Then again, as one of the 'new men' brought to the fore by the increasingly flexible outlook of the sixteenth century, he had developed a cutting edge, based upon a simple knack for grasping the internal logic of policies and the momentum of events, which would prove invaluable in any position of impasse. Endowed with great energy and vision, Cromwell displayed, finally, an unerring determination to pursue to the bitter end all he attempted, and not altogether surprisingly, therefore, we next hear of him operating between 1520 and 1524 as a thriving solicitor, whose expertise in the common law was bringing him important business from Wolsey himself. By 1525, indeed, he was established as one of the leading lights of the cardinal's household, where he was employed – somewhat portentously – upon the task of suppressing twenty-nine monasteries.

It would be in Wolsey's service, in fact, that the really substantial opportunities for advancement materialised and, upon the cardinal's fall, Cromwell was fortunate to be able, at long odds, to sustain his rise. With the Duke of Norfolk's help he was duly elected to the first session of the Reformation Parliament as the new member for Taunton and now, in addition to the talented beavering that had already carried him far, he demonstrated both an intuitive grasp of the epoch he would help to shape and what amounted to a sixth sense for timing. In particular, Cromwell's prominent role in the anticlerical debates that occupied Parliament during November and December 1529 happened to coincide perfectly with the king's mood and needs. At the same time, Cromwell was given ample opportunity to engage in the kind of earnest posturing that is so vital for any aspiring public servant. Unlike others, such as Stephen Gardiner, for instance, who fled Wolsey's cause at the first hint of impending disaster, Cromwell chose to remain steadfast until the last possible moment. Indeed, while the vultures circled hungrily, he alone of Wolsey's household was prepared to speak up on his master's behalf, persuading the Commons to reject the Lords' bill of attainder against him and engineering ultimately a formal pardon for the beleaguered cardinal under the Great Seal.

In this way, the blacksmith's son fuelled his reputation for loyalty, and hereafter his rise was swift. By the autumn of 1530, Cromwell had at last become personally known to his sovereign as a dependable man of service. Moreover, in helping Henry replenish the treasury with the spoils from Wolsey's forfeited see of Winchester and abbacy of St Albans, this rising political star gave clear notice of his ability to deliver – something which, as we have seen, seemed sorely lacking in Henry's existing aristocratic advisers. He now demonstrated, too, that infinite capacity for taking pains, which would always be one of his outstanding characteristics. Whether drafting laws, overhauling the machinery of government or vigorously pursuing enemies of the State, Cromwell's meticulous eye for detail would never waver. Towards the end of 1530, therefore, he joined the king's council and within a year he belonged to its inner ring. In fact, as he wove his subtle magic in loosing Henry's bonds to Rome during the next few years, his ascent would prove unstoppable. By early 1533 he was the king's chief minister and in 1534 came the really decisive consolidation of his influence when he was appointed principal secretary to Henry himself. His father, Walter, might well have been proud, though by now the son had bigger thoughts than this to fill his head.

Throughout 1531 the government's blind and unavailing threshing had continued, as had the rancour it engendered, for the second session of the Reformation Parliament, which began in January, had yielded only resistance and altercation. On 30 March, Sir Brian Tuke had brought the House of Lords an unexpected and unwelcome message from his sovereign in the form of a long letter, exposing the troubled state of the king's conscience and reiterating the opinions of the universities against his marriage. The Bishop of Lincoln, Henry's confessor, also delivered a carefully prepared speech in favour of the king's divorce which was solemnly seconded by the Bishop of London. To the dismay of the government, however, two other bishops, Bath and St Asaph's, offered instant hot rebuttal and Sir Thomas More, when appealed to, also refused to support the divorce. Thereafter, it was left to George Talbot, Earl of Shrewsbury, to voice his displeasure in no uncertain terms, and the general hum of comment which accompanied his words left no doubt concerning the overall opposition of the peers. In a hasty and less than dexterous face-saving manoeuvre, the Duke of Norfolk then rose awkwardly on the Crown's behalf in a vain attempt to reassure all present that the king's message was only for the information of the Lords rather than for their action. And at an uncomfortable signal from the duke, Tuke swiftly retreated, flanked by his supporting bishops, to try his luck in the Commons. There, once again, he read the king's long-winded message and again the two bishops spoke in turn, taking it upon their consciences that the king's marriage was null. But the MPs 'little edified, returned no answer'. Even the Speaker, it seems, was silent, and Tuke and his bishops beat a second retreat before Henry abruptly prorogued Parliament until October.

Nor were Henry's continued assaults upon the queen's resolve any more fruitful, even though the pope's procrastination in opening the case in Rome was placing her under untold pressure. Having informed the emperor that the hearing was to begin not later than September 1530, Clement had still done nothing by June 1531, at which point Henry embarked upon another frontal attack upon his wife's determined stand. The tactic this time involved a mob-handed harangue, which was delivered as Catherine prepared for bed on the Tuesday evening after Whitsunday. Led by the Dukes of Norfolk and Suffolk and the Earl of Wiltshire, a party of some thirty privy councillors, reinforced by half a dozen bishops and a clutch of frowning canonists, attended upon the queen to convince her of her folly. It was Norfolk, in fact, who began proceedings by launching into a characteristically pompous and garbled prelection, which soon trailed off into a maze-like account of how her father's conquest of Navarre had been made possible only by English assistance. Eventually regaining a tenuous thread of sorts, Norfolk then emphasised the king's pain and surprise at his wife's continued insistence that her case should be opened at Rome. That the pope should have summoned Henry there in person was, said the duke, an unparalleled humiliation and if she was determined not to abandon her vain request for a legal judgement, she should at least be content with a neutral hearing in England conducted by impartial judges.

Predictably, perhaps, Catherine's response to this rambling attack upon her judgement was as unflinchingly resolute as her confidence in her cause. Though no living person, she said, could regret Henry's inconvenience more than she, it was, nevertheless, her husband who had first laid this case before the pope. Besides which, she added with scarcely concealed bitterness, she had no especial reason to expect favour at the hands of His Holiness, for he had so far offered her little succour and, if anything, had caused her much injury by his persistent delay. Concerning the king's new title of Supreme Head of the Church of England, which Norfolk had touched upon, Catherine readily accepted that her husband was lord and master of the whole kingdom in things temporal, but as for spiritual matters it was the pope alone who 'has the power of Our Lord Jesus Christ on this earth, and is, in consequence, the mirror image of eternal truth'. On this principle she could never bend, and she prayed God that her husband would never think otherwise.

This, then, was the point at which Henry's rubicon was finally reached. Standing in her nightclothes, the portly and embattled queen had seen off an assemblage of England's great and mighty with consummate ease and loosed the first pebble in a landslide of undreamed magnitude. Unquestionably, the costs of a breach with the papacy were difficult to estimate. If it did entail war with Charles V and a subsequent severing of commercial relations between England and Flanders, the government might well be thrown into the most serious danger. The projected marriage with Anne was, of course, already notoriously unpopular in its own right, and if it was to be accompanied by the burden of war taxation and a grievous disruption to trade, there was no telling where things might end. The events of the year had, after all, shown that public opinion was being violently stirred and when the *praemunire* fine was demanded of the London clergy, a riotous assault upon the bishop's palace ensued. Mutinous words had also been voiced in the House of Commons, when it was suspected that the laity might, too, be mulcted under the pretext of *praemunire*. 'The King', it was said, 'had burdened and oppressed his kingdom with more imposts and exactions than any three or four of his predecessors and should consider that his strength lay in the affections of his people.' At the same time, the threat from without continued to loom, since the defences of the Scottish border were weak and in Ireland a Spanish envoy had appeared just at the time when the Earl of Desmond was throwing off his allegiance to Henry.

Nevertheless, while England waited on the brink of come-what-may, its king settled for what amounted to little more than an aimless mish-mash of displacement activities. Any action rather than effective action would apparently suffice it seemed. One whole day in June, from nine in the morning till seven at night, Henry was locked tight in examining a lone heretic. At other times he chose to lose himself in laboured attempts at polemics, the ultimate result of which was the publication in November of a pamphlet entitled *A Glass of Truth*. Couched in the form of a dialogue between a lawyer and a divine, it rehearsed the same tired old arguments that had already lost any efficacy they may ever have had. Moreover, even the production of such a lame work was, it seems, beyond his meagre reserves of stamina. 'My book', he had informed Anne at the height of his efforts, 'maketh substantially for my matter in looking whereof I have spent above four hours this day, which caused me now to write the shorter letter to you at this time, because of some pain in my head.' In the event, his day's writing had had more impact on his libido than upon the progress of the divorce, for he ended his letter 'wishing myself in my sweetheart's arms whose pretty ducks [breasts] I trust shortly to kiss'. By December Henry was occupying his time with little else beyond random proclamations against beggars, heretics and crossbows.

And as events unfolded around him there was growing evidence of outright opposition in Parliament to any further assault upon the Church's status. To be sure, there was anticlericalism among MPs and for some it ran deep but it was far from unalloyed, and disapproval of clerical abuses was more than balanced by fear of the unknown. Furthermore, the Church seemed at this very time to be making every effort to put its own house in order. Needless to say, such measures would neither please nor satisfy those who were bent upon seeing it subordinated for good. But even now Convocation was embarking upon an impressive programme of reform, placing tighter controls on clerical residence and the qualifications of ordinands, increasing the penalties for fornication and imposing a weekly minimum of six hours' scriptural study on incumbents.

From January 1532 onwards, therefore, when the third session of the Reformation Parliament began, there were ominous rumblings concerning government policy. There were, for instance, unwelcome warnings from the lower chamber about attempts to extract further taxation, as well as a call for Henry to restore his wife and daughter to favour. Nor, perhaps, was the king's insipid response to such impertinence any less unexpected, for underneath his imperious posturing he remained baffled and perplexed before the delicate balance of forces now confronting him. Declaring that he 'marvelled not a little' that matters pertaining to his soul should have been mooted in Parliament, he deigned, nonetheless, to explain to MPs why his conscience was troubled, rejecting in the process any claims that his motives were carnal in origin: 'I am forty-one years old', he reminded the Commons, 'at which age the lust of a man is not so quick as in lusty youth.' Henry's tone was, then, more overawed than overbearing and the implication was plain enough. Far from speeding hot-footed to his destiny, he was edging his way gingerly down an unknown path of eggshells.

Nor was the government's case advanced any more successfully by its campaign of bribery and intimidation or by its attempt to flood the country with books and pamphlets. A priest who was inveighing against the divorce at St Paul's was arrested in full flow, but when Henry commanded every priest in the kingdom to preach in his favour, few dared to do so, and at Salisbury one who did was hissed and torn from the pulpit. In the Commons, meanwhile, an MP named Temse took the occasion of a money bill to say that if the king would take back his true wife, he would not have an enemy in Christendom and would not need to oppress his people with exactions. More worryingly still, the London merchants who traded with Flanders and feared war with the emperor applauded this opinion. Likewise, among the lay peers Anne's insolence had alienated many of her earlier supporters, and though for a year she fought back at them, forcing Sir Henry Guildford's dismissal from the council and boasting always that a few months would see her married, she could not cow or neutralise them all. Even the Duke of Norfolk, Chapuys thought, was so disgusted with his niece, and so frightened by the popular outcry, that he, too, would have opposed the king's divorce except that he was 'one of those men who will do anything to cling to power'.

In fact, the annulment issue seems to have been taking a particularly heavy toll upon the unity of the nation's elites around this time. In February, when Norfolk had summoned his own noble allies to enlist their support for the claim that matrimonial suits should be under secular rather than ecclesiastical jurisdiction, the suggestion was angrily dismissed, and Lord Darcy, who had once been Norfolk's keen backer, roundly dismissed his proposal as preposterous. But this was actually only one incident among a number, which reflected a whole range of divisions at the highest level. Noble women, for instance, were consistently among the most forthright supporters of the queen's cause and the Duchess of Norfolk, who by now had become estranged from her husband, as well as the Marchioness of Exeter and the Countess of Salisbury all stood firm on Catherine's behalf.

Men, on the other hand, tended to be more combustible in expressing their partisanship and flaring tempers now gave rise to a serious flashpoint. Charles Brandon, Duke of Suffolk, had long opposed Henry's plan to make Anne his queen and in 1530, he had been banished from court after bringing the king a disturbing story about Anne Boleyn's illicit relations with a courtier. After his return, however, the coals were fanned once more when his wife, Mary, was responsible for 'opprobrious language' against the king's mistress. As a result, in April 1532, a mob of the Duke of Norfolk's retainers, led by the three Southwell brothers, had chased William Pennington, a member of Suffolk's suite, into the sanctuary of Westminster and there stabbed him to death, at which point Suffolk himself sought bloody revenge before the king intervened personally to suppress the vendetta. In the end, however, as so often happened, it was Anne who had the last word when she proceeded to accuse the vengeful duke of seducing his own daughter.

Against this background, then, Thomas Cromwell was set at the head of a rudderless and foundering cause. With the opening of the third session of the Reformation Parliament, Cromwell soon emerged, in fact, as the manager of government business and now for the first time, as his sovereign's frustration reached breaking point, he would be given the green light to implement his more radical plans. This is not to suggest, however, that he was the originator of the idea of a unilateral break with Rome, for Edward Foxe and Cranmer had already preceded him on the council with the broad principle. Neither, however, had shown any real inkling of how, in practice, the destruction of the Church's jurisdiction might be effected, for the mechanics of demolition were, at one and the same time, too subtle and too crude to be encompassed by men who were themselves so much products of the institution they now sought to undo. It would be up to Cromwell, therefore, during the course of the coming year to devise new tools for the task and show both his counterparts and his king the way forward.

For the time being, however, Henry still seems to have been thinking more in terms of action than outcomes and this was to have the most momentous consequences, for he now appears to have slipped all too readily into the new and fateful path laid down for him by his servant. With great craft, Cromwell deliberately decided to stir the one issue that he knew still smarted with the swarms of common lawyers so influential in the Commons: the activities of the Church courts. Linking this with the legislative power of Convocation, which the Crown wished to control, he thus devised a powerful bait which even the most vacillating of MPs would find difficult to resist. Therefore, on 18 March, Cromwell's 'Supplication of the Commons against the Ordinaries' was drawn up. It was a list which incorported a wide range of ones linked to the episcopacy, but concentrated mainly on abuses associated with ecclesiastical courts and particularly those relating to the expense of litigation and the delays involved. In particular it attacked nepotism, the free use of excommunication, the number of secular posts held by clergy and Convocation's independent power to frame canon law. And in the process the singularly potent demands for a single sovereignty and individual allegiance within the realm were slipped in almost innocently – so innocently, in fact, that few, if any, of those who lent their names to the measure could have fully realised what they were now committing themselves to so irrevocably.

And so on 11 May, Henry, flanked by his chief councillors, ordered Convocation to submit all its legislation, past and present, for his consent. Five days later Convocation submitted and presented the king with the so-called 'Submission of the Clergy', in which they acceded to all his demands. At a stroke, then, the English Church had been subordinated, Henry had been offered a way forward and Thomas Cromwell had found his niche. As Chapuys put it, churchmen were now of less account than cobblers, for such tradesmen could still assemble and make their own rules for their craft guild, which the clergy no longer could. The next day, More resigned the Chancellorship, promising, nevertheless, to keep silent and never more 'to study nor meddle with any matter of this world'. Henry, meanwhile, had gone against everything he had supported for most of his life and was purring with vengeful satisfaction.

The period between May 1532 (when Parliament was prorogued) and February 1533 (when it reassembled) was a crucial time. Though a wave of suicides in London was seen as a malign portent 'foreboding future evil', Cromwell planned coolly and purposefully, aware that events were now proceeding to their ordained climax. It was true that Rome remained intransigent, but nevertheless, the Church had been cowed domestically and there were other signs that the strategic initiative was shifting decisively in favour of the Crown. Thomas More's resignation had, for instance, removed for the time being a passive but nevertheless influential and implacable opponent. More importantly still, perhaps, Archbishop Warham, who had obstructed Henry at every turn, died on 23 August 1532 after Henry's threats had already extracted from the pope the necessary bulls for his replacement by the ever-amenable Cranmer. With an archbishop properly consecrated and granted the authority of *legatus natus*, Henry was now in a position to have his previous marriage annulled in a way that satisfied his curious desire to abide by 'legality'. Only the formalities remained and accordingly in January 1533, after a stint as ambassador to the imperial court, Thomas Cranmer became Archbishop of Canterbury. Predictably, at his consecration on 30 March, he left no doubt where his loyalties lay by declaring that his oath to the pope could not bind him to violate England's laws or God's prerogative. With all this in the bag, Cromwell could duly proceed to ponder the endgame, which now developed a new momentum.

Around September 1532, Anne had finally consented to share the king's bed with the result that in December 1532 or January 1533, she became pregnant. Then, on 25 January, Henry married her in secret within his private chapel at Whitehall. In a hushed ceremony quite unlike the one she had wished for, only four or five witnesses were said to have been present, one of whom, ironically, was Henry Norris of the king's privy chamber, who would later be accused of adulterous dealings with the new bride. But while the king now had his wedding, he also required something much more important: a subtle and compelling case for the validity of the marriage that would satisfy a majority of the Commons, temporal peers and moderate episcopacy alike. Equally importantly, he required a statesmanlike justification of his actions for the benefit of those outside England. For these purposes the case had to be self-evident and without pleading, and as such, it would be necessary to go to the source of the issues in a way that Henry himself had never conceived. It would require, in fact, all Thomas Cromwell's expertise as lawyer and manager of parliamentary business to bring such things to pass.

Ultimately, however, once the necessary imagination and rigour had been applied to the problem, the solution was simple enough. Cromwell was, after all, an unsurpassed reader of political runes and he demonstrated this to perfection as events now ran their course. Constitutional granite rather than theological quicksand was to be the foundation of his approach. While the Almighty's preferences were to be taken as read, the invalidity of papal claims would be demonstrated on legal grounds backed up by historical precedent. They would be undermined more pragmatically, too, in terms of the delays, expense and general inconvenience entailed by papal jurisdiction. In a nutshell, the pope and his cronies were to be beaten out of the undergrowth of canon law and scriptural interpretation, and then clinically despatched in the cool, clear daylight of hard historical fact and practical necessity.

All of these principles were evident in the Act in Restraint of Appeals to Rome, which was passed in March 1533. With one deft magician's tug, this seminal measure pulled the carpet from under both Catherine and the pope by denying her right to seek legal recourse to Rome in the matter of her divorce. The Act also outlined the theoretical underpinning of the entire Henrician Reformation that would follow. The key to all was the 'imperial idea', that is, the principle that England was a self-contained political unit wholly insulated and independent from the legal authority of any 'foreign prince'. In an age that was uneasy with change or novelty of any kind, it was wholly predictable, of course, that Henry's imperial aspirations should have been justified by reference to 'old authentic histories and chronicles', even if this did involve nothing less than a series of blatant fabrications. Indeed, if ever any measure achieved an irresistible momentum from the self-confidence of its assertion rather than the self-evidence of its content, this applied to the so-called Act of Appeals. It was predictable, too, that the break with Rome would be presented more as a routine tidying exercise than as a moral crusade or historical watershed. Its true nature and implications were not dwelt upon to any degree and, as such, for the nation at large (and to some extent for the king, too) the measure became law almost, as it were, in a fit of absent-mindedness.

But with Catherine's legal options irretrievably hamstrung, she could now be dealt with unceremoniously. On 2 April a depleted Convocation speedily declared that it was unlawful for a man to marry his deceased brother's wife, that papal dispensations were void and that the consummation of Catherine's marriage to Prince Arthur had been proven beyond doubt. Within a few days she was also told of her husband's new marriage, as a consequence of which she would revert to the status of Princess of Wales. She may well have come to hear, too, how, on Easter Eve, Anne was attended in greater state than she herself had ever been. Preceded by trumpeters and with sixty ladies in her suite, she made her way in glory to a service at the Chapel Royal where she was prayed for publicly as queen. To seal proceedings, on 23 May Thomas Cranmer delivered his verdict at Dunstable that Henry's union with Queen Catherine had been invalid from the outset. At the last, then, the queen had been trapped and trussed unfussily enough. Spanish pride, honour and obduracy had proven no more a defence against the budding constitutional revolution than control of the moral high ground had been or would be during the traumatic months ahead.

All that remained was the finishing touch and on 1 June, Whit Sunday, Anne Boleyn was crowned Queen of England. But not, it must be said, amid the warmth and ardour that she craved so much. Instead, the ceremonies and festivities were described by the imperial ambassador as 'cold, meagre and uncomfortable and dissatisfying to everybody'. 'Sitting in her hair' as a maiden bride and wearing a string of pearls 'bigger than chick peas', she was borne in a litter from the Tower to Westminster Abbey through crowds that refused to cheer her. The customary cry of *'Dieu garde la reine'* was not to be heard anywhere along the route and when one of Anne's suite asked the Lord Mayor to teach his citizens better manners, he is said to have retorted sharply that he could not command people's hearts any more than the king was able. It was left to Anne's fool, a much travelled woman who had visited Jerusalem in her younger days, to defend her mistress with her best attempt at sarcasm. Seeing how few of the onlookers took off their hats to the queen, she yelled, 'I think you all have scurvy heads and dare not uncover!'

Nor should Henry have been surprised at the general display of popular disfavour. He had, after all, married Anne against the advice of his councillors and in flagrant disregard of both Catherine's dignity and status. He had blatantly ignored, too, the considerable threat posed by pope and emperor. 'All the world is astonished at it', wrote one contemporary of Henry's marriage to Anne, 'for it looks like a dream and even those who take her part know not whether to laugh or cry.' At best, the court had for years shown only feigned deference to the new queen for her royal lover's sake. Indeed, during that time she had progressively alienated most leading men and women, including her own blood relatives. Anne's aunt, the Duchess of Norfolk, for example, now refused to attend her niece's coronation. Furthermore, Anne's free-flowing vitriol had offended not only her father but also her uncle, the Duke of Norfolk, who considered her a 'she-devil' – and not without reason, it might be added, for she was said to have heaped more insults upon him 'than a dog'. It was little wonder, therefore, that at her Eastertide appearance in 1533, the king was reported to be 'very watchful' of his courtiers' reaction to his second wife, even begging them afterwards 'to go and visit and make their court to the new queen'.

Certainly, if Henry's courtiers held Anne in low esteem, the commons roundly hated her 'It is a thing to note that the common people always dislike her', wrote the Spanish merchant de Guaras, and even if this Spaniard's observation was not entirely impartial, it was confirmed by other reports. The Venetian ambassador, for example, was expecting in August 1530 that a rebellion would actually occur in the event of Henry's marriage to Anne. In the same year, too, Chapuys was reporting 'the wishes of the whole country for the preservation of the marriage and the downfall of the Lady'. Women, it seems, remained particularly hostile to Anne, although that hearty misogynist Edward Hall attributed this solely to the fact that they were 'more wilful than wise or learned'. Nevertheless, royal representatives who came to Oxford to advance the case for the annulment were met by furious females armed with rocks, and a preacher in Salisbury who supported the king's actions had to be rescued before he 'suffered much at the hands of women'. Meanwhile at St Paul's in London, a woman responded to a sermon favouring the divorce by calling the preacher a liar and claiming that the king should be chastised for undermining the institution of marriage.

Not altogether surprisingly, of course, some concerns about the marriage were less rational. In 1532, a Colchester man was questioned about his prophecy that a 'battle between priests' was imminent, as a result of the king's abandonment of his true wife. Under other circumstances, his dementia might surely have passed unchallenged, but during this period of invasive uncertainty and tension, even such agitated ramblings attracted the keen notice of the authorities. Elsewhere many simple people were 'greatly agitated' by another prediction, which had begun to circulate from around 1530 onwards, to the effect that the kingdom was to be destroyed by a woman. And all the while a series of occult marvels and heavenly portents seemed to confirm the imminence of grave danger. A monstrous dead fish, said to be some 90 feet in length was beached on the northern coast and not long afterwards a freak tide flowed into the Thames for nine straight hours, causing the river to rise higher than ever before, to the very steps of the chapel at Greenwich. Even more ominously, there was talk of a ball of fire falling from the sky near the same place and for some weeks a comet with a long tail 'in the form of a luminous silver beard', was visible before daybreak.

If the subdued silence of the coronation and the supernatural portents were perplexing enough, any slender hope that Henry may have harboured that the pope would accept Cranmer's annulment of the marriage was soon shattered. The archbishop had delivered his verdict as a 'Legate of the Apostolic See', but such a claim lacked all credibility, of course. Furthermore, the pope's idea of legality, on this occasion at least, was far less supple than the king's and his willingness to play piggy in the middle to Charles V's genuine political might and Henry VIII's rude banter was waning fast. In July, therefore, Clement declared that Anne was not the King of England's wife and Henry was excommunicated. Though the sentence was suspended until September to give him time to put away his mistress and repent, this was purely a notional gesture. For half a decade, Henry had been vandalising the bridges between England and Rome and, seeing no good purpose in further attempts at repair, the pope himself had burnt the last one. In any case, by the time that Clement's deadline expired events had moved on again, for on 7 September, Henry's second daughter was born.

Letters announcing the birth of an heir had been produced in advance of its occurrence but now, in all cases, the word 'prince' was wistfully altered by the addition of a solitary 's'. The depth of Henry's dismay at the birth of Princess Elizabeth should not be underestimated, 'God has forgotten him entirely', noted Chapuys, 'hardening him in his obstinacy to punish and ruin him.' At Princess Mary's birth seventeen years earlier, Henry had made light of his disappointment, confident that sons would follow. Now in middle age there was more anxiety, more frustration, more impatience and less time. Anne had, after all, already experienced one unsuccessful pregnancy and the newborn Princess Elizabeth was no real consolation. In the event, neither Henry nor Anne attended the christening at Greenwich, and Chapuys considered the christening of the 'little bastard' to have been 'cold and disagreeable'. With barefaced cheek, Henry had actually demanded the use of the Princess Mary's christening robe, though Catherine refused to give up the garment, which had been brought initially from Spain and was her own property. Even spite could not moderate the king's gloom on this occasion, however. The tournament he had planned was abandoned and the fireworks unlit, as were the traditional celebratory bonfires of the City of London. And predictably there were jibes. Two friars, for instance, were arrested for saying they had heard that Princess Elizabeth had been christened in hot water but that 'it was not hot enough'.

Thereafter, the final threads linking England to Rome were systematically severed during the fifth session of the Reformation Parliament, which opened in mid-January 1534 and lasted until March. One of the new laws, the Act for the Submission of the Clergy, put the clergy's submission following the Supplication Against the Ordinaries of 1532 into statutory form and the penalty of fine or imprisonment was imposed on all who acted contrary to its provisions. Similarly, appeals to Rome, which the Act of the previous year had prohibited only in certain cases, were now forbidden under all circumstances. Pleas from the archbishop's court would now be made, instead, to the Court of Chancery and a fresh Annates Act confirmed the conditional measure of the previous July, thus ensuring that these dues could no longer be paid to Rome and enforcing the acceptance of bishops nominated by the Crown. Pennies as well as principles were also at issue in the Dispensations Act, which stopped all payments to Rome, including Peter's Pence. At the same time, the act laid down that dispensations allowing departures from canon law should, in future, be issued by the Archbishop of Canterbury. And for all her dogged resistance, Catherine of Aragon was now to be reduced, as planned, to the status of Dowager Princess of Wales.

Strangely, though, even at this remarkably late stage, Henry may still have been entertaining some vain remnant of hope for reconciliation with Rome, since the Dispensations Act was not to take effect until the feast of John the Baptist, some three months later, unless the king should decide to the contrary. In addition, the king was enabled to annul the whole or any part of the Act at any time before the feast day. There was, however, no such eventuality, for on 23 March 1534, the very day of Parliament's ratification of Henry's marriage to Anne, Pope Clement once again demonstrated his control of the initiative. With what by now must have become relief rather than remorse, he closed the royal case, which had been 'under consideration' all this time in Rome, by solemnly pronouncing Henry's first marriage valid. One month later, the pope died and by September 1535, Paul III, his replacement, had confirmed Henry's excommunication. Ironically, then, the Henrician Reformation was from some perspectives ultimately the tale of Rome's break with England rather than vice versa. Perhaps, in view of Henry's almost pathological incapacity for decisive action, there could have been no other way. But, of course, having temporised agonisingly until the decisive moves were taken by the pontiff, Henry now duly responded with an empty show of vigour. A proclamation was immediately drawn up, which ordered the pope's name to be struck out of all prayer books, so that it be 'never more (except in contumely and reproach) remembered, but perpetually suppressed and obscured'. Though the final goal in the match had, in effect, been scored by the opposition, Henry could not be denied his triumphal pose.

In March 1534, the political objective that, ostensibly at least, had driven Henry during the preceding years of trouble was at last attained. The Act of Succession now stipulated that any offspring from Henry's marriage to Anne would become undisputed direct heirs to the throne of England. This was in its own right, of course, hardly a surprising measure. Henry could take or leave a new Church, perhaps, but from his own perspective at least, a healthy male heir by the woman upon whom he had hung his conscience was an utter necessity. More significantly, however, the Act also contained an oath to the succession, which any subject could be called upon to swear and which included in its preamble clear-cut recognition of the royal supremacy. Surely enough, it was within this oath rather than the outer casing of the Act that the terrorist explosive was, in fact, subtly packed by Cromwell.

For the time being, the formal process of religious nationalisation was finally completed in November 1534 by the Act of Supremacy. In the course of its long development, the Catholic Church had been empowered by a doctrinal and financial monopoly and a comprehensive system of discipline, which tethered the thoughts and purses of its flock to Rome. Now Henry sought to finalise his authority both in practice as well as in theory by a concerted programme of expropriation, involving both funds and minds. The Act of Supremacy granted the king control of clerical discipline and the right to correct the opinions of preachers. More importantly still, it accorded him the right to try heresy cases and, as such, confirmed his ultimate control of all religious teaching. From this point onwards, technically at least, Henry not only controlled how his people behaved, but also what they believed.

The so-called Act of First Fruits and Tenths, which followed, was a necessary accompanying measure. Taxes formerly paid to the pope were now made payable to the Crown and all beneficed clergy were to pay a tenth of their net income to the king annually. Furthermore, the king would not be content, as the pope had been, with an assessment of income made in 1292, which was, naturally enough, completely unattuned to the inflationary spirals of the sixteenth century. If Henry now owned his Church, then the yield would have to be a rich one and to ensure that he received what was fully his due, the new Vicegerent in ecclesiastical matters, Thomas Cromwell, ordered the compilation of the so-called *Valor Ecclesiasticus*, a detailed account of all clerical incomes. Cromwell would, in this case, rob Peter to pay Henry, and he would do so without compunction. 'The Latin Papa', wrote Henry Brinklow in *The Complaynt of Roderick Mors*, 'had been translated into the English Pay Pay.'

But much more ominously still – simultaneously with the passage of the Act of Supremacy through Parliament in November 1534 – Cromwell also created the means for silencing all opposition. His Treason Act involved an unprecedented broadening of the concept of treason to encompass all types of 'malicious' attack on the king, Queen Anne or the succession, including those made even orally or in writing. This so-called 'law of words' was designed to root out the seditious 'imps of the said bishop of Rome', and it left few, if any, hiding places within the legal foliage. It was now made treasonable, for instance, to call the king a heretic, schismatic, tyrant, infidel or usurper, and though it was not made an offence to refuse to answer questions relating to the supremacy until 1536, with the Act Extinguishing the Authority of the Bishop of Rome, there was little refuge to be had even in honourable silence, as Sir Thomas More would find to his cost, 'It was', said Lord Montague at the time, 'a strange world as words were made treason.'

Significantly, the Treason Act would be repealed in the very first

Parliament of the next reign on the grounds that it was likely to 'appear to men of exterior realms and many of the king's majesty's subjects very strait, sore, extreme and terrible'. Yet there was no denying, of course, that men had been executed for words rather than actions well before 1534 when their words had been 'constructed' as treason. And dubious evidence had, for that matter, always been a feature of political trials, too: the cases of Clarence in 1478 and of Warwick in 1499 are striking examples of such miscarriages. Nor, it must be said, were all those arraigned under the new law of treason necessarily subjected to its full rigours. In the event, only one in every three prosecutions led to condemnation. When Cromwell heard, for instance, that an absent-minded canon nearing his eightieth year had mistakenly prayed for 'Catherine the Queen' instead of Anne, he did not press for punishment. Similarly, a drunken servant of the Duchess of Northumberland who had been 'in danger of his limbs' for criticising the king was eventually released from prison when his mistress interceded for him on the grounds that he had been insensible at the time and now had no memory of his offence.

Nevertheless, the arrest or interrogation of the king's subjects for such ill-considered remarks served to create what would become by degrees a pervasive culture of suspicion and denunciation. And even if some two-thirds of those accused of treason were acquitted, pardoned or had their cases dropped, up to 130 people still lost their lives for 'treasonable words' between 1534 and 1540. Moreover, the real significance of Henry VIII's terror lies not so much in its scale as in its very nature, for this was a terror inflicted mainly upon victims of conscience who were readily condemned on the basis of false witness and subsequently executed with the utmost cruelty. No less reprehensibly, it was also a form of terror employed not so much to preserve the king and his realm, but as a cynical weapon of everyday politics. 'It is rumoured', a correspondent wrote to the king's aunt Lady Lisle in 1538, 'that a person should be committed to the Tower for saying that this month will be rainy and full of wet, next month, death, and the third month, war. He will be kept there till experience shows the truth of his policy.' And it was Henry himself who once told Cranmer that 'if they have you once in prison, three or four knaves will soon be procured to witness against you'. Perhaps it was hardly surprising, then, that when Anne Boleyn heard from the lieutenant of the Tower how 'the poorest subject the King hath, hath justice', she laughed.

II

The Lion Learns His Strength

'The Bishop of Rome's authority is good and lawful within this realm according to the old trade and that is the true way. And the contrary of the King's part but usurpations, deceived by flattery and adulation [...] It is marvellous that the King's grace could not be contented with that noble queen, his very true and undoubted wife, Queen Catherine.'

Words attributed to Robert Hobbes, Abbot of Woburn, which led to his trial on 14 June 1538, and for which he was sentenced to be hung, drawn and quartered.

As the 1530s ran their tumultuous course, the news of England's season of bloodshed would resound throughout Europe. 'The affairs of England', wrote one Italian, 'are commonly managed more than barbarously.' 'In England, death has snatched away everyone of worth, or fear has shrunk them up', commented another, while Marillac, the French ambassador, would observe in March 1540 that 'every accusation in this country is called treason'. Closer to home there was equal shock and dismay. 'Thy father's father never saw such a world', a Berkshire man observed ruefully. Here, then, was a country ruled by a king whose parliaments enacted forty-four penal statutes between 1529 and 1539, who expelled the gypsies and sanctioned the execution of those who remained, who made ready use of the verbal treason law (which allowed conviction on the strength of only one witness) and who caused honest monks and friars to suffer the grisly fate of traitors at Glastonbury, Norwich and elsewhere. This, too, was a king who was said to revel at times in his inhumanity. On the eve of St John in 1535, for instance, a parody of the apocalypse was performed in London, in which an actor playing the king featured prominently. So eager was Henry to see the spectacle, we are told, that he came in from the country especially, travelling 'ten miles at two o'clock one night'. Nor were his efforts wasted, it seems, for as the players depicted him boisterously beheading the clergy, we hear that he 'discovered himself' to the audience, so that he could laugh at greater ease.

No doubt, this was a violent time when torture and brutality conformed neatly with the social realities of the day. Did not a thronging crowd of 20,000 people gather one Sunday in July 1539 to savour the gruesome spectacle of Cratwell, London's hangman, dancing on a gibbet for robbing a booth at Bartholomew Fair? And when four years earlier thirteen Dutch Anabaptists had been burnt at the stake, they went to their fate not only unlamented, but without even an official record of their names. All Tudor Englishmen knew full well that, in the king's own words, 'living in a commonwealth, men must conform themselves to the more part in authority'. Nevertheless, when Henry suggested to the Earl of Derby that the abbot and monks of Sawley be hung from a 'long piece of timber [...] out of the steeple of their monastery', he seemed, as on so many other occasions, to be less than fully driven by the dictates of social order and political justice. It was savage enough that John Wyot, a carpenter from Essex who had bad-mouthed the king, should be set upon the pillory with one of his ears nailed to a board behind his head. It was degrading enough that he should have to stand in public with a dunce's hat upon his head inscribed with the legend 'for lewd words'. But what kind of mocking cruelty was it that required the man to remain thus until he found the courage to sever the ear himself? A better ruler would have trodden the path of religious revolution wrapped in a swarm of misgivings but in Henry's case, such misgivings were always dispelled ultimately by a deadly combination of implacable conceit and blind machismo.

Like so many consuming addictions, Henry VIII's dependence on brutality began modestly enough and was fuelled by the dutiful compliance of those around him. Being a staunch upholder of the law, if not justice, Henry could identify his victims swiftly and unequivocally. Meanwhile, Thomas Cromwell, as the chief executant of the king's wrath, was fully prepared, out of loyalty and cold-blooded pragmatism, to cut a swathe through those who refused to swear allegiance to the new order that he was fashioning on his master's behalf. For both Henry and Cromwell, there were neither unworldly people, nor any such thing as innocent non-compliance in these dangerous times. The government's elaborate spy system therefore threatened great nobles and drunken yokels alike, and just as the Franciscan Observants of Greenwich, the Bridgettines of Syon and above all the London Carthusians might not be allowed to keep their austere, contemplative isolation from events, so Sir Thomas More's studied silence, which echoed throughout Europe, would have to be quashed by all necessary means.

The king's descent into manic repression had begun, in fact, with the case of Elizabeth Barton, a deluded epileptic girl who had visions that rarely came true. Known to her devotees as the Nun or Holy Maid of Kent, she had been employed as a domestic servant to one Thomas Cobb, a steward of the archiepiscopal estates in the parish of Aldington, approximately 12 miles from Canterbury. Barton was some eighteen years of age when, around Easter 1525, she was first seized by serious illness, and from that time forth she began to experience trance-like states that soon brought her a curious form of venerated celebrity status. It was said that 'while lying unconscious she uttered mysterious words', and that, on other occasions, as her tongue lolled and her eyes stood out wondrously from their sockets, 'a voice came out of her belly speaking sweetly of heaven and terribly of hell'. Prophecies became her particular speciality after she happened to forecast the impending death of a child belonging to her employer, and the cash value of these exalted states was quickly perceived by Richard Masters, the rector of Aldington. Soon enough, the shrine of Our Lady at Court-Le-Street, which was the scene of her inspired ecstasies, became irresistibly attractive to pilgrims and equally lucrative to the neighbourhood. Before long, too, she had acquired the services of one Edward Bocking, monk and cellarer of Christchurch, who became by turns her confessor, spiritual adviser and impresario.

The king himself paid little heed to Barton's revelations until her prophetic gaze was finally turned on him, for she was soon visited by those anxious to hear from heaven upon the royal marriage, as well as the heresies and schisms that were then dividing the realm. To such inquirers she declared that Henry would not survive his second marriage more than a month, and that once united to Anne he would no longer be king in the eyes of God. Her prophecies then began to take an even more sinister turn when, in 1532, she had visions of Christ re-crucified, as a result of the king's adultery, and of Anne Boleyn as a Jezebel whom dogs would eat. She also claimed that angels had shown her the place reserved in hell for Henry and in October 1532, at Canterbury, actually succeeded in forcing herself into the royal presence. Though plainly directed by Bocking, and like many deluded people given to subtle forms of deception, Elizabeth Barton became the focus of a genuine moral protest against the divorce and in the process her head was turned. Now she entered into communication with papal ambassadors and wrote to the pope himself.

So it was that in July 1533, the government determined that the 'mad maid' or 'hypocrite nun' would have to be dealt with as an enemy of the State. Following their imprisonment in London, Barton and her companions, including Bocking and Masters, were examined in Star Chamber and forced under torture to confess their guilt. Accordingly on 23 November 1533, the nun and six of her associates were made to do public penance. But this was by no means the end of the matter, for although the nun had been thwarted, the sentiments she embodied were not, and the government's only remedy, therefore, was to follow the tenuous threads linking the Holy Maid to the king's other 'enemies'. With this object in mind the chancellor, Thomas Audley, spoke publicly in November of the great personages implicated in the affair, while Henry pressed for a judicial declaration that it was heresy to believe the political revelations of the nun, and high treason to fail to report them. In the meantime, on 20 March 1534, Barton herself was attainted of high treason with five others and on 20 April all were drawn on hurdles to the gallows at Tyburn. There they were hanged, cut down while still alive and beheaded before great crowds.

Around this time there were also other ripples of defiance from less high-profile opponents of the marriage. In April, an Oxford midwife was imprisoned for referring to the 'goggle-eyed whore Nan Bullen', and Robert Feron, a priest, was also jailed for declaring that 'the King's wife in fornication, this matron Anne, be more stinking than a sow'. Later, a Mrs Burgyn of Watlington in Oxfordshire was interrogated before three justices for exclaiming to her midwife, whilst in the extremes of labour, that 'for her honesty and cunning [...] she might be midwife to the Queen of England, if it were Queen Catherine, and, if it were Queen Anne, she was too good to be her midwife, for she was a whore and a harlot for her living'. Nor was the king himself spared entirely from the lash of scurrilous tongues. John Garle, master of Manton College in Rutland, ascribed Henry's difficulties in fathering children to the fact that he 'did occupy so many whores and harlots', while Dr Maydland, a grey friar of London, vented his displeasure at both Henry and Anne by declaring his hope 'to see the King suffer a violent and shameful death and [...] the mischievous whore, the Queen, buried'. Just how far these colourful fulminations represented a general distaste for events among the general populace is, of course, impossible to gauge. Some of the protesters, like a certain Mrs Amadas, for instance, appear to have been driven less by righteous indignation than by some form of morbid derangement. Having declared that the king was 'cursed with God's own mouth', she went on to affirm that he had for some time been plying her with gifts, in order that she, too, might succumb to his lewd advances.

Nevertheless, the most significant resistance to government policy would, of course, prove to be the least hysterical. The Charterhouse of London stood just outside the city wall and close to Smithfield. It was an abode of peace where the Carthusian monks, whose home it was, spent their time in prayer and adoration, immured until this time from the world and its distracted political turnings. Predictably, therefore, when the king's commissioners arrived to make the monks swear to the oath of succession, the prior, John Houghton, told them with steely humility that 'it pertained not to his vocation and calling, nor that of his subjects, to meddle in or discuss the King's business'. Under pressure, however, Houghton admitted that he could not see how the first marriage could be invalid, since it had been duly solemnised and for so many years unquestioned. For thus complying with the request that he express an honest opinion, Houghton would now be subjected to the full violence of the new Treason Act.

Accordingly, on 4 May he was dragged through the city to Tyburn on a hurdle, along with Dr Reynolds, the Bridgettine from Syon, John Hale, the parson of Isleworth and the Carthusian priors of Axholme and Beauvale. Thomas More, from his prison window, saw them go and commented to Margaret Roper who was visiting him, 'So! Dost not thou see, Meg, that these blessed fellows be now as cheerfully going to their deaths as bridegrooms to their marriages.' Not all spectators were so benevolent, however. Upon the victims' arrival at Tyburn, it was found that the whole Boleyn clique had turned out to see the show. Norfolk was there with his nephew, Viscount Rochford, and the Duke of Richmond was also present. Next arrived the chamberlain, Henry Norris, with forty horsemen who were, no doubt for additional dramatic effect, all masked. It was something new, wrote Chapuys, that young Richmond, Norfolk, Wiltshire and other magnates had stood 'quite near the sufferers'. Rumour had it that the king himself was among this ghoulish congregation, 'which was very probable', added Chapuys, 'seeing that all the court were there'. Indeed, among some courtiers, disguised as Scottish borderers, there had been, it was claimed, one to whom extraordinary deference had been paid.

And so the dreadful spectacle proceeded. Houghton, perhaps fortunately for him, was the first to suffer. When, as was the custom, the executioner asked for forgiveness, the monk duly kissed him and prayed as well for the bystanders. He was then hanged and almost immediately cut down. Revived with vinegar, he was next stripped of the gown of his Order, except for his hair shirt. Finally, he was castrated and disembowelled before having his heart torn out and rubbed in his face. One arm was later sent to be nailed above the door of the Charterhouse as a gory admonition to the remaining monks within and the world at large without. Meanwhile, the other victims had been made to watch in patient fortitude until their turn came. 'No change', said one eyewitness, 'was noticed in their colour or tone of speech, and while the execution was going on they preached and exhorted the bystanders with the greatest boldness to do well and obey the king in everything that was not against the honour of God or the Church.' In contempt for the clerical estate, all were butchered in the gowns of their orders.

Incredibly, such intimidation was unavailing in numerous cases. In May 1535, three more monks, Humphrey Middlemore, William Exmew and Sebastian Newdigate were locked up in the Tower and thence sent to a stinking dungeon in Newgate jail. By no means all the martyrs were, in fact, spiritual athletes by background and training, avidly embracing the scaffold as a blessed release from lifelong privation. Newdigate, for instance, had once been a carefree young man of Henry's court, but now he and the others were tied to posts with iron collars around their necks and 'great fetters' riveted to their legs. There they were left for seventeen days, loaded with lead, unable to sit and 'never loosed for any natural necessity' before being executed at Tyburn in the same manner as Houghton. Under such extreme duress some monks did, indeed, submit, but ten more persisted and were starved to death at Newgate.

Meanwhile, John Fisher's eventual decapitation at Smithfield on the morning of 22 June 1535 came as no surprise. Described by Chapuys as the 'paragon of Christian prelates, both for learning and holiness', to his enemies in high places Fisher was wilful, deluded and dangerous. For his part, the chronicler Edward Hall thought the bishop 'a man of very good life, but wonderfully deceived therein'. Fisher had, in fact, been from the outset an outspoken opponent of the divorce, defending Catherine at

Blackfriars in 1529 and declaring openly that he would willingly die like St John the Baptist on behalf of the indissolubility of her marriage. Certainly, death held no terror for a soul of his calibre. On the contrary, it had been the somewhat obsessive object of his daily meditation for many a year. 'And lest that the memory of death might hap to slip from his mind', wrote one contemporary, 'he always accustomed to set upon one end of the altar a dead man's skull which was also set before him at his table as he dined or supped.' Clearly, this was not the man to settle for the submissive silence observed by most other public figures.

There had already been a second attempt on Fisher's life – this time involving an unknown sharpshooter – before he was imprisoned in April 1533 to gag his protests at the annulment of Henry's marriage and Queen Anne's coronation. But after this temporary confinement, the bishop was still no more pliant and he now took a step, which guaranteed him either a martyr's or a traitor's end, depending upon chosen perspective. Ultimately, he had entered into treasonous correspondence with Charles V, which was intercepted on the Continent by Cromwell's spies, and in this rare instance royal justice was actually impeccable, since Fisher had called for nothing less than holy war. Indeed by September 1533 he was urging the emperor to invade England and depose the king: a crusade, which, he maintained, would be as pleasing to God as war against the Turk. As such, his refusal to take the oath of succession, which brought about his final incarceration, merely confirmed the inevitable. The Bishop of Rochester's case was, of course, indefensible in law and when, in May 1535, Henry heard the infuriating news that the new pope, Paul III, had appointed him a cardinal in blatant defiance, the matter was hermetically sealed. With his usual bravado, the king swore that by the time the cardinal's hat arrived, the old man for whom it was intended would have no head to wear it. And on this occasion, at least, Henry was true to his word.

The scaffold was still being erected when, on 22 June, Fisher rode into view on Tower Hill. One who was present at the execution considered the emaciated victim 'a very image of death and (as one might say) Death in a man's shape and using a man's voice'. He had awaited the day of his ordeal in dread ever since Cromwell informed him of it, telling him at the same time that the pope had made him a cardinal. Now he had still longer to wait as he sat astride his mule in heavy silence watching the unfinished preparations. When, however, the arena for his suffering was finally ready, Fisher 'spoke to the people boldly', said the Bishop of Faenza, telling them to be loving and obedient to the king, who was good by nature but had been deceived in this matter. As for himself, he confessed that since he was only flesh, he feared death as any man would. But, in the event, Fisher seems to have found the courage to 'suffer cheerfully his impending punishment'. As the onlookers prayed, he knelt down with all the difficulty of an elderly man, and laid his head on the block and died. Thereafter, we are told, the 'headless carcass of the Chancellor [of Cambridge] was left naked on the scaffold for the rest of the hot June day, saving that one, for pity and humanity, cast a little straw upon it'.

The king was heard to remark afterwards that Fisher's death had been the least cruel that could be devised. He had, after all, been neither poisoned nor boiled in lead, nor hanged, nor burned nor tortured, but 'sworded'. The bishop's few personal possessions were duly taken to the king's use, among them a small book with a gilt cover and the French king's arms on the inside, a mitre set with a worthless stone and pearl, knitted gloves embossed with gold, and some plate of silver gilt. The bishop's head, meanwhile, was placed on a pike on London Bridge amid the others that were perched there in putrefaction. Curiously, however, after a fortnight it remained 'fresher' than the rest, according to a Spanish report, and was therefore knocked into the Thames to quell suspicion among the credulous of divine approval for the victim. In just over a fortnight, the head of Thomas More would take its place on the self-same pike.

When called to Lambeth on 13 April 1534 to take the oath to the succession, More had maintained that he could not do so 'without the jeopardy of my soul to perpetual damnation'. Four days later, therefore, he was sent to the Tower. Time and again in the second half of 1534 he was coaxed and cajoled by Cromwell and a string of skilled interrogators, but refused absolutely to be drawn on his opinions, for they were, he said, 'secret in my conscience'. Naturally, as an outstanding authority on the law and former bosom friend of the king, More would have to be cowed or culled. Even so, the principal secretary was by no means a sadistic man and he very likely assumed that his prisoner, as a rational political player, would be capable of weighing realities and balancing them to personal advantage. For Cromwell, after all, a man might sell his soul for a worthy cause and, with a good conscience, live from the proceeds for many a year. In view of all this, it is not, perhaps, so surprising that he apparently went to considerable lengths to accommodate his adversary's intransigence. On 7 May 1535, for instance, he is said to have led a deputation to the Tower to seek More's compliance and it seems that on this occasion he spoke 'full gently' to him.

The forbearance of any ambitious pragmatist is not, however, dependable and surely enough Cromwell returned to More's lodging in the Tower on 3 June in very different circumstances and with very different ends in mind. Since the previous interrogation, news of Fisher's cardinalate had reached England and the king now demanded that both he and More pay the appropriate price for the pope's provocation. Therefore, Cromwell was no longer amenable and informed More that the king considered 'he had been the occasion of much grudge and harm in the realm'. Accordingly, the time for prevarication was at an end and a straightforward answer regarding the supremacy was demanded of him. More said in response that the choice confronting him was an impossible one – either to affirm the statute 'against my conscience to the loss of my soul, or precisely against it to the destruction of my body'. However, Cromwell, unlike his master, knew a bottom line when he saw one and now became bent upon his adversary's destruction. Almost at once, then, he began to contrive what he knew would be, on technical grounds, a difficult case for a State trial. In the meantime, now that kindness was an irrelevance to 'progress', More could be punished by removal of his books, which was carried out promptly by the Solicitor General, Sir Richard Rich, on 12 June.

At his trial the accused defended himself with considerable skill and fortitude. Challenging the prosecution to prove its case and claiming the right of silence to avoid incriminating himself, his strategy was as subtle as it was simple. Nevertheless, he foundered ultimately upon Rich's claim that on 12 June, when he had been relieved of the books that were such a source of consolation to him, he had spoken treasonous words. Whether or not this evidence was accurate is unknown. Certainly, More denied it vehemently and the two other men present at the time, Southwell and Palmer, could not confirm it. However, it might well have been that Rich, who was a skilled legal practitioner and, like many of that kind, an artful tickler of human frailty, did indeed entice More into an indiscreet form of words that could be construed as a denial of the royal supremacy. More's fondness for hypothetical 'putting of cases' may well have led to a fatal slip of wording that technically, at least, questioned the royal supremacy. With supreme irony, then, More's barefaced cleverness may thus have been his ultimate undoing. Whatever the case, the jury appear to have been convinced readily enough, for, after they retired, they needed no more than a quarter of an hour to return a verdict of guilty.

As he lay in prison awaiting death another attempt was made to wring a retraction from him, but More's mind was composed, and he now wished only to be released from the troubles of this world. While in the Tower, he told his friends, he was chiefly concerned with preparing for death. To lighten his sorrow he wrote songs. He often thought, too, of his sovereign who had in turn, befriended him, coerced him, dispossessed him and finally condemned him to death. But his thoughts remained charitable, for loyalty to the king was as deeply ingrained in More as loyalty to his conscience. He had prayed again and again, it seems, kneeling on the stone floor of his cell, until prayer banished all resentment. In fact, even if More's modern detractors are correct and he had, indeed, been an all-too-human man of ambition in his earlier life and no mean persecutor of heretics himself, it was precisely his former worldliness that now made the innocent mirth and unaffected piety of his final days all the more impressive. And if, as seems likely, true saintliness derives not so much from innate perfection as from the honest struggle against inner weakness, then perhaps More's later canonisation was not inapt after all.

On the morning of 6 July, while the king was hunting outside Reading, the sometime Lord Chancellor of England was conducted to Tower Hill, clad in an old frieze gown and carrying a red cross. Prematurely aged, he needed a staff as he tottered on his way and required assistance to mount the rickety scaffold. Reproached by a spectator for a legal judgement he had once made, he said he would make it again, and made some wry jokes. As the sheriff's officers helped him up the scaffold, he thanked them, adding that when it was time to come down, he could be left to 'shift for myself'. Finally, after tipping the headsman a gold angel, he told him he had a short neck, and asked that he be allowed to lay his beard over the block away from the fall of the axe, since it had done no harm. 'I die', he said, 'the King's good servant, but God's first.'

The treatment of Henry's high-profile opponents should not, of course, obscure the fact that they themselves represented a tiny minority of active, overt opponents to the breach with Rome. The Carthusians, for instance, were most definitely the exception rather than the rule. Unlike them, the Observant Franciscans, whom Henry had attacked first, because of the danger they posed as itinerant preachers, were soon neutralised. A number were imprisoned, but the rest fled the country and their seven houses were appropriated to the Crown. Similarly, only the Bridgettine leaders were arrested, after which their brothers, faced with the rigours of the Newgate and Marshalsea prisons, submitted. The episcopacy, too, toed the line. Although individuals like Bishop Stokesley of London harboured grave misgivings, they did not join John Fisher in outright resistance. Bishop Gardiner, indeed, even emerged as an ardent spokesman in favour of the royal supremacy, publishing in 1535, his *De Vera Obedientia*. England's bishops were, after all, the king's servants before all else and the badgering they had endured at Wolsey's hands made them all the more inclined to comply. Meanwhile, the response of the English nobility was weaker still. Prominent conservatives, such as the Duke of Norfolk, booked their passage as fellow travellers and enjoyed their first class accommodation. Doubtless, many others were also attracted by the prospect of material gain and they would not be disappointed.

Thomas Cromwell had been appointed Vicar-General or 'Vicegerent' in 1535, a post which placed him in control of all non-spiritual matters relating to the new Church of England, and one of his first actions in this new role had been to order the compilation of the so-called *Valor Ecclesiasticus* – a hungry assessment of all clerical incomes, which would serve before long to underpin the case for a swingeing attack on the monasteries. Ultimately, the survey showed that religious houses owned at least 10 per cent of the land in England and were the beneficiaries of a total annual revenue that, at £136,000, exceeded the Crown's in normal years. In view of this, the financial incentive for some degree of dissolution was manifest. Predictably, however, the preamble to the first Act of dissolution in 1536, which dealt with the smaller monasteries, adorned the move with stirring talk of noble aims and rational necessity. Any money accruing, it was claimed, would be turned to charitable and educational purposes. It was said, too, that the dissolution was occurring in order to develop a better disciplined and more streamlined monasticism.

This willingness to combine principle with ulterior motives was well demonstrated by the nature of the visitations organised in 1535 to report on the moral condition and status of the nation's monasteries. The commissioners who were to conduct these visitations were appointed with the avowed intention of remedying abuses and the ulterior purpose of providing a watertight pretext for wholesale destruction. As such, Cromwell chose his men well. They were for the most part doctors of law with experience in the work of the ecclesiastical courts, fully qualified at any time to act as counsel for the prosecution, and skilled in all the arts necessary to obtain a convenient verdict to their boss's liking. Their task was, of course, all the easier, since there was to be, in this case, no counsel for the defence.

The visitors were, with few exceptions, typical of their species. Dr Layton was a clubbable fellow who evidently loved to hear and tell a dirty story. He expected, as he said, that monks would be human, by which he meant that they would not be far removed from beasts. He died a pluralist and Dean of York, having ended his life of bureaucratic pillage by secretly pawning the Minster plate, which the chapter had to redeem strenuously after his death. Dr Legh, on the other hand, was an overbearing young don, who expected to be met by a procession at the west door of an abbey when he made his appearance in his velvet gown with retainers in attendance. He not only accused monks of immorality, but was notorious for the filthy suggestions he made to nuns. Dr ap Rice, who travelled in tow with Legh, was a coward with a murky past, while Dr London, Warden of New College, Oxford, was a bustling, choleric man, who was, in fairness, one of the better sort among his colleagues. Although he enjoyed destroying spurious relics and defacing monuments, he did at least spare the tomb of Blanche of Lancaster, because it was 'very beautiful'. He also showed some compassion for the friars he dismissed and wrote on their behalf to Cromwell. Even so, he was twice convicted of adultery and once of perjury, ending his life miserably in the Fleet Prison.

The reports produced by these luminaries of the inspectorial craft were said by some authorities to have been presented to Parliament in the form of a 'Black Book', which no longer exists. Now, however, they are to be found in the form of the fragmentary *Comperta*. In fairness, not all the reports that issued from these men were entirely negative. Layton, for example, reported well on Durham, and ap Rice commended the abbey at Laycock. Moreover, almost twenty years before Cromwell's inspectors brandished their quills in anger, some of their comments had already been anticipated by a string of predecessors. A contemporary letter of the Abbot of Warden about ignorance, drunkenness, fornication, violence and insubordination amongst his own monks does not make pretty reading. Similarly, in 1526, the Abbot of Waverley had been sent to investigate the monks of Thame and left no doubt about the widespread misdoing. The abbot there was accused of scandalous relations with a boy, running the estates in the interests of his favourites, letting buildings decay, keeping too many servants and too good a table, and failing to prevent his monks from enjoying themselves in the town. Again, the many charges of homosexuality made later (especially in the North) by Legh and Layton may well be multiplied through malice, yet a number of such cases do occur in the reports of earlier bishops' visitations and other reliable sources.

For all this, though, nowhere is there evidence of such general depravity as is found in the *Comperta* of Cromwell's visitors, who neatly classified the monks as sodomites, adulterers, thieves and superstitious. The disproportionate focus upon sexual misdemeanours betrays the underlying desire of the commissioners to slur and besmirch rather than to investigate and reform. Moreover, the underlying purpose of these visitations is further neatly demonstrated by the fact that when eventually those properties that passed to the king were resurveyed by new local commissioners, these men soon had to be replaced by the old gang, because they submitted reports utterly at variance with Cromwell's stooges. When, for instance, Henry received a report that the nuns of Catesby in Northamptonshire were as 'religious, decent and of as good obedience as we in time have seen or be like to see', he immediately accused the authors of taking bribes.

The overall tone of the reports found in the *Comperta* is, in fact, cheap and nasty like the men who, in the main, produced them. Both the smaller and greater monasteries alike were treated to the same demeaning and biased invasion, and the same grimy mantra of decadence and degeneracy drones on throughout the findings. At the convent at Lampley, 'Mariana Whyte had given birth three times, and Johanna Snaden, six'. At Lichfield 'two of the nuns were with child'. Abbot Hexham of Whitby 'took his cut at the proceeds from piracy' and the prior of Abbotsbury was caught 'wrongfully selling timber'. Perhaps the monks at Pershore had heard of the commissioners' approach, for they were reported to be 'drunk at mass'. In all, a day was generally sufficient for a bullying cross-examiner to extort damaging admissions from someone or other. Occasionally, however, Layton had to allot a second day, as at Newark College, Leicester, where he confessed he had discovered nothing. However, even here he went on to tell his sovereign: 'Tomorrow I will object against divers of them buggery and adultery.'

Layton, in fact, went about his distasteful task with especial gusto. Having exposed the Abbot of Langdon with his 'tender demoiselle', he wrote to Cromwell that 'it was a comedy for me, but a tragedy for the Abbot'. There is also, of course, Layton's famous report concerning Jennings, prior of

Maiden Bradley in Wiltshire: 'The prior hath but six children, and but one daughter yet married out of the goods of the monastery, trusting shortly to marry the rest. His sons be tall men, and he thanks God he never meddled with married women, but with all maidens the fairest could be gotten, and always married them right well.' Maiden Bradley was dissolved and Prior Jennings, who went quietly, was presented to the living of Shipton Moyne in Gloucester, for the moralists could afford to wink at sin after gaining possession of the sinner's property.

Along this shoddy path, then, Cromwell and his visitors made their way and accordingly, in March 1536, Parliament passed an Act dissolving all those smaller foundations, about 300 in all, with a net annual income of under £200. This first suppression, along with the dissolution of the greater monasteries formalised by a second Act in 1539, brought the king lands worth £100,000 per year, around one-fifth of England's landed wealth. Nor should the bonanza of jewels and precious metal from expropriated religious paraphernalia be forgotten. It was no coincidence, of course, that when Drs Legh and Henley arrived at Durham to deal with St Cuthbert's tomb, they did so with a gaggle of goldsmiths and lapidaries in tow. Meanwhile, at St Thomas Becket's shrine at Canterbury, where only twelve years earlier Henry and Charles V had worshipped together, the tidy haul amounted to some twenty-six wagon loads of precious items. A ruby, which had adorned the saint's tomb at Canterbury since 1179 when it had been donated by Louis VII of France, would be set in a thumb ring for Henry, and as a parting gesture to the saint, the king's men burnt his bones, mingled the ashes with earth and blew them heavenwards from the mouth of a cannon. Perhaps, if St Thomas' mortal remains could have been peddled profitably, their treatment might have been more respectful.

Material advantage was, then, the warmly pulsing vein driving the dissolution process at all levels and, predictably, all expectations generated by government propaganda proved depressingly hollow. There was, for instance, no real sign of the much mooted bounteous windfall for 'commonwealth' projects. Progressive social thinkers like Thomas Starkey had harboured passionate hopes that funds accruing from the dissolution might create the foundations for a truly equitable Christian commonwealth. In June 1536, he wrote to Henry thus: 'And finally I trust now to see all such superfluous riches, which among them that bear the name of spiritual nourished nothing but idleness and vice, to be converted and turned by your gracious goodness to the increase of all virtue and honesty.' Such optimism seemed justified in the light of the preamble to the 1539 Act, which was possibly drafted by the king himself. Here it had been promised that the purpose of dissolution was to ensure, amongst other things, that 'God's word might the better be set forth' and that 'children be brought up in learning'. Furthermore, Henry had held out hopes for 'daily alms to be administered' and there was also to be provision for 'old servants decayed to have livings', as well as 'almshouses for poor folk to be sustained in' and funds for the 'mending of highways'. None of these promised boons were forthcoming on any significant scale, however, just as Cranmer's oft-repeated promises at St Paul's Cross that the dissolution would mean an end to taxation were never fulfilled.

And where, of course, valiant resistance was offered to the dissolution, it proved largely futile in forestalling the full bureaucratic momentum of the State. The abbots of Glastonbury, Reading and Colchester refused to give up their abbeys voluntarily and it was decided, therefore, that these had 'otherwise to come into the King's hands'. An infamous note in Cromwell's memoranda, which has been used down the years to darken his reputation, continues to do so. 'The Abbot of Reading to be sent down to be tried *and executed* at Reading with his complices, similarly the Abbot of Glaston at Glaston', Cromwell noted in advance of the trial. Clearly, the outcome of due process of law was, in this case, not in doubt. Whiting, the elderly Abbot of Glastonbury was thus dragged through the streets of his little abbey town and hanged, drawn and quartered on the Tor overlooking the abbey. Hugh Cook, Abbot of Reading, was hung on the same day. Thereafter, Thomas Beche, Abbot of Colchester, was convicted on the slender evidence of John Scrope, a priest in the town. He was hanged under the Treason Act on 1 December 1539, a fortnight after Cook and Whiting.

Further butchery proved unnecessary, however, and as early as 1538, even before the larger monasteries had been formally dismantled, the signs of monastic decay were already plain. We learn from *The Chronicle of the Grey Friars of London* that the bells of Jesus Tower no longer rang, since they had been won at dice by Sir Miles Partridge, and according to John Bale, precious books of all kinds were now mainly in the hands of grocers and soap-sellers, 'some to serve their jakes, some to scour their candlesticks, and some to rub their boots'. At the same time, convent buildings erected for pious contemplation were housing factories, while friary churches had found a new role as government storehouses. In one case, the church of the Crutched Friars was serving as a stone quarry for the repair of the Tower, and in another, St Mary Grace's was bursting with ship's biscuits baked in the huge ovens that had been installed there. The church of the Austin Friars, on the other hand, had been bought by an enterprising nobleman to store his corn and coal supplies in the steeple. At the Charterhouse behind the doors where Houghton's severed arm had been nailed, the king was keeping his hunting nets and tents.

If, however, the monks went quietly on the whole, the people of England, and especially those of the conservative North, proved less accommodating. Initially, there had been general disquiet in response to a leftward swing in religion, which gathered pace during 1536. The Ten Articles had already reduced the seven sacraments to three when a further series of religious injunctions, drawn up by Cromwell, had clamped down on 'popular superstitions'. At the same time, in the upper echelons of society, the elites were bristling over what were perceived as direct assaults upon their status, brought about by social upstarts. To add fuel to the fire, there was economic discontent caused by high prices in the aftermath of the bad harvests of 1535–36, and recent taxation measures had also been particularly unpopular, as had enclosures and tithes. All this formed a crucial backcloth for the rebellion that would now present Henry with what was, arguably, the most dangerous test of his reign: a massive popular insurrection directed by frustrated elements of the old feudal nobility of England. Between October 1536 and March 1537, at least 40,000 Englishmen of all classes would take up arms in a backlash that would shake the Tudor State to its very foundations. For the first time Henry VIII was reaping the whirlwind that he himself had sown.

The rising that marked the beginning of the rebellion known today as the 'Pilgrimage of Grace' broke out spontaneously in October 1536 with what is sometimes referred to as the 'Lincolnshire rising'. Cromwell had already sent clear signals of his intentions and in an atmosphere of seething suspicion rumours were rife about taxes on baptisms, marriages and burials, and reductions in the number of parish churches and numbers of saints' days. 'There can be no better way to beat the King's authority into the heads of the rude people of the North', he wrote, 'than to show them that the King intends reformation and correction of religion. They are more superstitious than virtuous, long accustomed to frantic fantasies and ceremonies, which they regard more than either God or their prince.' Therefore, when two tax collectors arrived at Louth on 1 October, the consequences were predictable. The lucky one was hanged, while the other was allegedly wrapped in a freshly stripped cow skin and fed to dogs. Within days a gathering of around 10,000 peasants, craftsmen, parish priests and gentlemen was occupying Lincoln and by 4 October a group of at least eighteen local gentry was exercising a leading role.

When Henry first heard of these events, he responded with a characteristic combination of majestic fury and incomprehension. On 10 October a letter from the king was read out to the men of Lincolnshire in which he told them that 'I never have read, heard nor known that princes, counsellors and prelates should be appointed by rude and ignorant common people; nor that they were meet, or of ability to discern meet and sufficient counsellors for a prince.' This hectoring tone was maintained throughout: 'How presumptuous [...] are ye, the rude commons of one shire, and that one of the most brute and beastly of the whole realm, to find fault with your prince ...' It was Parliament, said Henry, not he who had suppressed the monasteries and in any case only those 'where abominable living was used'. Having rejected all their demands out of hand, he then ordered the rebels to 'remember your duty of allegiance, and that ye are bound to obey us, your King, both by God's commandment and the law of nature'. They were ordered, too, to hand over 100 persons 'on penalty of condign punishment and the indignation of almighty God'. Though always an adept trimmer of other necks, Henry's own could still, when required, obviously project as far as ever.

At first, his show of regal disdain appeared to work. By the time the king's words were heard by the rebels, the Duke of Suffolk was already hastening northwards at the head of a royal force with instructions from Henry to hang many 'for a terrible example of like offenders'. Faced, then, with the king's intransigence and the approach of a royal army, the rebels' courage failed them and the Lincolnshire rising appeared to fizzle out as quickly as it had begun. When Suffolk entered Lincoln, therefore, he rode through sullen crowds who refused to doff their hats, but encountered no resistance. Even so, forty-six people were executed, including the vicar of Louth, who was hanged from the steeple of the parish church. And twelve more were taken to London where they were sentenced 'to be hanged, cut down alive, disembowelled, their entrails burned while they were still alive, and beheaded'. 'As the gates of London are full of quarters not consumed', the Lord Chancellor wrote to Cromwell, 'I have ordered the heads of these prisoners to be set up over London Bridge and at every gate.' But the sparks from the fenlands had already flown northwards and ignited a far more menacing conflagration, which spread like wildfire and turned into what would now become the Pilgrimage of Grace proper.

It was Robert Aske, a one-eyed Yorkshire barrister, who emerged at this point as the rebellion's unlikely leader and gave it the religious characteristics for which it is usually remembered. The rebels now styled themselves 'pilgrims' and, by and large, they behaved as such, singing hymns on their way and carrying banners displaying the Five Wounds of Christ. However, it was soon clear that they had in their number those who had the potential for something altogether more rousing than pious tunes. Aske's supporters were, in fact, soon joined by the men of Hull and, as Aske himself began a march on York, his forces were further augmented by the retainers of Lords Latimer, Lumley and Neville in full armour. When, a few days later, Sir Thomas Percy came with 5,000 men from Northumbria, Aske had an army rather than a mob under his command, with the initiative fully his. He entered York, therefore, on 16 October, full of confidence and brimming with hope, and within three days appeared before the royal castle at Pontefract, where Lord Darcy surrendered tamely enough to confirm that he, too, was in sympathy with the insurgents.

In this situation of extreme tension, the king now despatched the Duke of Norfolk northwards. As he entered enemy territory, however, it was apparent that the duke could win no immediate victory. His force of 8,000 men was outnumbered five to one and the rebels already controlled York and Pontefract Castle. Moreover, in the country beyond, several great marcher lords had given their allegiance to the rebellion. Therefore, when Norfolk joined the Earl of Shrewsbury at Doncaster, a temporary compromise seemed the only sensible course of action, though there was still at least the option of deceit and double-dealing. After first rejecting the pilgrims' petition, the king at last instructed Norfolk to accept it, and the duke duly informed the rebels that he was ready to go to London with two of their representatives, Sir Robert Bowes and Sir Ralph Ellerkar, to intercede for them and their petition, on condition that there should be a temporary armistice. This, however, was the guarantee of a thoroughly dishonest broker, and almost immediately after his offer had been made, Norfolk wrote to Henry, matching the duplicity of his sovereign's mind to perfection, 'I would', he said, 'esteem no promise that I made to them, nor think my honour touched in breach of the same.'

In reality, of course, Henry dealt neither in mercy nor compromise, especially when his own 'honour' was in question. And though the rebel envoys were graciously entertained in the capital for fully two weeks after their arrival, the king's real intention was delay in the confident expectation that the onset of a northern winter would numb rebel passions. In early December, therefore, Aske was informed that his demands would be met and reassured 'with comfortable words' that Norfolk would be sent north to deal with the details. Henry even agreed, for good measure, to call a free parliament. At the same time, however, Cromwell was writing to Sir Ralph Evers 'that there should be such vengeance taken, that the whole world should speak thereof'. As part of the grand deception, moreover, Aske was formally pardoned on 8 December and became the king's guest at court over Christmas. Indeed, after much good cheer and friendly pampering, he was sent back to Doncaster with the gift of a new crimson jacket – a choice of colour that would soon prove most apt.

In fact, when Aske returned to Yorkshire, a horrifyingly unexpected spectacle greeted him. Far from being treated to a hero's return, he found the whole county smouldering with suspicion and the ground utterly cut from under him. The king's commissioners who had been the initial flashpoint for the rebellion were actually still active and nor had any pardons arrived. In panic, therefore, Aske wrote to Henry to plead that he implement his promises and then tried himself to calm the hotheads who were urging renewed rebellion. In both respects, however, he failed miserably. Firstly, in January 1537, another rising did indeed break out in the East Riding, led this time by the heedless rabble-rouser Sir Francis Bigod. Worse still, this new conflagration, with its distinct class undertones, had thoroughly alienated the gentry and nobility from the common people and, as Aske well knew, in such division lay calamity. To seal matters, further disorders also erupted in Westmorland and Cumberland for which the original 'pilgrims' were now quite wrongly held responsible.

In such circumstances, the isolation of the rebels from their social betters furnished the king with the perfect opportunity for symbolic retribution against all and sundry, which would restore his wounded pride and re-establish his flagging credentials as a mighty and 'puissant' ruler. Now Henry could and would strut vengefully and his instructions to the Duke of Norfolk made this all too chillingly clear:

> Before you close up our said banner again you shall in any wise cause such dreadful execution to be done upon a good number of every town, village and hamlet that have offended in this rebellion, as well by the hanging them

up in trees, as by the quartering them, and the setting up of their heads and quarters in every town, great and small, and in all such other places, as they may be in fearful spectacle to all other hereafter that would practise in any like manner.

In the event, Norfolk had little difficulty in crushing the torpid ripples of disorganised resistance that he now encountered, and ruthless suppression followed in which 178 rebels were executed. Sir Robert Constable, who was among the first of the rebel leaders to be taken, was condemned to death in June. He was butchered in Hull, where he had been briefly in command of the royal garrison, and his remains were duly hung from the Beverley Gate. Shortly afterwards, Norfolk, who was in charge of the arrangements, gloated that Sir Robert 'doth hang above the highest gate in the town, so trimmed with chains [...] that I think his bones will hang there this hundred year'. Aske, in his turn, suffered a similar fate at York a month later on a market day, and Darcy, Lord Hussey, Sir Thomas Percy, Sir John Bulmer and his wife were also all executed – Lady Bulmer being burnt alive. When Henry learned later that, in Cumberland, the wives and mothers of the executed were removing the bodies of their loved ones from the gibbets where they were displayed, he ordered that these women, too, be punished for their insolence.

12

Who Hastes to Climb Seeks to Revert

'For how many servants did he advance in haste but for what virtue no man could suspect, and with the changes of his fancy ruined them again no man knowing for what offence. To how many others of more desert gave he abundant flowers from whence to gather honey, and in the end of the harvest burned them in the hive. How many wives did he cut off, and cast off, as his fancy and his affection changed?'

Sir Walter Raleigh, *History of the World*.

On 7 January 1536, the long-suffering Catherine of Aragon breathed her last and launched a year of great personal and political significance for Henry VIII. In the early days after Wolsey's fall, Catherine had continued to follow her husband each day on the hunt, but by 1531 even common civilities were irksome to him and he saw her for the last time in July of that year. Riding off from Windsor at dawn to follow the hounds at Woodstock with the Lady Anne, Henry had dismissed his wife's messenger brusquely. 'Tell the Queen', he shouted, 'that I do not want any of her goodbyes.' Then, in the wake of his eventual divorce, the king clinically and comprehensively severed all links with his former spouse. Catherine's insignia were stripped from the royal barge in preparation for its use at Anne's coronation, and for good measure they were even removed from the stone gate of the great hall at Westminster – an ignominy reserved hitherto for traitors to the Crown. By May 1534, the former Queen of England was 'often sickly' and found herself despatched eventually to Kimbolton castle in the remote fenlands of Huntingdonshire where she was placed under the governorship of Sir Edward Bedingfield and Sir Edward Chamberlayne. Surrounded by spies and deprived of her comforts, she ground out her final days in comparative penury, preparing her own meals for fear of poisoning. And when at last she was finally freed from the earthly trials that had dogged her, her body was hurriedly sealed in lead and buried.

Lord Herbert of Cherbury, Henry's seventeenth-century biographer, would claim that the king wept when he read Catherine's last letter, in which she had told him that 'mine eyes desire you above all things'. But his tears, if ever shed, were soon dry. It was Chapuys who brought Henry news of the death and the ambassador was appalled by the response, for there was, it seems, no grief, but merely unsuppressed elation. 'God be praised that we are free from all suspicion of war', Henry exclaimed, and shortly afterwards the Princess Elizabeth was escorted to Mass with a triumphant fanfare. Nor was this the sum of the king's cold-blooded disregard, since the very little that was Catherine's to give was appropriated on his behalf perfectly legitimately and equally cynically thanks to the legal artistry of Sir Richard Rich. The former queen's favourite Franciscan convent was not to receive her gowns as she had hoped, and Henry refused to comply with any of her other bequests of clothes and property until he had seen 'what the robes and furs were like'. She was to be buried, the king commanded, not at St Paul's, because that would cost more 'than was either needful or requisite', but at Peterborough Cathedral.

This, though, was an age of exquisite ironies. It was ironic, for instance, that through his alliance with Anne Boleyn, Henry's dynastic position had worsened markedly rather than improved. In September 1533, Elizabeth had been born, but Anne produced no other heirs, and without the arrival of the son that he had now made crucial, Henry would bequeath a disputed succession in the event of his sudden death. It was ironic, too, that seventeen days after Catherine's death, Henry came within a hair's breadth of triggering this nightmarish scenario. At that very tournament held to mark the triumph of his first wife's demise, the king fell heavily from his horse, remaining unconscious for more than two hours. Most ironic of all, however, was what followed hard upon this event, for although Charles Wriothesley recorded untruthfully in his *Chronicle* that the king 'took no hurt', he also noted that Queen Anne 'took a fright' upon learning of the king's fall and 'was brought abed and delivered of a man child, as it was said, afore her time'. This 'man child' – later alleged by the Catholic propagandist Nicholas Sander to be nothing more than 'a shapeless mass of flesh' – represented a grievous blow to the queen's long-term prospects for survival. It was, Henry reflected later, 'God's punishing him for having been snared into a marriage by a bad woman who practised unlawful arts', and when, after some tarrying, Henry at last visited Anne's bedside, he told her harshly how he now saw that God would not grant them a son. This time, however, there were no scriptural strings for the king to pull and as such there was only one way out for him. Therefore, within a year of the death of her enemy Thomas More, Anne, too, would kneel in the executioner's shadow.

With hindsight, Anne's status in Henry's affections was always fragile. It was based essentially upon passion and pregnancy, and when she failed to deliver in either department, her days were numbered. In fact, those qualities that made Anne so exciting as a lover made her intolerably exasperating as a wife. She played the shrew consummately and without effort, but this was the only role in her repertoire, whilst Henry, as a husband, was entirely conventional, expecting and demanding self-effacing obedience from his spouse. Cromwell, too, it seems, had become a butt of the tantrums and abuse that were Anne's stock-in-trade. In June 1535, for instance, he told Chapuys that the queen had threatened to have his head. The plain fact was that she was arrogant, vain, emotional and jarringly disputatious, always vying for the last word. Worse still, she was sometimes inclined to indulge these faults in public. When Henry accused her of having been responsible for the executions of More and Fisher and for causing all the present troubles in the kingdom, she responded by claiming that, without her, he could not have reformed the Church and that, consequently, she had made him the richest prince in Christendom. Not surprisingly, after Anne had lost her second child in June 1535, the Venetian ambassador reported that Henry was 'tired to satiety' of her.

To any outside observer, Henry's court was now quite unlike the one that Erasmus had described so enthusiastically twenty years earlier. It had become, in fact, a long whispering gallery of scandal and spiteful gossip, built on constantly shifting sands. Cromwell, for instance, who had once been Anne Boleyn's close ally, was by this time quite ready to ruin her at the king's convenience. Moreover, the queen's behaviour in recent months made his task an easy one, for among others, Henry Norris (principal gentleman of the chamber) and Mark Smeaton (the queen's musician) had begun to indulge in the most dangerous badinage with her. Norris, above all others, should have been much more circumspect. He had for years been Henry's most trusted companion, the one official with ready access to the king's bedchamber. However, enchanted by the fairytale domain of the queen's private lodgings, he had played foolishly with emotional fire by leading Anne to feel that, if the king died, he would look to have her for himself. Such comments would provide more than ample ammunition for the commission, led by Cromwell and Norfolk, that Henry appointed on 24 April to discover sufficient evidence against Anne to bring about her downfall. When the time came, then, it was easy enough to convince the self-serving conscience of the king that he had been 'seduced and forced into his second marriage by means of sortileges and charms' and for good measure Cromwell would also persuade his master that Anne's brother, Viscount Rochford, had been the father of the aborted child.

The Duke of Norfolk, who had once dangled his niece as a laughing girl before the king, now presided at her trial and, although she eventually made a good defence, there could be but one outcome. With stone-cold detachment, therefore, Norfolk pronounced her guilty in court and condemned her to death. It had been suggested that

> bearing malice against the king and following her frail and carnal lust, she did falsely and traitorously procure by means of indecent language, gifts and other arts [...] divers of the king's daily and familiar servants to be her adulterers and concubines, so that several of them, by most vile provocation and invitation, became given and inclined to the said Queen.

Though guilt was, in the king's view, mainly the queen's, blame naturally descended on all concerned. Smeaton alone confessed his crimes, albeit after his tongue was loosened on the rack, and though there was no real evidence against the other men, Cromwell visited them separately to attempt to lure each one into incriminating admissions. In any case, their fate was sealed, irrespective of any formalities regarding due process of law. The treatment of William Brereton, another of those accused, was, perhaps, especially despicable, since Cromwell resented his territorial influence in North Wales and Cheshire, and wanted him out of the way. The contemporary observer Cavendish was in no doubt that he was executed 'shamefully, only of old rancour'.

Anne, meanwhile, paid the ultimate price for her indiscretions on 18 May. Deferential as ever, Norfolk had left it to the king's pleasure to decide whether she should be beheaded or burned alive, but 'for mercy's sake' Henry opted to despatch her by means of the blade. For this purpose, an expert headsman was imported from Calais who, with a Gallic eye for style, rejected the axe as an unfitting instrument for his art and beheaded the queen, instead, with a single swing of a two-handed sword. In the event, Anne was said to have died 'boldly' rather than 'well'. Characteristically, her bearing, though dignified, was impenitent.

Some time before the deed itself, the king's legal laundrymen had already attended to his dirty linen. Two days after Anne had been condemned for adultery Cranmer presided over a court that deemed she had never been married, though three years earlier he himself had gladly sanctioned the union. Now with claims of fresh evidence that was never disclosed, but which probably centred upon Henry's earlier relationship with Mary Boleyn, Anne's marriage was rendered null and void. Upon hearing Cranmer's decision, Henry declared that it was a great relief to his conscience to find that he was and always had been a bachelor, and so had never broken the seventh commandment. Indeed, so light was the king's conscience that he soon felt impelled to lecture his sister, Margaret, on her sinful life, reminding her of 'the divine ordinance of inseparable matrimony first instituted in paradise', and urging her to avoid 'the inevitable damnation threatened against avouterers'.

In spite of the Archbishop of Canterbury's concern for what he assumed must be the king's 'lamentable heaviness' upon the execution of his wife, Henry had actually enjoyed the highest spirits from the time that Anne was first sentenced. While his wife awaited the scaffold, he gave a series of river pageants and amused himself by writing a tragedy with Anne as heroine, which he showed to the Bishop of Carlisle. Moreover, on the day before Anne's execution, he sent word to Jane Seymour that she would hear good news at three o' clock and that he would sup with her soon afterwards. The following day, he and Jane were betrothed and before a week had passed they were married. As it transpired, his new wife had been 'assured' to him for six months already.

Though Henry's third queen had risen from sound if unillustrious aristocratic stock, the Seymours were prolific breeders, particularly in terms of male progeny, and this was no small consideration in sealing Henry's new choice of bride. As for Jane herself, she was around 25 years of age, plain, pale, diffident, discreet and, in the words of the king, 'inclined to peace', which, after the protracted marital buffetings he had already undergone, was recommendation in itself. Indeed, during her brief reign the new queen seems to have cultivated quite consciously the image of a shy and unassuming woman, rather overwhelmed by her status. It was no coincidence, therefore, that where Anne's motto had been, ironically, 'The Happiest of Women', Jane chose 'Bound to Obey and Serve'. Her one and only priority, it seemed, was pregnancy, which she had duly achieved by Trinity Sunday in 1537, when the joyous news of her quickening with child resounded across the country and plunged her husband once more into adolescent raptures of optimism and affection.

However, when the future Edward VI was, indeed, finally born at Hampton Court at two o'clock in the morning of 12 October 1537, his mother had already endured an agonising labour lasting two days and three nights. And though she had been attended throughout by royal doctors, the men concerned were merely distinguished academics with limited practical experience who had, in all likelihood, failed to check that her afterbirth had been properly extruded. Curiously, then, a woman of inferior station might well have received better treatment at the hands of her friends and relatives than that accorded to the most revered female in the land.

Even so, the news of the birth suggested that Divine Providence, as manifested by the new God of the Church of England, was, after all, with the king. Accordingly, the bells of London's churches, great and small, rang out triumphantly, garlands were hung from windows and 2,000 salvoes sounded from the Tower's arsenal. All that afternoon and evening and throughout the night and next day, conduits and hogsheads gushed ale and wine in the packed streets of the capital as the poor were exhorted 'to drink as long as they listed'. Even cutthroats and common pickpockets had cause for celebration in confident expectation of a general pardon that would surely be announced imminently. 'We all hungered after a prince so long', said the preacher Hugh Latimer, 'that there was so much rejoicing as at the birth of John the Baptist.'

Yet less than a fortnight after she had borne her husband's only legitimate son, Jane Seymour's ashen corpse lay in the presence chamber at Hampton Court in a robe of gold tissue, jewelled and crowned. Eight days after the christening on 15 October, at which the queen had been displayed on a state pallet throughout five hours of elaborate ritual, she had been stricken by fever and delirium. Soon afterwards she experienced what was described as 'an naturall laxe', or in other words, a catastrophic haemorrhage consistent with the onset of puerperal fever. Such was the gravity of the situation that the king, who had intended to leave for Esher to hunt, was forced to remain at Hampton Court for one more day, though he determined nevertheless to leave on the morrow, because, according to the Duke of Norfolk, 'he could not find it in his heart to tarry'. This time, however, fate was to cheat him of the pleasure of his favourite pastime as well as a wife, for early in the morning of the day of his rearranged departure, Jane was being shriven by her confessor and receiving the last sacrament.

For all his heavy-duty egotism, the news of his third wife's death was a bitter draught for the king to swallow. And though her jewels were soon given away, and her jointure reclaimed, Henry would never forget the mother of his only legitimate son. Twice, in 1539 and again in 1543, he paid nostalgic pilgrimages to the cramped medieval manor house of Wulfhall in Savernake Forest, where Sir John Seymour had served his daughter her betrothal feast. And in his will, Henry would order that 'the bones and body of our true and loving wife Queen Jane' be committed to his own tomb.

Amid the sadness, however, there were also more pressing concerns surrounding the well-being of the newborn prince, whose life had been won at such high cost. In the regulations laid down for his safekeeping, there was a particularly noteworthy preamble, stating that whereas 'God hath the devil repugnant to Him and Christ hath antichrist', so the prince notwithstanding his innocence, may have adversaries who because of 'ambition for their own promotion' might endanger his person. And indeed there were stirrings in the country at large, which gave some grounds for caution. Shortly after Edward's birth, for instance, one of the humbler instruments of Thomas Cromwell's ubiquitous spy system reported that there had been beery grumbling amid the clink of tankards at the Bell Inn on Tower Hill. A mariner had, it seems, repeated the prophecy that the prince would be as great a murderer as his father, adding: 'He must be a murderer by kind, for he murdered his mother at birth.' Elsewhere, under interrogation, one Richard Guercey confessed that he had spoken, in the kitchen of Corpus Christi College, Oxford, about information given to him by a man called Osmond, 'one of Peckwater's Inn', that there was 'a wax image found in London way with a knife sticking through his head or heart, representing the prince, and as that did consume, so likewise the prince'.

But if the danger at home lay mainly in drunken rambling and backstreet curses, the threat from abroad was of an altogether different order.

Throughout the 1530s, in fact, the whole emphasis of England's foreign policy would switch from the strident adventurism of Wolsey's day to a nervous, low-profile shuffling for security from any quarter. The breach with Rome had, after all, ended any former hopes that Henry may have had of posing as the arbiter of Europe. On the contrary, it had isolated him from the Catholic superpowers whom he had once sought to manipulate for his own ends and had rendered him a hostage to the vagaries of European power politics. Above all, it had placed him in irretrievable enmity with Charles V, of whom he was now chiefly afraid. His residing concern, then, was that European peace might spawn a crushing coalition against him between the Empire and France, and his only hope lay in the prospect of a measly alliance with a ragbag medley of German Lutheran states who, like England, were hopelessly casting around for any and every diplomatic lifeline.

Nevertheless, over the next three years or so, Henry's negotiations with the German Lutherans would continue to bob lifelessly in the water. 'The King', said Cromwell, 'knowing himself to be the learnedest prince in Europe, thought it became not him to submit unto them; but he expected they should submit to him.' And all the while that Henry found himself uneasily protesting his zeal for 'the pure word of God' to his German 'allies', he continued to shower the King of France with firm assurances that he had departed not one jot from Catholic faith and practice by repudiating the pope. Moreover, as the testy hair-splitting wound on between English and German divines over the true Protestant way, the prospect of peace between Francis and Charles seemed increasingly likely. The third war between them, begun in 1536, was steadily dying down after the imperial troops had originally advanced as far as Marseille, and now, in November 1537, a three-month truce was concluded between the old adversaries, which seemed especially ominous of peace between them.

Lacking any more imaginative options, Henry therefore chose at this point to dabble in the usual weary talk of marriage. His opening gambit was to bore Charles V with a proposal of marriage to Christina, Duchess of Milan. A 16-year-old virgin widow, she was described as 'very tall, of competent beauty, soft of speech, and gentle of countenance'. And when this match quickly foundered on reality's reef, Henry resumed his gallant quest, unabashed, with an embassy to his old enemy, Francis. Could not a train of French beauties be duly despatched to Calais or some such spot, where the intending bridegroom might conveniently inspect them for himself? When, however, it was objected that French ladies were not to be trotted out like so much horse flesh, Henry quickly rejected the idea of sending trustworthy representatives. 'By God', he said, 'I trust no one but myself. The thing touches me too near. I wish to see them and know them some time before deciding.'

In the meantime, as the King of England wriggled aimlessly, events abroad once more outpaced him. In June 1538, a ten-year truce was arranged at Nice between Charles and Francis through the mediation of the pope; and in July the understanding was confirmed by a personal meeting between the two sovereigns at Aigues-Mortes. There they exchanged their respective emblems of the Golden Fleece and St Michael, and gave each other mutual tokens of warm friendship. Much more worryingly still, the two rulers committed themselves to a joint crusade against heresy, at home and abroad, while in December Paul III finally launched the Bull of Excommunication and deposition against the King of England drawn up in 1535. For good measure, he also proposed a coalition of the emperor, the French and the Scots against the heretical English. As one English observer reporting from Nice put it, 'the Emperor and the French King and the Bishop of Rome assembled, pretending a union of the world'.

However, while war fears mounted, Henry's response was merely to turn his concerns to 'malice domestic', and this boded ill for certain guileless suspects. The two most likely candidates for sedition, or so at least Henry believed in his semi-delusional state, were Henry Courtenay, Marquess of Exeter, and Henry Pole, Lord Montague – the chief thorns of a White Rose that had, in fact, long since withered on the branch. There was no denying, of course, that Courtenay, who was Henry's first cousin and descended from a daughter of Edward IV, possessed vast estates in the West Country and was regarded by some as a potential contender for the throne. Indeed, one of his servants had actually blabbed to royal spies in 1531, when the divorce was causing outrage, that 'our master shall wear the garland at the last'. And though Courtenay himself had long been reconciled to Henry, his wife had been intimate with Queen Dowager Catherine and involved with the Maid of Kent, so that Henry had already warned the marquess and his friends that they 'must not trip or vary for fear of losing their heads'. Meanwhile, Montague had been seriously compromised by the activities of his brother Reginald on the Continent. In fact, Reginald Pole's gradual estrangement from the king over relations with the pope had ultimately assumed the proportions of an unbridgeable and treasonable gulf. If his departure from England and eventual residence in Rome had placed him under a cloud of royal displeasure, the publication of his manifesto on Church unity in 1536 and denunciation of the government's crimes, not to mention his promotion to cardinal in the same year and his intrigues with Francis I and Charles V, had left Henry implacably hostile.

Yet in reality neither Courtenay nor Montague, possessed the stuff of which true conspirators and rebels are made. Though they both sympathised with Reginald Pole's views, they deplored his conduct and feared, quite rightly, that 'the King, to be avenged of Reynold, will kill us all'. Prudently submissive at all times, then, Montague and his mother, the Countess of Salisbury, were even ready, at the behest of the council, to write to the vexatious black sheep of their family in abhorrence at his treasonable conduct.

Nevertheless, when it suited him, as it frequently did, Henry was wholly capable of conjuring forest fire from the slightest wisp of smoke, especially when the fanning was assisted by Cromwell. And the flimsy pretext for action was conveniently supplied by Sir Geoffrey Pole, a weak and inconstant man whose bold words betokened more than he was fitted for. He had postured as a spy for Catherine of Aragon's cause and sounded Chapuys on the possibility of the emperor's intervention by force. Then, during the Pilgrimage of Grace, he had been with Norfolk at Doncaster and whispered that he meant to desert if there was battle. All this, of course, was damp leaves rather than dry tinder, but it was enough, all the same, to consume both him and his family.

In August, therefore, Sir Geoffrey was arrested and once caged he sang like a bird. Constantly probed and in fear of torture, he confessed to what his relations and friends had said in private. Courtenay, it seems, had declared that 'knaves rule about the king' and that he trusted some day 'to give them a buffet'. Worse still, Montague had gone on to suggest that 'Cardinal Wolsey had been an honest man if he had had an honest master'. Most offensively and dangerously of all, however, Sir Edward Neville, Henry's boyhood companion, was alleged to have voiced the view that 'the king is a beast and worse than a beast'.

During these days when words were considered mortal treasonable weapons, even if uttered within earshot of only a single individual, the king's revenge would be both swift and complete. At the trial, Sir Geoffrey Pole was, in fact, the only witness, but the marquess, Montague and

Neville were convicted and executed nonetheless under the law of verbal treason. Also hewn was Sir Nicholas Carew, who had already fallen from favour after responding in anger to insulting remarks made by the king after a game of bowls. Not coincidentally, Henry was known to covet the estates in Surrey where Carew was creating a vast hunting domain. In due course, Gertrude, Marchioness of Exeter, and her 12-year-old son Edward Courtenay would be other victims taken to the Tower, while Lord Montague's young son was also arrested, dying later at some unrecorded date. Most reprehensibly of all, perhaps, the 'aged and feeble' Countess of Salisbury, whom the king had 'once venerated no less than his mother', was incarcerated on the evidence of an apparently seditious banner before being executed for treason two years later. A Londoner, writing to a German acquaintance in 1541, observed: 'I do not hear that any of the royal race are left except a nephew of the Cardinal and another boy, the son of the Marquess of Exeter. They are both children and in prison and condemned.'

In fact, the so-called 'Exeter Conspiracy', far from demonstrating the fragility of the king's dynastic position, was actually proof of its inherent strength. The threat presented by the Marquess of Exeter, the king's first cousin, was not, of course, entirely imaginary. If a papal crusade against Henry had indeed ever materialised, opposition in Devon and Cornwall might well have proved crucial. The Nevilles, in their turn, owned much property in Kent and the Poles were powerful in Hampshire and Sussex. Moreover, Henry was now in his late forties, an advanced age by contemporary standards. Exeter's threat could not therefore be measured only in terms of this reign. Yet such potential threats remained precisely that, and fear of the possible has tended to grease many a slippery slope to tyranny down the years. As for Cromwell, his spy networks, treason legislation, craft and opportunism had been demonstrated to perfection and a dangerous nest of his enemies had been conveniently flushed.

But if the principal secretary's choice of victim was always eagle-eyed, his grasp of his master's taste in women would now prove much less acute. For Cromwell, a marriage between Henry and Anne of Cleves was a matter of political expediency. For the king himself, however, it was of altogether more personal significance and he was very anxious to know what the lady involved was like. Indeed, the king seems to have taken an unusually intense interest in the physical attributes of all the females that were now arrayed before him as prospective brides. He was anxious, for instance, to ascertain whether Christina of Milan was pock-marked, whilst his perspective on Marie de Guise was more that of a stock breeder than suitor. Did she, he asked earnestly, have wide hips for child-bearing? And as always bulk in general continued to be an issue of particular significance to the king in his identification of a worthy mate. 'I am big in person', he is known to have declared, 'and have need of a big wife.'

In the end, of course, Henry was forced to settle for a bride whom he would loudly defame as an aesthetic non-starter. But how far Anne of Cleves deserved her husband's jibes or how far those jibes were a cover for her husband's flagging potency is anyone's guess. Certainly, Nicholas Wotton had sent an unflattering report about her, which the king probably never saw. In it, he told how the lady had been very strictly brought up and how she spoke no language but her own. He pointed out, too, that she could neither dance, sing, nor play an instrument, since Germans regarded such accomplishments below the dignity of the well born. Her only real recommendations, in Wotton's view, were her skill with the needle and the fact that she was not given to drink. The issue of her looks was not dwelt upon, however, and Cromwell, not altogether surprisingly, preferred to send on to Henry the glowing description of Christopher Mont, who boldly claimed that 'every one praiseth the beauty of the same lady, as well for the face as the body'.

Ultimately, Henry would meet Anne of Cleves for the first time shortly after Christmas in 1539, only to leave the encounter after a few minutes, exclaiming famously, 'I am ashamed that men have praised her as they have done. I love her not.' Nevertheless, the marriage did appear to make sound diplomatic sense, at least initially. Since the beginning of 1539, Charles V and Francis I had been advertising their growing accord and the Duke of Cleves, as inheritor of Jülich and Berg and possessor of Guelderland, held territories of strategic importance that were a barrier between Charles's possessions in the Netherlands and Germany. It was, therefore, diplomatic necessity as adumbrated by Thomas Cromwell that made Henry accept 'I must needs put my head into the yoke'. Sadly for him, however, and more unfortunately still for Cromwell, the pressing diplomatic necessity evaporated almost as soon as the nuptials were solemnised by Cranmer on 6 January.

The marriage to Anne of Cleves, for which Cromwell was responsible, certainly infuriated Henry in its own right. But the fact that it had occurred on the basis of what soon proved to be a wholly false political premise magnified the effect enormously. During Christmas of 1539, Charles V was being feasted in Paris and the Cleves marriage made sound good sense. By February 1540, however, Charles and Francis were at daggers drawn, since, after subduing Ghent, the former had repudiated his promise that the French king's son, the Duke of Orléans, should be invested with the Duchy of Milan. Though Henry now wished for an imperial alliance, the Cleves marriage proved an insuperable obstacle. Cromwell had therefore wangled himself into a corner in which he was dangerously exposed to the whims of his master and the wiles of his enemies. Moreover, the principal secretary's problem now was not so much that he had married Henry to Anne of Cleves, but that this time he could not so readily assist in 'un-marrying' the king as he had done before. Indeed, the agonising logic of the situation was all too manifest, for once free from Anne, Henry would be sure to marry his new fancy, Catherine Howard, niece of Cromwell's conservative opponent, the Duke of Norfolk. Once installed, she would be employed to wreak the ultimate vengeance upon him.

In the meantime, though, the king's new wife certainly behaved compliantly and when asked was wholly content to forgo her marriage and become, instead, her husband's 'beloved sister'. In fact, the marriage was actually dissolved so amenably that Henry appears to have been more than a little hurt by his latest wife's readiness to be parted from him. Ultimately the special commission appointed by Convocation took only two days to annul the 'pretended' marriage and once Anne was assured of a princely income, she reacted like any lottery winner surely should. A month later, the French ambassador, Marillac, captured her reaction thus: 'Madam of Cleves has a more joyous countenance than ever. She wears a great variety of dresses and passes all her time in sports and recreations.' By the time the Frenchman made his observation, however, the minister who had bought Anne her ticket to a life of anonymous leisure was already headless and cold in the ground.

In April 1540, Thomas Cromwell was at the zenith of his power. On the fourteenth day of the month, he was created Earl of Essex and Lord Chamberlain of England and given thirty manors in recognition of his services. But while Henry may not as yet have been consciously pondering his right-hand man's destruction, the seeds of Cromwell's fall were already safely sown. To the principal secretary's great cost, his master was, in fact, a perfect example of the five-minute enthusiast who commits those around him to courses of action with which he eventually finds himself unhappy.

Worse still, he would then be fully prepared to condemn his associates for pursuing a direction that he himself had tired of condoning. Quite apart from his grievously flawed matchmaking exercise with Anne of Cleves, Cromwell's religious policies had for some time been outpacing Henry's own inclinations, even though the king had only fully realised this after the event.

The Ten Articles of religious faith, for instance, which had been drawn up by Convocation in 1536, appeared to have had the king's full support in speaking the language of 'justification by faith alone' and reducing the seven sacraments to three. And though the so-called *Bishops' Book* of the following year was calculated to soothe conservative opinion in the aftermath of the Pilgrimage of Grace, it too hinted that England's progress along the road to Wittenberg was far from over. Meanwhile, Cromwell's injunctions as Vicar-General, which amongst other things required a copy of the Bible in English to be placed in every parish church, seemed to confirm beyond all question the emphatically scriptural basis of the Reformed Church over which Henry was now presiding. Indeed, even to outspokenly reformist clergy like Hugh Latimer and Nicholas Shaxton, there seemed little doubt that the King of England was calling his people out of darkness and into the marvellous light of Christ.

But even Thomas Cromwell, it seems, could not always be relied upon to interpret the inner workings of his master's thinking on the basis of his external behaviour. Therefore, when the Six Articles Act of 1539, which represented a clear conservative reaction against the leftward religious manoeuvrings of the previous few years, was forced upon the principal secretary like a bolt from the blue, it was clear at once that the symmetry of outlook between himself and the king, on which he depended and of which he had so far been completely confident, was nothing more than a dangerous mirage. In fact, only a mixture of creeping self-deception and lassitude had probably prevented Henry from thwarting the Protestant initiative earlier and even more decisively. Certainly, his reservations about an authorised vernacular Bible remained especially deep-seated, even though the publication of Miles Coverdale's version in October 1535 had received official sanction and its successor, the so-called 'Matthew Bible', would still be installed in all parish churches. Since the fourteenth century, after all, Lollard heretics in England had claimed to need no priesthood because of their unauthorised access to 'the sweetness of God's Holy Word' in the native tongue. An English Bible, therefore, had a long heretical pedigree to live down, which neither could nor would be wholly ignored by the king.

But most worrying of all from Henry's perspective was the general religious ferment that now seemed to be bubbling ominously throughout his realm. Among the popular preachers of the time the loudest and most violent form of the Lollard tradition was being combined with further scraps from the table of German theology. Some hotheads maintained, for instance, that priests and churches were redundant, others that all goods should be held in common. Then there were those who proclaimed that 'the singing and saying of mass, matins and evensong is but a roaring, howling, whining, murmuring, conjuring and juggling', and that the playing of organs was a 'foolish vanity'. 'It is as much available', said one observer, 'to pray unto saints as to hurl a stone against the wind.' The newfangled men poured scorn, too, on the 'dumb' clergy, 'the strawberry preachers' as they were afterwards called, because, as Hugh Latimer said, their sermons came 'like strawberries, but once a year'. On the other hand, old-fashioned priests were increasingly scandalised by the plague of sermonising and by young fellows who imbibed scripture rather than ale in taphouses. Loud-mouthed women were also making their mark, it seems. One Margaret Tofts, for instance, had sealed her place in history by declaring that her daughter could piss holy water every bit as good as that produced by any priest's blessing.

Having succumbed, therefore, to a stillborn marriage and facing a popular religious tide he found as repugnant as his most recent bride, Henry VIII did not hesitate to be swung by vengeful counsel. So it was that on 10 June, without warning, the Captain of the Guard entered the room at Westminster where the council was assembled and arrested Cromwell on a charge of high treason. In response, the wretched victim leapt to his feet and dashed his bonnet to the ground, calling on his colleagues to confirm his loyalty. But Cromwell's despairing outburst was to no avail as Norfolk snatched the medal of St George from his neck while Southampton stripped the Garter from his knee. Thereafter he was taken by river to the Tower to suffer the justice of the bloody laws that he himself had fashioned. Meanwhile, Londoners only learned the news later that evening when the king's archers were seen outside Cromwell's house. Within, men who were packing plate and money for the king's use found that the accused had salted away Church jewels to the value of £7,000.

Needless to say, Cromwell's subsequent frantic appeals to the king went unheeded. On 3 July he wrote to Henry as his 'poor slave'. 'Most gracious Prince', he implored, 'I cry for mercy, mercy, mercy', but no succour was forthcoming. Instead, Sir Richard Rich, whose testimony had once undone Sir Thomas More, was now eager to report the treasonable sayings of the patron who had made his fortune. In the meantime, Cromwell was not allowed to be heard in his own defence, and in the trial that followed he was condemned to die by Act of Attainder – not for the numerous crimes of which he had been genuinely guilty, since the king himself had been party to them, but on the false accusation that he had opposed the master whom he himself had helped to make a tyrant. 'Full of pride' Cromwell had, it was said, dealt in 'weighty causes' and, though of 'very base and low degree', he had boasted too freely of his power and influence. Early in 1540, when taunted about his origins, for example, he was alleged to have responded with a threat to the effect that 'if the Lords would handle him so, he would give them such a breakfast as never was made in England and that the proudest should know'. Predictably, he was accused also of heretical leanings, demonstrated by his encouragement of 'combinations' and 'conventicles'. But most damagingly of all, perhaps, he was said to have revealed intimate secrets about Henry's relationship with Anne Boleyn to an unspecified third party. In his desperation to make a success of the king's latest marriage, then, Cromwell had, it seems, made a clumsy attempt to tutor Anne of Cleves in the arts of seduction by confiding to her certain sexual preferences of her husband. And more than any other single factor it was quite possibly this last revelation that had rendered the king's fury uncontrollable.

Furthermore, Cromwell, unlike Wolsey, had only been the king's man of business and never his friend. True, no one else could work so hard and no one else could conform England to the royal will so effectively. No one else, for that matter, was such a power in the City, acceptable to both English and foreign merchants. But however crucial he may have been to Henry's needs, he was always essentially an object of contempt. Long before the marriage to Anne of Cleves, gossip had it that 'the King beknaveth him twice a week, and sometimes knocks him well about the pate', although Cromwell would invariably emerge from his routine lambastings 'with as merry countenance as though he might rule all the roost'. Likewise, in May 1538, Henry described his principal secretary to the French ambassador as 'a good household manager, but not fit to meddle in the affairs of Kings'. Above all, however, there remained a grubbiness about Cromwell that was not confined to his social origins and would prove just as damaging to his prospects in the long run. For Henry suffered occasionally from delusions of morality and at such times his right-hand man seemed less than appetising.

At bottom, after all, the principal secretary remained a chameleon with a roving eye for opportunity. To this extent, Henry, and the circumstances that he had fashioned, had made Cromwell what he was in exactly the same way that the latter's strategy for dealing with these circumstances encouraged the king to fulfil his unwholesome potential. In a very real sense, therefore, both men had made monsters of each other. But as the king's fixer-in-chief, Cromwell had ultimately proven too cold-blooded a pragmatist for his own good and in glimpsing this uncomfortable truth from time to time Henry seems to have decided that by purging Cromwell he might thereby cleanse himself. Given the king's innate volatility, then, Cromwell's sudden sorry fall was probably only a matter of time, foreshortened with every bold step upwards that he made on the ladder of success.

In some respects, of course, the brewer's son from Putney had been the classic embodiment of Machiavellian 'virtue'. He understood the dynamics of situations and understood, too, that satisfactory solutions could sometimes be derived only by altering the premises upon which they were based. Equally, he was always too preoccupied with outcomes to be considered cruel in the narrow sense. Yet he was, nevertheless, a master of rationalisation, who demonstrated a ruthless capacity for dealing with individuals in terms of broader wholes. And the more Cromwell achieved, the more convinced Henry became of his own infallibility until ultimately the one who had designed the imperial mantle was casually discarded for his efforts. The strident self-confidence, which Cromwell's policies had magnified in Henry, was amply demonstrated by the latter's claim in 1536 that 'God has not only made us King by inheritance, but has given us wisdom, policy and other graces in most plentiful sort, necessary for a prince to direct his affairs to his honour and glory'. Unmindful, therefore, of Sir Thomas More's advice, Cromwell had indeed taught the lion his strength and been mauled to death in the process.

In all, six weeks would eventually elapse between Cromwell's condemnation and his eventual execution, because the king was determined to be rid of Anne of Cleves and in this regard there was still a final service to be had from the fallen minister. Determined to squeeze out the last drop of his usefulness, Henry sent him fourteen questions concerning his marriage, which would confirm, among other things, that he had entered the match unwillingly and that the marriage had never been consummated. Clutching at straws, Cromwell supplied all the required details and threw himself once more on the king's mercy. As a result, Henry read his appeal for clemency three times before substituting the block for the gallows.

It was on 28 July 1540, therefore, that Thomas Cromwell was gruesomely hacked by a bungling headsman who required two blows to complete the task. In John Foxe's opinion, 'he patiently suffered the stroke of the axe, by a ragged, butcherly miser, which very ungodly performed the office'. Nor was it long, of course, before Henry's tortuous judgement was bemoaning Cromwell's fate. Soon enough, he was looking back on Cromwell as 'the best servant he ever had' and convincing himself that he had been condemned 'on light pretexts'. But although Henry was apparently incapable of perceiving the manifest link between his own arbitrariness and his servant's fate, he was in other essentials right. Cromwell was invaluable to him and had been wantonly erased. Yet again the king had proven accessible to gusts of influence and in a fit of pique had rid himself of his ablest adviser: thereafter he would have to rely on the slender political resources of an ailing incompetent – himself.

Nor would Henry be any more successful from this point onwards in achieving the personal fulfilment that had largely eluded him. His own explanation of his many disappointments and frustrations was always founded, of course, upon the disloyalty of others or the vagaries of fortune. But when, for example, he later proclaimed that he 'regretted his ill luck in meeting with such ill-conditioned wives', he was typically deluded. Impulsiveness and ego are, after all, powerful hallucinogens, which, in Henry's case, far from opening the gates of perception, locked them firmly shut. And if, indeed, he was a sitting duck to misfortune, he had only himself to blame. Who else, having been so niftily freed from Anne of Cleves, would have selected as her successor Catherine Howard, the niece of that great pander, the Duke of Norfolk?

The story of Henry's penultimate bride is, in fact, both sad and simple. As a child, she had been placed inadvisedly in the dormitory of unfit waiting women who indulged themselves by corrupting her morals, and the consequences were predictable. First of all, she had developed a childish passion for her music master, Henry Mannox, who trifled with her innocence. Then, at fifteen, she became the mistress of Francis Dereham, a bounder of more grotesque proportions, who loaded her with presents and called her 'wife'. When Dereham's dealings became known, he was forced to leave Catherine's company and opted, appropriately, for a brief career of piracy in Ireland. Later there was gossip, too, about Catherine's relations with her cousin Thomas Culpeper.

Yet in spite of these indiscretions, Catherine remained a valuable marital asset and at the age of 19 was duly introduced at court, where she soon attracted the attention of the king. Though not, according to Marillac, especially beautiful, she had nonetheless a winning countenance and was also kindly. Most significantly of all, however, she had puppy fat for brains and this had two crucial consequences. Firstly, it rendered her a palpable liability to any discerning prospective husband. Secondly, it made her irresistible to the inadequate and rapidly ageing would-be sensualist who now occupied the throne of England.

Trinkets and idle petting were, it seems, the highways to Catherine Howard's heart and she was married to Henry only sixteen days after his divorce from Anne of Cleves. As the new queen was soon to find, however, it was no easy thing for a woman to hide her past reputation, least of all at the Tudor court, where every alcove and portico was discreetly nested with nods and side-glances. Like moths to the flame, therefore, Catherine's former associates descended upon her. Mannox, Dereham, Culpeper and Mrs Bulmer, her former secretary (who had acted previously as a go-between during the Dereham affair), were all appeased with places at court. And Catherine was now encouraged and assisted in fresh misbehaviour by none other than Lady Rochford, the widow of the self-same Viscount Rochford, brother of Anne Boleyn, who had been executed for alleged incest with the former queen. This good lady now had opportunity aplenty for the most condign revenge upon the king, even if it would entail the forfeit of the life of his new spouse. As a Howard, Catherine had more powerful enemies, too, and now they made hay.

It was at Mass on All Souls' Day 1541 that Henry was told by Cranmer how his 'rose without a thorn' had lived 'most corruptly and sensually' prior to her marriage to him. Later when it was proven by intimate love letters that she had been adulterous with her cousin Thomas Culpeper, who was a gentleman of the king's bedchamber, Henry is said to have become hysterical. Weeping so violently that he lost all control, he vomited on a table in front of Cranmer and the other advisers present. Then he called for a sword that he might kill Catherine, Culpeper and himself, threatening that his wicked wife 'never had such delight in her incontinency as she should have torture in her death'.

For her part, meanwhile, Catherine went from one frenzy to another when Cranmer was sent to question her, at first disputing everything and then confessing fully to at least her pre-marital adventures whilst denying any outright unfaithfulness to Henry himself. However, when given the option to have her marriage rendered invalid by admitting to an earlier pre-contract with Francis Dereham, Catherine unwisely refused and in doing so lost her best opportunity to save herself. Thereafter, her fate was sealed when it was discovered that she had written to Culpeper stating that she would marry him, if only she were free of Henry. At a time when it was treason even to mention the death of the king, her punishment was clear.

Though Dereham and Culpeper refused, even on the rack, to acknowledge any illicit connection with the queen after her marriage, they were condemned to die. Meanwhile, the Duchess of Norfolk and several of the Howards were, in their turn, found guilty of misprision, since they had not told the king of Catherine's past. Culpeper, as a gentleman, was beheaded, though Mannox and Dereham would suffer the full rigour of traitors' deaths by being hung, drawn and quartered.

Naturally enough, the queen and Lady Rochford soon followed. Catherine, for her part, seems to have met her fate with a self-control that was especially admirable in one so young and naive. The night before her own execution in February 1542, not wanting to appear ungainly on the scaffold, she requested that the block be brought to her chambers, so that she could practise how she would lay her head upon it. Next day, Lady Rochford would place her own head on the same block, which was by that time spattered with the gore of her former mistress. And shortly after the whole process of royal justice had run its course, the Duke of Norfolk duly wrote to the king deploring his relations. Railing against his 'ungracious' stepmother, his 'unhappy' brother, his 'lewd' sister and his 'abominable' nieces, he said not a word in their defence, but many in his own.

From the king's own perspective, Catherine Howard's casual promiscuity had rendered him a laughing stock and he emerged from this encounter irretrievably winded and worn. It had been clear, in fact, from Jane Seymour's death onwards that time was 'coming fast on' for Henry, and the burgeoning population growth of the sixteenth century, which meant that by the later years of his reign at least half of his subjects were under the age of 18, only served to heighten, in its way, the king's increasingly painful awareness of his own finite span. The court teemed, after all, with youngsters and the emphasis upon youth, vitality, tourneying, hunting, glorious warfare and, for that matter, vigorous impregnation continued unabated. It was enough to dampen the spirits of any sickly has-been. But now to compound his growing gloom, Henry had yet again felt the full force of the old adage that marriage is not so much a word as a sentence.

13

Opinionate and Wilful

'We are at war with France and Scotland, we have enmity with the bishop of Rome [...] Our war is noisome to our realm and to all our merchants that traffic through the Narrow Seas [...] We are in a world where reason and learning prevail not and covenants are little regarded.'

From Stephen Gardiner to Sir William Paget,
November 1545.

In his later years, it was not so much marital commotion that tormented Henry VIII as the passage of time and all that it entailed. For high and low alike in mid-Tudor England, age and suffering danced a triumphant galliard, and particularly from March 1541 onwards, when his ulcerating leg brought him to the brink of the grave, the king's health deteriorated steadily. His medical record now became, in effect, a rising chart of recurrent colds, headaches, abdominal griping, shivering fits, watery discharges, fevers and 'sickly waxings'. And though the specific cause of this decline must remain uncertain, there is no doubting either the scale of its impact or the depth of the morbid obsessions that it fuelled in the king's mind. On the one hand, his increasing fear of the plague, which had taken six of his advisers in two years, is well documented. In the autumn of 1540, for example, with 300 people dying every week in the capital, Henry sequestered himself at Windsor, ordering that all victims be removed from the town, so that many were dragged from their beds and left to die in fields around about. Likewise, the manuscripts are heavier than ever at this time with evidence to confirm the king's growing obsession with physical ailments of all kinds, and not only his own. He seems, for instance, to have personally concocted remedies for a host of disorders including ruptures, testicular tumours, gravels, wheezing lungs, ringworm, eczema, corns, raw eyes, toothache and haemorrhoids. Various unguents, consisting mainly of rose and honeysuckle water, white wine, calf's marrow and ground pearls, were also painstakingly devised by him for a range of other maladies. All in all, then, Henry's growing realisation that 'time slippeth and flieth away marvellously' appears to have been dawning upon him ever more pressingly and as he continued to muse anxiously upon the transience of both himself and those around him, his realm would be transformed by turns into a hospice for an old man's fevered dreams.

Now, for instance, that the exercise of his manhood in the marriage chamber was no longer a pressing requirement or, for that matter, a practical option, Henry opted instead to prove his mettle on another field of honour. By this time, of course, both the Holy Roman Emperor and the King of France were similarly shadowed by old age and sickness. Racked by gout and ruined by galloping consumption of pickled eels, live oysters, Spanish sausages and huge tankards of iced German ale taken at whim both day and night, Charles V carried his huge empire on his back like a geriatric tortoise. It was at this time, as he tottered agonisingly on his stick around the imperial court, that he was inclined to reflect all too wistfully upon those former fine images of him as a dashing knight-errant. His French counterpart, meanwhile, was suffering from a stricture of the urethra, probably caused by gonorrhoea, and what the imperial ambassador called a 'gathering under the lower parts'. Articulate only in his insults, his teeth had rotted and he blathered his words out of a florid and distended caricature of a face. Nevertheless, like Charles, he too was intent upon renewing the Habsburg-Valois wars, which had already lumbered on for half a century, and though, as Thomas Wriothesley aptly remarked, England was 'but a morsel between these choppers', the eighth Henry was also set upon a final martial bow. All three rulers were, in fact, as intoxicated as ever by a bitter cocktail of chivalric fantasy and base ambition, and in spite of their many infirmities this meant war.

In Henry's case, the essential preliminary to any final marauding fling against the French foe was, by necessity, the neutralisation of Scotland. To this end, in an effort to protect his back, he first sought 'full brotherly' alliance with James V of Scotland before quickly settling upon an 'honourable enterprise' to crush him. The resulting military campaign achieved an outstanding English success at Solway Moss in November 1542, which was said to have been so spectacular that it cured Sir William

Paget's sciatica in London. In other respects, however, it achieved little of profit. On the field of battle 3,000 English troops had almost casually routed some 18,000 Scots, and in return for the capture of 1,200 Scottish prisoners – including 2 earls, 5 lords and 500 gentlemen – only 7 Englishmen had been killed. But though the conflict was also followed by the death of King James the next month, Henry consistently missed opportunities to gain ground politically. True, the Treaty of Greenwich, which betrothed James' daughter (the future Mary Queen of Scots) to Prince Edward, represented an uncharacteristic attempt at subtlety on Henry's part. Yet within the year English demands for physical possession of the princess's person had proved so insensitive that the Scots had reaffirmed their alliance with the French and were bent on retribution.

Faced with such 'ingratitude', Henry at first responded flaccidly with offers of pensions and then with characteristic brutality when an army under Edward Seymour, Earl of Hertford, was despatched north to destroy every house and village within 7 miles of Edinburgh. The English king's orders to Seymour still make truly harrowing reading across the centuries. He was 'to sack Leith and burn and subvert it and all the rest, putting man, woman and child to fire and sword without exception [...] and extend the like extremities and destruction in all towns and villages whereunto you may reach conveniently'. 'Furthermore', the instructions ran:

> you shall take order with the Wardens that the borderers in Scotland may be still tormented and occupied as much as can be conveniently, now specially that it is seed-time, from which if they may be kept and not suffered to sow their grounds, they shall by the next year be brought to such penury as they shall not be able to live nor abide the country.

Seymour, for his part, counselled Henry that the proposed destruction would be sure to breed greater desperation and resistance, and recorded that he 'could not sleep this night for thinking of the king's determination for Leith'. Nevertheless, Henry was typically obdurate and heartily condoned the calculated carnage of the civilian population, in accordance with Leviticus (xxvi 36), whereby 'the sound of a shaken leaf' might so terrify the survivors that they would 'flee, as fleeing from a sword'.

Accordingly, in May, Lord Evers' horsemen burned and devastated their way to Edinburgh, stormed it, set the surrounding countryside ablaze and returned whence they had come, part by land and part by sea, pillaging every port and gutting some fifty towns, abbeys, chapels, nunneries and castles in their path. At Dunbar, we are told, the inhabitants had been caught unawares by a surprise raid at night 'so that their first sleeps closed in with the fire' and they were duly 'suffocated and burnt'. Hertford himself was especially appreciative of his Irish troops who, he told his master, 'have done great service and are dreaded by the Scots as they take no prisoners'. Not surprisingly, this 'great season of notable victories' was perceived by Henry and his subjects as 'rather a miracle than otherwise', and the chronicler Edward Hall, in keeping with the sentiments of the time, loyally trumpeted the exact number of buildings demolished by his rampaging countrymen so that the Earl of Hertford's 'great exploit' might 'be the better known'. Thus ended the earl's 'prosperous adventures' in Scotland, though now, of course, at least the way to France was clear.

In the summer of 1544, therefore, Henry returned at last to his time-honoured passion and personally led the attack on his bitterest enemy, regardless of the fact that by now his gross physical condition made it difficult for him even to negotiate a normal doorway. According to one account, he had 'a body and a half, very abdominous and unwieldy with fat'. 'And', the account went on, 'it was death to him to be dieted, and death to him not to be dieted, so great his corpulence.' Edward Hall, in his turn, spoke of the king's need at this stage for 'an engine' to carry him upstairs, although, in the main, he appears to have been manhandled around his various residences in a type of sedan chair 'covered with tawny velvet and all over quilted'. This, then, was the monarch portrayed by Cornelis Matsys, his eyes embedded like arrow slits above his bloated jowls. This also was the king whose tilt armour, made for him at Greenwich in 1540, measured 57 inches across the chest. Now, on those rare occasions that he edged forth from the specially constructed litter in which he was to make his curious French odyssey, he would have to be winched by crane into the royal saddle. Nor was there any denying that the king's ambitions were every bit as inflated as his ailing bulk.

The entire campaign in the 'ungracious dog-holes' of France was, of course, a wildly improbable enterprise, fought mainly to muffle the ticking clocks that disturbed Henry's sleep and mocked his waking hours. From the time that it began in earnest, it is difficult to discern any coherent plan of attack. Only a week or so after setting out from Calais, the Duke of Norfolk wrote in desperation to the Privy Council that he had expected to know before this where he was supposed to be going, and although

Boulogne was captured in September, none of the projected huge gains in northern and south-western France were achieved. Then, to compound matters, the emperor rapidly withdrew from the war, leaving Henry to face a possible French invasion in 1545, along with an actual French landing on the Isle of Wight, the prelude to which was the sinking of the *Mary Rose*. And though Henry's French adventures ended in 1546 with Francis agreeing to uncommonly generous peace terms, the Treaty of Camp, which yielded Boulogne to England for eight years, was in reality no more than a face-saving sop afforded by a French government that was sufficiently triumphant for generosity. No glory was won, no gain accrued. In short, the English tyrannosaur had once again begotten a tadpole.

All things considered, the King of England would have done well to heed the advice given some time earlier to Louis XII of France that in war 'three things must be made ready: money, money and, once again, money'. A military revolution of sorts was currently outstripping royal revenues and the gap between princely posturing and harsh economic reality was starker than ever. The cost of mercenaries, in particular, was out of control and armies of 10,000, which once consumed whole kingdoms, had by now swollen drastically. The English force, which campaigned for three months in France in 1544, for instance, consisted of 42,000 men and cost just under £587,000, while the total expense of Henry's wars between 1542 and 1546 amounted to £2,144,000 – some ten times as much as the expenditure on the French campaigns that had followed his accession. Apart from the unexpected length of the wars, the economic planning of Henry VIII's council, such as it was, also foundered on the huge standing cost of maintaining defences at Berwick, Calais, Boulogne and the south-coast ports. In this regard, even victory brought with it crippling costs. After it had been won, Boulogne, for instance, would cost another £426,306 to defend and this at a time when the best that Henry could depend upon annually from his normal peacetime revenues was a mere £200,000.

Ultimately, the king would resort to any and every financial expedient to subsidise his new venture. The man who had begun his reign safe and solvent now went cap-in-hand to the money lenders of Antwerp to raise, at rates of 10 and 14 per cent, loans totalling £75,000 at his death. And, on top of all this, he would still need to impose taxes and forced loans upon his country that were heavier than any hitherto. Wolsey's earlier extortions, for example, were nothing compared to the levies of Henry's last years, even excluding the 'benevolences' screwed from both clergy and laity with no honest intention of repayment. Worst of all, over half of the necessary war expenditure would be paid for by resort to a grievous debasement of the coinage and by the sale of crown lands. The coins minted in 1544, for example, contained only half their weight in fine silver, while those of 1546 consisted of no more than a third, and though this attempted fraud made the war possible in the short term, it did so, of course, only by stoking rampant inflation later on. In effect, Henry and his ministers mortgaged the economic security of the nation with a crude and counter-productive financial scam, and as the new 'silver' coins turned copper red with use in the hands of their holders, so a desperate government grew increasingly discredited by its own antics.

The dangers involved in the government's fiscal mismanagement were actually quite apparent to all but the king himself. In 1545, Wriothesley, the Lord Chancellor, informed the council that 'this year and last year the king has spent about £1,300,000. His subsidy and benevolence ministering scant £300,000, and the lands being consumed and the plate of the realm molten and coined, I lament the danger of the time to come...' Furthermore, the groans without as well as within the corridors of power were now growing increasingly audible. After two London aldermen had refused to contribute to Henry's escapades, one of them was incarcerated in Fleet Prison until he did, while the other, Richard Reid, was ordered to the Scottish wars with a 'following' raised at his own expense. When Reid was subsequently captured and forced to pay a ransom to the Scots, the king was quick to share the joke with his cronies. Clearly, though, there were no broader grounds for mirth, since Henry's vain pursuit of shadows abroad was creating a dismal tapestry of mounting problems, all of which would weigh most heavily upon his successor. Plainly, the exploits were few, the exploited many, and all the while, as the commons wheezed under the weight of their corpulent ruler's ambitions, a select few wheedled for the nation's religious future.

In 1539, the French ambassador, Marillac, wrote that the English 'protest that in all points but the papal supremacy and the religious orders their creed is identical with ours'. Henry had, indeed, always claimed that in breaking with Rome he never intended to 'touch the sacraments' or follow the 'Lutheran sect' and it is true that, officially, there was much formal similarity between the old and new devotional forms. The so-called 'King's Book' of 1543, for instance, would be positively anti-Lutheran in tone, especially upon the central issue of justification by faith: 'Men may not think we be justified by faith as it is a several virtue separated from hope and charity, fear of God and repentance; but by it is meant faith neither only or alone, but with the foresaid virtues coupled together.' Meanwhile, in terms of external forms, Henry's Church of England was both scriptural and sacramental, denouncing superstition, but maintaining ancient tradition as vigorously as ever. The English Church still upheld, for example, the symbol of St Athanasius and the Nicaean Creed, while the laity, for their part, heard the familiar Mass in Latin and were mainly satisfied. They went also to confession, made their communion at Easter, abstained from flesh on Fridays and Saturdays, observed the Lenten fast and kept the Ember seasons. And just as there was still holy water to be found in church porches, so, at Candlemas, the priest continued to bless the sanctifying lights dressed in familiar vestments.

But perhaps the most significant evidence for Henry's continuing lack of commitment to genuine evangelical reform is provided by those who desired it most, for after their earlier optimism, many Protestants now despaired of the King of England's leanings. The future Protestant martyr John Hooper, for instance, wrote bitterly to Bullinger in Germany that

> as far as religion is concerned, idolatry is nowhere in greater vigour. Our king has destroyed the Pope, but not popery; he has expelled all the monks and nuns, pulled down their monasteries; he has caused all their possessions to be transferred into his exchequer, and yet they are bound, even the fragile female sex [...] to perpetual chastity [...] The impious mass, the most shameful celibacy of the clergy, the invocation of Saints, auricular confession, superstitions, abstinence from meats, and purgatory, were never held by the people in greater esteem than at the moment.

Fearing unruly 'reformation from below', then, Henry held the orthodox line on all fundamental ideas, including transubstantiation. He would also prove unwavering in his insistence upon restricting access to the English Bible on the grounds that the free availability of the gospel to the uneducated commons might well lead to challenges to the social hierarchy. To this end, he gave his assent in 1543 to an Act of Parliament seriously curtailing the study of Scripture in English, which was entitled, somewhat paradoxically perhaps, the 'Act for the advancement of true religion'. In justification, Henry complained to Parliament that the 'most precious jewel, the Word of God, is disputed, rhymed, sung and jangled in every alehouse and tavern', since it was in such places that Bible readings for the illiterate took place chiefly.

The Act of Six Articles had, of course, already shaken the religious left, and in its wake, the radical Nicholas Shaxton was deprived of his see and Hugh Latimer, too, was induced to resign. As the conservative cloud descended, even Mrs Cranmer was forced to slip off to see her relations in Germany. Yet until the very end of his reign, the king also continued to sow confusion by flirting in a most damaging way with certain features of Protestantism. Not only did he become doubtful about purgatory, for instance, but he outrightly decried the sacraments of ordination, extreme unction and ultimately confession. Likewise, Henry considered himself to be carrying out an avid assault on superstitious practices as well. In 1546, for instance, creeping to the Cross was added to the list of forbidden practices, though he himself had earlier encouraged this particular ritual in his proclamation of February 1539 and would continue the practice in his own chapel on the grounds that he was less inclined to error than his subjects. In his last years, too, much to the satisfaction of supporters of Protestant reform, he continued to urge the teaching of the Creed, the Lord's Prayer and the Ten Commandments in English. In effect, then, the Act of Six Articles proved another lost opportunity to cut the clear course to left or right that was required by circumstances. Instead, flying in the face of what had been attempted in 1539, Henry sought throughout the 1540s to impose his own idiosyncratic, hybrid version of doctrine which contained elements both to satisfy and at the same time frustrate all sides.

In reality, Henry's professed intention to hold a 'mean, indifferent, true and virtuous way' between the errors of Rome and the excesses of continental Europe was a sure-fire recipe for increasing dissent and division. And Erasmus' belief that faith and charity alone might dispel religious differences would prove a fond delusion unsuited to the times, for when dealing with religion, as indeed most things, Tudor Englishmen did not seek accommodation and compromise. Instead, they dealt unequivocally in categorical certainties, universal authorities and monopolies of spiritual truths. The debate 'between Tyndale and me', Thomas More had written, was 'nothing else in effect but to find out which Church was the very Church'. And this was a mindset well attuned – in theory at least – to Henry's own. But the king was also a hesitant character, intermittently beset by insecurities and rarely prepared to grasp nettles when occasion demanded. So when the proponents of reform rightly repeated that the king could not expect to 'throw a man headlong from the top of a high tower and bid him stay where he was, half-way down', this would not prevent him from attempting to do precisely that.

Paradoxically, then, Henry's problem and the problem for his successor was that, in rejecting the old religion, he had not been enough of a heretic. Either Henry the Catholic or Henry the Protestant would have meant scope for the imposition of order and stability, but Henry the imperious religious dabbler meant oppression in the here and now, and a stock of trouble for the future. On July 1540, he demonstrated very aptly what his 'mean, indifferent' and 'virtuous' route in religion entailed when he burnt the evangelicals, Barnes, Garrett and Jerome at the same time that the conservatives, Abel, Featherstone and Powell were being hanged, drawn and quartered elsewhere. 'What a country England is to live in', a foreigner is said to have exclaimed to John Foxe, 'when they hang papists and burn Anabaptists.' In reality, the king's religious thinking in these years grew out of and epitomised his egocentricity and arbitrariness, as well as the ultimately unsystematic nature of his thinking. Henry remained, indeed, a dilettante in religion concerned primarily with issues relating to royal control *per se* and the satisfaction of his personal inklings, prejudices and vanities. The fact, for instance, that he frequently challenged the doctrine of purgatory during these years, but nevertheless ordered in his will that masses be said for his soul 'for ever perpetually' says everything.

The extent of the religious divisions bred by the king's indecision was particularly evident in his famous speech to Parliament of 1545:

> What love and charity is there among you when one calleth another heretic and Anabaptist, and he calleth him again papist, hypocrite and Pharisee? […] I hear daily that you of the clergy preach one against another, without charity or discretion […] Be not judges of yourselves of your fantastical opinions and vain expositions […] Be in charity with one another like brother and brother.

Henry's concerns are understandable. He now ruled a society where some believed in justification by faith and others in the efficacy of good works; some that the Mass was a sacrifice of Christ, others that it was a memorial of the last supper; some that the consecrated bread and wine of the Eucharist became Christ's body and blood, others that they remained materially unaltered; some in auricular confession and priestly absolution, others in the priesthood of all believers. Cromwell's call in his injunctions of 1538 that Englishmen should 'most commodiously resort' to reading of the English Bible and 'avoid all contention and altercation therein' had therefore proved singularly unsuccessful. However, if Henry's concerns make sense, his failure to acknowledge the Crown's responsibility for this state of affairs does not. The new Church of England, with its Latin liturgy and English scriptures, was even linguistically at odds with itself. Moreover, any attempt to construe Henry's religious policies as an attempt to achieve a *via media* is fundamentally deceptive, for a middle path is just that and not one which oscillates wildly and incessantly from side to side. Moreover, as Henry's Church rattled along on its doctrinal rollercoaster ride, there was every danger, that without his bulk as ballast, it might at some point after his death be in serious danger of derailment.

Certainly, this religious ambivalence would cause the court to darken, as ambitious courtiers looked increasingly to the future and the king found himself fighting more and more viciously to maintain some control of the present. Two main contending groups orbited the throne at this time, each jockeying for position and cagily probing the weak spots of its foe. On the one hand, there were religious conservatives, led by the Duke of Norfolk and Stephen Gardiner, Bishop of Winchester, who wished to resist further Protestant advance. Having hitched themselves to the Church of England pragmatically in the 1530s, and accepted the royal supremacy in political terms, they now, nevertheless, baulked at any prospect of the introduction of newfangled doctrines from Europe. In the opposing camp, meanwhile, were the radicals, led by Edward Seymour and Thomas Cranmer, both of whom wished to press forward the pace of religious reform with a genuinely Protestant onslaught that would reach well beyond Henry's own religious instincts. For both sides, this faction war would be waged remorselessly by means of character assassination, scaremongering, rumour, innuendo, and of course fawning deceit. And as the protagonists tussled for high stakes, the king, for his part, derived a failing old man's delight in observing, frustrating and mocking them.

The opening assault in the vendetta was made by the conservatives when they attempted in the spring of 1543 to bring about the arrest of Thomas Cranmer on grounds of heresy. On this occasion the so-called Prebendaries' Plot, which had originated with Stephen Gardiner and a member of the cathedral chapter at Canterbury whom Cranmer had sentenced for denouncing the English Bible, eventually fizzled out harmlessly after a commission had duly investigated the matter. When the storm first broke, however, the archbishop had been treated to the kind of chilled joviality that is the favourite hors-d'oeuvre of many gangland bosses. 'Ah my chaplain', Henry remarked as he took the articles of accusation from his sleeve, 'I have news for you. I now know who is the greatest heretic in Kent.' Although the archbishop appears to have maintained an outward calm throughout, the inner impact of what must surely have appeared the first chime of his death-knell may well be imagined.

But a far graver danger arose before the year was out when the council obtained Henry's consent to examine Cranmer and send him to the Tower. Summoned suddenly to the king's presence during the night at 'about 11 of the clock', the primate appears to have responded, once again, not with a feverish defence of his position and counter-accusations against his enemies, but with what Henry dubbed 'fond simplicity', thanking his master for the opportunity to explain his ideas before his accusers. Clearly, he had not learned that at the mid-Tudor court, a scholarly knowledge of mankind was no substitute for a hard-edged understanding of men, and his naivety could well have meant an end to him. In effect, the archbishop was like a vegan offering to discuss the virtues of a low cholesterol diet with a pack of half-starved slavering wolves. Nevertheless a mixture of sentimentality born of old familiarity with his archbishop and spiteful glee at foiling the wiles of Gardiner and Norfolk had already swung Henry to Cranmer's defence. Promising the archbishop his support in the ensuing face-off, he presented the cleric with one of his rings and instructed him to display it before the council at the appropriate time next day, as a token that he enjoyed unwavering royal protection.

Around eight hours later, the vultures duly gathered, confident of the king's support and hungry for an easy kill, though Henry had all the time been relishing the farce in prospect. When finally admitted to the council meeting, Cranmer was told in no uncertain terms by his enemies that he had infected the whole realm with heresy and was to be committed to the Tower and examined as a common heretic. Having been refused access to the witnesses against him and just prior to what would have been his brusque removal, Cranmer now responded to script. And though the primate was, by nature, a scholar of the grey and reticent kind rather than a political virtuoso skilled in the flourishes of that trade, the saving ring was brandished with aplomb and the ship of rats not only sunk but deserted in a trice. Lord John Russell, the Lord Privy Seal and a key player in the conspiracy against Cranmer, at once took it upon himself to declare to his colleagues how he had warned them 'what would come of this matter'. No doubt with puffed out chest, he added: 'I knew right well that the king would never permit my Lord of Canterbury to have such a blemish as to be imprisoned.' Then, as the icy water reached his nostrils, the Duke of Norfolk, in his turn, explained that the council had desired the imprisonment of Cranmer only so that he might 'after his trial be set at liberty to his more glory'.

Thereafter, however, the factional merry-go-round continued to spin. In 1544, it had been the turn of the conservatives to feel the brunt of radical counter-plotting and the king's capriciousness was once more much in evidence. The victim this time was Stephen Gardiner. Nor was it surprising that he should have been a man marked for infamy by his opponents. The bishop, after all, generated strong antipathies, as John Ponet's famous description of him amply demonstrates. He was, wrote Ponet, 'of a swart colour, with a hanging look, frowning brows, deep-set eyes, a nose hooked like a buzzard, great paws (like a devil), an outward monster with a vengeable wit'. So when his nephew and secretary, Germain, was condemned for denying the royal supremacy, Gardiner himself was soon implicated, only to be saved by a display of utter submission fully worthy of him, but demonstrating, nevertheless, the cold fear that his master still generated. Falling to his knees in front of Henry he is said to have declared timorously that, though he had once harboured some of the evil views of his kinsman, he would now 'become a new man'. The king, no doubt relishing another opportunity to dominate his councillors, immediately granted a full pardon and once again failed to inform the intended victim's accusers, simultaneously humiliating and infuriating them in the process.

However, if Stephen Gardiner might willingly kneel down under such duress, he would not, it seems, lie down for long. Was he not after all, according to his enemies, a man who would never relent, never forgive a rebuff, never forget an imagined injustice done unto him, or remember friendship? Indeed, such was his unyielding nature that John Dudley, a rising star of the radical faction, would be banned from court in November 1546 for rendering him a full-blooded clout within the confines of the council chamber itself. Therefore, once the dust had settled on his own case, Gardiner duly decided to go for broke. Sensing the growing ascendancy of the radicals in the intervening period and working in cahoots with Thomas

Wriothesley, it was time, he concluded, for a last-ditch attack on none other than the queen herself over her allegedly heretical activities.

The queen concerned was, of course, Catherine Parr, whom Henry had married in July 1543, some eighteen months after the execution of Catherine Howard. Aged 31 at that time, Henry's new wife had already buried two elderly husbands after nursing both dutifully. However, the final Queen Catherine had now been chosen more as an intellectual companion and ideal stepmother rather than as a nursemaid, in the way that is often assumed. Though childless herself, she had found herself living with stepchildren, albeit much older than she, in both her previous marriages, and it says much for her tact that she maintained good relations with them. She had also received an excellent education in the liberal, Renaissance tradition and spoke Latin fluently. Moreover, as well as being acquainted with modern languages, she was known to be theologically inquisitive. Sad to relate, it was this last quality that would nearly cost the queen her life.

In truth, Catherine Parr was always wholly unsympathetic to so-called 'hot gospellers', who claimed what she termed a 'carnal liberty' for themselves. But, as John Foxe later pointed out, she was undeniably 'very zealous' to God's word and had made her private apartments the roost of a flock of young radical sympathisers from the time of her marriage. Worst of all, in a Tudor court that was all ears, she had voiced her opinions too freely, even to the extent of making them known to her unreceptive husband. The king had, of course, already been 'taught' to his cost by some of his former wives and he had been anything but a good or willing learner on previous occasions. Nor was he prepared to risk further humiliation. Therefore, Gardiner, working in league with Wriothesley, was told to investigate Catherine's heretical activities and search her rooms at once. If any damning evidence were uncovered, she should be 'carried by night unto the Tower'.

Once again, however, things unfolded strangely, as a result of what appears to have been yet another double game on Henry's part. The warrant for the queen's arrest was, it seems, 'mislaid' shortly after it had been drawn up, only to find its way to her 'by accident'. At this, Catherine is said to have 'fell incontinent into a great melancholy and agony' which Henry now used as a pretext for a stage-managed public spectacle designed both to subordinate and save his wife at one and the same time. When, therefore, the queen duly offered him her remorseful and humble prostration, along with guarantees of perpetual subservience before a carefully selected audience, Henry was only too pleased to respond with gushing offers of forgiveness, making them once more 'perfect friends'. Of course, the little matter of condign punishment for the plot's perpetrators remained, and that very afternoon Henry duly greeted Wriothesley with blows from his hat before forcing him to his knees amid cries that he was an 'arrant-knave, beast and fool'.

But if the Lord Chancellor would at least be spared the fleeting hospitality of the gallows, the same could not be said for the son of his fellow conservative, the Duke of Norfolk. Henry Howard, Earl of Surrey, is known today, of course, as a poet of considerable talent, but he was woefully lacking in any kind of self-control and would discover soon enough that heedless ambition and presumption were mortally dangerous vices for any courtier, regardless of birth or connection. Touched by the 'fury of his restless youth' and a 'heady will', Surrey was once described by one of Cromwell's agents as 'the most foolish proud boy in England' and now, at the age of 30, nothing, it seems, had changed. Indeed, though he popularised the Petrarchan sonnet and introduced blank verse into the English language, it is still difficult not to conclude that he remained, at bottom, a drama queen with a serious attitude problem. Furthermore, in spite of the fact that he himself was a religious radical, he remained the son of a leading conservative and was, as such, a rich prize for the radical faction at court whose ascendancy was increasingly apparent. This, then, was not the man to make old bones at the court of Henry VIII and when at last, during 1546, he began to vaunt his Plantagenet blood too brazenly, the king had him arrested and paraded publicly through the streets of London.

Howard's eventual defence at his trial was a superb, but unavailing, display of aristocratic sauce. Advancing the principle that the proof of the pudding was in the pedigree, he claimed simply that a true nobleman, such as he, would not lie. The honour of his line did not, however, prevent him from an unenviable escape attempt involving a slippery slide down the privy of his cell in the Tower to a waiting boat. In the event, he was apprehended just after his messy descent and then further compounded his predicament by announcing that he had escaped, because 'they always find the innocent guilty' – a clear and grievous aspersion on the king's justice. So it was that, on 19 January, as his sovereign neared death, Henry Howard went with uncharacteristic resignation to the scaffold where he, too, learned the truth of the dictum that 'one had a little pain in the head and heart, then all is over'.

Naturally, the Duke of Norfolk himself would not be able to remain unscathed after this catastrophe for his family. Norfolk was by this time an odious old man, still very crafty and still, naturally, of limited ability. His main problem now, however, was the trickle of royal blood in his own veins, which had been noised too broadly by his careless son. Knowing, of course, from long service to the Crown that the outcomes of State trials under Henry VIII were a foregone conclusion, this time he was to be on the receiving end of royal justice. Sensibly, therefore, he opted for a guilty plea and a strategy of abject surrender, which came as easily to him as it had done to Gardiner. The day before his son's trial, therefore, Norfolk drew up a confession about his own faults in concealing his son's treasonable use of Edward the Confessor's arms. Then, after he was attainted, he wrote to the king in the hope of mollifying him by asking that his vast estates be granted to Prince Edward. Nevertheless, Henry was not appeased and he fixed Norfolk's execution for 28 January: the day, as it transpired, before his own death. Ultimately, it was this alone which would save the duke at the very last.

With Norfolk's disgrace finally sealed, there could be no doubt that events had taken on a momentum of their own and that the radicals had won their protracted struggle for power comprehensively. They had secured vital positions in the privy chamber, which controlled access to the king, and they had also obtained the exclusion of Gardiner from the council. Meanwhile, the Howards had fallen utterly. In fact, all that was left of the house of Howard now was the considerable booty left by their fall, and the crows were swift in swooping. Hertford even pilfered Surrey's parliament cap, his spurs and two pairs of stockings, while his brother, Thomas Seymour, seized the hapless earl's shirts and shoes.

The key factor in the radicals' success was simply Hertford's personal standing and credibility as a potential leader over that of Norfolk. Whereas the latter had not emerged with credit from his French campaigns, the former had appeared to shine in Scotland. Similarly, Catherine Howard's disgrace continued to hang like a soiled pall over Norfolk's family line. By the 1540s the Duke of Norfolk was an ageing figure who should have been handing over his influence to the younger generation, but his son, the Earl of Surrey, had been too blatantly irresponsible to be considered a future leader. Bishop Gardiner, on the other hand, was distrusted by Henry and in any case had spent all of 1541 out of the country as ambassador to Charles V. Then again, other conservatives like Wriothesley and Lord

Russell were essentially herd creatures. Ultimately, therefore, the radicals emerged victorious at the end of the reign in spite of rather than because of their religious stance. Though Henry's religious position should logically have dictated otherwise, his commitment to what he perceived to be his son's interests had dictated his final affiliations. And now that his end was edging ever nearer, the king was, of course, more prepared than ever to sacrifice religious principle for his dynasty's sake.

That Henry's existence was, indeed, winding down was unmistakable. More than ever, as he slipped into the semi-retired life of an elderly invalid, the king's private hours were now spent in the company of his favourite fool, Will Somers, who for twenty years had made his master laugh and acted as his confidant. On those increasingly frequent occasions when Henry was in pain, only Somers could cheer him and it was no coincidence that the artist who illustrated the king's personal psalter in 1540, chose to depict him in the company of the diminutive Shropshireman. Such was Somers' status that he was paid handsomely as a servant of the privy chamber and performed for his master only in private. Yet in spite of his fool's antics and saws, the king had continued to be jarred by regular reminders of his mortality. Thomas Audley, Lord Chancellor since 1533 and an uncommonly loyal servant, had died in 1544, while the commander of Boulogne, Lord Poynings, died the following year, along with Henry's longtime physician Dr Butts. Most wounding of all, perhaps, was the death of Charles Brandon, who finally abandoned his hounds in 1545 while the king was away from court on progess.

In Henry's own case, when the Angel of Death finally chose to descend, it did not so much swoop as flutter randomly in a lengthy and painful descent. Grievous collapses were punctuated by apparent recoveries, which, in turn, were followed by further breakdowns. Gradually the intervals between the king's bouts of disease became shorter, his periods of convalescence longer, and more and more often he was forced to keep to his bed or at least to the confines of his private apartments. Ten years earlier, Lord Montague had been executed for remarking that 'his leg will kill him', and in March 1546 this prophecy began to take on a renewed significance. In Chapuys' view, it was already remarkable that Henry could get about at all, for he had 'the worst legs in the world' and when, therefore, yet another seizure followed, the portents were not good. Admitting that he had a fever in his left leg, the king said nonetheless that his robust constitution would sustain him. But his 'visage', an observer reported, 'showed it was worse than he pretended', and left no doubt that his last illness had begun.

From March onwards Henry was forced to seek shelter away from the public eye at Whitehall and as he did so the court itself settled into an increasingly melancholy routine, the impact of which was actually heightened by the pretence of normality that it involved. The privy chamber at Whitehall was located in a block of apartments running parallel to the river, and in the nearby guard chamber fifty gentlemen pensioners were in constant attendance upon the ailing king, with poleaxes at the ready, lest anyone should attempt to disturb him. Outside in the presence chamber, however, merely a shadow court held sway. Even so, all due reverence was paid to the empty throne as steaming dishes of meat were served at the unoccupied dining table only to be removed later with full ceremony. Moreover, in deference to the king's symbolic presence, courtiers and servants alike continued to go bareheaded and in every other way behaved as if their master's dreaded eye was still upon them.

Henry did not, however, go lightly into oblivion. Though he had been ill in July (and for a time shut himself away in deep depression) he was soon speaking of undertaking an extensive progress to the far corners of the realm and making plans for a spree of hawking. Furthermore, when his health permitted, Henry still managed to hobble in acute discomfort about his gardens, where in 1546 he ordered the planting of 4,000 rosebushes, presumably in the expectation that he would live to see them blossom. He also had strength enough to order the weeding of the strawberry beds and continued to grow the large artichokes he loved so much. And there was time, too, for him to supervise the care of his animals: his gerfalcons, peregrines and canary birds, his beagles, harthounds and spaniels, not to mention the eighty or so horses in his stables, the pride of which were four Arabian stallions. Remarkably, even at this late stage, he was actually able to ride, as is demonstrated by the expenses for the king's horses in August 1546, where there is a payment for 'a new stool of walnotry for the king to light upon horseback'. Indeed, on 4 September, Henry left for his customary autumnal hunting tour, on which he planned to visit 'houses remote from towns'. Travelling first to Oatlands, he took his turn among the hunters shooting from fixed standings, whereby the beasts were herded together as sitting targets to be shot in comfort. Three days later he was still spending long hours in the fields, 'always at the chase'.

Predictably, however, he paid a heavy price for these exertions, as he became seriously ill soon afterwards. And though visitors to the itinerant court were told it was only a cold, van der Delft, the new imperial ambassador, found out from his informants that the king was really in 'great danger'. Now, in the foggy London winter, Henry grew steadily worse. For several weeks, from late December to mid-January, he was kept in the utmost seclusion and there was no word of his condition. Rumour even had it that he was already dead. But if these murmurings were wide of the mark, the French ambassador remained in no doubt that the king's illness 'can only be bad and will not last long'. With the queen instructed to remain at Greenwich and the royal children banished to country houses far from court, the physicians now governed all and did what little they could. Unable to pronounce the king's imminent death, which was treason, they feared, too, to give false hope lest they be blamed when the end came. Instead, they warbled the time-honoured blandishments of their profession and played at remedy. Rose water, 'eyebright' water, mouthwashes, fomentations, liquorice, ointment for piles, a soothing powder, known as 'Christ's hands', were all prescribed. There were also cinnamon comfits and green ginger, as well as regular spongings of the king's great frame.

So passed Christmas before Henry made one last rally to turn his attention, albeit much too late, to the business of his will. Ostensibly, it was nothing short of incredible that the succession arrangements had not been sealed long before this time. But from other perspectives, it was, perhaps, all too predictable that one who had been so driven in life by his own purposes and so ensnared by the expedients of the short term should have failed to make satisfactory provision for his demise. The fevered obsession of Henry's quest for an heir did not, it seems, descend to the detail of contriving sound arrangements for the succession of his beloved son. Fear, of course, may well have underlain the postponement, for even during his final days Henry had been 'loth to hear any mention of his death'. The fact that there were actually references in the will both to the possibility of the king's begetting further children and to the eventuality of his dying overseas certainly suggests that the king himself was refusing to acknowledge the inevitable. It is also known, that, at the very time he called for his will to be drafted in late December 1546, Henry was actually contemplating a further attack upon Scotland. But whatever the cause of the delay, such unwillingness to concede his own mortality would, of course, further impair what was already a potentially disastrous political bequest to his successors. Moreover, as a result of his last-minute tampering and tinkering, Henry's will was ultimately never sealed with his signature and was, in many other respects, far from watertight.

It was laid down eventually that the crown should be left to Edward and then, if necessary, to Mary and Elizabeth in turn. At the same time, sixteen of Henry's 'well beloved' ministers were to form a Council of Regency with full powers to govern in the name of the boy who was commanded by his father never 'to change, molest, trouble nor disquiet' his legally appointed councillors. As with everything that Henry did, however, the details were highly problematic and the will was in no way a serious blueprint for addressing the intricacies consequent upon minority government. In the first place, Henry imposed a system of majority decision-making in respect of anything specifically designated *within* the will. This did not necessarily mean, therefore, as has sometimes been mistakenly assumed, that all day-to-day political decisions of the Council of Regency would be hamstrung by indecision and political haggling in the search for shaky majorities. Nevertheless, there was a worrying absence of specific information about the precise process of policy-making and the fuzziness was magnified by the will's heavy insistence upon the equality of each councillor: a principle wholly out of kilter with the prevailing political notions of the day, which were authoritarian to the core. In these, as in all other respects, the will was a reflection of Henry's undisciplined mind and unwieldy ego, which inclined him always to opt for a snap of the fingers rather than more painstaking approaches. Whilst living, the force of his personality might, of course, extract some mileage from ill-considered policies, but any momentum of this kind could not extend beyond the grave, even for him.

Likewise, Henry failed to create any machinery by which the council could create new members. Since Edward could not come of age until he was eighteen, this meant that its personnel would, in theory at least, have to remain unchanged for nigh on a decade. And to make matters worse the Council of Regency in any case possessed no constitutional powers beyond an arbitrary assumption and wish on Henry's part that the king's authority be identified with it. There were no precedents, nor was there anything self-evident about the council's status in the way that the king seemed to assume. Indeed, whether the king could simply found the status of the new council upon his prerogative was doubtful. Furthermore, its absolute status was seriously undermined by the provision that all laws created in the minority of the new king, along with all major administrative decisions enacted were to be subject to repeal upon his coming of age.

That the signature of the will was so badly mishandled was simply one more item in a tale of general incompetence. The delay until 26 December for the last draft might, of course, be taken to indicate that the king was merely using the will as a tool to manipulate the factions that continued to buzz around him. However, even if this might explain his tardiness and the shortcomings in terms of concrete provision, it does nothing to release him from the charge that he was starkly remiss in failing to lay sound foundations for the next reign much earlier. Equally, if, as is sometimes suggested, the will had little to do with Henry but was largely produced under the conspiratorial influence of Seymour and Paget, then the king still remains culpable for sinking into irrelevance at what was, arguably, the pivotal point of the whole reign. According to whichever of the available readings is chosen, Henry is rendered either an incompetent, misguided, egotistical Machiavellian or an aged, sickly spectator, outmanoeuvred at the last by the very councillors whom he had consistently treated with such contempt.

As the power-brokers of the next reign hovered solicitously, the king grew steadily worse throughout January. Some thirty-eight years earlier, he had ascended the throne of England, the epitome of health and vitality, with 'hair plenty and red' and with 'pulse great and full, digestion perfect, anger short, sweat abundant'. Now, however, his former vigour had finally deserted him and neither the constant examination of his stools and sputum, nor the continual letting of his blood in accordance with the waxing and waning of the moon could save him. Between August and December the medical expenses of the privy chamber had increased more than fivefold and judging by the rising expenditure on rhubarb, which was considered a sure remedy for the excessive yellow bile of a choleric disposition, the king's physicians had been ministering to an increasingly desperate and irascible patient. But any attempts at remedy were wholly unavailing.

The specific cause of the king's final disintegration has, of course, long exercised the imagination of historians. Osteomyelitis, cardial infection, scurvy, malaria and alcoholism have all been suggested as possible causes. Syphilis, too, has been touted, though there is not a scrap of documentary evidence to confirm that Henry had indeed fallen prey to love's rogue bacillus. Significantly, the accounts of the king's physician, Thomas Alport, contain no mention of mercury, the standard cure of the day. Nor does any ambassador's report even hint that Henry had been stricken by what the English called the French disease, the French termed the Italian pox, the Italians dubbed the Spanish complaint and the Spanish, in their turn, duly designated the English disease. In any case, all that counted now was outcomes rather than causes, for by the night of 27 January the end was imminent. By this stage, indeed, the only priority was to fetch the cleric whom Henry knew and loved best. Therefore, as the king was overcome by a final paralysing weakness, Thomas Cranmer rode at breakneck pace from Croydon in the small hours of a bitter night when the rivers across Europe were frozen hard.

The scene that greeted the archbishop upon his breathless arrival is a matter of some conjecture, but the resonances of the past were unlikely to have gone entirely unnoticed by him. All around at Whitehall were keen reminders of those who had died infamously at his master's behest. Down the years, countless items 'from sundry persons attainted' had been delivered to the Crown's receivers for them to distribute as they saw fit and much that had been confiscated from the estates of 'traitors' had found its way to the palace where Henry now lay. Among the furnishings arranged so painstakingly by Catherine Howard were Nicholas Carew's former bedcoverings of purple velvet, embroidered cushions once belonging to Lord Montague and further bedchamber goods snatched from the estate of Edward Neville. All kinds of ornaments that had once been Wolsey's, many of them still bearing his arms, were also everywhere to be seen.

Around about, too, were hushed voices of the kind that had once stirred the king to frenzy but could now no longer touch him. The death of a sovereign was, after all, a public spectacle and since Henry's will was unlikely to have been finalised until the evening of his death, its eleven witnesses, which included the ever-present Patrec, his lutanist, may well have been in attendance to watch him die. Doubtless, all the unmistakable tokens of mortal sickness will also have been evident: the oppressive aroma of grey amber and musk to smother the stench of physical decay, the shadowy gloom created by the window tapestries, which were tightly drawn to bar the invasive damp, and the stifling fug generated by the great wood fire that was fed continually to eliminate all 'evil vapours'. Surely, too, the king's physicians were still hovering vainly, with their potions and plasters, their ointments and decoctions, now awaiting what they knew must surely come before the rising of another sun.

Concerning the actual manner of the king's passing, however, there is rather more doubt, for the chroniclers, predictably, were keen to spin his final moments with posterity in mind. In the account given by Godwin in his *Annales*, which is the one most frequently rendered today, it is suggested that Cranmer found the king speechless and already beyond help. When the prelate grasped the king's hand and begged his sovereign to give some token of dying 'in the faith of Christ', the cold fingers are said to have given a last spasm of assent. John Foxe, in his turn, paints an equally edifying scene. Having conveniently set aside the empty ritual of the old church, Henry, it seems, firmly stated his confidence in Christ's willingness to cleanse his soul before slipping fearlessly into the welcoming embrace of his maker. Even the *Spanish Chronicle* concedes the serenity with which Henry faced his redeemer, though here we learn that before commending himself to God, the king duly 'confessed and took the holy sacrament'. Catherine Parr is also added to the bedside scene to receive a fond farewell from her husband, along with brave assurances of how 'it is God's will that we should part'.

But if such descriptions of Henry's death square uneasily with what we have heard of him in life, there is one other account of his extinction which is strikingly different. While others are tinged with triumphal Protestant undertones or tainted by the heavy odour of sanctity, the account of Henry's final hours in the British Library's Hargrave manuscript is much less tranquil and altogether less hopeful. Needless to say, it is largely ignored at this present time when experts are still inclined to end their accounts with talk of Henry's 'greatness'. Here we read of a tormented soul, hovering on the brink of the abyss and wavering frantically between fear and fury. As the victim endures an agonisingly drawn-out struggle against his final fate, his flaws and weaknesses are laid bare at last. His bold impenitence is apparent, his moral worthlessness manifest. Cosmic justice, it seems, prevails on all sides. In mortal panic, Henry calls at last for a final draught of white wine to slake his raging thirst and raves deliriously about monks and clerics before bellowing hopelessly that 'all is lost'.

Doubtless, this particular version is no less awash with wishful thinking than its blander alternatives. Death is, after all, apt to be a prosaic enough affair even for the mighty. But perhaps the Hargrave account is still not without some residing value of a kind, since in one way at least, it may satisfy posterity's deeper needs. For if myths are all there are when the facts themselves are absent, it is surely better that the myths concerned should have a fitting moral edge than otherwise. This, it should be remembered, was the king who had fumed, broken and wrecked through almost forty years of rule – the individual who, in the words of Sir Robert Naunton, had spared neither man in his anger nor woman in his lust. If, then, the Hargrave manuscript plays too freely with events, at least its virtue is to convey in some small measure the essential bankruptcy of a man unfit for power and the ultimate vanity of his hopes.

Epilogue

'But when we remember our mortality and that we must die, then we think that all our doings in our lifetime are clearly defaced and worthy of no memory if we leave you in trouble at the time of our death.'

Henry VIII, speaking in November 1528 to 'his nobility, judges and counsellors with divers other persons'.

'In this confusion of wives, so many noblemen and great personages were beheaded, so much church plunder committed and so many acts of disobedience perpetrated that it may be said that all that ensued and is still going on, is the penalty of that first sin.'

Daniel Barbaro to the Venetian Senate (1551).

Though Henry VIII had finally achieved that 'most precious jewel' of a healthy male heir in October 1537, his son had sprung too late from his weary loins, for by the time of the birth Henry was already forty-six in an age when a fleeting earthly span of less than forty was the norm. Merely nine years later, therefore, Edward VI, the much-heralded 'boy of wondrous hope', was left a vulnerable orphan cast adrift amid the surging sectarian and faction-ridden currents of mid-Tudor politics. Nor was it altogether surprising that within six and a half years of his accession in 1547, the heirless boy-king on whom all hinged should himself be ailing mortally at the unripe age of 15. This, after all, was almost the identical age at which his father's elder brother, Arthur, and bastard son, Henry Fitzroy, had been plucked from life. In the summer of 1553, therefore, a politically and religiously torn country hovered on the brink of a bloody war of succession.

For some months, Edward had been enduring an agonising and prolonged approach to death from what contemporaries termed 'a consumption of the lights'. What was until recently still considered to have been tuberculosis is now known with more certainty to have been a suppurating pulmonary infection, which would lead in due course to the ghastly traumas associated with generalised septicaemia and renal failure. His first biographer, John Hayward, bemoaned 'the invincible malignity' of Edward's affliction and those who tended him have left harrowing testimony to the disease's relentless progress. John Banister, a young medical student attached to the royal household, noted at the time that the king was 'steadily pining away' and added that he could not sleep 'except he be stuffed with drugs'. Banister further observed that 'the sputum which he brings up is livid, black and fetid' smelling 'beyond measure'. The king's feet were, it seems, 'swollen all over' and it was acknowledged without reservation that 'to the doctors all these things portend death'.

In fact, both time and the times had conspired from the outset against the stricken youth who would play his role so dutifully until the very end. First, under the partly right-minded but wholly wrong-headed stewardship of his uncle and Lord Protector, Edward Seymour, England had continued its agonising descent into foreign war and economic upheaval. Then, after Seymour's ouster in the aftermath of the rebellions of 1549, the desperate quest for the restoration of law and order became too often the pretext for the abuse of justice under John Dudley, Duke of Northumberland. As religious commotion added to the unwholesome mix, so the corridors of power heaved with faction and ambition, and in the wider world, dearth and the unfamiliar scourge of inflation racked the common people and strained social bonds to the limit. Amid the general hardship, landlords, it was said, 'bred a decay of people' and 'returned to their old vomit' in spite of government invocations that they mend their ways. Meanwhile, the radical Protestant John Ponet lamented, 'the people driven of hunger to grind acorns for bread and drink water instead of ale'. To cap all, as the 'hideous monster of base moneys', first unleashed in the previous reign, had continued to stalk the land, even nature herself seemed to assume an unforgiving aspect as 'sweating sickness' cut two consecutive morbid swathes through high and low alike in 1551 and 1552. Though, ultimately, there would be no apocalypse in mid-Tudor England, there were, nevertheless, many who felt keenly enough the passing of the four horsemen.

As dusk fell on 6 July 1553, just after Edward had breathed his last, rain is said to have fallen in torrents, sweeping houses away and hurling trees heavenwards from their roots. In the City forked lightning, that most evil of ill omens, struck down the steeple of the church where the heretic service had first been heard, and hail, said to be the colour of blood, covered the gardens by the Thames. Nor, it seems, were such signs and wonders confined to London. At Middleton Stoney in Oxfordshire, anxious whispers circulated that a child had been born that same day with one body, two heads, four feet and four hands. Elsewhere, it was thought to be of no little moment that in a churchyard near St Neots a landslide had rudely exposed a clutch of newly buried corpses. Later, too, the superstitious multitude would be readily convinced that the dead king's father had himself sent the storm and risen from the grave in anger at the subversion of his wishes.

These contemporary descriptions of such dramatic portents, however colourfully embellished, were, in fact, by no means inappropriate, for with his son's passing Henry VIII's all-too-fragile plans appeared to have been shattered totally and irrevocably. Indeed, the House of Tudor, divided against itself by a father's caprice, would now be abruptly refashioned against that father's hopes. At a single stroke the male heir and the new national Church, which Henry had sought so strenuously (and at such a cost to others), were extinguished. Jane Seymour's Protestant son was no more and in his stead there loomed imminently the succession of the other, unfavoured half of this fractured legacy: Mary, Catholic daughter of Catherine of Aragon, whom Henry had striven so remorselessly to undermine. But before that time, of course, the supporters of another 'Queen' Jane would also be ripe for culling.

Source Notes and Bibliographical Information

1. Collections of documents

If Henry James was right in claiming that 'the historian, essentially, wants more documents than he can really use', then those scholars involved in unravelling the many threads of Henry VIII's reign must be happy indeed with the abundance of printed sources available to them. What might well be considered merely the 'core' material consists of at least 50,000 documents and at this level the calendars of State papers compiled by our admirably diligent Victorian forebears remain of fundamental importance. Every historian of Henrician England depends upon the *Letters and Papers, Foreign and Domestic, of the Reign of Henry VIII*, edited in twenty-one volumes by J.S. Brewer, J. Gairdner, R.H. Brodie (London, 1862–1932), which remains and will continue to remain the consummate source of detail for the period. Another great mine of contemporary source material is the eleven-volume collection of *State Papers* compiled by the Record Commission from 1830–52. But, in addition to these mighty publications, there are, of course, the calendars containing the correspondence of foreign ambassadors preserved in the archives of Spain and Italy, the various collections of treaties, laws, decrees and ecclesiastical statutes, as well as the acts of the Privy Council, parliamentary records and contemporary chronicles. This enormous mass of documents has been further augmented by the publication of private archives and the additional contributions of various historical societies, such as the Camden, Parker, Selden and Royal Historical Societies.

J.S. Brewer has as good a claim as any to be considered the godfather of modern scholarship on the reign of Henry VIII. A high-minded and many-sided man of letters, he had held the chair of classical literature at King's College, London, before spending the whole of the latter part of his life in the task of calendaring Henry VIII's State papers for the so-called Rolls Series. The first four volumes of the *Letters and Papers* (usually referred to as *L&P*) were edited by him and the remaining seventeen by J. Gairdner, assisted towards the end by R.H. Brodie. They are arranged in chronological order and embrace every type of primary evidence relating to the reign. However, while the *Letters and Papers* serve as an unsurpassed introduction to the historical literature of the period, it should not be forgotten that Brewer and his successors only cited in full those passages that they considered to be of special interest, though in all cases the process of abridgement was conducted with the utmost sensitivity and integrity.

By contrast, the *State Papers* are narrower in scope and arranged according to subject (vol. i, domestic correspondence; vols. ii–iii, correspondence relating to Ireland; vols. iv–v, correspondence relating to Scotland; vols. vi–xi, correspondence between England and other courts) and though this method of categorisation was well intentioned, it did not, of course, reflect the actual thinking of Tudor politicians who had, by necessity, to think in terms of wholes and overviews. Unlike the *Letters and Papers*, however, the *State Papers* are unabridged.

Two other calendars are of particular worth. The *Calendar of State Papers, Venetian*, ed. R. Brown et al. (9 vols., London, 1864–98) is especially relevant for the earlier part of the reign, while the later years are covered by the *Calendar of State Papers, Spanish*, ed. G.A. Bergenroth et al. (13 vols. and 2 supplements, London, 1862–69). The *Calendar of State Papers, Milan*, ed. A.B. Hinds (London, 1913) is also of considerable interest.

Other important collections of sources relating to the reign of Henry VIII are contained in: J. Strype, *Ecclesiastical Memorials, Relating Chiefly to Religion, and the Reformation [...] under King Henry VIII, King Edward VI, and Queen Mary I* (3 vols., Oxford, 1822); N. Pocock, *Records of the Reformation, the Divorce, 1527–1533* (2 vols., Oxford, 1870); G. Burnet, *History of the Reformation of the Church of England*, ed. N. Pocock (6 vols., Oxford, 1865); *The Antiquarian Repertory: A Miscellany Intended to Preserve and illustrate several valuable Remains of Old Times*, ed. F. Grose and T. Astle (4 vols.,

London, 1808); J. Kaulek, *Correspondence Politique de MM. de Castillon and Marillac* (Paris, 1885); R.B. Merriman, *Life and Letters of Thomas Cromwell* (2 vols., Oxford, 1902; reprinted Oxford, 2000); *Correspondencia de Gutierre Gomez de Fuensalida*, ed. duque de Berwick y de Alba (Madrid, 1907); the *Ambassades en Angleterre de Jean du Bellay*, eds. V.L. Bourilly and P. de Vaissiere (Paris, 1905); and A Luders et al. eds., *Statutes of the Realm*, vols. ii and iv, ed. T.E. Tomlins and W.E. Taunton for the Record Commission (1817–19). The development of religious policy can be traced through *Formularies of Faith put forth by Authority during the reign of Henry VIII*, ed. C. Lloyd (Oxford, 1825), while the official records of Convocation are to be found in D. Wilkins, *Concilia magna Britanniae et Hiberniae a synodo Verulamiens A.D. 446 ad Londiniensem, A.D. 1717*, vol. iii (4 vols., London, 1737). Regarding contemporary correspondence, Sir H. E. Ellis, *Original Letters Illustrative of English History* (London, 1835–46) contains a good deal of particularly illuminating material.

A special mention should also be made of T. Rymer, *Foedera* (16 vols., London, 1704–13). As historiographer royal, Thomas Rymer undertook the research and transcription of 'all the leagues, treaties, alliances, capitulations and confederacies, which have at any time been made between the Crown of England and any other kingdoms and states', an immense labour which occupied the last twenty years of his life.

More recent collections of sources, which are therefore more readily accessible, include: P.L. Hughes and J.F. Larkin, *Tudor Royal Proclamations*, vol. i (3 vols., New Haven and London, 1964); G.R. Elton, *The Tudor Constitution: Documents and Commentary* (Cambridge, 1960); M. St Clare Byrne ed., *The Letters of King Henry VIII: A Selection with a Few Other Documents* (London, 1936); H. Savage ed., *Love Letters of Henry VIII* (London, 1945); E. Surtz and V. Murphy eds., *Divorce Tracts of Henry VIII* (Angers, 1988); G. Bray ed., *Documents of the English Reformation* (Cambridge, 1994).

Sadly, the information on Parliament's activities during the Henrician period is much sparser than we might wish for. The *Journals of the House of Lords* (vol. i) contain the Rolls of Parliament from 1513 to 1533 and the Lords' Journals from 1509 to 1513 and from 1533 to 1547. However, the journals are somewhat scanty, detailing the peers in attendance and the bills debated and enacted, but providing no information on the debates themselves or the division lists. For the House of Commons at this time there are no journals at all until the reign of Edward VI and as such, information concerning its proceedings must be gleaned from unofficial sources, such as Merriman's collection of Cromwell's letters (see above), Hall's *Chronicle* (see below), Foxe's *Acts and Monuments* (see below), Roper's *Life of More* (see below) and the correspondence of foreign ambassadors.

For the history of the Privy Council, vols. i–iv of *The Acts of the Privy Council of England*, ed. J.R. Dasent (46 vols., London, 1890–1964) are invaluable, and vol. ii of I.S. Leadam ed., *Select Cases before the King's Council in the Star Chamber* (Selden Society, 1911) may be another source of interest. There is also H. Nicholas ed., *Proceedings and Ordinances of the Privy Council, 1386–1542* (7 vols., London, 1837).

It should be remembered, of course, that 'state' records were often private papers in this period and as such, remained in the hands of elite families. Certainly the most outstanding of such collections published by the Historical Manuscripts Commission remains part one of the *Calendar of the MSS of the Marquess of Salisbury at Hatfield House* (24 vols., London, 1883–1976). Also worthy of mention are *The Manuscripts of his grace the duke of Rutland* (4 vols., Historical Manuscripts Commission, London, 1888–95).

For Henry VIII's youth and background, J. Gairdner ed., *Letters and Papers Illustrative of the Reigns of Richard III and Henry VII* (2 vols., Rolls Series, 1861) is very useful, while the chief printed sources for Ireland are contained in the *Calendar of State Papers Ireland*, 1509–1603, ed. H.C. Hamilton et al. (11 vols., London, 1860–1912). For Scotland, consult *The Hamilton Papers – Letters and Papers Illustrating the Political Relations of England and Scotland in the XVIth Century*, ed. J. Bain (2 vols., 1890–92).

2. Contemporary histories and chronicles

Polydore Vergil's *Anglica Historia*, translated and edited by David Hay, Camden Society, LXXIV (1950), is the first chronicle of English history by a Renaissance humanist. Born at Urbino in 1470, the author came to England in 1503 in the household of Castelli, Bishop of Hereford, as Deputy Collector of Peter's Pence. When Castelli became a cardinal and Bishop of Bath and Wells, Polydore Vergil became archdeacon of Wells and a prebendary of St Paul's, an appointment which brought him into the thick of affairs. Having helped to secure the papal bull for the foundation of St John's College, Cambridge, he also helped to secure the cardinalate for Wolsey, whom he later came to detest. His *Anglica Historia* first appeared in

1534 and is important for the reigns of both Henry VII and Henry VIII up to 1537. It glorifies the Tudors and is unashamedly hostile to Wolsey.

Edward Hall's *The Union of the two noble and Illustre Famelies of Lancastre and York* first appeared in 1542, and was continued and republished by Richard Grafton in 1548 and 1550. It was then edited by Sir Henry Ellis in six volumes in 1809, after which the part concerned with the 'triumphant' reign of Henry VIII was edited into two volumes by C.A. Whibley (London and Edinburgh, 1904). Hall was heavily influenced by the *Anglica Historia*, but while Vergil's outlook was Catholic and cosmopolitan, Hall's was militantly Protestant and nationalistic. Once described as a 'creature of most illuminating limitations', Hall came of Shropshire gentry and was educated at Eton and King's College, Cambridge (1514–18), and at Gray's Inn. He established himself as a lawyer and a Londoner, with a flair for detail and dialogue, and became MP for Bridgnorth in 1542. An ardent royalist, priest-hater, and lover of gorgeous sights and sounds, his is undoubtedly the richest and most comprehensive narrative for the period up to 1532. Hall glorifies the king, vindicates the Reformation and reflects Protestant opinion in contemporary London like no other. He died in 1547.

Compared to Hall, the other contemporary chroniclers, though often contributing useful scraps of information are tame and jejune. They were published in the main by the Camden Society as part of the so-called 'Camden Miscellany' and consist, most notably, of *The Chronicle of the Grey Friars of London*, ed. J.G. Nichols (Camden Society, liii, 1859); *The Chronicle of Calais*, ed. J.G. Nichols (Camden Society, 1846); *The London Chronicle*, ed. C. Hopper (Camden Society, 1859); *The Great Chronicle of London*, ed. A.H. Thomas and I.D. Thornley (London, 1938); and *The Chronicle of Charles Wriothesley*, ed. D.W. Hamilton (Camden Society, 1875). Of these Wriothesley is the most useful, especially for the later years of Henry VIII's life, becoming fuller at the point at which Hall becomes thin in Grafton's continuation.

Though neither is contemporary in the strict sense, two other chronicles warrant attention. John Stow's *Annals* first appeared in 1580 under the title *The Chronicles of England from Brutus unto the present Year of Christ*, but though he was only a London tailor, and a young one at that when Henry VIII died, his accounts are full and reliable. Likewise, Ralph Holinshed's *Chronicles of England, Scotland and Ireland* did not appear until 1577. Nevertheless, feelings and impressions of Henry VIII's reign were far from effaced by that time.

Although not, strictly speaking, a chronicle, Sebastiano Giustiniani's *Four Years at the Court of Henry VIII*, trans. R. Brown (2 vols., London, 1854) is also invaluable. Giustiniani's 226 letters from England convey the complexities of contemporary diplomacy, but are perhaps more interesting in terms of the social observations they contain. His early despatches of 1515 praise Henry, but by the time they cease in July 1519, the Venetian diplomat is expressing greater wariness. He assesses Wolsey, meanwhile, with both hostility and admiration, noting the cardinal's efforts to intimidate and upset him.

3. Contemporary sources relating to prominent individuals

George Cavendish's *Life of Cardinal Wolsey* was written around thirty years after the cardinal's death, but its observations were compiled on the basis of the closest personal acquaintance. Some time before 1522, Cavendish had entered Wolsey's household as gentleman usher, and he stayed in his master's service up to the time of the cardinal's death. Throughout this period, Cavendish took notes of Wolsey's conversations and movements and, as a result, he was able to produce what many have considered to be the earliest of the great English biographies. Though written very much from the perspective of a 'loyal servitor', it is nevertheless the sole authentic record of its kind.

Thomas More also enjoys the distinction of having his own contemporary biographer. About 1557, More's son-in-law William Roper wrote a series of notes, which eventually emerged as his famous *Life of Sir Thomas More*. Based upon his personal recollections and those of his wife, Margaret More, it has been criticised for its hagiographical tendencies. Nevertheless, this is certainly the most direct and intimate source, since Roper had lived with his father-in-law for fifteen years under the paternal roof at Chelsea.

More's works have been gathered in *The Yale Edition of the Complete Works of St Thomas More* (New Haven and London, 1963–79), and Roper's account of his life, as well as Cavendish's life of Wolsey, have been reproduced in R.S. Sylvester and D.P. Harding eds., *Two Early Tudor Lives* (New Haven and London, 1962).

Much useful information on Thomas Cromwell's rise can be gleaned from Cavendish's *Life of Cardinal Wolsey*, and Chapuys' letter to Granvelle (*L&P,* vol. v., No. 228) gives some details on the secretary's origins and early struggles. From the time he came to power, all the publications of documents relating to the reign, and especially the *Letters and Papers*, speak of him. In his *Acts and Monuments*, ed. S.R. Cattley and G. Townsend (8 vols., London, 1837–41), John Foxe (1516–87) gave a *Life of the Lord Cromwell*, in which there are some interesting details, although his work is unashamedly polemical in tone. Foxe was, of course, an earnest and passionate Protestant, who had given up an Oxford fellowship on religious grounds, and preferred exile to conformity in the reign of Mary. He hated popery, pursued Stephen Gardiner with special vehemence as the figurehead of religious conservatism and eulogised Cromwell. His authority has often been impugned, and not without some justification when it is remembered that he was capable of forgetting the date of the Act of Six Articles. Marillac (Kaulek op. cit.) gives us the most precise account of Cromwell's fall.

Aside from the *Letters and Papers*, one of the best authorities for Thomas Cranmer's life is Ralph Morice, Cranmer's secretary, who supplied Foxe with much information. Cranmer's works were edited by H. Jenkyns, *Remains of Thomas Cranmer* (Oxford, 1833), while Strype was the first to write a Life of Cranmer in 1694, *Memorials of the Most Reverend Father in God, Thomas Cranmer* (3 vols., Oxford, 1848–54). The latter work made use of 'documents, registers, letters and other original manuscripts', which are given in great number in the appendix.

The oldest complete biography of Fisher was written in English about 1570 and is believed to have been penned by former students of Christ Church or St John's, Cambridge. One of those involved, Thomas Watson, was Stephen Gardiner's chaplain. Another of Fisher's contemporaries, Richard Hilliard, priest and secretary to Bishop Tunstall, was condemned to death in Parliament in 1543 before taking refuge in Rome, where he wrote a book on Henry VIII's reign, which dealt with Fisher's activities and treatment. Though this work has been lost, an extract was preserved by the British Museum in the Arundel MSS 152. Another of Fisher's contemporaries, who was present at his martyrdom, Mr Justice William Rastell, wrote a life of Thomas More, his uncle, in which many pages refer to the Bishop of Rochester. Though the manuscript has once again been lost, numerous extracts are preserved from it in the Arundel MS. Another biography of Fisher, *The Life and Death of that renowned John Fisher, Bishop of Rochester*, was produced in 1655 but not published until 1893 by the Jesuit Francis van Ortroy in the *Analecta Bollandiana*.

***

There follows a summary of material specifically relevant to each chapter. Most of the books mentioned are secondary works, but there are also references to particular contemporary sources not cited in the preceding section.

The Child Within the Man

M.L. Bruce, *The Making of Henry VIII* (Glasgow, 1977), is one of the few books to focus extensively upon the king's childhood and contains a number of intriguing nuggets of detail, which have been incorporated into this chapter. For the background and personalities of Henry VII and Elizabeth of York, see S.B. Chrimes, *Henry VII*, (London, 1981); R.L. Storey, *The Reign of Henry VII* (London, 1968); and S. Cunningham, Henry VII (London, 2007). Further light is shed upon the mother of Henry VIII by N.H. Nicholas, *The Privy Purse Expenses of Elizabeth of York with a Memoir* (Pickering, 1830). The various complexities of Lady Margaret Beaufort are dealt with in E.M.G. Routh, *Lady Margaret, Mother of Henry VII*, (Oxford, 1924), while a more modern perspective is provided by M.K. Jones and M.G. Underwood, *The King's Mother* (Cambridge, 1993). Vols. iv and v of John Leland's *De Rebus Britannicis Collectanea*, ed. T. Hearne (6 vols., Oxford, 1715), give details of her ordinances. For Lady Margaret's hostility towards the French, consult John Fisher's funeral sermon, published in 1708. Henry's nurse Anne Luke is mentioned in the *Calendar of Patent Rolls* (HMSO, 1911), 11, 46, 345, 422, 488, 489, 581, while aspects of contemporary child care are outlined in the treatises of Thomas Phaer, Felix Wurtz and Bartholomaeus Metlinger, which can be found in John Ruhrah, *Pediatrics of the Past*, (New York, 1925). On the other hand, surviving examples of the jousting toys mentioned in this chapter are to be found today in the Kuntshistorisches Museum, Vienna. Henry's flight to the Tower before the advancing Cornish rebels is described in the *Great Chronicle of London*, ed. A.H. Thomas and I.D. Thorley (London, 1938), 275–6, and A.L. Rowse's *Tudor Cornwall* (London, 1969) contains a discussion of the revolt itself. For the ethos of Henry VIII's early development see the following works of S. Anglo: *Spectacle, Pageantry and Early Tudor Policy* (Oxford 1969); 'The British History in Early Tudor

Propaganda', *Bulletin of the John Rylands Library*, 44 (1961); and 'The Court Festivals of Henry VII', *Bulletin of the John Rylands Library*, 43 (1960–61). Maurice Pollet's *John Skelton, Poet of Tudor England* (1971) is useful, and H.L.R. Edwards, *Skelton, The Life and Times of a Tudor Poet* (New York, 1971) is another valuable source of information, along with A.F. Kinney, *John Skelton, Priest as Poet: Seasons of Discovery* (North Carolina, 1987). See also 'Skelton's Speculum Principis' by F.M. Salter in *Speculum, a Journal of Medieval Studies*, IX (1934). The purchase of Codnor Castle is mentioned in the *Calendar of the Close Rolls, 1500–1509* (HMSO, 1963), 160, and the *Calendar of Patent Rolls, 1494–1509* (London, 1916), 583.

A Prince Beyond Improvement

M.L. Bruce is once again a major source of information for this chapter. See also *Materials for a History of the Reign of Henry VII*, ed. William Campbell (London, 1873), vols. i and iii of A. F. Pollard's *The Reign of Henry VII from Contemporary Sources* (London, 1913), *Memorials of Henry VII*, ed. J. Gairdner (London, 1858), and F.A. Mumby, *The Youth of Henry VIII: A Narrative in Contemporary Letters* (Boston, 1913). Fuensalida's *Correspondencia* (Madrid, 1907) is the main contemporary source dealing with the relationship between Henry VII and his second son. For Prince Henry's personal household arrangements, see *Patent Rolls*, 126, 127, 386, 387, 391 and S. Anglo, 'The Court Festivals of Henry VII', *Bulletin of the John Rylands Library*, xliii (1960), 40, 43, 44. For questions relating to the prince's education, consult N. Orme, *From Childhood to Chivalry: The Education of English Kings and Aristocracy, 1066–1530* (Cambridge, 1984). An analysis of contemporary love literature is given in R. Barber, *The Knight and Chivalry* (London, 1970) and the chapter entitled 'The Game of Love' in J. Stevens, *Music and Poetry in the Early Tudor Court* (Cambridge, 1961) is also useful. For a typically romantic reading list of a contemporary nobleman, consult the *Household Books of John Duke of Norfolk and Thomas Earl of Surrey 1481–1490*, ed. J. Payne Collier (London, 1844). A.B. Ferguson, *The Indian Summer of English Chivalry* (North Carolina, 1960), also contains interesting observations. M.H. Keen's *Chivalry* (New Haven, 1984) provides many useful insights, as does M. Vale, *War and Chivalry: Warfare and Aristocratic Culture in England, France and Burgundy at the End of the Middle Ages* (London, 1981). Relevant information relating to Lord

Mountjoy can be found in H. Miller, *Henry VIII and the English Nobility* (Oxford, 1989) and M. Dowling, *Humanism in the Age of Henry VIII* (London, 1986). Mountjoy's relationship with Prince Henry is mentioned in *Excerpta Historica*, ed. S. Bentley (London, 1831). For Henry's protest in Latin against his betrothal to Catherine see J. Collier, *Ecclesiastical History*, vol. ix (London, 1847). The papal brief giving Henry authority over his wife is printed in S. Ehses, *Romische Dokumente zur Geschichte der Ehescheidung Heinrichs VIII 1527–1534* (Paderborn, 1893). For the young Henry's hostility to France, see vol. i of Pollard, op. cit., and Erasmus' *Epistles*, trans. F. Morgan Nichols (London, 1962). For Henry's double-edged compliment to the French envoy, see L.P. Gachard, *Collection des Voyages des Souverains des Pays Bas* (Brussels, 1874–82). Etiquette for a king's brother is outlined in the *Collection of Ordinances and Regulations for the Government of the Royal Household*, Society of the Antiquaries of London (London, 1790). More information about Catherine of Aragon's parents can be found in J. Edwards, *Ferdinand and Isabella* (Harlow, 2004).

The Golden World of Coeur Loyall

A useful starting point is S.J. Gunn, 'The accession of Henry VIII', *Historical Research* 64 (1991), 278–88. For the treatment of Edmund Dudley, see C.J. Harrison, 'The Petition of Edmund Dudley', *English Historical Review*, vol. lxxxvii (1972). Dudley's *The Tree of Commonwealth*, ed. D.M. Brodie (Cambridge, 1948) is also of interest. Catherine of Aragon's early relationship with Henry VIII is dealt with very comprehensively in D. Starkey, *Six Wives: The Queens of Henry VIII* (London, 2004) and Alison Weir, *The Six Wives of Henry VIII* (London, 1991). See also G. Mattingly, *Catherine of Aragon* (London, 1942).

R.B. Wernham, *Before the Armada: The Emergence of the English Nation, 1485–1588* (New York, 1966) is still a useful introduction to Tudor foreign policy, but there is also *Tudor England and its Neighbours*, eds. S. Doran and G. Richardson (Basingstoke, 2005) and S. Doran, *England and Europe in the Sixteenth Century* (New York, 1999). All aspects of the condition of Europe are discussed in M. Mallett and C. Shaw, *The Italian Wars, 1494–1559: War, State and Society in Early Modern Europe* (Harlow, 2012), while for Henry VIII's relationships with Francis I and Charles V, the following pieces by G. Richardson should be consulted: '"Good friends and brothers"?: Francis I and Henry VIII', *History Today*, 44/9 (1994) and *Renaissance Monarchy: The Reigns of Henry VIII, Francis I and Charles V* (London, 2002).

The most comprehensive study of Henry VIII's campaign of 1513 is C. Cruickshank, *Henry VIII and the Invasion of France* (Stroud, 1990), although Sir Charles Oman's *A history of the art of war in the sixteenth century* (London, 1937) is still valuable, too. From the French perspective, there are the *Memoires du Chevalier Bayard dit le Chevalier sans peur et sans reproche: Memoires particuliers relatifs a l'histoire de France*, xv (London and Paris, 1786), as well as the *Memoires du maréchal de Florange dit le jeune adventureux*, eds. R. Goubaux and P.-A. Lemoisne (Paris, 1913). For Louis XII, see F.J. Baumgartner, *Louis XII* (Basingstoke, 1996). See also J.R. Hale: *The Art of War and Renaissance England* (Washington, 1961) and 'Sixteenth-century explanations of war and violence', *Past and Present*, 1971. A. Hocquet, *Tournai et l'occupation anglaise* (Bibliothèque de l'École de chartes, 1900) contains a good deal of interesting information, and much light is thrown on Flodden by *The Days of James IV, 1488–1513*, ed. G.G. Smith (London, 1890), W. Mackenzie, *The Secret of Flodden* (Edinburgh, 1931), and more recently N. Bevor, *The Scottish Invasion of Henry VIII's England* (Stroud, 2001).

Biographies of the Emperor Maximilian are provided by R.W. Seton-Watson, *Maximilian I, Holy Roman Emperor* (London, 1902), C. Hare, *Maximilian the Dreamer* (London, 1913), and G.E. Waas, *The Legendary Character of Kaiser Maximilian* (New York, 1941). There is also L. Silver, *Marketing Maximilian: The Visual Ideology of a Holy Roman Emperor* (Princeton, 2008). F. Fernandez-Armesto, *Ferdinand and Isabella* (New York, 1975) helps set Catherine of Aragon in context and also provides further information on the king who was so influential in shaping Henry VIII's early foreign policy.

Brought Up Out of Nought

The most authoritative text on Wolsey today is undoubtedly P. Gwyn, *The King's Cardinal: The Rise and Fall of Thomas Wolsey* (London, 1990), which deals comprehensively with all areas of his activity. However, in the attempt to redress once and for all the dark legends surrounding his subject, the author has perhaps overcompensated. To appreciate the kind of interpretation that Gwyn was attacking, it is necessary to read A.F. Pollard's vitriolic *Wolsey* (London, 1929), which echoes Shakespeare's assessment of the 'bold, bad man' first advanced by contemporaries like Polydore Vergil and Edward Hall. Although it is very dated now, Mandell Creighton, *Cardinal Wolsey* (London, 1891) is still worth consulting, and for an assessment of Wolsey's performance as Lord Chancellor, see J. A. Guy, *The Cardinal's Court: The Impact of Thomas Wolsey in Star Chamber* (Sussex, 1977). A variety of important essays can be found in S.J. Gunn and P.G. Lindley, *Cardinal Wolsey: church, state and art* (Cambridge and New York, 1991). For Wolsey's background, T.W. Campbell, 'The early life of Thomas Wolsey', *English Historical Review*, iii (1888) contains much useful information which remains largely unchallenged. The cardinal's relationship with the king and his influence over government policy is explored from differing perspectives by J.J. Scarisbrick, *Henry VIII*, (New Haven, 1968; 2nd edn., 1997) and G.R. Elton, *England Under the Tudors* (London, 1953). While Scarisbrick is inclined to emphasise Henry's 'commanding partnership' with his minister, Elton is more inclined to recognise that Henry 'often relied on others for ideas'. The events of May 1517 are analysed in M. Holmes, 'Evil May Day, 1517', *History Today*, 15 (1965), and interesting material on Wolsey's fall from power is to be found in L.R. Gardiner, 'Further News of Cardinal Wolsey's End, November–December 1530', *Bulletin of the Institute of Historical Research*, lvii (1984). In addition to the wealth of material contained in the *Letters and Papers* and Cavendish, the *Calendar of Carew Manuscripts, 1515–74*, ed. J.S. Brewer and W. Bullen (London, 1870) also contains relevant material.

By contrast, Charles Brandon has been largely neglected in the literature of the period, since historians have been rather too inclined, by and large, to associate influence with *ex officio* authority rather than in terms of personal relationships. Undoubtedly, the most comprehensive study is S.J. Gunn, *Charles Brandon, Duke of Suffolk c.1484–1545*, (Oxford, 1988), although it is doubtful whether this treatment fully encompasses the nature of the psychological bond between the two men. There are further details on Brandon's relationship with Henry's sister Mary in W.C. Richardson's *Mary Tudor, The White Queen* (London, 1970), Hester W. Chapman, *The Sisters of Henry VIII* (London, 1969), and M. Perry, *The Sisters of Henry VIII: The Tumultuous Lives of Margaret of Scotland and Mary of France* (London, 1998). For Mary's French marriage, see C. Giry-Deloison, 'Mary Tudor's marriage to Louis XII' in D. Grummitt (ed.), *The English Experience in France, c. 1450–1558* (Basingstoke, 2000), 132–59.

The standard biography of Francis I remains R.J. Knecht, *Renaissance Warrior and Patron: The Reign of Francis I* (Cambridge, 1996). D. Seward, *Prince of the Renaissance: The Life of Francis I* (New York, 1973) makes excellent reading. See also G. Richardson, *Renaissance Monarchy: The Reigns of Henry VIII, Francis I and Charles V* (London, 2002).

Palace of Illusions

The best account of Henry VIII's quest to become Holy Roman Emperor is to be found in J.J. Scarisbrick's biography. The nature of the Empire and the electoral process is dealt with in H.G. Koenigsburger, *The Habsburgs and Europe, 1516–1660* (London, 1971). Charles V's eventual success is explained in K. Brandi, *The Emperor Charles V*, trans. C.V. Wedgewood (London, 1965). More recent works on Charles include W. Blockmans, *Emperor Charles V, 1500–1558* (London, 2002) and J.D. Tracy, *Emperor Charles V, Impresario of War: Campaign Strategy, International Finance and Domestic Politics* (Cambridge, 2002). See also *Correspondence of the Emperor Charles V*, ed. W. Bradford (London, 1850). An interesting view of what it was like to be one of the hapless toilers on Henry's behalf can be found in J. Wegg, *Richard Pace: a Tudor Diplomatist* (London, 1932).

For the purge of Henry VIII's minions in 1519, see D. Starkey, *The Reign of Henry VIII: Personalities and Politics* (London, 1985). Contemporary sources providing details are Hall, pp. 597–98, *L&P*, iii, 246–50, and the *Venetian Calendar*, ii, 1220 and 1230.

The *Spanish Calendar*, *Venetian Calendar* and *The Chronicle of Calais* contain a wealth of material on the Field of Cloth of Gold, as well as the preliminary meeting between Henry and Charles. There is an interesting account by S. Anglo, 'Le Camp du Drap d'Or et les Entrevues d'Henri VIII et de Charles Quint' (Paris, 1959), although the best general account in English remains J.G. Russell, *The Field of Cloth of Gold: Men and Manners in 1520* (London, 1969). Not altogether surprisingly, the English accounts are silent on the issue of the royal wrestling match, although it is described in detail in the memoirs of the Seigneur de Florange, who was an eyewitness. See the *Memoires du maréchal de Florange dit le jeune adventureux*, eds. R. Goubaux and P.-A. Lemoisne (Paris, 1913). The details concerning provisioning of food for the English party are contained in *L&P*, iii, 919.

The Duke of Buckingham's career and ultimate fall is well charted in: B. Harris, *Edward Stafford, Third Duke of Buckingham, 1478–1521* (Stanford, 1986); C. Rawcliffe, *The Staffords, Earls of Stafford and Dukes of Buckingham, 1394–1521* (Cambridge, 1978) and M. Levine, 'The fall of Edward Duke of Buckingham' in *Tudor Men and Institutions*, ed. A.J. Flavin (Louisiana, 1972).

Defender of the Faith

Long-standing opinions concerning Henry VIII's religious attitudes and influence have been fundamentally challenged in recent times. For the new perspective, which depicts the king as an active advocate of Protestant thinking, see G. W. Bernard, *The King's Reformation: Henry VIII and the Re-Making of the English Church* (New Haven and London, 2005) and Bernard's essay, 'The piety of Henry VIII' in *The Education of a Christian Society: Humanism and the Reformation in Britain and the Netherlands*, eds. N.S. Amos, A. Pettegree and H. van Nierop (Aldershot, 1999), 62–88. R. Rex, *Henry VIII and the English Reformation* (Basingstoke, 1993) is also required reading. However, in order to gain some appreciation of the broader context of contemporary religious thinking, it is worth consulting K. Thomas, *Religion and the Decline of Magic* (Harmondsworth, 1991).

Not surprisingly, other aspects of the religious history of this period have also generated deep controversy. The competing perspectives on a range of issues are discussed in R. O'Day, *The Debate on the Reformation* (London, 1986) and R. Rex, *Henry VIII and the English Reformation* (Basingstoke, 1993). What can justifiably be termed the old view on the state of the pre-Reformation Church, which emphasised its decadence and inevitable decline, can be found in A.G. Dickens, *The English Reformation* (Pennsylvania, 1989). The current view that the Church continued to enjoy widespread support is presented in J.J. Scarisbrick, *The Reformation and the English People* (Oxford, 1984), E. Duffy, *The Stripping of the Altars: Traditional Religion in England 1400–1580* (New Haven, 1992), and C.A. Haigh, *English Reformations* (Oxford, 1993).

Other useful sources of information on the state of the Church in England at the start of the sixteenth century include: A. Savine, *The English Monasteries on the Eve of the Dissolution* (Oxford, 1909); F. Gasquet: *The Eve of the Reformation* (London, 1900); P. Heath, *The English Parish Clergy on the*

Eve of the Reformation (London, 1969); R. Houlbrooke, *Church Courts and the People during the English Reformation, 1520–70* (Oxford, 1979); J.A.F. Thomson, *The Later Lollards, 1414–1520* (Oxford, 1965); J. McConica, *English Humanists and Reformation Politics under Henry VIII* (Oxford, 1965); C. Haigh, 'Anticlericalism and the English Reformation', *History*, lxviii (1985); C. Marsh, *Popular Religion in Sixteenth-Century England* (Basingstoke, 1998); S. Brigden, *London and the Reformation* (Oxford, 1989); P. Marshall, *Religious Identities in Henry VIII's England* (Aldershot, 2006); and P. Marshall, *Reformation England 1480–1642* (London, 2012). Some valuable material for this chapter has also been gleaned from H. Maynard-Smith's *Henry VIII and the Reformation* (London, 1963). For those wishing to read some anticlerical literature in the original, Simon Fish's 'Supplication for the beggars' can be found in Thomas More, *The Supplication of Souls* (London, 1970).

The best biography of Martin Luther in English is probably M. Mullett, *Martin Luther* (London, 2004). Other books well worth reading are R. Bainton, *Here I Stand* (New York, 1950) and H. Boehmer, *Martin Luther: Road to Reformation*, trans. J.W. Doberstein and T.G. Tappert (Philadelphia, 1957). For Henry VIII's relationship with the German reformer, consult E. Doernburg, *Henry VIII and Luther* (Stanford, 1961), N.S. Tjernagel, *Henry VIII and the Lutherans: A Study in Anglo-Lutheran Relations from 1521 to 1547* (St Louis, 1965), and R. Rex, 'The English campaign against Luther in the 1520s', *Trans. Royal Hist. Soc.*, 5th ser., 39 (1989). For those wishing to experience Henry VIII's own personal contribution, see *Assertio Septem Sacramentorum* or *Defence of the Seven Sacraments by Henry VIII, King of England*, ed. Rev. L. O'Donovan (New York, 1908 edn.).

Puissance and Penury

Wolsey has often been presented, most notably by J.J. Scarisbrick, as a sincere peacemaker. This line of interpretation is explored further in J. G. Russell, 'The search for universal peace: the conferences at Calais and Bruges in 1521', *Bulletin of the Institute of Historical Research*, xliv (1971) and P.J. Gwyn, 'Wolsey's foreign policy: the conferences of Calais and Bruges reconsidered', *Historical Journal*, 23. For a discussion of Wolsey's involvement in the quest for the papacy, see D.S. Chambers, 'Cardinal Wolsey and the Papal Tiara' in *Bull. Inst. Hist. Res.*, xxxv (1967).

More can be found out about events in Scotland from R.G. Eaves, *Henry VIII's Scottish Diplomacy, 1513–24* (New York, 1971) and J.D. Mackie, 'Henry VIII and Scotland', *Transactions of the Royal Hist. Soc.*, xxix, 4th ser. (1947). For Ireland, see S.G. Ellis, *Ireland in the Age of the Tudors, 1447–1603: English Expansion and the End of Gaelic Rule* (Harlow, 1998) and S.G. Ellis and C. Maginn, *The Making of the British Isles: The State of Britain and Ireland, 1450–1660* (Harlow, 2007).

For parliamentary opposition to the cost of the war, see J.A. Guy, 'Wolsey and the parliament of 1523' in *Law and Government under the Tudors*, ed. C. Cross, D. Loades and J J. Scarisbrick (Cambridge University Press, 1988) and G.W. Bernard, *War, Taxation and Rebellion in Early Tudor England: Henry VIII, Cardinal Wolsey and the Amicable Grant of 1525* (Brighton, 1983). See also R.S. Schofield, *Taxation under the Early Tudors, 1485–1547* (Cambridge, 2004).

M.H. Keen, *The Laws of War in the Late Middle Ages* (London, 1965) helps to set Surrey's campaign of 1522 in a broader context, while the subsequent military campaign is discussed by S.J. Gunn, 'The duke of Suffolk's march on Paris in 1523', *English Historical Review*, ci (1986), and in Gunn's essay, 'The Imperial Wars of Henry VIII', in *The Origins of War in Early Modern Europe*, ed. J. Black (Edinburgh, 1987). The resounding French victory of 1525 is dealt with in A. Konstam, *Pavia, 1525: The Climax of the Italian Wars* (Oxford, 1996).

There is further information on the Peasants' War in Germany in E.B. Bax, *The Peasants' War in Germany 1525–1526* (New York, 1968) and P. Blickle, *The Revolution of 1525: the German Peasants' War from a new perspective*, (Baltimore and London, 1981).

For the changing operation of the royal household, see A.P. Newton, 'Tudor reforms in the royal household' in R.W. Seton-Watson (ed.), *Tudor Studies* (London, 1924).

Impulse Born of Passion

One of the main contemporary sources for Anne Boleyn's life is George Wyatt's late sixteenth-century biography, *Extracts from the life of the Virtuous, Christian and Renowned Queen Anne Boleyn* (London, 1817). However, while Wyatt's treatment of Anne is extremely sympathetic, Reginald Pole's *Pro ecclesiasticae unitatis defensione libri quatuor* (Rome, *c.* 1555) contains views which are probably more indicative of contemporary opinion in general. For the most authoritative modern evaluation of her life, see E.W. Ives, *The Life and Death of Anne Boleyn: The Most Happy* (Oxford, 2005), while further light is shed on Anne's early life in J.H. Round, *The Early Life of Anne Boleyn* (London, 1886) and H. Paget, 'The Youth of Anne Boleyn', *Bulletin of the Institute of Historical Research*, 55, 1981. Two other books that the general reader may find worthwhile are C. Erickson, *Mistress Anne* (New York, 1984) and H.W. Chapman, *Anne Boleyn* (London, 1974). The standard biography for many years was P. Friedmann, *Anne Boleyn, a Chapter of English History, 1527–1536* (2 vols., London, 1884).

Henry's marital infidelities are thoroughly explored by David Starkey and Alison Weir in their books on his wives. See also Antonia Frasier, *The Six Wives of Henry VIII* (London, 2007). The story of Bessie Blount's bastard son, the Duke of Richmond, is told in B.A. Murphy, *Bastard Prince: Henry VIII's Lost Son* (Stroud, 2001).

The need for a male heir has rarely been discussed in depth by Henry's biographers, because its necessity has always been assumed. However, L. B. Smith in *Henry VIII: The Mask of Royalty* (Stroud, 2012) has made a number of interesting observations which coincide largely with the line of argument adopted here. Smith also emphasises the marital possibilities for Princess Mary.

On the issue of female rule in a sixteenth-century context, consult the following: S. Mendelson and P. Crawford, *Women in Early Modern England*, (Oxford, 2003); J. Eales, *Women in Early Modern England, 1500–1700* (London, 1998); B.J. Harris, *English Aristocratic Women, 1450–1550* (Oxford, 2002); M. Levine, 'The place of women in Tudor rule and revolution' in *Essays for G.R. Elton from his American friends*, eds. J. Guth and J.W. McKenna (Cambridge, 1982); R. M. Warnicke, 'Women of the English Renaissance and Reformation' in *Contributions to Women's Studies*, 38, 1983; and J.M. Richards, '"To Promote a Woman to Beare Rule": Talking of Queens in Mid-Tudor England', in *Sixteenth Century Journal*, xxviii (1997).

The main technicalities of Henry's divorce case are covered in G. de C. Parmiter, *The King's Great Matter: A Study of Anglo-Papal Relations* (London, 1967) and H. Thurston, 'The canon law of divorce', *English Historical Review* xix (1904). There is also a great deal of technical detail in N. Harpsfield, *A Treatise on the Pretended Divorce between Henry VIII and Catherine of Aragon*, ed. N. Pocock, Camden Society, 2nd ser, xxi (1878). See also E. Surtz and

V. Murphy (eds.), *The Divorce Tracts of Henry VIII* (Angers, 1988) and H. A. Kelly, *The Matrimonial Trials of Henry VIII* (Stanford, 1976). Chapter 7 of Scarisbrick's biography of Henry VIII remains the best starting point for any exploration of the canon law of the divorce.

Other broadly relevant work includes: V. Murphy, 'The Literature and Propaganda of Henry VIII's First Divorce' in D. MacCulloch (ed.), *The Reign of Henry VIII* (Basingstoke, 1995), 135–58; and J.C. Warner, *Henry VIII's Divorce: Literature and the Politics of the Printing Press* (Woodbridge, 1998).

For the key event in the collapse of English diplomacy, see J. Hook, *The Sack of Rome, 1527* (Basingstoke, 2004) and A. Chastel, *The Sack of Rome* (Princeton, 1983). An interesting account of the hidden mechanics of English diplomacy is to be found in C. Fletcher, *Our Man in Rome: Henry VIII and his Italian Ambassador* (London, 2012).

Wolsey's fall is discussed in E.W. Ives, 'The Fall of Wolsey' in *Cardinal Wolsey: Church, state and art*, ed. S.J. Gunn and P.G. Lindley (Cambridge, 1991) and G.W. Bernard, 'The Fall of Wolsey Reconsidered', *Journal of British Studies*, 35 (1996), 277–310.

The Infinite Clamour of Deadlock

For Catherine's life at Kimbolton, see *The Kimbolton Papers in the Collection of the Duke of Manchester* (London, 1864). Mattingly's biography of the queen charts this period of her life thoroughly and full details can also be found in David Starkey, *Six Wives: The Queens of Henry VIII* (London, 2004*)* and Alison Weir, *The Six Wives of Henry VIII* (London, 1991). See also J.E. Paul, *Catherine of Aragon and her Friends* (London, 1965).

Anne's background is, of course, explored in all the biographical works dealing with her, as are her general unpopularity and deteriorating relationship with Henry. The failed attack on her by the London mob is recorded only in the *Venetian Calendar*, although *L&P* provides substantial evidence of widespread opposition to the divorce. Anne's creation as Marquess of Pembroke is described in T. Milles, *Catalogue of Honour* (London, 1610).

The best collective examination of the key figures of this period is D. Wilson, *In the Lion's Court: Power, Ambition and Sudden Death in the Court of Henry VIII* (London, 2002). For the Duke of Suffolk, there is

S.J. Gunn, *Charles Brandon, Duke of Suffolk c.1484–1545* (Oxford, 1988) and for the Duke of Norfolk there is also a useful entry by M.A.R. Graves in the Oxford Dictionary of National Biography (2008). Enough material on Sir Thomas Boleyn can be found in *L&P* to confirm the low opinion of him presented here.

Thomas More's reputation has, of course, undergone considerable revision in recent times. Over many years the standard biography was R.W. Chambers, *Thomas More* (London, 1935), but for the modern perspective readers should consult J.A. Guy, *Thomas More* (London, 2000).

Those interested in the activities of Parliament during these years should read S.E. Lehmberg, *The Reformation Parliament, 1529–36* (Cambridge, 1970) and M.A.R. Graves, *Tudor Parliaments: Crowns, Lords and Commons, 1485–1603* (London, 1985). The Rolls of Parliament, *Rotuli Parliamentorum*, ed. J. Strachey et al. (London, 1767–1832) remain a major source of primary evidence. See also the *Acts of the Court of the Mercers' Company, 1453–1527*, eds. L. Lyell and F.D. Watney (Cambridge, 1936).

On Cranmer, there is J. Ridley, *Thomas Cranmer* (Oxford, 1962), although this book has now been superseded by D. MacCulloch, *Thomas Cranmer: A Life* (New Haven and London, 1996). See also MacCulloch's article, 'Cranmer's Ambiguous Legacy', *History Today* (June 1996). An early biography which is still of some value is A.F. Pollard, *Thomas Cranmer and the English Reformation, 1489–1556* (London, 1905).

For the early manoeuvres in Henry's struggle with Rome, the following are all very useful: J.A. Guy, 'Henry VIII and the praemunire manoeuvres of 1530–31', *English Historical Review*, xvii (1982); J.J. Scarisbrick, 'Henry VIII and the Vatican Library', *Bibliothèque d'Humanisme et Renaissance*, xxiv (Geneva, 1962); and V. Murphy, 'The literature and propaganda of Henry VIII's first divorce' in *The Reign of Henry VIII: Politics, Policy and Piety*, ed. D. MacCulloch (London, 1995). Rome's position on the divorce is encapsulated in *Acta Curiae Romana in cause matrimoniale Regis cum Katherina Regina* (1531).

Plenary, Whole and Entire Power

Although many of his ideas have been and are still being subjected to revision, G.R. Elton remains the starting point for any student of Thomas Cromwell. The following of Elton's articles are particularly relevant to this chapter: 'King or Minister? The man behind the Henrician Reformation' in *History* xxxiv (1954)'; 'The Political Creed of Thomas Cromwell' in *Trans. Royal Hist. Soc.*, 5th ser., vi (1956); 'The Evolution of a Reformation Statute' in *English Hist. Review*, lxix (1949); 'Parliamentary Drafts, 1529–40', in *Bulletin of the Institute of Hist. Research*, xxv (1952); 'The Commons' Supplication of 1532' in *English Hist. Review*, lxvi (1952).

Other relevant articles pertaining to Cromwell's activities in Parliament include: M. Bowker, 'The Commons Supplication Against the Ordinaries in the Light of Some Archidiaconal Acta' in *Trans. Royal Hist. Soc.*, 5th ser., xxi (1971); M. Kelly, 'The Submission of the Clergy' in *Trans. Royal Hist. Soc.*, 5th ser., xv (1965); J.J. Scarisbrick, 'The Pardon of the Clergy, 1531' in *Cambridge Historical Journal*, xii (1956); and R. Koebner, '"The Imperial Crown of This Realm"; Henry VIII, Constantine the Great, and Polydore Vergil', *Bulletin of the Institute of Historical Research*, xxvi (1953). See also T.M. Parker, 'Was Thomas Cromwell a Machiavellian?' in *Jnl. Eccles. Hist.*, (1950) and J. A. Guy, 'Thomas Cromwell and the Intellectual Origins of the Henrician Revolution' in *Reassessing the Henrician Age*, eds. A. Fox and J. A. Guy (Oxford, 1986), 151–78.

A.G. Dickens' masterfully concise *Thomas Cromwell and the English Reformation* (London, 1974) should also be consulted, along with B. Beckingsale, *Thomas Cromwell: Tudor Minister* (London, 1978). The most recent books on Cromwell are: Robert Hutchinson, *Thomas Cromwell: Henry VIII's Most Notorious Minister* (London, 2007); J. Schofield, *The Rise and Fall of Thomas Cromwell: Henry VIII's Most Faithful Servant* (Stroud, 2011); and J.P. Coby, *Thomas Cromwell* (Stroud, 2012).

On contemporary political theory, see: W.G. Zeeveld, *Foundations of Tudor Policy* (Cambridge, Mass., 1948) and F. Le Van Baumer, *The Early Tudor Theory of Kingship* (Cambridge, Mass., 1938). More general accounts are to be found in J.W. Allen, *History of Political Thought in the Sixteenth Century* (London, 1960) and in C. Morris, *Political Thought in England: Tyndale to Hooker* (Oxford, 1953). See also W. Ullmann, *Principles of Government and Politics in the Middle Ages* (London, 1961).

For anyone interested in legal intricacies, there is J. Bellamy, *The Tudor Law of Treason: An Introduction* (Toronto, 1979).

Henry VIII's *A Glasse of the Truthe* and other contemporary works are contained in N. Pocock, *Records of the Reformation: The Divorce 1527–1533* (Oxford, 1870). For Catherine's stand-off with Norfolk and members of the council in 1531, see Edward Hall, the *Spanish Calendar* and *L&P*.

The Lion Learns His Strength

Henry's brutality has been shifted well away from the centre of discussion for many years now, as has Cromwell's reputation for ruthlessness. G.R. Elton's attempt to recast the agenda in the interests of 'objective' history and 'bigger' issues has been extremely influential in this respect and though, perhaps, this trend has now itself begun to distort as much as enlighten, there is no doubting its initial importance in enhancing our understanding of the period. For a view of Cromwell very different to the one advanced here, see G.R. Elton, *Policy and Police: The Enforcement of the Reformation in the Age of Thomas Cromwell* (Cambridge, 1972).

The most detailed account of the Nun of Kent's activities is to be found in A. Neame, *The Holy Maid of Kent: The Life of Elizabeth Barton 1506–1534* (London, 1971), and the Rolls of Parliament, *Rotuli Parliamentorum*, ed. J. Strachey et al. (London, 1767–1832), also provide useful information. See also A.D. Cheney, 'The Holy Maid of Kent' in *Trans. Royal Hist. Soc.*, 2nd ser., xviii (1904); L.E. Whatmore, 'The sermon against the Holy Maid of Kent and her adherents, 1533', *English Historical Review*, vol. lviii (1943); and E.J. Devereux, 'Elizabeth Barton and Tudor Censorship', *Bull. John Rylands Library*, 49 (1966).

The attack on Thomas More's reputation as 'a man of singular virtue' began with J. Ridley, *The Statesman and the Fanatic* (London, 1982) and has culminated in John Guy's interpretation, which is summarised in J.A. Guy, *Thomas More* (London, 2000). Another critical work is R. Marius, *Thomas More*, (New York, 1984). See also A. Fox, *Thomas More: History and Providence* (Oxford, 1982), G.R. Elton, 'Sir Thomas More and the opposition to Henry VIII', *Studies in Tudor Politics and Government*, I (1974), and D.M. Derrett, 'The Trial of Sir Thomas More', *English Historical Review*, 79 (1964), 449–72. More's letters can be examined in *The Correspondence of Sir Thomas More*, ed. E.F. Rogers (Princeton, 1947).

John Fisher is still, it seems, awaiting his ultimate biographer, though a range of eminent historians have dealt with aspects of his activity. The best starting point is J.J. Scarisbrick, 'Fisher, Henry VIII and the Reformation Crisis' in *Humanism, Reform and the Reformation: The Career of Bishop John Fisher*, eds. B. Bradshaw and E. Duffy (Cambridge, 1989), while Richard Rex has dealt with Fisher as a theologian in *The Theology of John Fisher* (Cambridge, 1991). For Fisher the man, however, we are left mainly with books like P. Hughes, *The Earliest English Life of John Fisher* (London,

1935) and E.E. Reynolds, *St John Fisher* (London, 1955). Two books worthy of recommendation are E. Surtz, *The Works and Days of John Fisher* (Cambridge, Mass., 1967) and M. Dowling, *Fisher of Men: A Life of John Fisher, 1469–1535* (Cambridge, 1991).

J. Youings, *The Dissolution of the Monasteries* (London, 1971) is still a first-class work devoted solely to the dissolution, although a broader treatment is to be found in D. Knowles, *The Religious Orders in England* (3 vols., Cambridge, 1947–59). F.A. Gasquet, *Henry VIII and the Dissolution of the Monasteries* (2 vols., London, 1906), remains useful, too, and there is also E. Duffy, *The Stripping of the Altars: Traditional Religion in England, 1400–1580* (New Haven, 1992) and J.G. Clark (ed.), *The Religious Orders in Pre-Reformation England* (Woodbridge, 2003). For individual religious orders see E.M. Thompson, *The Carthusian Order in England* (London, 1930) and J.R. Fletcher, *The Story of the English Bridgettines of Syon Abbey* (Bristol, 1933). Further insight into the resistance of prominent individuals is provided in J.E. Paul, 'The last abbots of Reading and Colchester', *Bulletin of the Institute of Historical Research*, xxxiii (1960). Contemporary sources may be consulted in *Letters Relating to the Suppression of the Monasteries*, ed. T. Wright (Camden Society xxvi, 1843).

The classic work on the Pilgrimage of Grace was for many years, M.H. and R. Dodds, *The Pilgrimage of Grace, 1536–7, and the Exeter Conspiracy 1538* (2 vols., Cambridge, 1915). Their interpretation has been largely undermined by modern research, however, and for a more up-to-date view readers should consult the following: R.W. Hoyle, *The Pilgrimage of Grace and the Politics of the 1530s* (Oxford, 2001); A. Fletcher and D. MacCulloch, *Tudor Rebellions*, 4th edn., (London, 1997); C.S.L. Davies, 'The Pilgrimage of Grace reconsidered', *Past and Present,* 41 (1968); and M. E. James, 'Obedience and dissent in Henrician England: the Lincolnshire Rebellion 1536', *Past and Present* lxvii (1970), 3–78. There is also G. Moorhouse, *The Pilgrimage of Grace: The Rebellion that Shook Henry VIII's Throne* (London, 2002). The nature of popular politics in general is dealt with in E. Shagan, *Popular Politics and the English Reformation* (Cambridge, 2002), A. Wood, *Riot, Rebellion and Popular Politics in Early Modern England* (Basingstoke, 2002), and T. Harris (ed.), *The Politics of the Excluded c. 1500–1850* (Basingstoke and New York, 2001).

Other books of relevance to this chapter include: G. Walker, *Writing Under Tyranny: English Literature and the Henrician Reformation* (Oxford, 2005); D.A. Dillon, *The Construction of Martyrdom in the English Catholic*

Community, 1535–1603 (Aldershot, 2002); S.L. Jansen, *Political Control and Protest under Henry VIII* (Woodbridge, 1991)'; and K.J. Kesselring, *Mercy and Authority in the Tudor State* (Cambridge, 2003).

Who Hastes to Climb Seeks to Revert

Suspicions of poisoning have always surrounded Catherine of Aragon's death, since her clumsy dissection in the immediate aftermath of her demise. The growth found on her heart at that time is now believed to be a cardial carcinoma. For one of the earliest scientific discussions of her condition, see Sir Norman Moore, 'The Death of Catherine of Aragon', *The Athenaeum* (1885).

After E.W. Ives' biography, readers interested in Anne's fall from grace should consult Retha M. Warnicke, *The Rise and Fall of Anne Boleyn: Family Politics at the Court of Henry VIII* (Cambridge 1989). There is also G.W. Bernard, 'The Fall of Anne Boleyn', *English Historical Review,* cvi (1990) and G. Walker, 'Rethinking the Fall of Anne Boleyn', *Historical Journal*, 45 (2002), 1–29. Henry's growing disillusionment with Anne is well documented in the *Spanish Calendar*, the *Venetian Calendar*, Roper's *Life of More*, as well as George Wyatt's biography. Henry Clifford's *The Life of Jane Dormer*, ed. J. Stevenson, S.J. (London, 1887), suggests that Henry blamed Anne for More's death.

The best contemporary source of information regarding Anne's imprisonment is the dispatches of Sir William Kingston, the Constable of the Tower, to Thomas Cromwell, which are to be found in the Cotton MSS in the British Library. The arrests and imprisonment of those implicated in her adultery are described in the *Histoire de la Royne Anne de Boullant* (Bibliothèque Nationale, c. 1550). The details of her trial were recorded by Sir John Spelman, an eyewitness, and have been preserved in the *Reports of Sir John Spelman*, ed. J.A. Baker (Selden Society, 1977–78).

In recent years, Henry's wives after Anne Boleyn have tended to be dealt with collectively in books such as D. Starkey, *Six Wives: The Queens of Henry VIII* (London, 2004), Alison Weir, *The Six Wives of Henry VIII* (London, 1991), Antonia Fraser, *The Six Wives of Henry VIII* (London, 1992) and D. Loades, *Henry VIII and His Queens* (Stroud, 2000). Individual biographies of Jane Seymour are for some reason particularly scarce, although there is a good deal of helpful information on her life and family in William

Seymour, *Ordeal by Ambition: An English Family in the Shadow of the Tudors* (London, 1972). There is also P.M. Gross, *Jane, The Quene, Third Consort of King Henry VIII* (New York, 1999). Contemporary sources of information are contained in the *Seymour Papers 1532–1686, Report on the Manuscripts of the Most Honourable the Marquess of Bath preserved at Longleat*, vol. iv, ed. M. Blatcher (Historical Manuscripts Commission, 1968) and H. St Maur, *Annals of the Seymours* (London, 1902). Over the last decade or so, Anne of Cleves has at last begun to be seen more and more in her own right. A particularly interesting study of her marriage and its broader significance is to be found in R.M. Warnicke, *The Marrying of Anne of Cleves: Royal Protocol in Early Modern England* (Cambridge, 2000). Mary Saaler places particular emphasis upon Anne's later years of independence as 'a queen unqueened' in *Anne of Cleves: Fourth Wife of Henry VIII* (London, 1997). The best available treatment of Catherine Howard remains L.B. Smith, *A Tudor Tragedy: The Life and Times of Catherine Howard* (London, 1961).

For the Exeter Conspiracy, see H. Durant's *Sorrowful Captives* (Pontypool, 1960), and on Cromwell's end, consult G.R. Elton, 'Thomas Cromwell's Decline and Fall', *Cambridge Hist. Journal*, x (1951) and S. Brigden, 'Popular Disturbance and the Fall of Thomas Cromwell and the Reformers, 1539–40', *Historical Journal*, xxxv (1992). More information on the Pole family can be found in H. Pierce, *Margaret Pole, Countess of Salisbury 1473–1541: Loyalty, Lineage and Leadership* (Cardiff, 2009) and T.F. Mayer, *Reginald Pole: Prince and Prophet* (Cambridge, 2000).

Opinionate and Wilful

The most absorbing account of Henry's declining years remains L.B. Smith's *Henry VIII: The Mask of Royalty* (Stroud, 2012). There is a wealth of fascinating information and analysis, much of which has been drawn upon in this chapter. Robert Hutchinson, *The Last Days of Henry VIII* (London, 2005) also contains a good deal of relevant information.

Ove Brinch, 'The Medical Problems of Henry VIII', *Centaurus*, 5 (1958) and J.F.D. Shrewsbury, 'Henry VIII: A Medical Study', *Journal of the History of Medicine and Allied Sciences*, vii (1952) are useful starting points for the morbid tale of Henry VIII's ailments. L.B. Smith's *Henry VIII* also contains a good deal of interesting discussion on the king's deteriorating physical condition and growing obsession with his own transience, which this chapter has drawn upon. See also Sir A.S. MacNalty, *Henry VIII: A Difficult Patient* (London, 1952), R. Lamont-Brown, *Royal Poxes and Potions: The Lives of Court Physicians, Surgeons and Apothecaries* (Stroud, 2001), and L.G. Matthews, 'Royal Apothecaries of the Tudor Period', *Medical History*, 3 (1964). For Charles V and Francis I in their dotage, see K. Brandi *The Emperor Charles V*, trans. C.V. Wedgewood (London, 1965) and R.J. Knecht, *Renaissance Warrior and Patron: The Reign of Francis I* (Cambridge, 1996).

Additional information concerning Henry VIII's last campaigns in Scotland can be found in G. Donaldson, *Scotland: James V to James VII* (Edinburgh, 1965) and C.P. Hotle, *Thorns and Thistles: Diplomacy between Henry VIII and James V, 1528–1542* (Lanham, Maryland and London, 1996). Some of the implications of Henry's military spending on his final French campaign are dealt with in F. Dietz, *English Public Finance, 1485– 1558* (2nd edn., London, 1964). Likewise, the broader aspects of Henry's wars during these years are covered in J. Raymond, *Henry VIII's Military Revolution: The Armies of Sixteenth-Century Britain and Europe* (London, 2007). Further details on the debasement of the coinage are to be found in J.D. Gould, *The Great Debasement: Currency and the Economy in Mid-Tudor England* (Oxford, 1970).

A very different interpretation of Henry's religious position in these years is provided in G.W. Bernard, *The King's Reformation: Henry VIII and the Re-Making of the English Church* (New Haven and London, 2005). Those readers wishing to reach their own conclusions might begin by consulting *The King's Book or A Necessary Doctrine and Erudition for any Christian Man, 1543*, ed. T.A. Lacey (London, 1932). See also A. Ryrie, *The Gospel and Henry VIII: Evangelicals in the Early English Reformation* (Cambridge, 2003).

The faction fighting of the period is discussed in D. Starkey, *The Reign of Henry VIII: Personalities and Politics* (London, 1985) and in E.W. Ives, *Faction in Tudor England, Historical Appreciation VI* (1979). See also E.W. Ives, 'Faction at the Court of Henry VIII', *History*, lvii (1972). A counterweight may be found in G. Walker, *Persuasive Fictions: Faction, Faith and Political Culture in the Reign of Henry VIII* (Aldershot, 1996), while S.J. Gunn, *Early Tudor Government, 1485–1558* (Basingstoke, 1995) provides a broader context. The cases of Cranmer and Gardiner are discussed in D. MacCulloch, *Thomas Cranmer: A Life* (New Haven and London, 1996) and G. Redworth, *In Defence of the Church Catholic: The Life of Stephen Gardiner* (Oxford 1990). For further information on Gardiner, consult J. Muller,

Stephen Gardiner and the Tudor Reaction (New York, 1926) and J.A. Muller ed., *The Letters of Stephen Gardiner* (Cambridge, 1933), while the fall of the Howards is explored in Jessie Childs, *Henry VIII's Last Victim: The Life and Times of Henry Howard, Earl of Surrey* (London, 2006). See also P.R. Moore, 'The Heraldic Charge Against the Earl of Surrey, 1546–7', *English Historical Review* (June, 2001) and J.M. Robinson, *The Dukes of Norfolk* (Chichester, 1995).

Two useful works on Henry's last queen are S.E. James, *Kateryn Parr: The Making of a Queen* (Aldershot, 1999), and W.J. Haugaard, 'Katherine Parr: The religious convictions of a Renaissance queen', *Renaissance Quarterly* 22 (1969). Above all, there is J. Mueller, *Katherine Parr: Complete Works and Correspondence* (Chicago, 2011).

For more information on the role of Will Somers, consult J. Doran, *History of Court Fools* (London, 1858) and J. Southworth, *Fools and Jesters at the English Court* (Stroud, 1998).

For the text of Henry's will, see *The Will of King Henry VIII*, ed. T. Astle (London, 1775). The following articles by E.W. Ives are also of particular importance in helping to unravel some of the problems associated with it: 'Henry VIII's Will: A Forensic Conundrum', *Historical Journal*, 35, 4 (1992), and 'Henry VIII's Will: The Protectorate Provisions of 1546–7', *Historical Journal* 37, 4 (1994). See also R.A. Houlbrooke, 'Henry VIII's Wills: A Comment', *Historical Journal*, 37, 4 (1994), H. Miller, 'Henry VIII's unwritten will' in E.W. Ives et al., ed., *Wealth and Power in Tudor England* (1978), and M. Levine, 'The Last Will and Testament of Henry VIII: A Reappraisal Reappraised', *Historian*, 26, 4 (August, 1964).

For accounts of Henry's death, see F. Godwin, *Annales of England containing the Reignes of Henry the Eighth, Edward the Sixth, Queen Mary* (London, 1630) and the British Library's Hargrave MSS 311, f. 125. The authorship of the so-called *Spanish Chronicle* referred to here is uncertain, but it was probably written from memory by one of the Spanish mercenary soldiers in Henry's pay at the end of the reign. Though interesting, it needs to be treated with extreme care.

Index